MW01629300

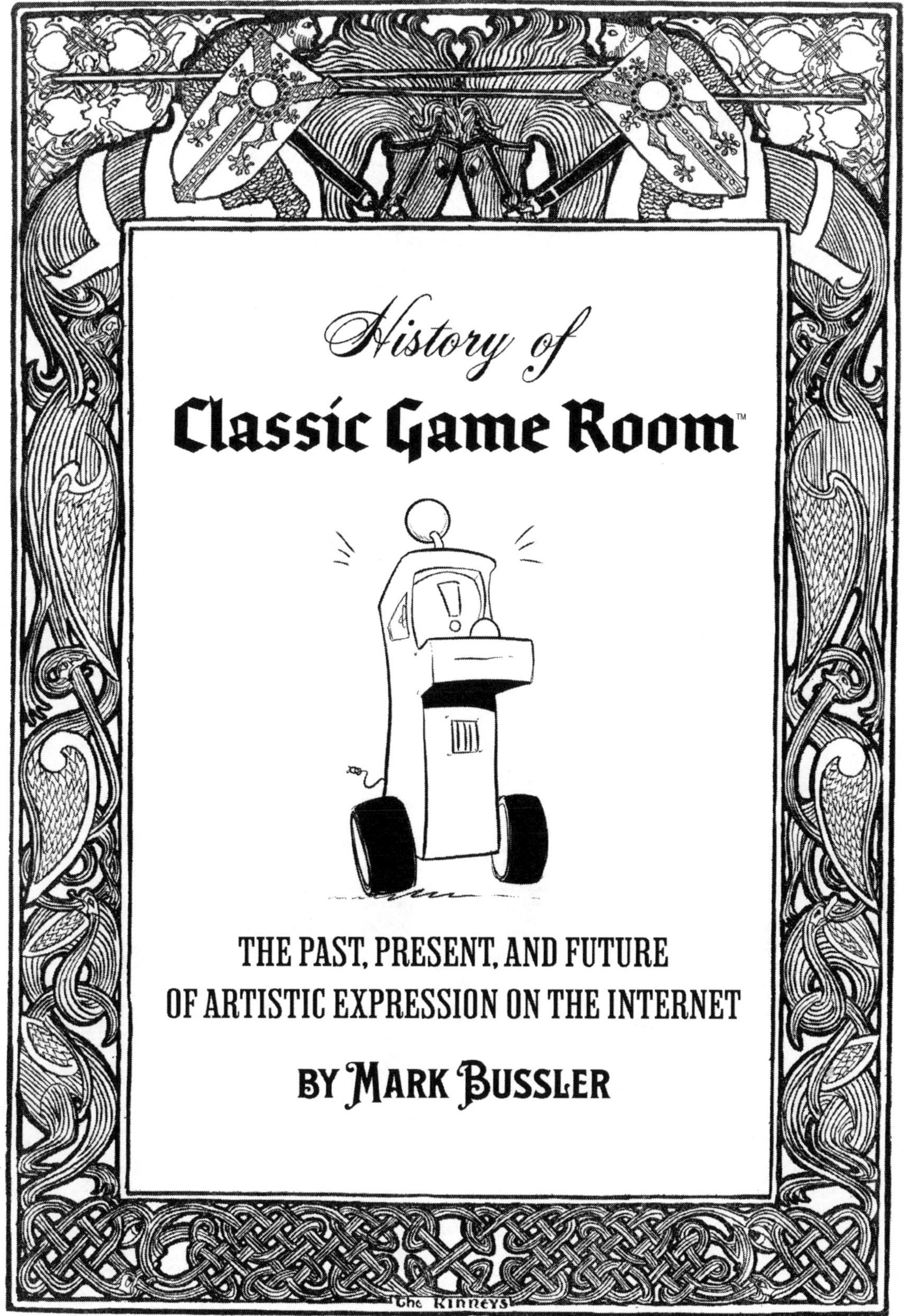

History of Classic Game Room™

THE PAST, PRESENT, AND FUTURE OF ARTISTIC EXPRESSION ON THE INTERNET

BY MARK BUSSLER

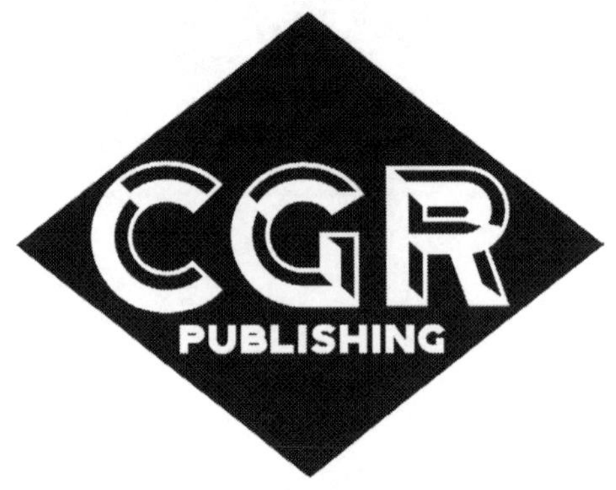

History of Classic Game Room™
The Past, Present, and Future of Artistic Expression on the Internet

Written and Illustrated by Mark Bussler
Cover Design by Mark Bussler

More Books by Mark Bussler at
CGRpublishing.com

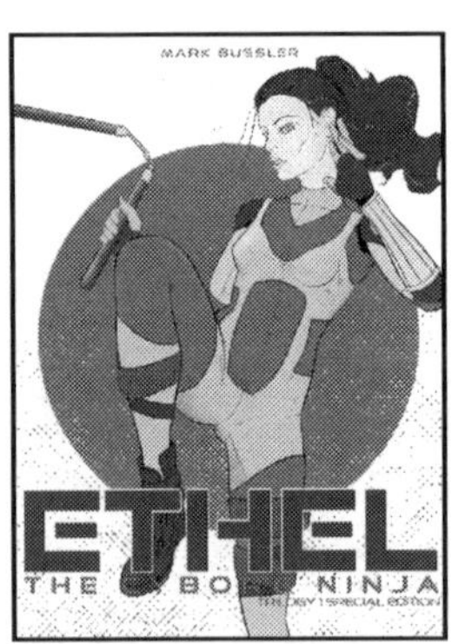

Ethel the Cyborg Ninja Trilogy 1
Hardcover Edition

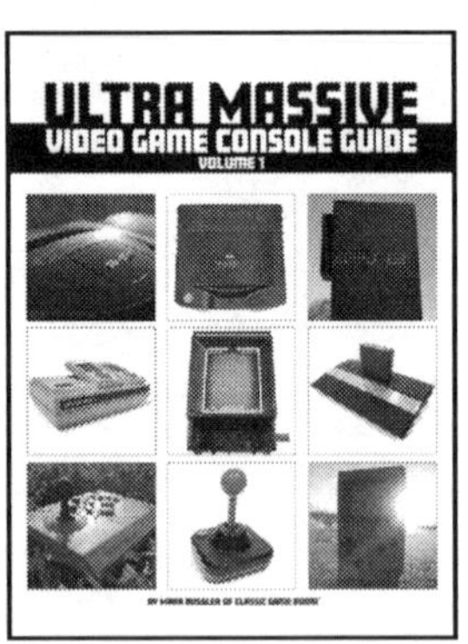

Ultra Massive Video Game
Console Guide Volume 1

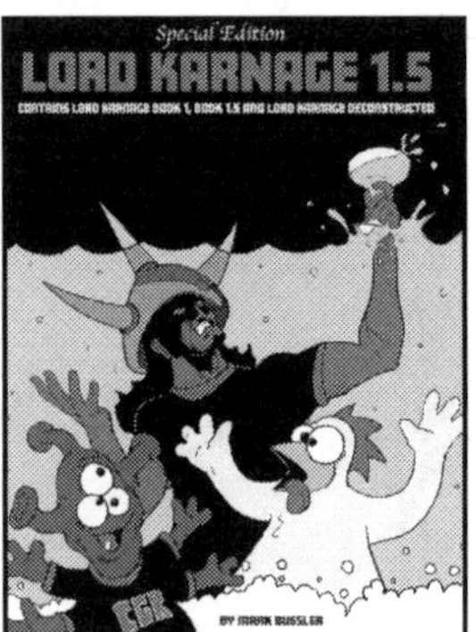

Lord Karnage 1.5
Special Edition

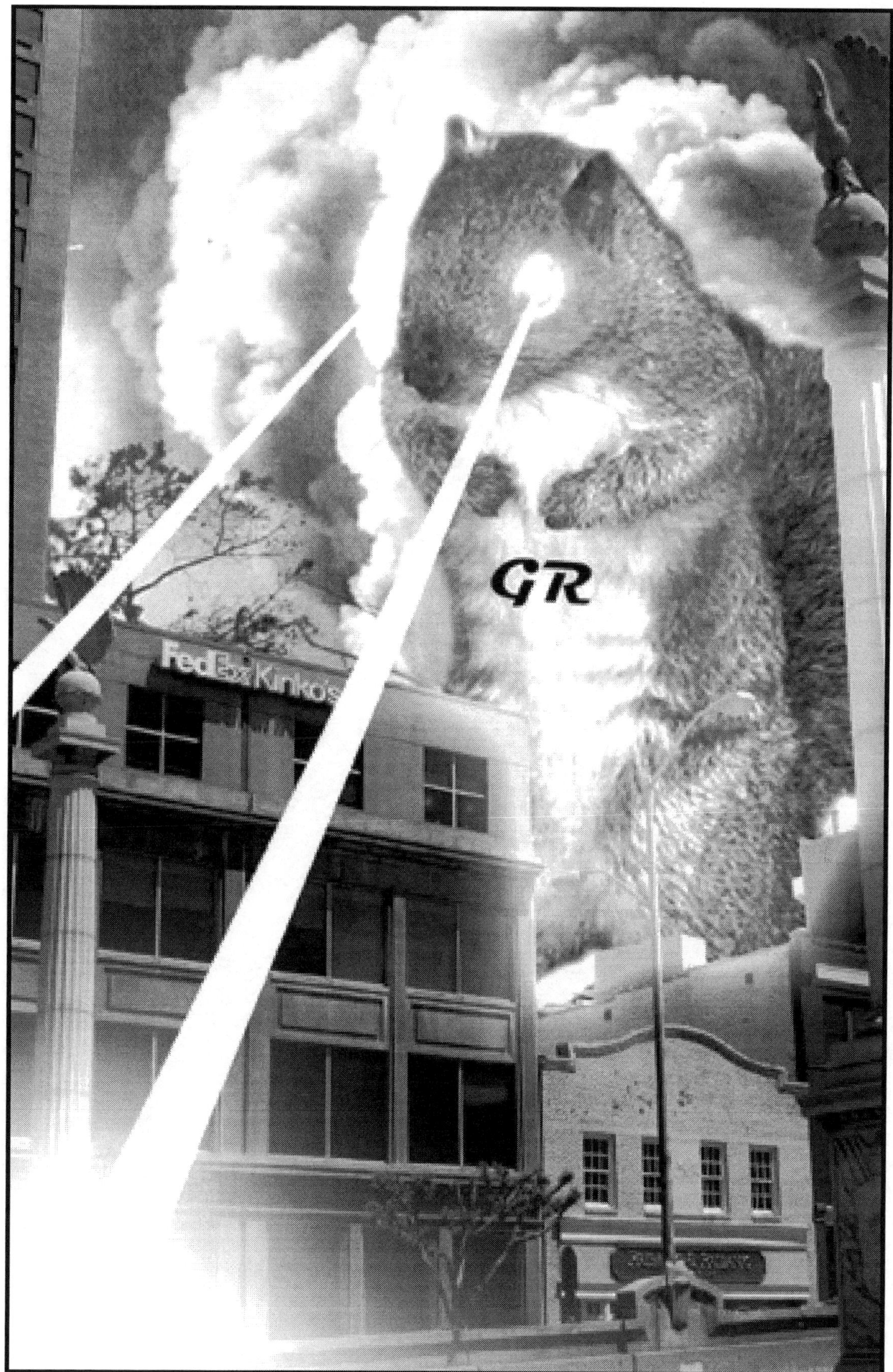
GR
FedEx Kinko's

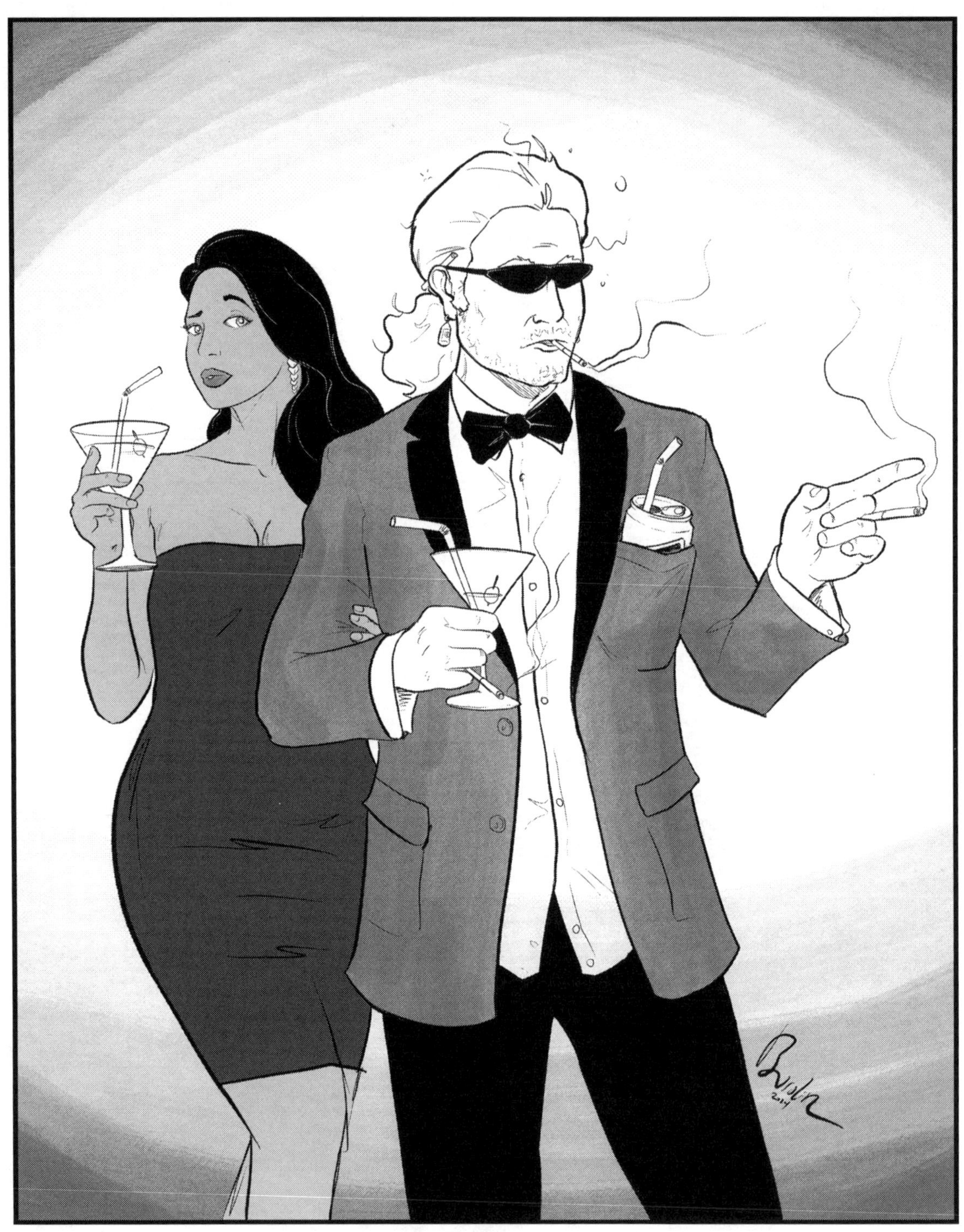

Agent 0040oz in
A View to Another Octopus Tomorrow that Never Dies (2024)

TABLE OF CONTENTS

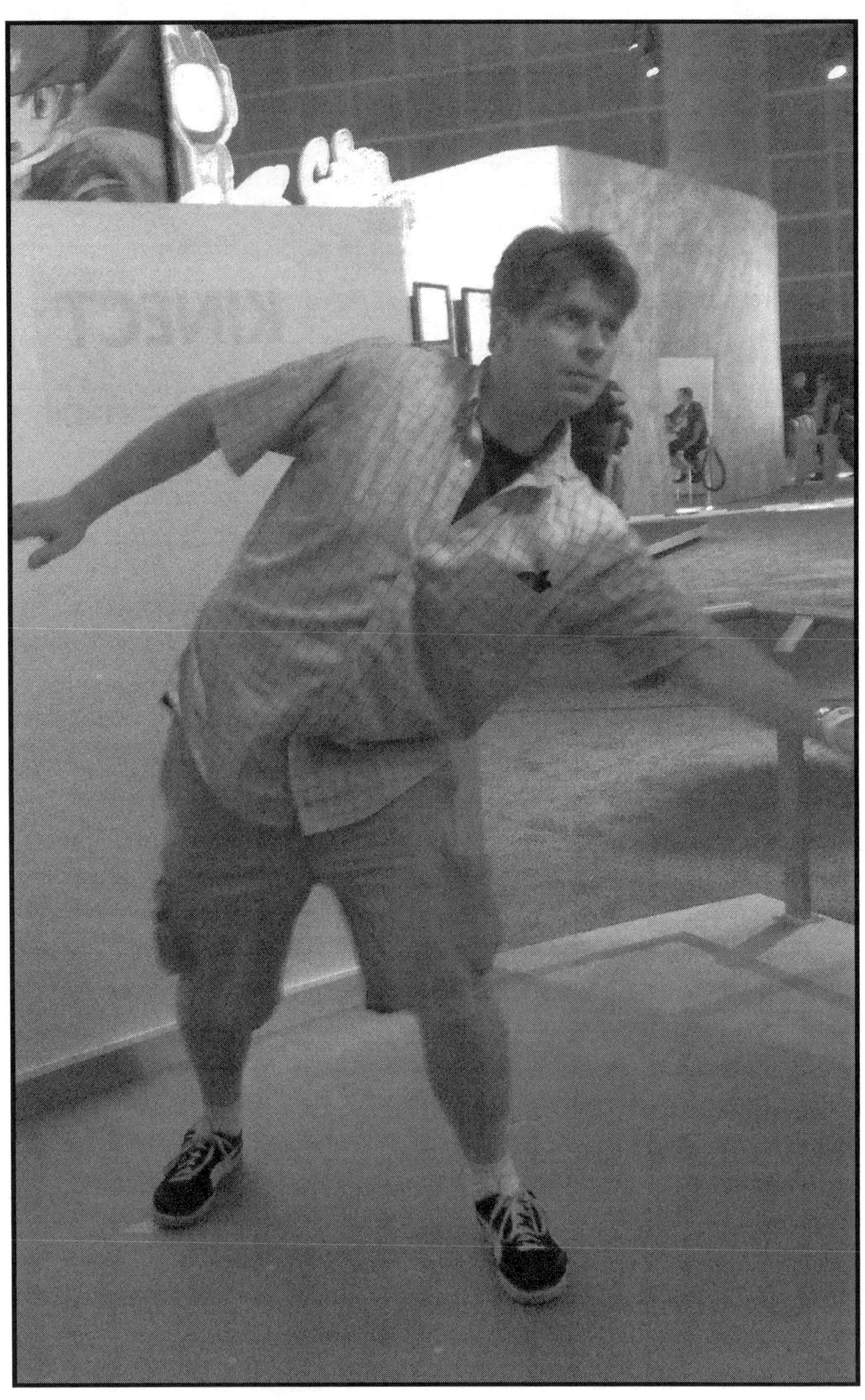

Mark Bussler at E3 2010 playing Kinect

PROLOGUE

"I don't like to lose."
-Captain Kirk

One can learn many life lessons from Star Trek II. For example, know how everything on your starship works. Don't make decisions on an empty stomach, and, most importantly, master the Kobayashi Maru scenario. (What is the Kobayashi Maru? Honestly, if you don't know, you're not going to fully understand this book.)

As I write this text, Classic Game Room turns 25 years old. Though not a household name, Classic Game Room is an interesting brand and a case study of surviving in business when the entire world changes around you overnight.

This book serves as a record of events to amuse and educate fans of the long-running Classic Game Room Internet series. Additionally, this book preserves, in detail, one story that took place during the earliest days of the online video entertainment industry.

I've seen a fair amount of discussion about Classic Game Room over the years and pretty much everyone misunderstands what "it" is. Classic Game Room is not a YouTube show. Classic Game Room is not a YouTube channel. It never was, and to view it as such puts the entire thing out of perspective. This is because Classic Game Room predates YouTube and all social media.

So, unlearn what you may have thought you learned. The actual story of Classic Game Room is a pragmatic case study of quickly adapting to changing situations, pivoting when necessary, and re-writing a business model that goes obsolete within hours.

What!? This is a business textbook!?

No, wait! Don't put it down! This is an entertaining journey through 25 years of nonsense. I have even included some doodles of a chicken high on drugs.

You'll laugh, you'll cry, you'll wish you were reading Garfield. Be forewarned, though, that the History of Classic Game Room is more than just a book about the rise and fall (and rise and fall and rise and fall and rise and fall and eventual evolution) of the Classic Game Room Internet show, it's a thorough look at one of the Internet's longest-running brands born on the Internet that dates back to the 20th century.

But wait, what actually *is* Classic Game Room?

Classic Game Room is, maybe, the longest-running Internet video game review show. I say "maybe" because it's hard to prove, and it doesn't matter anyway. There's no award and no marketing boost for being the "original Internet video game review show" because, for the most part, nobody cares about Internet history. Something popular last week is already viewed as obsolete, let alone 25 years ago. Dinosaurs may as well have roamed the earth.

It is well documented that Classic Game Room started life in November of 1999 as The Game Room on FromUSAlive and I was there to confirm this. There is solid video evidence of me looking much younger, much fatter, and with a thick mop of greasy young-man brown hair (it's now white and much easier to manage.)

In short, Classic Game Room is a VERY old Internet video game review show that ran the life cycle of all your favorite TV shows. It started, got popular, people lost interest, production costs went up, and it ended because it cost more to produce than it earned.

"Checkpoint!"

Founded in 1999, Classic Game Room predates social media, influencers, and "content creators." (FYI, the term content creators is a term meant to belittle artists working in the field of Internet video. It makes me sick. It makes me want to vomit. It is an insult to art.)

Classic Game Room predates YouTube.

Classic Game Room predates Facebook.

Classic Game Room predates TikTok, Twitter, Snapchat, Instagram, and even MySpace which debuted in 2003.

As I'm writing this, Classic Game Room continues to provide original gaming-related content in one form or another.

But seriously, what the "checkpoint" is it? (and where did this checkpoint thing come from??*)

*The "checkpoint" gag came from one of the Classic Game Room podcasts when I used a Sega Genesis sample from the Genesis synthesizer plugin for Korg Gadget to celebrate cracking a beer on mic. Checkpoint! From there, it also served as a good way to bleep foul language.

I suspect that many of you reading this think that Classic Game Room is a funny Vectrex-obsessed video game review show that ran on YouTube forever. That is true, but Classic Game Room is more than that.

Classic Game Room is a brand under the umbrella of CGR Publishing, which is the public-facing persona of a very boring company called Inecom, LLC. which also dates to 1999.

If you're taking notes, it's very important to understand that a brand isn't the same thing as a YouTube "show" or "channel."

A brand can be applied to any kind of product. Think Spaceballs the movie, Spaceballs the t-shirt, lunchbox, action figures, toilet paper, and Spaceballs the flamethrower.

Classic Game Room is one of many brands owned by CGR Publishing, and yes, I stole my business model from Spaceballs.

In this case, there's Classic Game Room the t-shirt, Classic Game Room the distribution company, Classic Game Room the beer stein, podcast, coffee mug, mousepad, and the show. Classic Game Room, by extension, also has connections to hundreds of books, thousands of songs, and tens of thousands of products sold around the world.

Classic Game Room sold out!

Classic Game Room sold out before the cameras even turned on in 1999. Get over it.

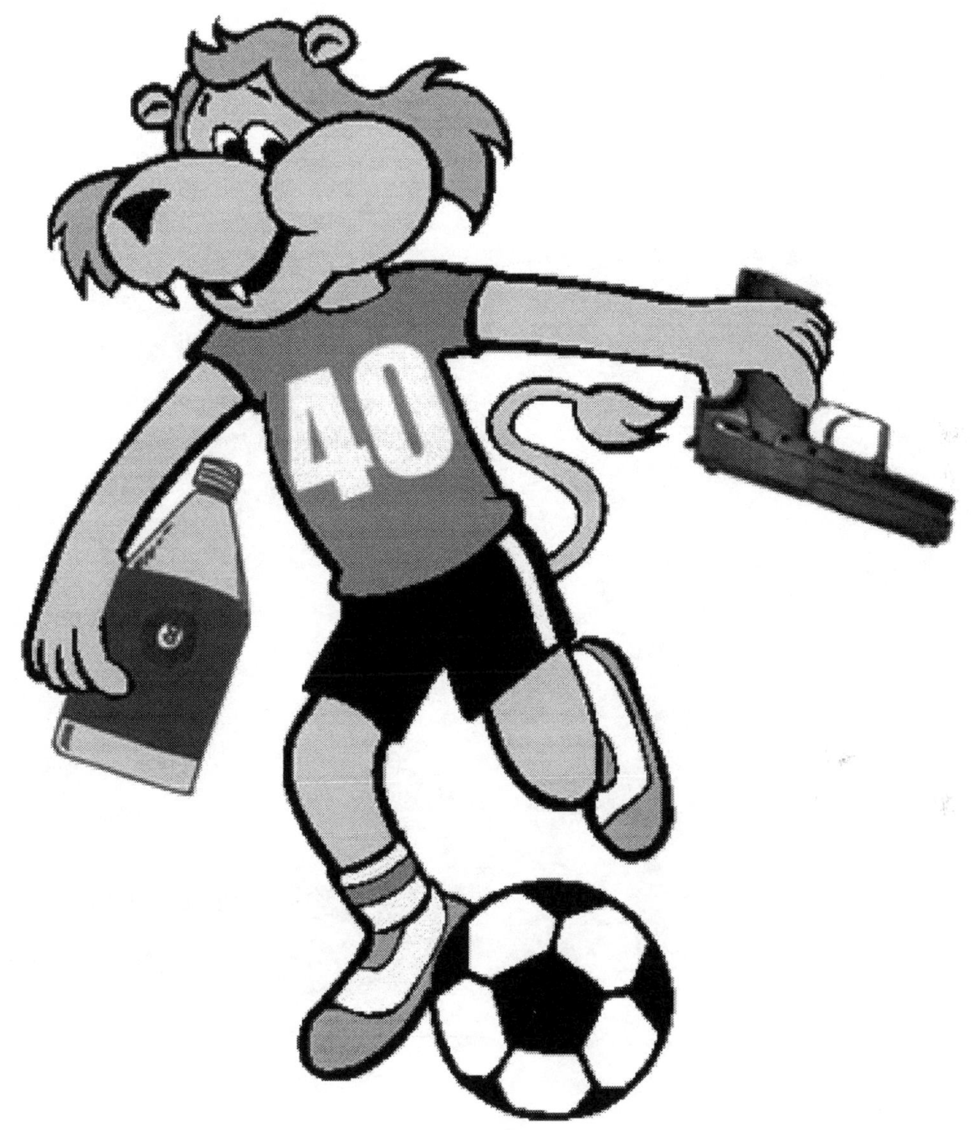

It's Larry the Lira Accepting Male Prostitute!
(Circa The Game Room 2000)

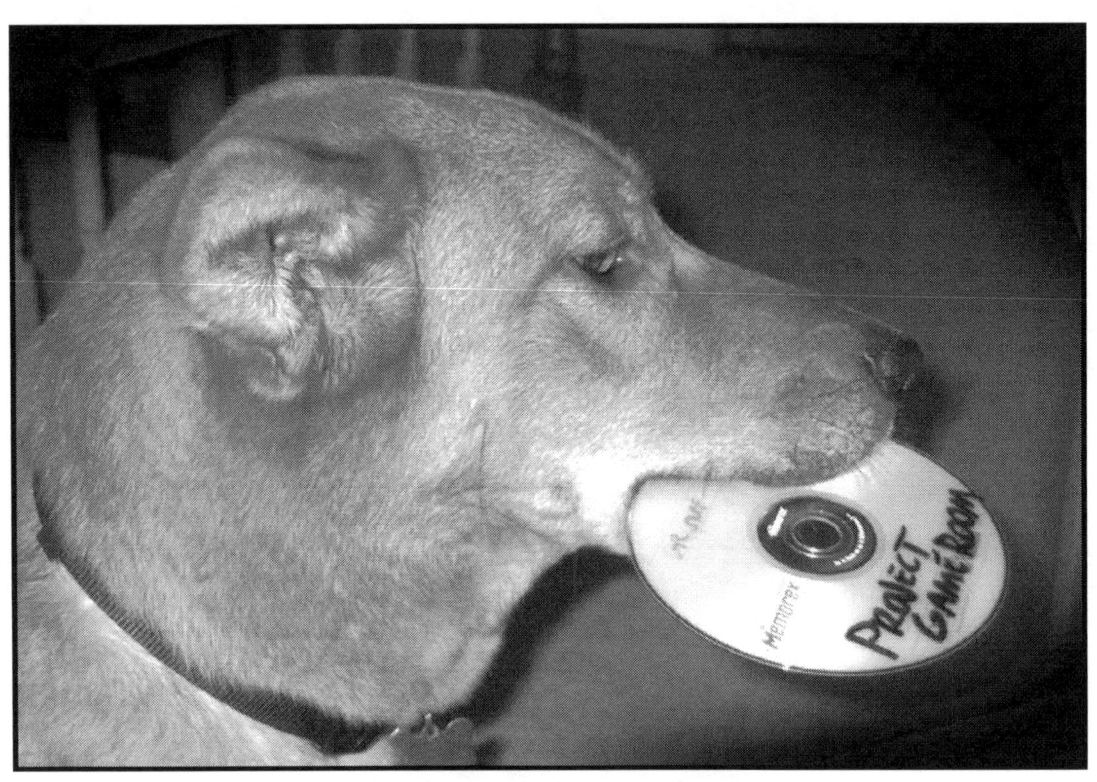

Viral Dog eating The Game Room

CHAPTER 1
AN INTRODUCTION TO CGR

As I write this in 2024, Classic Game Room the show is a very small part of CGR Publishing, but what is CGR Publishing? And why was the publishing company named after Classic Game Room when Classic Game Room is the bigger name but is somehow just a small part of the whole? More on that later. For now, let's talk publishing.

CGR Publishing is, as it sounds, a publishing company; An independent publishing company with a small footprint and relatively low overhead that bends and moves with the ever-changing breeze of consumer demands.

Ok, that's boring. What is a publishing company?

A publishing company does not make. A publishing company publishes. That's all that it does.

CGR Publishing can publish my work, your work, or the work of sentient artificially intelligent beings from the future. It is often difficult for people, including me, to compartmentalize that the publishing arm of this business only publishes. It does not create on its own.

Publishing can be complicated, or it can be very simple. It depends on the product. For my purposes, publishing is relatively simple and kept that way by design. (Once something is no longer simple, I don't want anything to do with it.)

Here's a fun breakdown:

WHAT IS PUBLISHING?

10. CGR Publishing takes a product (it doesn't matter what it is) and prepares it for sale.

20. CGR Publishing lists said product for sale somewhere that sells it.

30. CGR Publishing promotes the product so that people hear about it. Then it (hopefully) sells.

40. CGR Publishing ships or delivers the product to whoever buys it.

50. CGR Publishing earns money from selling products that it uses to publish more stuff.

60. Goto 10.

That is publishing in a nutshell.

Classic Game Room, Omega Ronin, Turbo Volcano, World's Fair books, glassware, t-shirts; it doesn't matter. Make, market, sell. Publish.

Now, let's go back to step 10. I said "Prepare it for sale" because that leaves the origin of the product wide open. I have, for the most part, made my own products for CGR Publishing, but that doesn't mean that I have to. I can also license products or publish things from other people. But, in the age of self-publishing, I tend to just make it myself or contract with someone to complete things under my direction.

The hardest part of publishing is step 30, promotion and marketing. Making stuff is easy, the promotional aspect of publishing is by far the costliest and most challenging aspect of this business. It doesn't matter how good your product is, if nobody hears about it, they'll never buy it.

Marketing is everything, and in the age of social media, marketing has gotten very, very complicated, and surprisingly expensive considering it's all supposed to be free. Nothing in life is free.

Social media appears free, but you're paying for it with your personal data and privacy. If you want to effectively market on social media, you have to pay to "boost" your posts. They still look free, but they aren't free. Free is an illusion.

Therefore, a brand with name recognition is worth its weight in gold (which is why we get endless movie sequels and reboots.)

Name recognition, for the purpose of marketing, is the only reason that Classic Game Room brand continues to this day, because otherwise it would have been shut down a decade ago.

The brand is associated with a video game review show, but there is no longer a need for video game review shows in the era of live streaming, Chat GPT, Google, Wikipedia, and no-barrier-to-entry influencers.

So, I must admit, the brand has been challenging to deal with for years because the entire world changed in the course of its existence. But it's still a brand, and that has value.

"I'm so confused! I thought you were just a one-dimensional idiot who played Atari games and yelled about Star Wars!"

I do like Atari and Star Wars, but I also like staying in business, and this book has a lot to do with staying in business. Perhaps, the greatest takeaway from this tome of knowledge is that staying in business requires sacrifice.

Like Spock repairing the radioactive do-hickey to save the Enterprise in Star Trek II, sometimes the ultimate price must be made.

So, before I really dig into this adventure from the beginning, let me give you a condensed timeline of the Classic Game Room history.

CLASSIC GAME ROOM: THE TIMELINE OF MAJOR EVENTS

1999: Classic Game Room starts life on FromUSAlive as The Game Room.

2000: FromUSAlive shuts down and with it, so does The Game Room after about 80 episodes.

2006: Production starts on Classic Game Room: The Rise and Fall of the Internet's Greatest Video Game Review Show.

2007: Classic Game Room: The Rise and Fall of the Internet's Greatest Video Game Review Show debuts on DVD.

2007: Classic Game Room starts to post old 1999-2000-era videos on YouTube.

2008: Classic Game Room HD debuts on YouTube with all-new video game reviews.

2008: Classic Game Room spins off from the parent company to expand and focus on video game reviews.

2009: Classic Game Room embarks on a mission to become a video game journalism empire and blows up on YouTube.

2010: Classic Game Room expands into a network of shows.

2011: Classic Game Room viewership peaks at roughly 1.5 million views a day. The brand continues to expand into a legitimate video game journalism company working with big-name game publishers such as Sega and Activision.

2012: Daily views start to decline.

2013: In the middle of expansion, Classic Game Room loses nearly half of its ad revenue within months. Classic Game Room discontinues YouTube production and launches its very-own website for video reviews. Views tank. The website crashes a lot but it works.

2014: Classic Game Room expands into products like Blu-Ray, glassware, and books. Views continue to plummet. Classic Game Room resumes YouTube content to the amusement of viewers laughing at us that we tried to do something different.

2015: After another disappointing year of falling views and evaporating ad revenue, Classic Game Room ceases operations. All shows are canceled, and the business prepares to close in December. Ethel the Cyborg Ninja Book 1 is crowdfunded and delivered to backers as the company is shuttered.

2016: Mark buys out Classic Game Room and reboots it with crowdfunding and product sales. It looks promising but crowdfunding turns off new viewers.

2017: Crowdfunding implodes, sales falter, views continue to plunge. Once again, the cost of production exceeds earnings. Mark reprints Ethel the Cyborg Ninja on Amazon and follows it by writing several non-fiction books. The books do well. Classic Game Room expands into clothing design on Amazon.

2018: Print publishing and clothing sales exceed video production. Classic Game Room launches as CGR 2085 on Amazon, a bigger budget show with television-quality production. Classic Game Room 2085 struggles to find an audience. Print publishing and clothing sales take over the company.

2019: CGR Publishing publishes dozens of books. Mark launches CGR Infinity as a low-budget, 60-second version of Classic Game Room. CGR Infinity bombs. Book sales grow. Mark shuts down video production after releasing a collection of reviews called CGR 20th. The CGR Publishing imprint begins. Mark shutters the video production company by the end of the year and liquidates production assets.

2020: Pandemic ravages the world. CGR Publishing digs in and continues to publish books and other non-video-related products. Record year for CGR Publishing.

2021: Same thing. Record year for CGR Publishing.

2022: Same thing. Record year for CGR Publishing. Mark starts to tinker with music production as a way to market products and adds music to commercials on various sales channels. Turbo Volcano releases Future Year 1982 in February. Omega Ronin debuts in April with Halcyon Sunrise.

2023: By 2023, everyone in the world wants to be an influencer and self-publishing guru. The cost of advertising explodes. Mark looks back to the Classic Game Room brand to market products with name recognition and launches a social media experiment across YouTube, TikTok, and Instagram. Omega Ronin continues to grow and finds success in music streaming services. Classic Game Room returns to YouTube with new video reviews to celebrate its 24th anniversary and launches Classic Game Room 2085 on Blu-Ray. Record year for CGR Publishing.

2024: Classic Game Room 2085 Season 2 debuts on YouTube and fails to reach an audience. Video viewership growth is negative. Production costs vastly exceed earnings. CGR ends its social media experiment and discontinues publishing free entertainment content on YouTube, TikTok, and Instagram. Mark prepares to end the final season of Classic Game Room and terminate the show once and for all. CGR Publishing continues to publish new clothing designs, books, and music releases. The website returns as an important marketing tool when social media is phased out.

Omega Ronin debuts as a graphic novel with a companion soundtrack album. Ethel the Cyborg Ninja returns in a new book. With the new focus on the website, Classic Game Room can justify the production of new, periodic shows exclusively on CGRpublishing.com. Classic Game Room begins the process of removing all content from YouTube and permanently archiving it on CGRpublishing.com.

After 25 years, Classic Game Room goes full circle and returns to its own website with gaming content, comic books, and beer mugs. Fun fact, writing this book helped me come up with this strategy because once I saw it all from a top-down perspective it made sense. CGR returned to its roots after a quarter century.

This is absurd!!

Is it?

I think all business development looks absurd in hindsight. One must remember that the person (or persons) running a company can only make estimated guesses about what will happen next, often leading to what looks like ridiculous decision-making.

Since day one in this business, there has been a disconnect between what people said they wanted, and what actually sold or earned views. It's just the way that people are, and the faster you figure that out, the better you will do in business. It took me a few years to figure this out.

Also, don't believe anything that a social media company tells you. Ever.

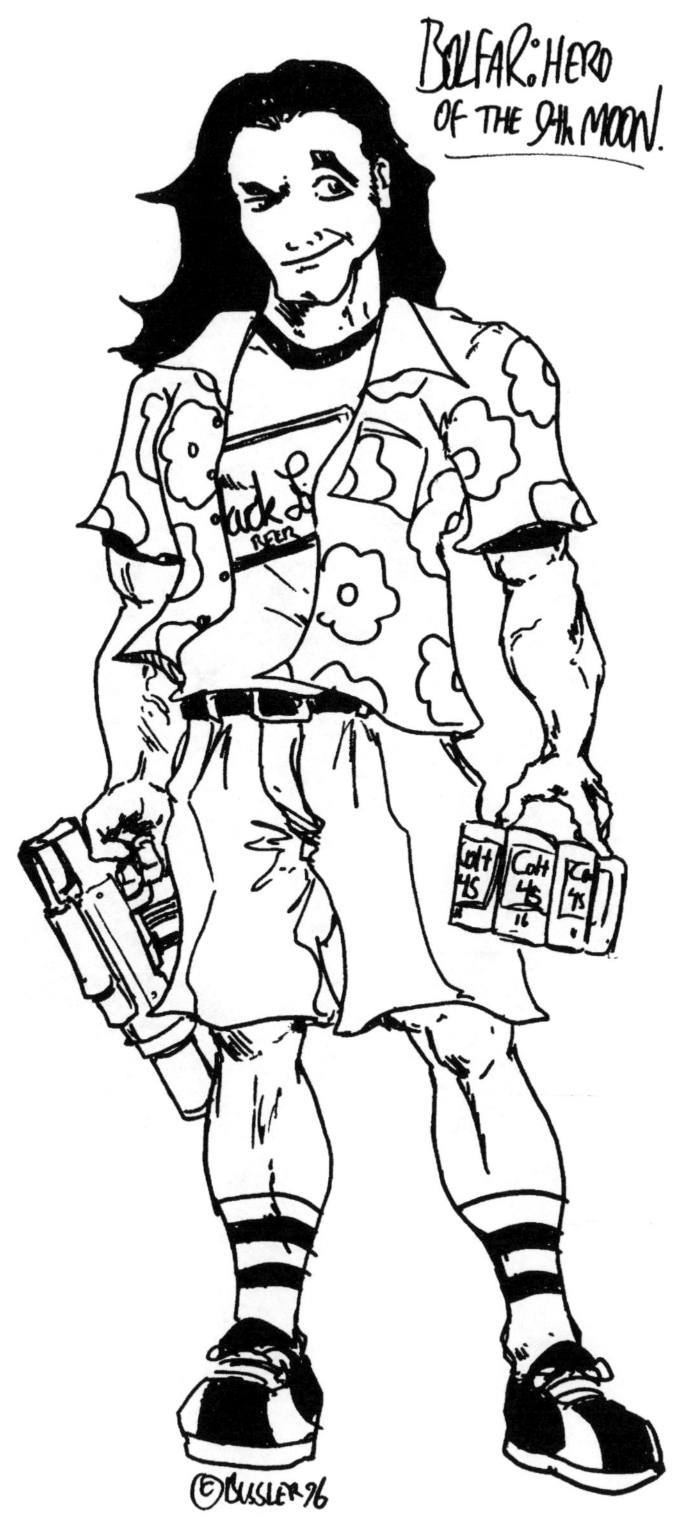

Bolfar: Hero of the 9th Moon (1996)

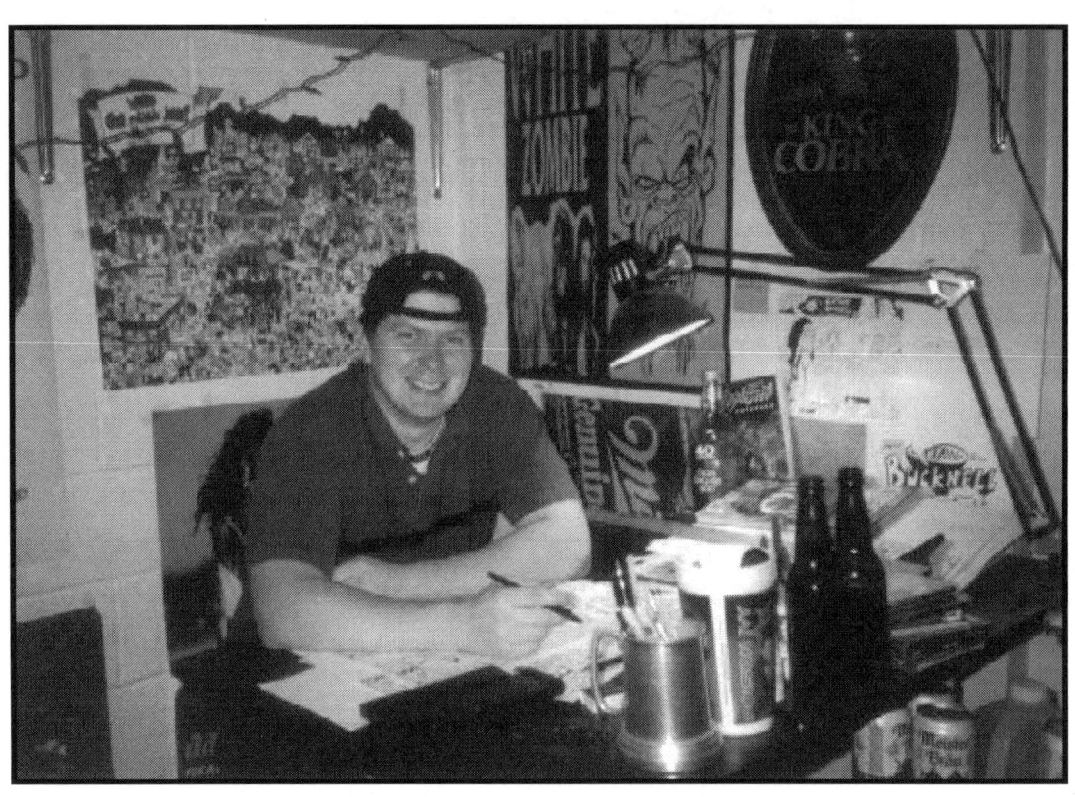

Mark Bussler circa 1997-1998 drawing comics in college.

CHAPTER 2
A COMPUTER LAB IN 1995

Let's take it way back to flannel shirts, Nirvana, dial-up modems, and Zima. It's the 90s!

I was born in 1975 which makes me a solid Gen X. This is an interesting age because I'm part of the last generation who grew up all the way through high school without the Internet. My formative years were influenced by Skeletor and Voltron, not TikTok dances and hate-for-profit podcasts.

I graduated from high school in the spring of 1994. I was an idiot in every possible way, but I do have a good memory and can recall being introduced to something called e-mail in the computer lab. It may have been 1993 or so, and I can't specifically say what we used it for, but the rudimentary green-text-on-black-screen computers were doing something beyond what they used to do. They were somehow magically connected to other computers and the people on those computers.

My attention was, for the most part, elsewhere in those years. I loathed high school, I detested classes, and I just wanted to get the hell out. I wanted to be an artist but knew enough to know that it was an impossible career choice. Not having a clear idea of what I wanted to do in life, I chose to go for a liberal arts degree in college focusing on business and marketing after graduation.

It wasn't until I started college in the fall of 1994 that I began to hear things about "surfing the web." I can vividly recall seeing a crappy printout hanging on the wall of my freshman dorm; A piece of blue paper with a clipart surfboard guy promoting a class about "The world wide web!"

What is this nonsense? Is the future turning into The Lawnmower Man mixed with Point Break? (And if so, right on.)

I had a computer in my dorm room freshman year and, when I wasn't playing Doom, got into old-school messaging and newsgroups. My college radio experience also started that year, and I remember hanging out with friends, going home, and then messaging them later, which in retrospect was dumb because we could have just continued hanging out in the real world.

But there was something so exciting about messaging someone. There was like this moment after sending a line of text where you'd stare at the screen and wait, with eager anticipation, for a reply.

So much change so quickly!

I was a strange fit for Bucknell University, a good liberal arts school with a good reputation, but also known for being a bit stuffy which wasn't me. I forget why I chose it. Probably because it was a good school and they didn't have a language requirement because I sword I'd never take a language again.

English was enough and I didn't need to speak some other dumb language like French to draw comic strips! (I was such an idiot in those years...)

Were it not for the Beastie Boys I would have transferred after my first semester because I met my buddies through this jackass who was wearing a B-Boys shirt.

I was like, "You like the Beastie Boys and beer?"

"Yeah man. You wanna drink beer and blast Brass Monkey?" (That's not word for word, but it may as well be.)

We're still great friends today.

I stayed and got hardcore into website design and taught myself HTML programming in their state-of-the-art computer labs. It took me a while to find my way in college. (One could argue that I'm still finding my way.)

I chose business marketing as a major. But, in retrospect, I should have majored in computer science and art. But, I went with the safe all-purpose major that probably wouldn't be too hard on my important social schedule (swilling beer and blasting Paul's Boutique.) How hard can economics and accounting be, anyway?

I had little interest in the science classes I had to take and certainly struggled through economics and accounting. Business law was at 8am which was VERY inconvenient (heavy sigh...) One could argue that if you aren't hungover in business law then you aren't really trying.

All that I wanted to do was create, and the Internet showed me how to combine creativity with computers.

I loved the Internet.

I learned how to make web pages by copying HTML (in Notepad, I think) and eventually started putting up my own art-related websites in 1995 or 1996. My computer science friends helped me host them, and in retrospect, I wish I had paid more attention to where the Internet was heading back then because I could have gotten in really early and made a buck.

In any event, in those years I was too busy pounding Black Label, playing video games, "frequenting social gatherings", and going to White Zombie concerts to care. It was the '90s. Had I known it would be the last decade that wasn't truly awful in every way, I would have enjoyed myself even more (which would have killed me.)

If someone could have showed me what the miserable 21st century would be like, I would have found a way to slow down time and stay in the 90s. I'd still be there, drinking beer and blasting Soundgarden, which is what I did last weekend... never mind.

Admittedly, I was short-sighted and immature at the time. I only saw website programming as a way to launch a comic strip and comic book art career.

In 1996 we couldn't Google how to do this stuff because Google didn't exist. Nor did Siri, Alexa, YouTube, Facebook, A.I. or any of it. We had Netscape, Alta Vista, and Lycos. None of them were good for anything except newsgroups and video game cheat codes (and for other kinds of lascivious searches.)

Anyway, somehow in my drink-addled mid-90s state of mind, I learned to design websites, got pretty good at it, and saw that it was a great way to get my creative work out there, beyond my college campus, into the computer monitors of readers around the world. It also looked good on a resume.

Indeed, this worked, and at one point I installed a thingy that showed me who was visiting my website. My comics had readers from England and Australia!

In 1997 I secured a national syndication deal for my Mass Media comic strip which ran in the school paper. I was like "Man, this is easy! I'm so good at this. Life is going to be a piece of cake."

I graduated in 1998. I was a fucking moron, there's just no other way to say it. I had a comic strip syndication deal with Creators Syndicate and I was going to be king of the world.

Instead of putting more time into a resume and job hunting on the East Coast like my friends, I was dumb and lazy and took a job with my dad's company in Pittsburgh after graduation because I just assumed I'd make it as a cartoonist. But I still needed a job to pay the bills until my comics started to earn millions of dollars like Calvin and Hobbes. The money just grows on money trees, right?

Yeah..... no.

My syndication deal fell apart that summer before ever going to print.

"Excuse me, this is messing up all my poorly planned plans."

In hindsight, Mass Media wasn't my best work, but also newspaper comic strips were in freefall by the late 90s. My dreams of being the next Berkely Breathed were just that, dreams. I may as well have dreamed about being the world's best buggy whip maker. The Internet killed newspapers overnight and the comics section got squeezed out of existence.

Thankfully I had a few useful real-world skills and learned more than perhaps I gave myself credit for in college. Not everyone could combine website programming with graphic design and I had that going for me.

By late 1998 working life was fine, but it certainly wasn't the glamorous career of artistic creative awesomeness that I thought it was going to be.

In 1998 and 1999 I wrote advertising copy for engineering magazines, I designed ad layouts, and I made websites. I even started to work in industrial videos.

Real work was hard, boring, and everyone hated me because I was the boss's idiot son like straight outta one of the Dilbert cartoons. I had one taped onto my fridge. "Boss's son = Moron."

Thankfully, I grew up quickly. I saw the awkward position I put myself in.

I was privileged enough to start my career and move things in the right direction, however, I wasn't privileged enough to travel to Europe at a whim or take a few years off to do drugs and soul-search. My plans rapidly changed from making the next Bloom County into just making it through the next week. I continued some art and website work as a hobby, but for the most part I just put on my tan pleated Dockers one leg at a time, drank three Cokes a day, and did an unfulfilling but perfectly acceptable job.

My intentions were good, and I worked hard, but I was definitely just going through the motions until I could figure out what was next in my life. I'm not very fond of who I was at 24.

My dad is a programming genius and one of those people who can often see the next big thing. It was in this period, late 1998 or so, when he converted a storage room (maybe it was a conference room) into a small studio in which to produce cheap VHS tapes for marketing and instructional purposes. He painted the walls beige because someone told him that beige looked good on video (I think they wanted to unload some beige paint because it looked awful.)

His company produced engineering computer aided design software for PCs. Instructional videos were a great way to show existing and potential customers how to use this stuff on-screen with step-by-step instructions and visual results.

Instructional videos on VHS were nothing new, but in 1998, my dad saw that posting these videos on the Internet was the future; and *that* was new.

I can't remember exactly how he figured out how to do it, but at some point in '98 he turned his little in-house production company into an online video experiment with one camera hooked up to the Internet for rudimentary marketing and live product demonstrations.

The thing about Internet video in the 90s is that there was no existing platform upon which to post it, and no way to effectively search for how to do it. Everyone knew that video existed on the Internet, because porn had been doing it for years, but nobody knew how to physically get a video signal onto the Internet.

We had to make it all up from scratch.

Somehow, behind the scenes, my dad and the tech people figured all of this out and we started broadcasting marketing and instructional videos regularly in late 1998 or early 1999.

Our audience was professionals who had access to the latest Internet tools like T-1 lines and stuff like that. We filmed weekly product announcements and gave weekly free training online.

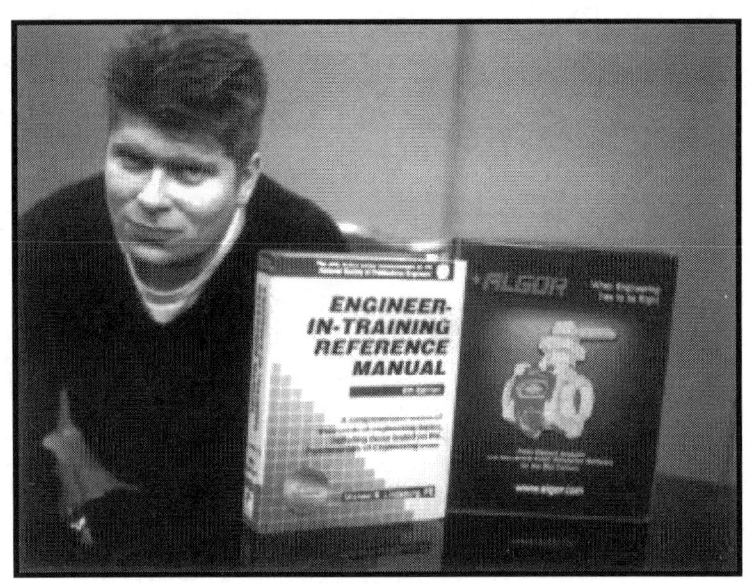

Mark circa 1999. What an asshole!

CHAPTER 3
TO FILM SCHOOL AND BEYOND

Somewhere around there, probably late 1998, I started film school at the now-defunct Pittsburgh Filmmakers to get some practical education in filming and editing for our corporate educational video productions. This was hilarious because, if I was the least-conservative, weirdest kid at Bucknell wearing a Ministry t-shirt with a beer in each hand reciting lines from Highlander, I was the most conservative business sell-out at film school coming off work in tan Dockers and a blue button up.

"What's up, ladies? Who wants to hang out and talk about Dave Matthews and J-Crew sweaters?"

How can one go to film school in the 90s without tattoos, a smoking habit, and a bad demeanor? I didn't even have blue hair.

All joking aside, I loved film school. It's a shame that I went in the years when I started to grow up a little bit. If I had gone to film school at 19, I'd probably be in jail or dead, so, maybe it's good I went a little bit later in life...

Film school rocks. We'd shoot super-8 videos on the weekends, hit up some crappy 90s clubs or dive bars at night, and end up at someone's apartment drinking, playing Unreal and watching Starship Troopers until 3 a.m. And then somehow, I would still make it to work at 7:30am with a raging hangover and orange drink bracelets on my wrists. Those were the days of unstoppable energy. It's amazing what one can do before middle age and kids kick the crap out of you.

In early 1999, I spent a few weekends working with my dad to start the conversion of a larger office space into a "real" production studio. This would eventually become the studio that you've seen in the original Game Room videos (reference page 86.)

This conference-room-turned-studio was awful but functional. It had gray carpet on the walls, brown carpeting on the floor, and a lonely plant sitting in the corner. The 1970s drop ceiling provided no soundproofing and the AC vents blasted air onto the microphones during recording. The sounds of real life and business poured through the walls.

Throughout that spring we hung lights on the ceiling and installed a mixing board for upcoming live engineering broadcasts. "Live" was going to be a big part of this plan because engineers watching our videos online could call in and ask questions that could be answered (this was before Zoom and Facetime, you know!)

The website and IT departments were furious with my dad because he made their safe and comfortable jobs complicated and busy.

You know Scotty from Star Trek. That's the IT department.

"There's no way we can get this done on time because we're stagger specting the wheels on the server for an email protocol testing dump. You wouldn't want to lose your emails for the week because of a time-flux tetrion particle inversion, would you? Well, then we have to be out by five. See ya." They were a funny crew. I liked them.

I'm not sure anyone around there was very excited about my dad's newfangled "Web TV" concept. In fact, I know they weren't. I thought it was neat, and perhaps a better way forward than writing marketing and website copy, which was painfully boring. So, I happily (or at least hungover and begrudgingly) went along for the ride.

After weeks of wiring, lighting, and rudimentary computer setups, we completed the construction of a low-budget TV studio in the middle of a conservative engineering company during that summer of 1999. This could have been one of the worst ideas that anyone has ever had, or maybe it was the best. How else could this have started?

It was 1999 after all, and people made millions of dollars out of thin air by making up websites with dumbass names like Amazon. Dad called his Internet production company Inecom.

Internet Entertainment and Communication.

Inecom seemed sufficiently professional if not super dull. (I wanted to call it something stupid like Starforce 9000 Death Ray Space Murder Factory, but I was an idiot.) Remember, this was originally set up for business-to-business webcasting, not entertainment.

Dear readers, this was not the "The Social Network." When you watch movies about early 2000s tech-bros creating social media companies in San Francisco you're only seeing one glamorized part of the story. Everyone is excited in those films, everything works out, and everything is awesome. There are parties and yachts, and spectacular scenery and a lavish California lifestyle.

We were the exact opposite.

No parties. No scenery. No boat rides. No drugs. Just Pittsburgh and maybe a half-empty bottle of Diet Pepsi.

We weren't Facebook, we were Office Space. Wasn't

the company in Office Space called Intertrode? Where ***are*** those TPS reports?

Inecom. Nobody could ever pronounce it, ever. EY-Enecom. EEEnecom. In-eh-com. Sigh....

The real shame is that we were just a few letters off from Encom, the company in Tron.

> We trailblazed the way for Internet entertainment in brown slacks without any cocaine.

So, throughout 1999, this tiny in-house production company called Inecom pivoted from instructional VHS tapes into Internet television, as he called it. I thought the concept was fascinating and loved the technical aspects of filming and editing, but my dad saw a bigger picture. To be fair, he's the only one who cared about the big picture.

But, it wasn't really what I was looking to do after getting a taste of film school and severely regretting not getting a real job in New York City like the rest of my friends.

By mid 1999, I was having second thoughts about moving back to sleepy Pittsburgh and being the boss's son working with my dad, which sounded like the biggest cop out ever when I admitted it out loud (in retrospect I should have cherished every second of it because you don't get that time back.)

My college friends lived in fun places like D.C., Philadelphia, and New York. In the 1990s, Pittsburgh was in freefall, losing significant chunks of its population every day after failing to recover from the steel mill shutdowns in the 1970s and 1980s. It had one of the oldest populations in the entire country, and people couldn't run away from its decaying infrastructure fast enough.

Late '90s Pittsburgh was a sausage-fest with no beaches, limited nightlife, and it took way too long to get to the Jersey Shore or Ocean City where the fun stuff was happening.

I'd road trip to visit my buddies in major cities where bars were full of 20-somethings and excitement. My friends went to the Jersey Shore on the weekends or happening places in Georgetown, Hoboken, and Manayunk.

I spent my weekends in an office with brown carpet and a lonely, depressed plant sitting on 1982 carpeting. I wore tan Dockers. I cried into my Mountain Dew when nobody was looking.

Film school was fun, but I knew there was no way it was going to get me into the film industry, that much was clear. Pittsburgh Filmmakers was, for the most part, a low-key operation with no studio connections whatsoever. If you wanted to get into real filmmaking, you needed to move to California or New York City.

Filmmakers always felt like it had this legacy to Romero's Night of the Living Dead and the outdated "you can do it all in Pittsburgh" attitude. I love that attitude, but no, it didn't work like that for anyone else in the film industry.

This is how I felt at the time. In retrospect, I have fond memories of that period of my life. It *was* fun.

We got to edit super-8 film in a building that looked like a post-apocalyptic set piece from Robocop. Everyone was pretty unhinged and moonlighting from other jobs or local colleges. After classes, we'd go bar hopping and smoke cigarettes at film screenings. I learned some good entry-level skills at film school and made some friends.

I took classes in photography, editing, and production planning. My worst grade was in cable management. That's a thing. I am truly awful at wrapping up cables. "Here, take this jumbled mess of cables and make it organized!" Everyone else could do it. I was like "Fuck this, just buy new cables." I think I got a D.

After the disappointment of watching my comic strip career dreams evaporate and the realization that I wasn't going to direct the next Star Wars, I seriously questioned where I was heading, professionally and personally.

That summer, I started to contemplate moving out to where my buddies were on the East Coast, but I still had a job to do, and I was too busy and scatterbrained to put together another resume. I brought it up with my dad who wanted to hear none of it, because he hates quitters and that was definitely a quitter's attitude.

Additionally, it was the fear of change that kept me rooted to Pittsburgh, which I loathed at the time (I like it now.) It would have been a big leap, and a bad decision, to leave a good job for stupid, juvenile reasons. I knew this.

Even though I hated the fact I worked with my dad, I actually liked working with my dad.

So, I dragged myself into the office on Saturdays and Sundays and got on board with his plan. I don't remember what we did exactly, but over the next few weeks, we completed our small studio.

Then he dropped it on me.

He called me in over a weekend in early-summer 1999 to discuss the design and launch of an Internet entertainment video-focused website called FromUSAlive.com. I was like... "seriously?"

From USA what?

Inecom was a bad name for a consumer website, so he came up with something even worse.

He insisted on FromUSAlive.com. I vehemently objected. He owned the company, so guess who got the naming rights?

The first time I told some friends what we were doing they couldn't even remember the website name by the end of the conversation. "USAfromlive what? LiveUSA? FromLiveWhat???"

I designed logos and graphics, and we built a website to host videos. In addition to the slowly dying plant, we added a new row of computers to broadcast live-streams over the Internet (though, nobody called it that, then.) We also installed a Betacam SP deck and a bunch of high-end audio gear that nobody knew how to use.

I wish I would have taken some photos, but I didn't envision a future where I'd be writing a book about this stuff in 2024.

Fun fact, I saw my dad earlier today, as I'm writing this. I asked him if he had any pictures of the studio and the computers. He looked at me like I had three heads and said "I built the studio to take pictures not to take pictures of the studio." Good answer.

It wasn't until a few months later that I realized his grand plan was to expand to specific locations like FromChicagoLive and FromNewYorkLive and whatever. He freely admits that he is terrible at naming things. The "live" component was intended to be a bigger part of the business than it ever became. Up to that point, most of our Internet broadcasts were live.

So, there we were at FromUSAlive sitting around a polished, circular wooden table in 1970s office chairs; the future of Internet video entertainment! There wasn't even a sign on the door. Nothing could have been less cool.

Nobody in his company understood what we were doing. I'm confident his management team thought this whole thing was a waste of time. The IT department hated us. I was having an existential crisis and suffering from #FOMO before #FOMO was a thing.

"Hey Mark, we're hitting Atlantic City this weekend, you in??"

"No. I'm programming a website and wiring microphones. There's a plant."

What was the exact date that FromUSAlive.com went on the air? I'm not exactly sure, but it was in August of 1999. Things moved quickly after that.

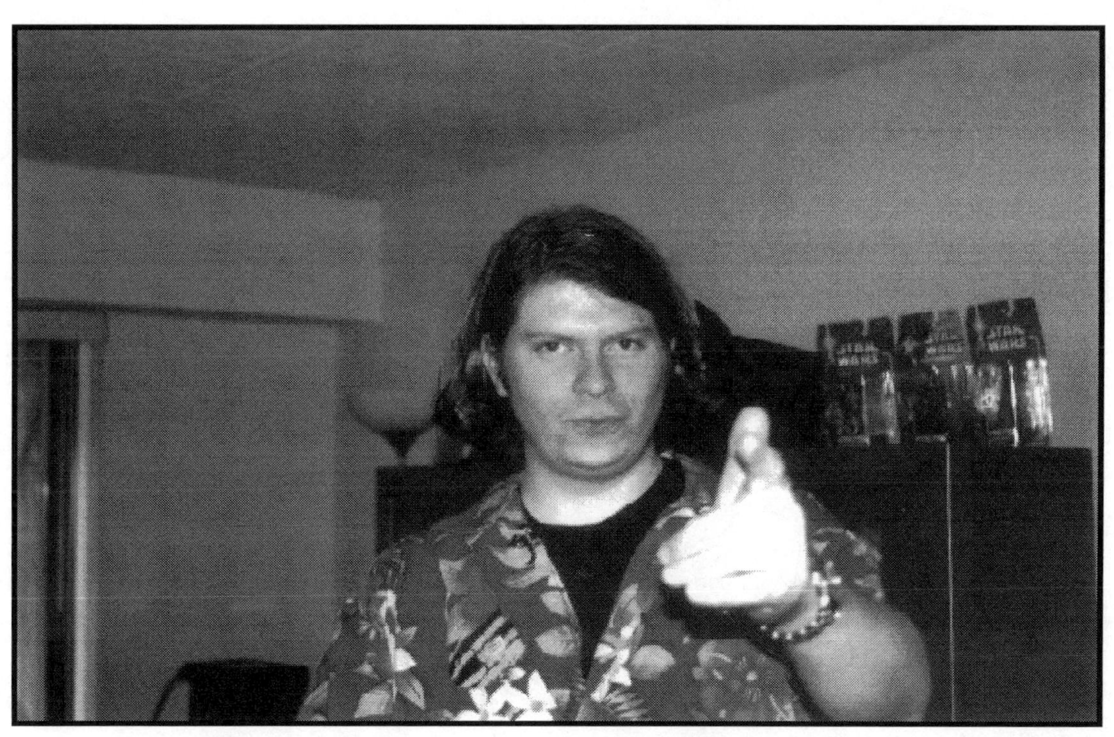

Mark in 2003 wearing The Game Room Hawaiian shirt.

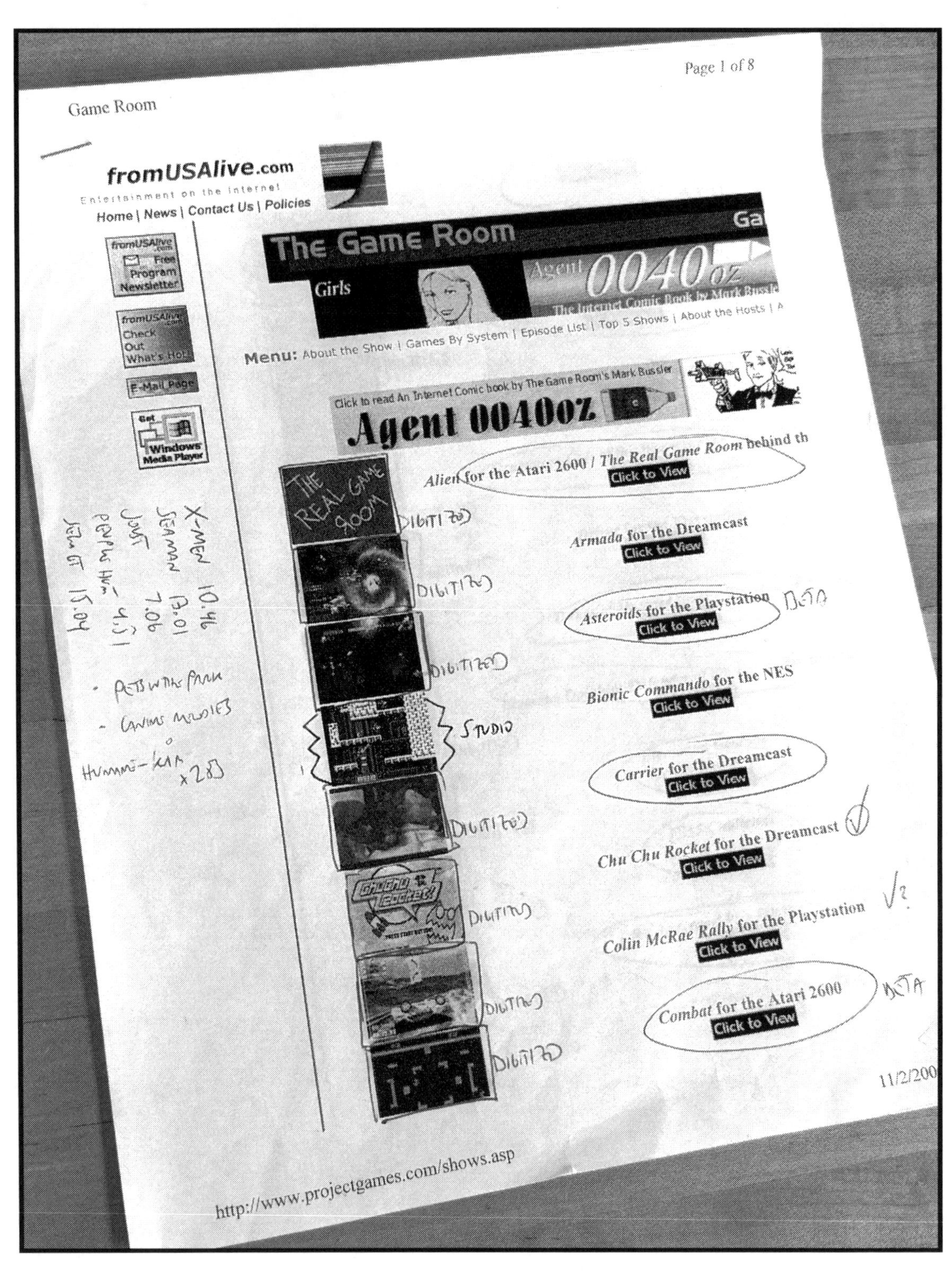
Game Room

Page 1 of 8

fromUSAlive.com

Entertainment on the internet

Home | News | Contact Us | Policies

The Game Room

Girls

Agent 0040oz

Menu: About the Show | Games By System | Episode List | Top 5 Shows | About the Hosts |

Click to read An Internet Comic book by The Game Room's Mark Bussler

Agent 0040oz

Alien for the Atari 2600 / *The Real Game Room* behind th

Click to View

Armada for the Dreamcast

Click to View

Asteroids for the Playstation

Click to View

Bionic Commando for the NES

Click to View

Carrier for the Dreamcast

Click to View

Chu Chu Rocket for the Dreamcast

Click to View

Colin McRae Rally for the Playstation

Click to View

Combat for the Atari 2600

Click to View

11/2/200

http://www.projectgames.com/shows.asp

FromUSAlive.com printout that I used for reference when assembling the Classic Game Room DVD in 2006.

CHAPTER 4
FROMUSALIVE.COM

Somehow, we hooked up with a few "producers" and local crews, people who made stuff for public television or regional religious TV stations or something. It was a motley crew. Pittsburgh still had the remnants of a film industry from the WQED Mr. Rogers days, but that was like 1,000 years ago. Everyone thought we were crazy. But apparently, we had money to spend, and that must have piqued their interest.

I don't recall what our first "entertainment" show was, but we cobbled together some dirt-cheap productions like Teen News USA, Let's Dance Salsa, Paintball whatever, Military Memoirs, some kind of show about mystery writers, and random stuff like that.... We even had a religious show and one about spirituality.

We shot stuff with an old Sony TV camera, I have no idea where he found it.

The recording quality was terrible, and it only went downhill from there once it went online. People viewed these broadcasts in tiny postage-stamp-sized windows because they watched them over a modem! But, it was still something.

It's probably best that you couldn't see the videos

since our color balance was usually off. We had no makeup, no crew, bad audio, an air conditioning hum on everything, and no quality control. Let's Dance Salsa was probably the only one of the early batch of shows where anyone looked like they knew what they were doing, though I can't believe we shot it on brown carpeting.

This was before LED lights were a thing, so the studio lights heated the place up to 100 degrees and I always burned myself when moving them. I melted many a cable.

At first, it was just me in the studio on Saturday mornings or late at night producing this myriad array of completely awful low budget programming. My friend nailed it when he said "this entire website is like the worst of late night cable access TV programming."

It was like Wayne's World except not funny (not intentionally, at least.)

He added a few people into the business to help with the website and marketing. It started to turn into something pretty quickly.

Some of our videos were ok, perhaps. Our history shows, Let's Dance Salsa and the paintball program were legit.

We produced some good stuff about Civil War history, World War II, and Gulf War veterans. But honestly, it's the crazy stuff that is always the most fun to talk about.

There was a mom who screamed at me in the hallway because we couldn't get her daughter famous and SHE DESERVED IT. She was going to be the next Brittany Spears. Someone needed to tell that lady that we were NOT the people who were going to get her daughter famous.

There was a woman who told us, on the invention program, about a device she worked with that would give the woman neck support during oral sex. One of our producers showed great interest in her after that segment.

A Civil War band played a song in the studio. In between takes I shouted "play Free Bird!" which, as it turns out, was some kind of trigger and the guy wanted to kill me afterward.

We filmed one segment where a psychic read a plant that was in the room when O.J. murdered someone or whatever. The plant said O.J. was innocent. THE PLANT SAID IT.

One of my favorite shows from our super-early batch of programming was The Board Room, the Internet's first board game show. The Board Room was actually very good.

Hosted by Bob Shwartz who ran a Pittsburgh-area board game shop called Games Unlimited, The Board Room was credible. The Board Room was also one of the first shows where we did multi-camera work and serious editing instead of focusing on "live."

We mounted an overhead camera on the ceiling to show how one played the board games that were covered in each episode, and we worked with a multi-camera TV switching board to make it look cool.

Bob knew his stuff, he was a good host, a nice guy, and he had real connections. We used our live broadcast equipment to conduct phone interviews with board game designers like Reiner Knizia.

A show like The Board Room did well compared to our other stuff. Like our entire concept, The Board Room was ahead of its time.

The live video component that we built into the studio never worked out as we had planned. Our first shows were all shot live, and we advertised a TV Guide-like schedule ahead of time on the website, but nobody ever watched them live. It quickly became clear that people only watched our shows after I'd do a quick edit, add title cards, and post them on the website.

I became an editing machine. We rapid-fire produced shows about bartending, karate, investing, and even had a live band or two in the studio. For a while there, the studio and editing suite were booked solid with back to back to back programming.

Most of our shows went nowhere. They were only viewed a couple of times and did not generate any following in the days before "followers". We had an e-mail newsletter that viewers could subscribe to, but of course, they had to discover our website in the first place.

A few of our shows did better, but the hosts grew disappointed that people weren't watching their work. "Producers" quickly dropped out.

I picked up the producing reigns on a bunch of in-house shows to fill the void and took charge of development. The studio ran smoothly enough, and none of the gear vanished, but we weren't bringing in new show concepts like those first few months. It's a weird business and I learned quickly that you want someone in the middle of it you can trust. As awful a human being as I was in 1999, I was trustworthy.

Suddenly I became a producer!

What is producing? In this context, producing is organizing and preparing a show and then getting it made. But I had no connections to speak of, so the best way to produce, in my mind, was to do it myself.

I started to make up animated shows, an Internet comic strip called Agent 00400z, and created a video game review show.

We had a small business team at that point in late

1999, and we'd toss ideas around in meetings. Basically, we made what we thought people would watch, and if the Board Room was doing okay, then surely The Game Room would do well. Everyone loves video games!

I had no idea how to make it but assumed that if I could show a video game on-screen and talk about it, that was good enough.

This classic formula dates all the way back to 1999. Play a game, record the game, talk about the game. It never really changed.

It was never posted, but I shot a pilot episode for The Game Room with me and one of the girls from another show talking about the Atari 7800 version of Dig Dug. It was terrible. If you thought the original Game Room episodes were poorly made, this was 1,000 times worse. I watched the pilot and I was like "nope."

All of our shows had at least two people on screen for back and forth banter and I needed a co-host. But, where to find a co-host?

I made a few friends in film school, including Dave, who you probably remember from the early Game Room episodes. Not only did we need more production help to keep up with the growing list of edited shows in late 1999, but I also wanted to make The Game Room, and Dave was excited to co-host. He came on board as our first production department hire and The Game Room co-host.

In real life, Dave is exactly who he is on screen. He's a funny guy and we got along great in film school. We were all young and single and hung out with a few fellow-minded film-nerd troublemakers who were into the same shit that we were into.

He was from New Jersey but had recently moved to

Pittsburgh because his dad was working in the city at the time. I remember crashing at his place numerous nights and using his Sega Dreamcast to play online video games like Chu Chu Rocket.

There were hardly any filmmaking jobs in Pittsburgh, so I think he was pretty jazzed about the chance to work in the industry, even if it was a crazy job for an upstart website. I don't want to put words in his mouth, but I think he enjoyed his time making low-budget videos in our former conference-room.

We hit the ground running. I don't think we even shot a test episode for The Game Room, we just made it up as we went along. (There was no YouTube to copy, or social media trends to rip off.)

The first Game Rooms were poorly made, but the onscreen charisma was good. I think the first games that we "reviewed" were Driver and Metal Gear VR Missions on PlayStation.

We played the games into a Betacam SP deck and then did a quick edit. Afterward, we hooked up RE-20 microphones through the mixing board into a second Betacam SP deck and did the audio recording freestyle. That's how I remember it at least, though maybe the first few were a little different...

Why did we do "reviews?" At the time we were a little bit concerned about showing video games online because of potential copyright issues. This was all ahead of the time, and we didn't want to pay lawyers to look into it, so journalism was our safely net. That's why we did reviews instead of something else.

It must have struck a chord with someone out there, though I'm not sure how anyone found it.

The Game Room immediately jumped into our top

10 shows after its unceremonious debut on November 11, 1999. I can date the show's release by the date on the Betacam SP tape which I still have in my archives. We shot the studio segments on November 7 and then edited it (so says my handwriting on the tape.) We did not have a live broadcast to mark the occasion.

Our next hurdle was promoting it in the age before social media.

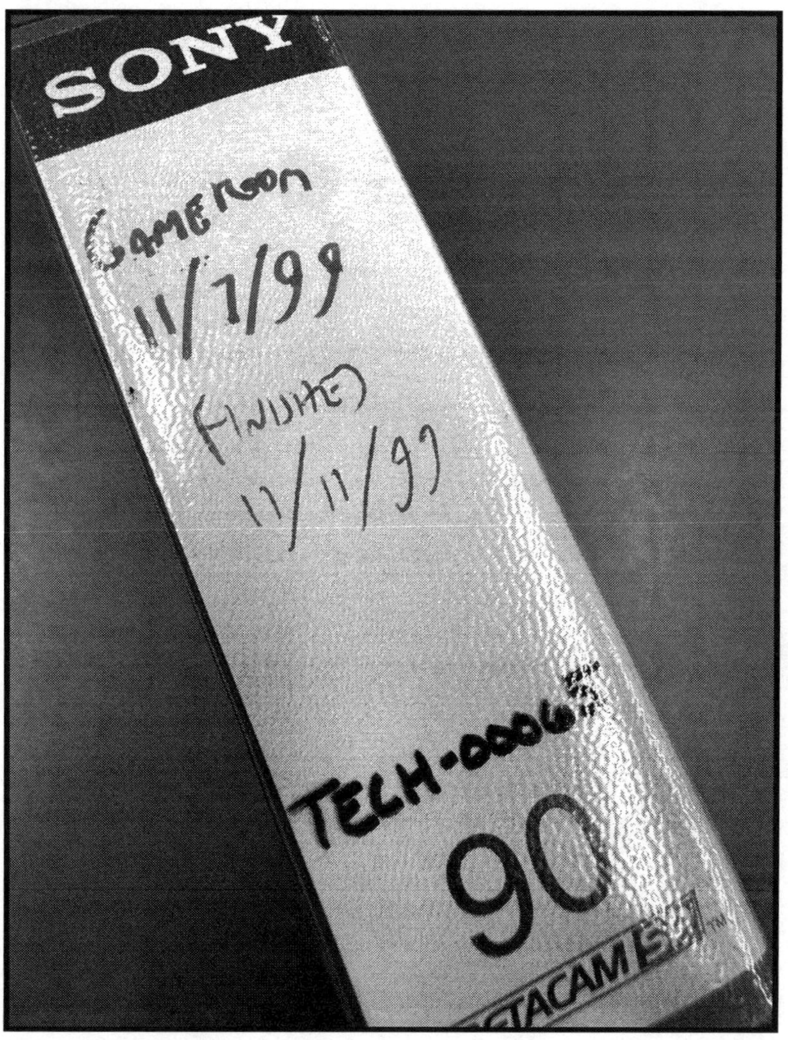

The first Game Room.

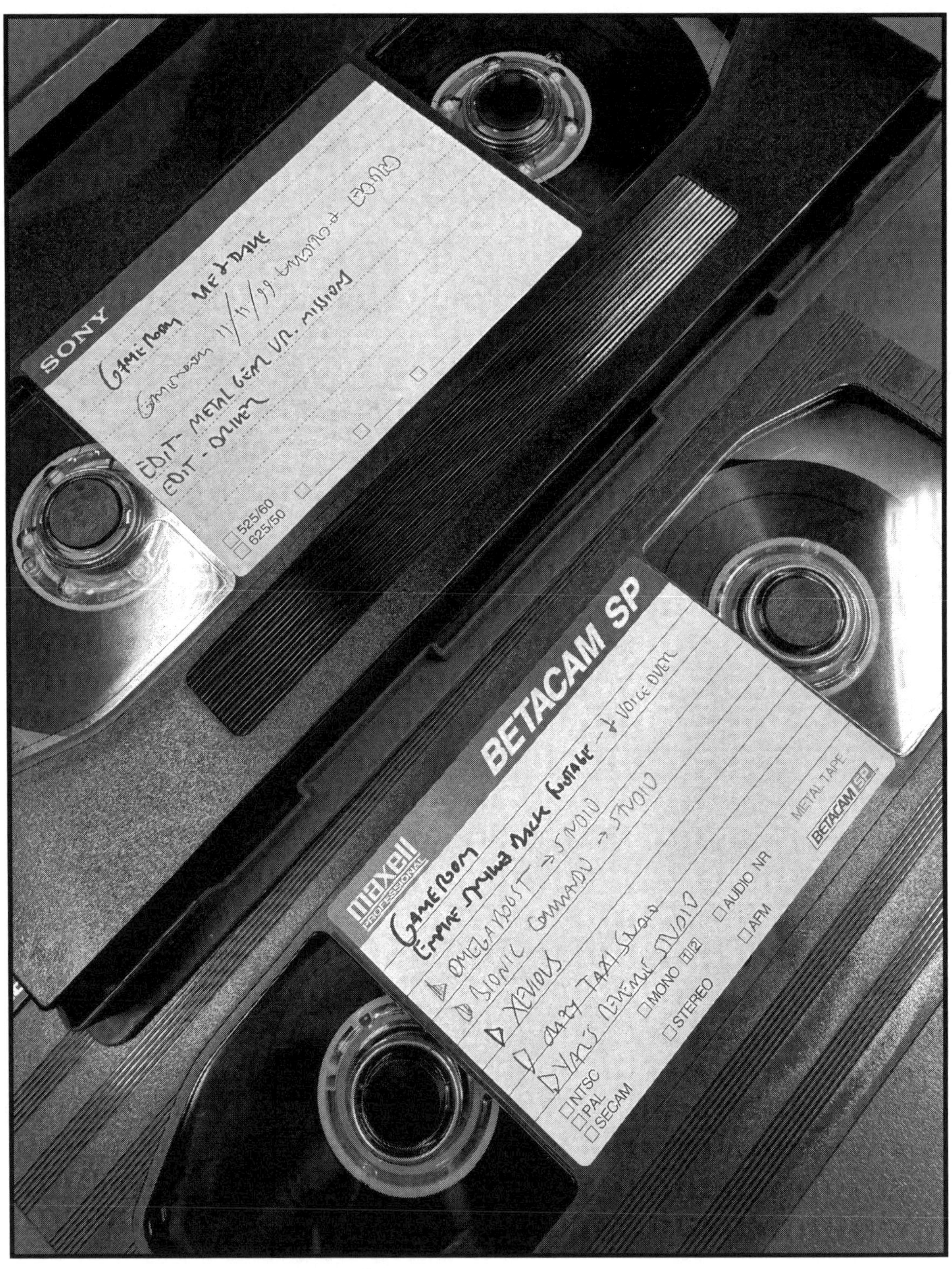

Original Game Room Betacam SP tapes.

CHAPTER 5
THE GAME ROOM, SUCKA

Dave and I would spam IGN forums back in 1999 in the hopes of drumming up new viewers until our account was banned or something. "Go watch the Game Room on FromUSAlive, sucka!"

He bought a brand-new Sega Dreamcast, and we started to raise a few eyebrows out there. "These clowns have a Dreamcast!?" Views went up. The Game Room was in effect.

But we also had to produce all of these other shows. It was nuts. How on earth did we do this? I don't know.

I spent New Year's Eve 1999 playing Gran Turismo 2 in the office because everyone else took that weekend off. It was great. I think I was chatting with some girls in Hong Kong over something (AOL Messenger?) and it was like "I can't believe we can talk to people on the other side of the world in real time!"

Then I went to a party when we all thought the world would end. It didn't, and I woke up on my friend's couch with a headache in future year 2000!

The Y2K bug turned out to be a load of bullshit and everything still worked. How about that...?

2000.

It's the dawn of the new millennium, and we're a bunch of inexperienced twenty-somethings running a TV studio under the watchful eye of a plant sitting in the corner of an old conference room. People watched our low-budget shows, and it worked. IT ACTUALLY WORKED. Sort of.

We weren't making any money, but functionally, it worked.

My memory is a little foggy here, but we'd have weekly meetings and discuss hits and website numbers. We had a consistent list of the top 10 best shows, and they were definitely the best shows with the people who knew what they were doing.

Shows like Let's Dance Salsa were killing it. If there was a breakout early show, it was Let's Dance Salsa. I think that salsa dancing was hot at the time, and there were dancing girls on screen.

The Board Room and The Game Room both did well, as did some of our history stuff like Civil War Minutes. Inventors Insider did well, and so did my obnoxious Agent 00400z comic strip.

The rest of the content, for the most part, went nowhere.

By early 2000, Our remaining "producers" flaked out one by one, and we couldn't get many new shows in the lineup with credible hosts, so I took a different approach.

"We're going to take the cameras outside and burn toy cars in the parking lot! We'll recreate live-action scenes from the X-Men Sega Genesis game! Let's bring real guns into the office and pretend to shoot the TV and drink bottles of gin on camera (it was water.)"

Early 2000 was awesome because we got more adventurous with our filmmaking and took it outside. We also got a green screen to make wacky backgrounds and even got a little bit better at filming and production. People seemed to like it, and the hits grew.

Dave and I shot and edited almost all of FromUSAlive's shows. When we weren't working on the other stuff, we'd spend our time on The Game Room. It was definitely a priority. We shot a Real World parody and murdered Sea Man with ease. "True storyeeee!"

The Game Room would be my first foray into music creation software. I discovered Acid Music, an ancient loop-based music program, and whipped up all of the FromUSAlive shows' theme songs and a bunch of sound effects. I spent a lot of time on Acid Music and got pretty good at mixing sick beats.

I composed the original Game Room theme in 1999 in Acid and made the spinning logo with Macromedia Flash.

It didn't take long for other hosts to get upset with The Game Room though. The few remaining producers blamed us for prioritizing Game Room editing and studio time. To be honest, we juggled it all pretty well. The best shows did the best, and the others sunk. I saw the hits and I saw the limited fan feedback (there weren't comments fields back in those days.)

I can't find any of the old studio sheets for this stuff, but we probably had 40-50 shows running at one time in 2000, in this tiny studio, with a 2-3 person crew and an IT department being pulled in seven different directions at once. When was the peak? I don't remember exactly, probably summer of 2000.

By that time, our once unsustainable crop of silly shows condensed to the remaining few that anyone was actually watching, namely Let's Dance Salsa, The Board Room, Civil War Minutes, Inventors Insider, and The Game

Room (as well as Agent 0040oz which had a following.)

Some of our programming showed real potential, but we needed to monetize it which meant that we needed to get bigger.

My dad was pleased that any of this worked at all, but he also needed it to turn a profit. We needed venture capital.

In early 2000 we started to run ads on our FromUSAlive.com website and the pennies flowed in, but not nearly fast enough. The studio and website were hemorrhaging cash throughout 2000. We needed something really big and popular, and it wasn't going to come from any of our existing shows. As good as some of them were, we struggled like hell to market them to an audience who wasn't able to view them on ancient dial-up modems and America Online.

Internet TV was starting to turn into a thing though, and competitors popped up. I think some of them even made video game shows (not as good as ours, obviously.)

The competitor that stands out is Pseudo.com from New York. We hated them because they always seemed to have bigger budgets and way more people than we did. They were in the middle of it all in New York City and we were based out of a dumpy conference room in Pittsburgh.

Did I mention that we had a plant, though?

While we had growth in fits and starts through 2000, and even ran ads for games like Perfect Dark on the Nintendo 64, we needed venture capital. That's how these things are funded.

One of the things my dad did at the time, which was pretty clever, was to market our overall concept of shooting and uploading videos to our website as a turnkey system. So, instead of trying to use our collection of low-budget programming as the selling point, it was the physical part of getting videos online that was our selling point. This kept a few of the shows, including The Game Room, going a little bit longer than they would have otherwise.

It didn't matter what the show was, at this point, it mattered that we could demonstrate the concept of filming and uploading to our website. That's where the value was.

So, instead of focusing on the next big show, by late summer of 2000, our mission changed to marketing this studio-in-a-box concept to investors.

He was five years into the future inventing YouTube before YouTube. His idea was brilliant and terrible.

You see, in 2000, you couldn't just upload a video from your phone because phones didn't do that for at least another 10-12 years. You couldn't even easily upload video from a video camera because cameras shot tape. In 2000, you needed to feed an analog tape format into a digital editing system and then make a rendered file to upload to the Internet.

In those years, we ran our video files through three "encoders" that would make a low, medium, and high-quality version of the master edit. Then, these three video files could be uploaded to our website where viewers would choose which quality version to watch depending on how awful their Internet connection was.

A lot of people assume that CGR started as a garage operation with no budget, and that's just not true. When you get down to it, this was a fairly well-funded outfit. Our shows had that low-cost Wayne's World vibe, but I know our gear was top notch. We focused on volume.

This shit was expensive back in the day, and complicated, which is why selling it as a studio-in-a-box was clever.

Once we saw this franchise concept that he had in his mind it all started to make sense. Sometime during that summer of 2000, we built a second, much smaller studio in our office space to prototype this studio-in-a-box. Imagine a 12' x 8' space (roughly) with a professional camera in the middle, green screen, microphones, and small mixing board. This setup was connected to our FromUSAlive rendering computers and website for uploading into our eco system. It really was brilliant.

I couldn't believe that he had this all figured out, except (and he's still mad about this) he never saw a future where people could upload cinema-quality videos from their phones for free from anywhere.

Additionally, none of us envisioned a future where people would just say "Hey, what's up?" and get millions of views just for being there.

The FromUSAlive studio-in-a-box concept was pitched to investors. Now "anyone can make an Internet TV show for the low price of $50,000!" or whatever the cost was. It was high by modern standards.

We met with venture capitalists who showed interest. Then we ran right into the Dot Com bust of 2000 in that spring/summer.

Venture capitalists ran for the hills, the stock market crashed, and any interest we had in FromUSAlive dried up late that summer. I recall a few meetings with interested parties who were genuinely impressed that we were able to make so many shows and post them online. But we couldn't secure the millions in financing that we actually needed to turn the concept into reality. We had planned to build these mini-studios and set them up in Chicago and

D.C. and Philadelphia for demonstration purposes, but it never happened.

Whether it was the Dot Com bust, our lack of quality programming, or the fact we were five years too early, I can't say. But, any hope of paying for FromUSAlive and the studio-in-a-box concept ended that summer.

Even if The Game Room was pretty awesome, and it was still growing, advertising didn't pay for much of it.

I'm not sure what happened to any of our competitors. They probably lost a lot more money than we did. Inecom weathered the storm pretty well because we rolled the studio-in-a-box right back into instructional videos, which actually did earn money. The engineering parent company loved our studio-in-a-box because all anyone had to do was walk into the studio, push a button, shoot a video, upload it, and leave. This was very ahead of its time, and it worked well for their purposes.

We continued to produce hundreds of engineering instructional videos, but the entertainment side had to go. Meetings were held and stern discussions discussed.

One by one the shows ended. Everyone knew it was coming.

The hammer fell in October of 2000, thus ending FromUSAlive.com for good. The Game Room review of Tokyo Xtreme Racer 2 on the Dreamcast was our last video. Sucks, because I think we really hit our stride that summer. The fact that some people still watch those videos and enjoy them says a lot.

There are old Betacam SP tapes in my storage locker filled with Shenmue footage that Dave recorded late one night. Sadly, we never finished the Shenmue review. In total, we made about 80 original Game Room episodes (there were a bunch that we never completed.)

It was fun while it lasted. FromUSAlive ran for more than a year!

My dad was right to shut it down and I'm not upset, and I never was. I knew it wasn't working and there was no way forward without external financing. After the last Game Room, it was a smooth and uneventful transition back into engineering instructional videos.

I don't recall what our viewership numbers were, but they were tiny compared to the kinds of numbers that big "influencers" get these days. Probably tens of thousands.... It was still growing at the end!

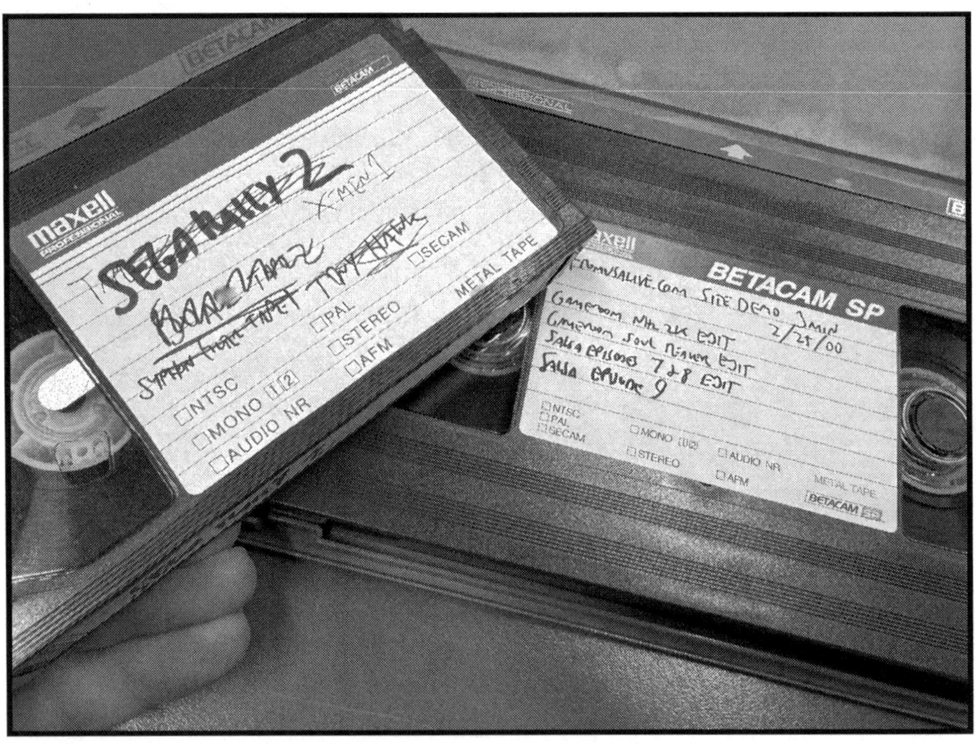

We re-used Betacam SP tapes in those days.

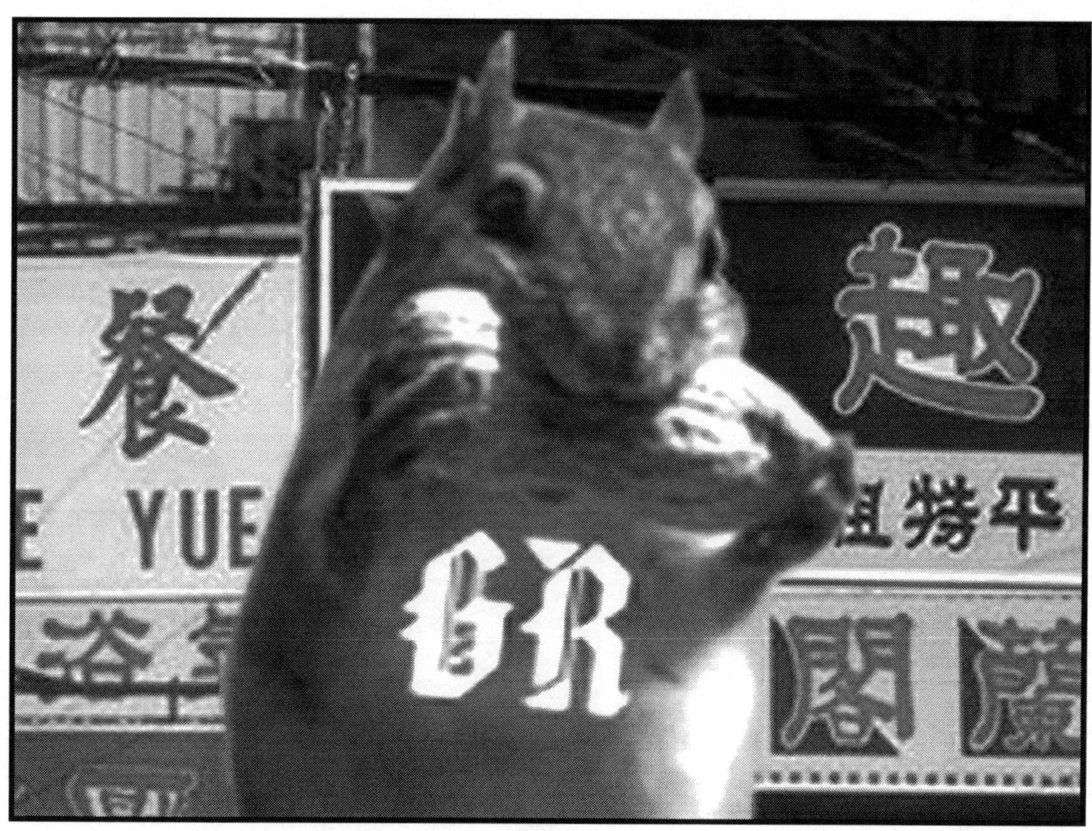

The green screen background for the Maken X review

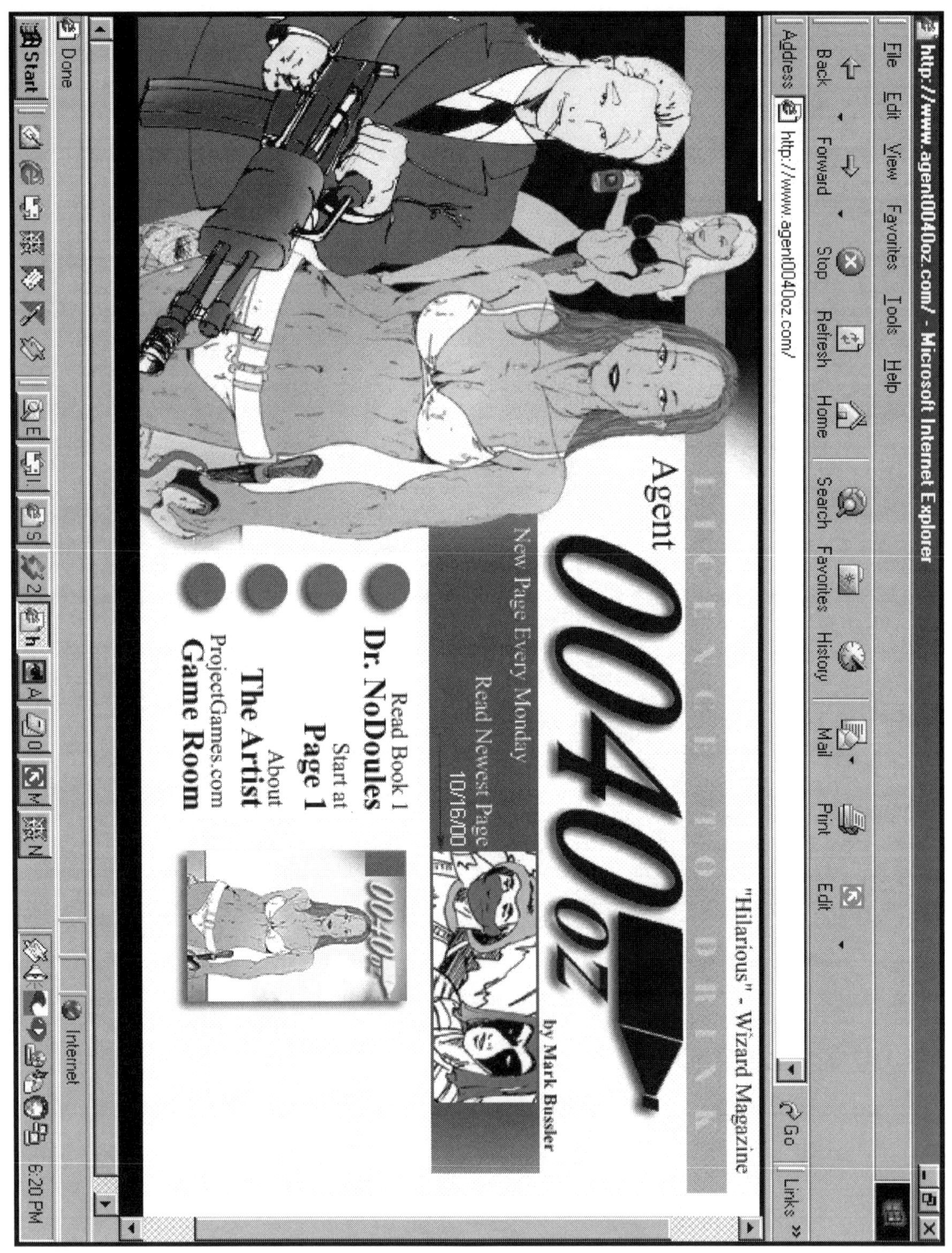

Agent 0040oz website in year 2000. Wow.

CHAPTER 6
AGENT 0040OZ

It wasn't video, but my weekly Agent 0040oz online comic strip was one of our most popular products by the end of the FromUSAlive era. People all over the world read about Agent James Brown and his boozy, sex-fueled adventures.

You know that episode of Star Trek TNG when Riker meets another version of Riker? I feel that way about 1999-2000 era Mark. He sucks. He was rude, sexist, obnoxious, and a person of ill repute. That being said, he was also wildly creative and Agent 0040oz is awesome (albeit, terrible.)

The concept emerged from one of my 1996 Captain Bucknell comic strips where Cap puts on a tux, drinks his way into oblivion, and battles bad guys to save the college while also "macking" on the ladies (I was such an awful shit.)

After school, I tried selling the concept to Maxim and they shot it down, so I did it myself and used our web platform to host it.

It ran for one complete book called Dr. NoDoules, with a second one in development called You Only See Double. Though I'm not particularly proud of the lewd nature of the book, which is absolutely juvenile and stupid, the parody aspect of 0040oz is terrific and people noticed.

One of our best plugs back in the day came from Wizard magazine who wrote a short article about Agent 0040oz in 2000 and called it "Hilarious!" They also mentioned The Game Room in the article and our old website, ProjectGames.com in passing.

0040oz was bigger than The Game Room, I love it. After 25 years of producing Classic Game Room, I think the Wizard plug is still the biggest mention CGR ever got in print.

After we stopped producing the FromUSAlive shows, 0040oz may have run for a little bit longer. I can't remember, but I do recall receiving a fair amount of fan mail from people who enjoyed it.

While I have no plans to continue the series today because I'm not that guy anymore, you can see the evolution from my college-era drawing into the early 2000s when I was batshit crazy creative and completely out there.

When I stopped the book, I also stopped drawing seriously for the next decade. It would not be until Lord Karnage in 2014 that I picked up pens and paper and took cartooning seriously once more.

0040 was awfully sexist and I'm not proud of that. Many of my leading characters these days are women, but they are strong and confident women. Ethel the Cyborg Ninja, Haylee Davenworth, and Cassandra lead the way in their books while the guys like Lord Karnage and Hunter Skywolf fumble about like incompetent drunken dipshits.

Maybe someday, depending on how things shake out, I'll consider getting back into some parody work again (albeit, with a more mature mindset.) Maybe the world needs James Brown and his El Camino to save the day with a case of 40s... or maybe the world is doing just fine without him.

That's stupid. The world totally needs more Agent 0040oz. (I just bought back the website URL minutes ago.) I'm confident there's a way to do a good parody without being quite so juvenile and overtly sexist and awful.

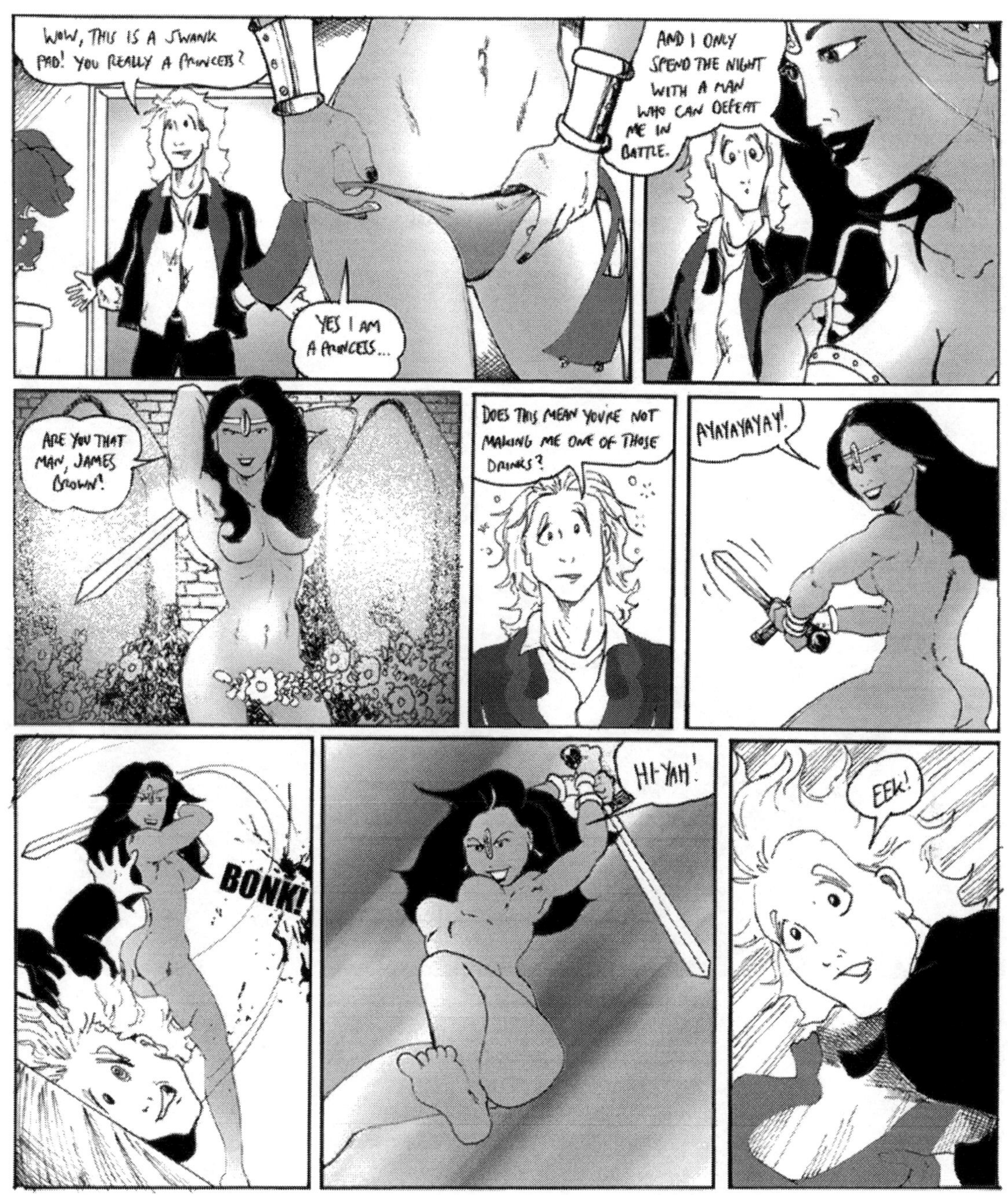

Agent 00400z battles Xima the Warrior Princess from 2000.

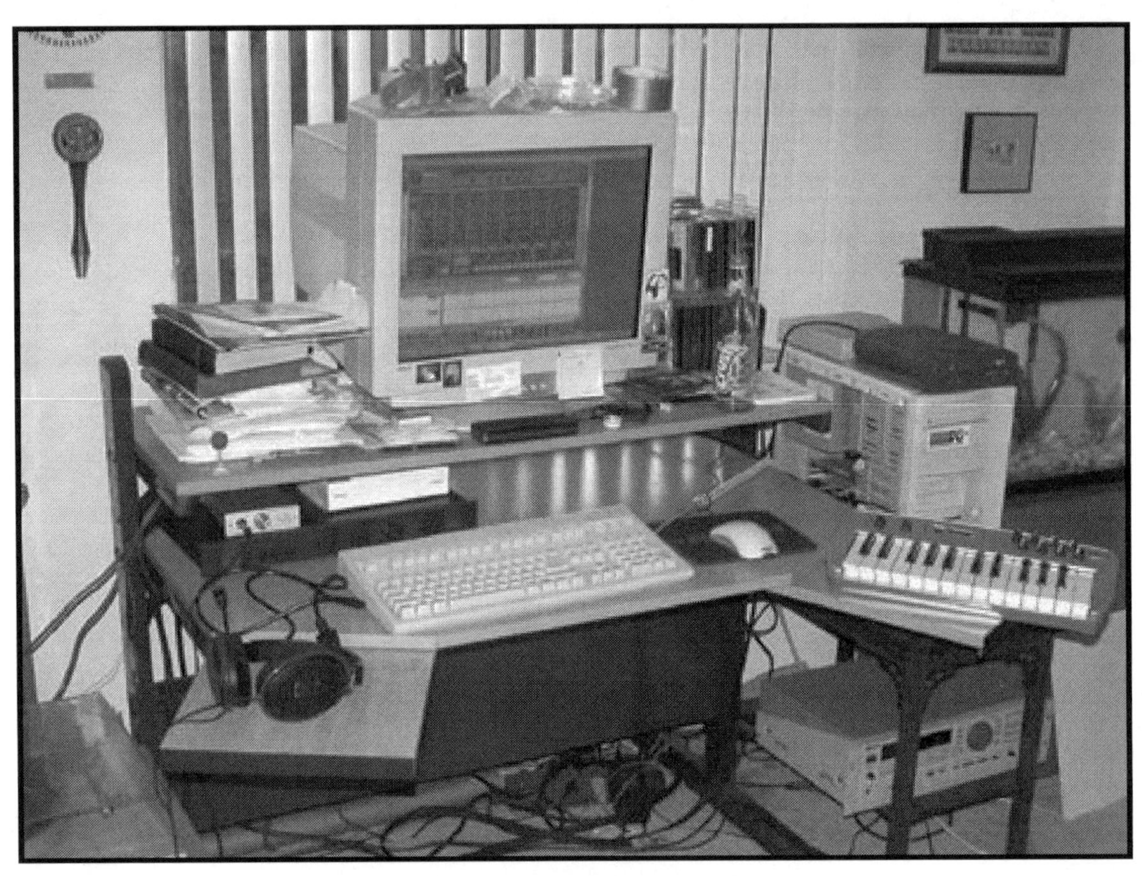

Music creation for (probably) Shot to Pieces, 2002-ish.

CHAPTER 7
FROM WEB TV TO DVD

Finally, it's over!

There was a collective sigh of relief throughout the engineering company when the dancing girls in miniskirts stopped walking around the building and discontinued using the first floor bathrooms as a makeup studio. There were no more paintball videos, swing dancing lessons, guys with guns, or roving mini bars. A conservative engineering company is where fun goes to die, but also where business returns to profitability.

What was next for The Game Room? Storage. (the first of many times The Game Room would end up in storage!)

I packed up all the tapes and stuffed them into a closet, assuming I'd never see them again. Without the constant pings, buzzing, and nagging of social media, nobody said much about it. A few people sent nice letters, but for the most part, The Game Room, and all of our other shows, died in silence.

When the studio pivoted back into business webcasting work and software instructional videos, I went along for the ride because it could have been worse. By 2000, I started to enjoy Pittsburgh a little bit more, and even met a girl who would put up with me (she still does.) Suddenly, I wasn't spending my weekends working on film school projects and Internet TV shows, I had other things to do.

I had that thing when you go outside and there's other stuff to do. I had that thing.

With The Game Room done, and the job changing completely, Dave decided to move back to New Jersey. The rest of our production resources dried up or moved on. All the expensive gear was re-purposed for the profitable engineering videos.

But, what about all that stuff we shot? What about this entire room full of hundreds of Betacam SP and DVC-pro tapes? We must have filmed thousands of hours of video.

Imagine the ending scene from Raiders of the Lost Ark, except instead of crates filled with priceless artifacts, our storage lockers remain full of plastic bins filled with poorly-filmed programs on Betacam SP tapes.

Remember what life was like before DVD? If you wanted to watch a movie at home, you had to rent a VHS tape, which was terrible.

Laserdisc was pretty awesome, but nobody had a Laserdisc player. They cost a small fortune and they were pretty much phased out by the late 90s.

The first DVD that I ever saw was Ninja Scroll. I remember it clearly because I was visiting my old roommate at Bucknell in 1998 or so, and he knew a kid who had a DVD player. Weren't they like $1000 then? Of course, the only person who could afford one would be a Bucknell student.

I was impressed with DVD, and thankfully the players dropped in price quickly. Eventually, I bought one at Circuit City which even played DIVX discs. Remember DIVX?

DVD was a huge improvement over VHS because the video looked good, movies played properly in widescreen, and the sound was great. Also, there were cool bonus features and commentary tracks. DVD was one of the most revolutionary things I ever saw when it was new, and I was super excited about the prospect of getting into the DVD business.

By late 2000 the DVD market was growing rapidly and at some point, in early 2001 or thereabouts, we hatched a plan to re-purpose our best FromUSAlive videos on physical media. Tapes were pulled out of storage and I quickly started to re-edit and re-package Let's Dance Salsa and Civil War Minutes into DVD box sets. We even made VHS tapes in those days (sadly, no Laserdisc.)

Civil War Minutes would become our first DVD set. It was like an ultra-low-budget History Channel show about Civil War stories and artifacts. The production quality was awful, but the information, artifacts, and the stories were good.

I worked with historians Mike Kraus and Dave Neville on the series, which was originally shot for the Internet. The three of us got along well and hit the ground running in 2001 with new Civil War Minutes episodes and reshoots. The first Civil War Minutes series, focusing on Union stories during the American Civil War, was comprised of mostly FromUSAlive-era shorts mixed with some re-editing and new footage.

The audio cleanup was a struggle because we got pretty good at recording Game Rooms with our RE-20s, but we always sucked at using lavalier mics with the incessant room noise. A bunch of the videos needed to be reshot, because what was acceptable over your 14,400 baud modem wasn't so awesome on a TV. This first box set took a while to make, but it turned out pretty good in the end considering the non-existent production budget.

I was on the phone working with the DVD authoring company on the morning of September 11, 2001. I remember that day all too well.

It was a weird couple months after that, and a bizarre time to launch a DVD set using an infomercial campaign about war. In early 2002, sales were good enough to justify a second series which turned into Civil War Minutes: Confederate.

These days the mere mention of us making Civil War Minutes: Confederate would imply that we're a bunch of racist pricks celebrating the Confederacy or conservative media, but that's not the case at all. We wanted to produce a similar set of stories focusing on Confederate artifacts to complement the Union series. I shot Civil War Minutes: Confederate from the ground up in our studio and I remember it selling well.

We did a lot of business with Northern and Southern Civil War battlefields and National Park stores. There is a huge jump in production quality between the Union and Confederate series because I got a hell of a let better at filming in that year thanks to Game Room.

It was about this time that I also shot a short, super-low budget action-documentary called Left for Dead, no relation to the video game.

Mike had this obscure book that he thought would make for a neat documentary film and we were like "Yeah, more DVDs, let's do that!" Left for Dead is a story about an obscure Civil War general named Oscar Jackson. I wanted to make it an action film because of course I did.

We combined the two ideas into one concept with a paltry budget and filmed Left for Dead, an action documentary, in the farmland surrounding Mike's studio space just north of Pittsburgh. And, when I say low budget, I'm thinking that we spent maybe $1,000 on production costs, reenactors, uniforms, ammunition, and camera rental.

The Civil War Minutes videos and Left for Dead sold well enough in the niche Civil War market to justify even more! Mike came up with the idea for Shot to Pieces, a much larger action documentary about a slightly-less-obscure Civil War general named William F. Bartlett.

We all had so much fun making Shot to Pieces. I was heavily into filmmaking by that point, after tasting a bit of success with our earlier DVDs, and I had a bigger budget. I took the producing reigns and put together a much larger production with detailed storyboards, epic battle scenes, location photography, horses, boats, and original music creation.

I produced and directed Shot to Pieces with a small crew and a bunch of Civil War reenactors. We filmed most of it in the summer of 2002 at a farm way north of Pittsburgh, up near Route 80. We shot some other scenes in Dave Neville's barn in Export, PA, and also in a historical museum near Harmony, PA.

The studio shots were filmed in our good, ole' brown carpeted low budget filming space. Patrick Jordan did the narration, and you can see him in Johnstown Flood, Expo: Magic of the White City, and he gets blown up in the third Christopher Nolan Batman movie.

If you ever see Shot to Pieces, pay attention to the filmmaking and the shots of nature, scenery, and wildlife. I tried to add some artistic flair to the production while also telling the story and keeping it within a realistic budget. I did all the sound design and editing myself, and learned more in a short span of time than I thought possible.

I filmed Shot to Pieces on Mini DV using the classic Canon XL1 with a manual lens for that cinematic look (as much as one can get with a one or two-person crew.) Some of the insert shots and b-roll were filmed on Hi-8. There's even an underwater shot or two!

We worked with a enthusiastic group of reenactors and filmed several battle scenes on top of a mountain, running down the mountain, into the river, beside the river, on a boat. There were horses! Nobody died. Our crew filmed a reenactment of The Battle of the Crater in a strip mine and even simulated some Civil War surgery. I still have the smoke machine that we used.

In the middle of production, Mike Kraus had to travel to Europe at one point because some little no-name film called Cold Mountain hired him as a historical consultant. You can see him as an extra on top of a pile of bodies in one prominent shot.

Shot to Pieces even features a little bit of original Mark Bussler synthesizer music, so it is the direct precursor to Omega Ronin. Who knew that the soundtrack for Shot to Pieces would evolve into future synthwave albums about space people mating with laser robots from another dimension?

The niche-market Civil War press enjoyed it, but Shot to Pieces failed to reach any kind of mainstream success. There's no way to make a low budget film look like a big budget film, so in that respect I'll always be a bit disappointed with it. But, Shot to Pieces was good enough to set the stage for my next serious documentary film project called Johnstown Flood.

By 2003 the Internet entertainment days seemed like a millennium ago. The Game Room was never on my mind, at all.

This was a great time for me. I learned every part of video production from the ground up, including the most important aspect, which is starting a project and then seeing it through to completion. You'd be surprised how many famous, seasoned professionals are unable to accomplish that. In our little TV studio, we did it every day.

Inecom continued to live inside an engineering company and for a while we existed in symbiotic harmony (provided I didn't ruffle any feathers.)

The engineering webcasts, for the most part, ran by themselves. Our DVD business grew along with the emerging DVD market. Gift shops at Civil War battlefields wanted our products. Our in-house direct-to-video department expanded into a few people who managed production, scheduling, marketing, fulfillment, and restocking.

We sold our films through Borders, Barnes and Noble, Amazon, and even sent massive spindles of unpackaged DVDs to this crazy outfit called Netflix. One wonders how many people learned to salsa dance from our Let's Dance Salsa DVDs at Netflix. Maybe that's where the term Netflix and Chill came from?

SALSA AND CHILL.

Our heads were still stuck in history though and, preferably, something that didn't involve too much expensive travel. We talked about making documentaries about the steel industry, the Whiskey Rebellion, Clara Barton, the Allegheny River, and the Western Pennsylvania oil rush in Oil City. Johnstown Flood won because it was relatively close to Pittsburgh and of national significance.

We got the Johnstown Flood Museum on board with

our ambitious concept, an action-packed documentary about the Johnstown Flood with the same kind of intensity as Shot to Pieces.

Our medium-sized-budget documentary proposal raised a few eyebrows locally when we went looking for crew and actors. They still thought we were crazy.

I attended a casting session at the University of Pittsburgh and a professor looked at me with scorn. He loudly asked in an incredulous tone of voice "Who ***ARE*** you?"

"I'm Mark Bussler, bitch. In the future, I'll draw comic books about half-naked space ninjas. Show some fucking respect."

Nobody knew what to make of us.

"Is this what Ken Burns would do?"

"Would Ken Burns blow shit up and film scenes of thugs cutting rings off fingers?"

"You guys are weird."

Maybe, but we also know how to make, market, and sell low-budget documentaries on DVD.

The Johnstown Flood took place on May 31, 1889, and remains one of the worst man-made disasters of all time. More than 2,200 people died during the flood after the South Fork dam collapsed, a dam used to hold back a recreational lake for people like Andrew Carnegie and Henry Clay Frick. It makes for quite a story, considering that maintaining the dam would have been pocket change for these people. (In the end, Carnegie built them a library, so there's that.)

A few people, including me, wrote the script which tells the story through eyewitness newspaper accounts in a dramatic 19th-century bombastic kind of way. The dam burst, trains tried to outrace the flood, horses ran for the hills, lots of people drowned, and thieves cut the fingers off hapless victims for their rings.

I built a clay model of the South Fork dam and then blew it up in slow motion. Who knew that my repeat viewing of Clash of the Titans would pay off? Miniatures are awesome.

We shot studio footage in our crappy studio, and I worked with a bunch of local actors to recite eyewitness accounts in the script's dramatic flair. I even traveled to Johnstown several times and filmed historical locations, the remnants of the dam, graves, rivers, and some beautiful Pennsylvania scenery.

It would have all worked out great except that we hired Richard Dreyfuss to do the narration and he was too good! He was such a great narrator that all my low-budget filmmaking ended up looking cheap by comparison.

In my opinion, the film is off balance because the narrator overpowers the low-budget filmmaking, but it still worked out. We held a screening in Johnstown and most of the crowd seemed to really enjoy it, except the one guy who left halfway through while clenching his fists and cursing. Most of the online reviewers enjoyed it, and it opened up a bunch of doors, but this was my first experience getting skewered on the Internet.

A few Internet reviews saw the same inconsistencies between the quality of the voice actor and filmmaking, and of course I got the blame for that.

Hey, assholes! My "I call you and your horse a coward!" line is one of the greatest pieces of dialog in cinema history. It's worthy of being in Robocop (it's not.)

Johnstown Flood was a great learning experience. I

went into the project planning to make Johnstown Flood a fast-paced, action-packed documentary with actors, animations, models, and action scenes. I had no idea that we'd be able to hire a big actor to narrate it.

Knowing what I know now, I would have reshot the entire film to bring it up to Richard Dreyfuss' level, but at the time, it's what I had to work with (and nobody would have paid for that anyway.)

Recording with Mr. Dreyfuss was a good experience and another big chance to learn. I enjoyed working with him even though I don't think I knew what I was doing during the recording, and I know he knew I didn't know what I was doing.

I think that Johnstown Flood might have been our first film edited on Avid. We never spent more than a few bucks on crew but blew thousands on hard drives. My girlfriend helped with the microphones during filming and did the lighting.

The same hard drives would be used to make Classic Game Room five years later.

I filmed the aftermath scene with the smoking wreckage on debris from a collapsed barn. We shot it in the winter and blew a smoke machine into piles of wood to create the look, the same smoke machine used in "The Crater" from Shot to Pieces.

I used a plastic watering can to sprinkle water in front of a large number of shots for that realistic rain effect. Using the same Canon XL-1 from Shot to Pieces, I filmed some gruesome flood wreckage after the Allegheny river flooded that year. I used out-of-copyright films to pad the edit with shots of rushing water and storm clouds.

We worked with a professional pianist on the soundtrack and, despite the unbalanced production, Johnstown Flood made its way to PBS and sold a fair amount of DVDs because of the hype and big-name actor. It was a success.

Some people really like it, all I see are flaws. I just can't take the inconsistency in the production, but that was a learning lesson for my next project. If we're going to use a big actor to narrate a film, then everything in the film has to be up to their level.

In the end it sold well and proved that we could get the job done. It showed that ***I*** could get the job done, and people, I think, stopped rolling their eyes at the boss's son playing movie director.

We did a bunch of local TV interviews and I'm terrible in all of them because, unlike the Game Room era, I was always trying to remember all of the history stuff while attempting to sound like I knew what I was talking about. I even did some talks and, I'm sure, was awful at all of them. This made me appreciate Classic Game Room talks years later because when discussing CGR I could walk out on stage and shout "Yo what up assheads!? EDF! Do you like Beer!? Truxton!!" and everyone always loved it.

Johnstown Flood opened the door to new and exciting projects over the next several years.

Also, in 2003, I started to film Gettysburg and Stories of Valor which went smoothly and without incident. For several weekends, the Civil War crew including me, Mike Kraus and Dave Neville, woke up early and captured gorgeous sunrises behind monuments at the Gettysburg Battlefield National Park. We'd drive around during the day and shoot places like Little Round Top and Pickett's Charge. At night we'd smoke cigars and film the sun going down behind giant statues or over firefly lit battlefields and scenic vistas. It was such an amazing experience.

I recorded the narration with actor, Keith Carradine, and wrapped up the editing, audio mix, and package design in 2004. The Gettysburg and Stories of Valor DVD set was well received by Internet critics and viewers. Most importantly, it sold well. Nothing made us feel better than watching crates of DVDs leaving the shipping department.

FromUSAlive was long gone. Most of the behind-the-scenes struggles regarding our little in-house production company called Inecom faded away. Everybody was in good spirits as we tackled our biggest documentary project of all, Expo: Magic of the White City.

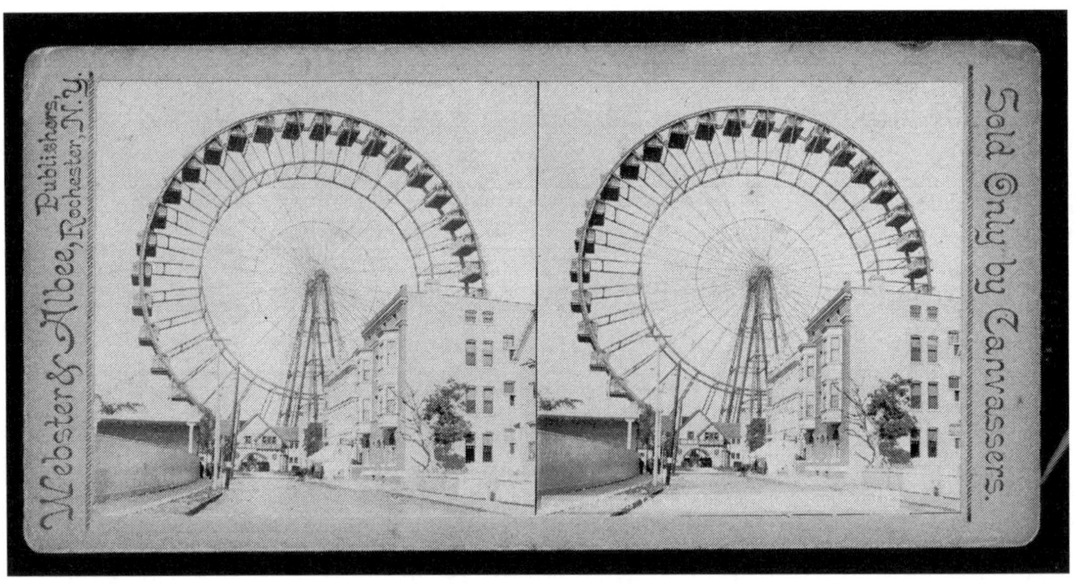

"Ride the Ferris Wheel!"

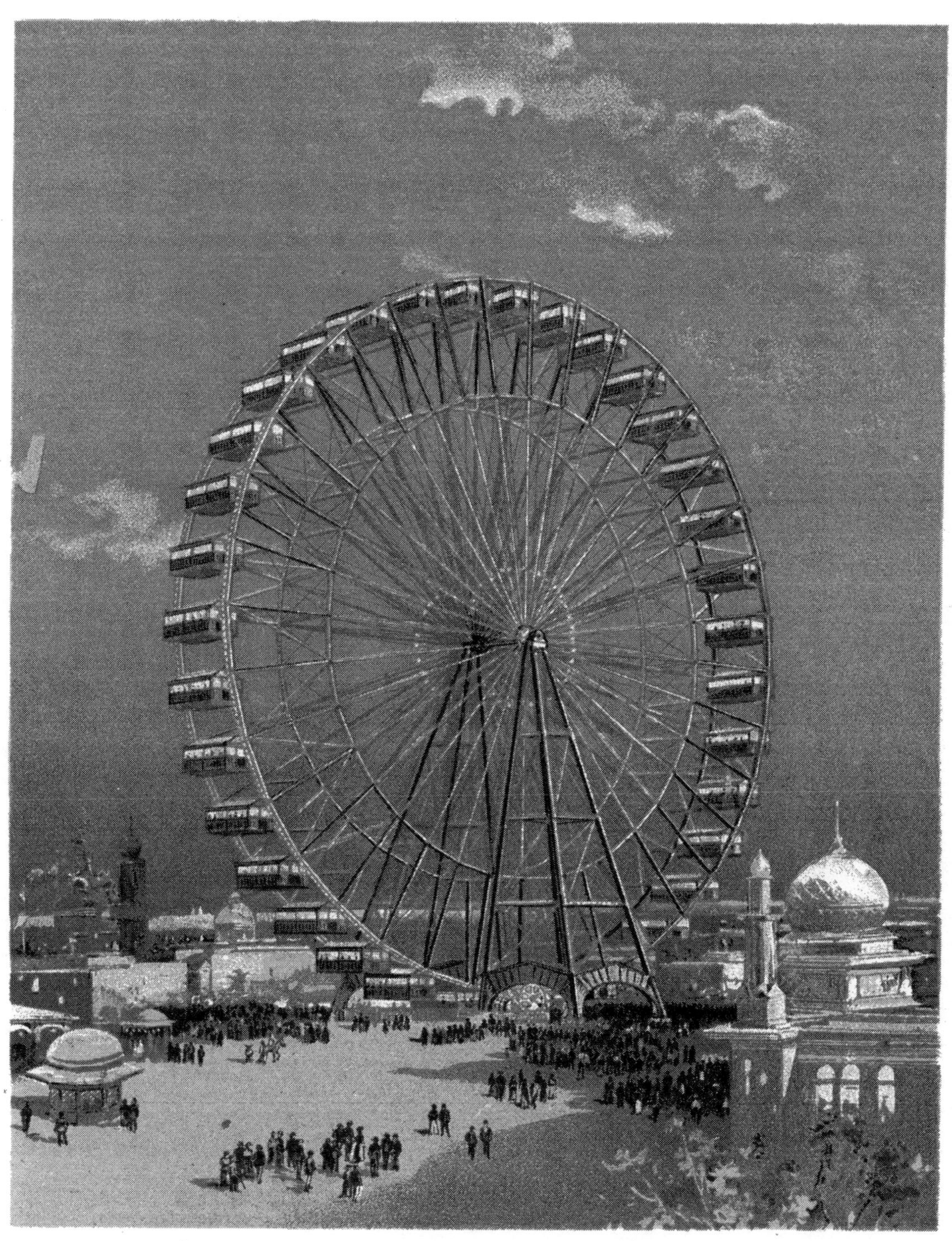

FERRIS WHEEL.

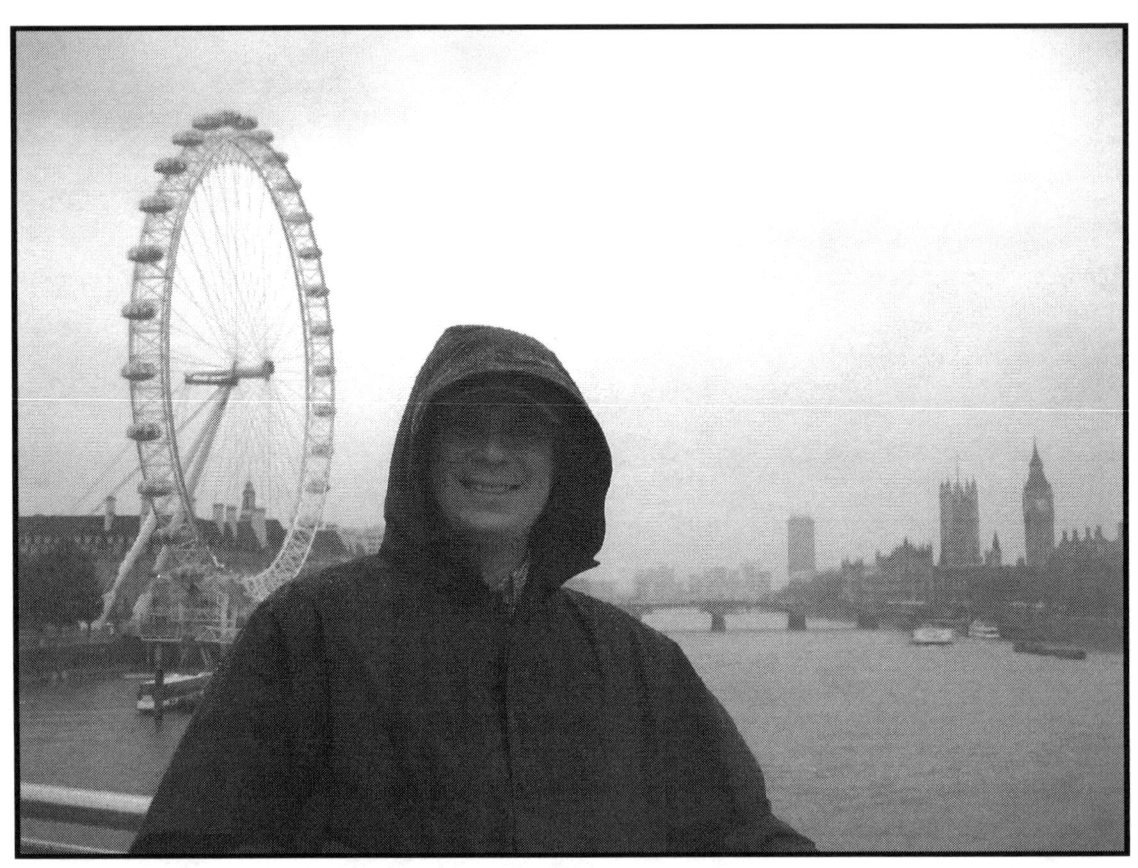

Mark in front of the London Eye, 2005.

CHAPTER 8
ADVANCED FILMMAKING

Some might think that we timed our White City film release with Erik Larson's popular book, The Devil in the White City, but I'm here to tell you we were clueless. I wasn't tuned into the possibility that we might be making a film about subject matter that would coincide with the release of a best-selling book. Sometimes you get lucky.

Our World's Fair project started years earlier, maybe in 2001. For some reason my dad had an idea to computer model and animate the 1893 Chicago fairgrounds after we secured a library of rare books and maps about the Exposition. That project never came to fruition, but in time, we collected a staggering amount of detail about the Columbian Exposition and hired a writer to create a documentary script about it after the success of Johnstown Flood.

In those days, before the Fair would become famous for serial killers and find itself featured in mainstream media like Loki and Bioshock, the Columbian Exposition of 1893 was curiosity. It was a rare chance for us to do something that was truly unique and uncovered, unlike the Civil War stuff which always ran into Ken Burns comparisons every step of the way.

I dug into the World's Fair source material and started to assemble pictures from our library of books based on the script. By early 2004, a rough edit emerged showing a spectacular event rich with amazing, colorful pictures. But I wanted more than just pictures.

Now, I have nothing against Ken Burns, but EVERYONE was doing the Ken Burns style with history projects back in the day. All of our Civil War projects were compared to Ken Burns, and my goal was to get as far away from the Ken Burns style as possible.

What is the Ken Burns style you might ask? The Ken Burns style is to approach a historical subject from an academic standpoint, discuss social matters, come to some kind of intellectual conclusion, and, most importantly, to slowly zoom in and out of old pictures.

The Mark Bussler style is to have fun with the subject matter, insert as many shots of beer as possible, and make the film flamboyant and loud. "Would Ken Burns film belly dancing and beer drinking?" Maybe, I don't know. But I certainly would, and I did!

What I thought was most fascinating about the 1893 World's Fair was its combination of low-brow entertainment and high-end technological progress. You could have beers and cigars by the lake while also witnessing the first large-scale use of electricity and gazing at priceless art. It must have been super cool to be there, and I tried to capture that experience on screen within a relatively small documentary-sized budget.

Now, I don't know how many people think about this kind of stuff, but filling up 90-120 minutes of screen time with hardly any production budget is no joke. Especially, when you're trying to recreate an event that no longer exists and for which no film exists. After the mishaps while making Johnstown Flood, I dropped any ultra-low-budget filmmaking aspirations and chose, instead, to fill up screen time with beautiful vistas and panoramas. Thankfully, at the time, my Gettysburg videos and Johnstown Flood gave me some leverage to negotiate a higher budget and film in HIGH DEFINITION.

This was a big deal in 2004, and it exploded the cost. It was worth it though.

Expecting a big narrator this time around, I hired a crew and lighting professionals and it shows. Also, I got smarter with photography and spent more time on close-up shots where I could control the lighting and every aspect of the video. The opening shots of beer and smoke are good examples of that (lots of production value for the cost of a case of beer!)

We filmed one action scene about a murder and hired a full crew for that. I still remember Patrick Jordan smacking the pistol off one of the chandeliers during filming, and we all stood there wide-eyed, hoping the thing didn't crash down on top of him (it didn't.) There's even a bit of special effects work in the background if you look closely at the shots of the moon.

Another fond memory is filming the belly dancing scenes, because I thought they turned out great and added a lot of motion to the film when mixed with the fireworks and smoke. But, after its release, a belly dancing group skewered me online because of my sick and distorted "James Bond" vision of belly dancing.

Did I read that right? My love of 1970s James Bond movies showed up on screen? Damn right it did. That's a huge compliment!

Thanks to Johnstown Flood and the Civil War documentaries, we had some street cred which opened up the door to more big actors. I'm not sure exactly how his name came up, but we talked to Gene Wilder's agent who said that he wanted to see the script. Then I'm at work one day and Gene Wilder calls me. I'm like... wait, seriously? It's not every day that one receives a phone call from Gene Wilder.

He liked the script and had some questions. We chatted and he was very nice. Maybe that's not the exact order of things, I can't remember, but he agreed to do the recording and that was that. Unlike Johnstown Flood, I had planned for a big-name actor, so my production values were much higher going into it.

I filmed Expo: Magic of the White City on DVCpro HD using the same camera equipment used to make Horses of Gettysburg and Westinghouse.

In 2004, I remember waiting in a Connecticut recording studio when Gene Wilder just casually strolls in and says hi to everyone. I've worked with some famous people before, but this was Gene freakin' Wilder! And he was super cool.

I think the recording took two days, and when you work with an actor like Gene Wilder, they're going to add their own thing to the recording, so for the most part, I stayed back and took notes and only offered a few comments with respect to the edit. Stuff like "Here's where the fountains light up, and you know, look, there's a bunch of people excited about electricity!"

We had lunch and chatted about some of his films. It was a cool experience, for sure.

Things went smoothly and from there I traveled with Jay (the cinematographer) to Chicago to film the remains of the fairgrounds in Jackson Park. I had a good eye for photography and learned a lot about scenic videography from our Gettysburg trips. Chicago's Jackson Park exploded from the screen in vibrant high definition colors. The shots of the sun over Like Michigan are gorgeous.

In 2005, we held a small release party in Chicago at the Museum of Science and Industry, the only remaining building from the Fair (it was originally the Fine Arts Palace.) Gene Wilder's narration got mainstream buzz, and the timing with Erik Larson's book helped too. Online review outlets enjoyed it, Amazon reviews were good, and the DVDs sold like hotcakes. There was even an article in Entertainment magazine!

One of the reasons I wanted to make Classic Game Room 2085, more than a decade later, is the positive experience I had filming Expo: Magic of the White City. It's a good-looking film, there's a lot of vibrant production value on screen, and it sounds great. That's the vibe I tried to capture with Classic Game Room 2085. I'm a sucker for high production values, even though they don't always add up to success.

Thankfully, in Expo's case, they did. We hit the high-definition-hungry television market with a much sought-after high definition documentary, and that helped sell DVDs and put our Inecom team in a great mood.

But remember, kids, you're only as good as your next project. What was my next project?

The years 2005 through 2007 were, for the most part, an exciting whirlwind in my life. Those are the years I got married, we moved into a house, we adopted a crazy mentally-challenged and destructive dog with anxiety issues, we traveled, and I enjoyed that time of life.

Somewhere in there I started blogging and tried to post a few things here and there about The Game Room.

Maybe my old blog is still out there? I don't even know.

In 2005 we produced Horses of Gettysburg, a cool documentary about horses in the Civil War. Coming off the high of Expo, I went batshit crazy with scenic photography and sunset bathed vistas.

The Civil War Minutes crew knew what we were doing by then and knew our way around Gettysburg. We caught all the best sunrises and sunsets to make it a spectacular-looking film. Horses of Gettysburg looks awesome, and the addition of live-action horse photography makes it even better.

Mike hooked us up with a bunch of cavalry reenactors and we worked for a few weekends on farms to tell the story of horses in the Civil War. I recorded the narration with Ron Maxwell, the director of Gettysburg, and Horses of Gettysburg went on to be a solid seller in our consistent niche-market channels.

While recording the narration for Horses of Gettysburg, I had lunch with Ron Maxwell. We chatted about films and his early career. Ron made a good point about media coverage. To paraphrase something he said to me, "All they ever wanted to talk about were the actors and drama. It's always who they're dating. Never the filmmaking."

I don't think I understood how right he was until much later in my career when all anyone wanted to talk about was view counts, fame, subscribers, and money. Never filmmaking. He was spot on.

2005 was the peak of my documentary filmmaking career. Like The Game Room, it was fun while it lasted.

Around 2006 or 2007 is the time when I realized that not only was I probably not going to make it big in filmmaking, but I wasn't sure that I wanted to anyway. Show business is a weird business.

I was an oddity as far as directors because I worked as an in-house director. I didn't have an agent, or a steady stream of commercial gigs, or connections, and there just wasn't a clear path forward.

Additionally, challenges grew as the DVD market rapidly changed.

Our Civil War team got busy with other stuff and Inecom started to take on more jobs from outside producers. Instead of making my own films, I started to assist other directors by finishing and polishing their films before we released them on DVD. Sales began to decline in 2006. We saw some of our best-selling outlets like Borders shut down, which greatly impacted on our business.

Remember how everyone was super-excited to see crates of DVDs go out the door? Well, they can also come back, and after Borders closed, a bunch did.

So, as bright as the future looked in 2005, by the end of 2006 it looked a lot less awesome.

By 2006, the DVD market become saturated with indie DVDs, and after Borders closed, nobody was willing to drop bigger bucks on a risky project that would tie me up for an entire year. We relied heavily on Internet review websites (in the days before Facebook and YouTube gobbled up all of the bandwidth) and these review sites weren't interested in many of the new titles that we had to offer.

This wasn't the end of days, but I could see that there wasn't going to be another Gene Wilder-level film in my career path.

We had one remaining bigger-budget documentary in the pipeline that I had started a few years earlier called World War 1 American Legacy. I worked on it steadily through 2006, but production never went as smoothly as

Expo or Gettysburg.

I only had grainy, old WW1 pictures to work with, and we couldn't budget live-action World War 1 reenactment footage, so the film just kinda ended up looking like "meh". Review websites didn't care, TV wouldn't touch it, and it ran over-budget and late. World War 1 American Legacy would be my least successful documentary project, despite the fact the audio mix is excellent and there are some great stories in there.

It was released in 2006 to crickets and sold maybe a handful of copies.

There was a definite moment in 2006 when I could see that my luck in bigger-budget documentary filmmaking may have run out.

It wasn't a hard choice to make. If I had really wanted to continue my documentary career, I would have had to take a major pay cut and throw away life as I knew it. I needed an agent, and I would have to throw away a good job working in our DVD business.

It's the "what's next?" moment in filmmaking that gets you. What's next? Uhhhh.... coming back down to Earth and maybe helping to grow our existing DVD sales?

Documentary filmmaking is a respectable career, and it looks good on a resume. But nobody can make a full-time living at it. Nobody. Anyone who says otherwise is lying.

In the background, between 2005 and 2007, we churned out a bunch of lower-budget documentaries and other DVDs from various producers. Inecom had a solid and growing catalog. That is where I directed my attention.

And this is where Classic Game Room came back (the first time.)

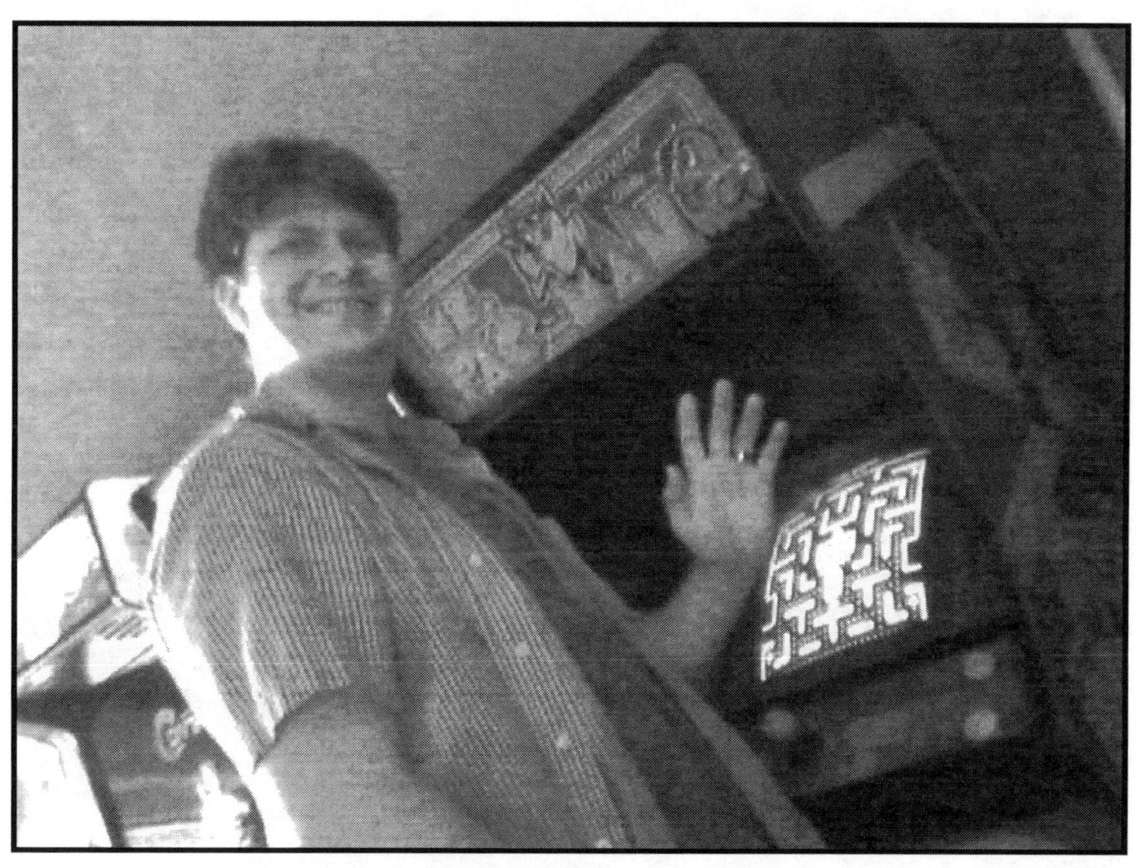

Mark Bussler and Ms. Pac-Man in 2006.

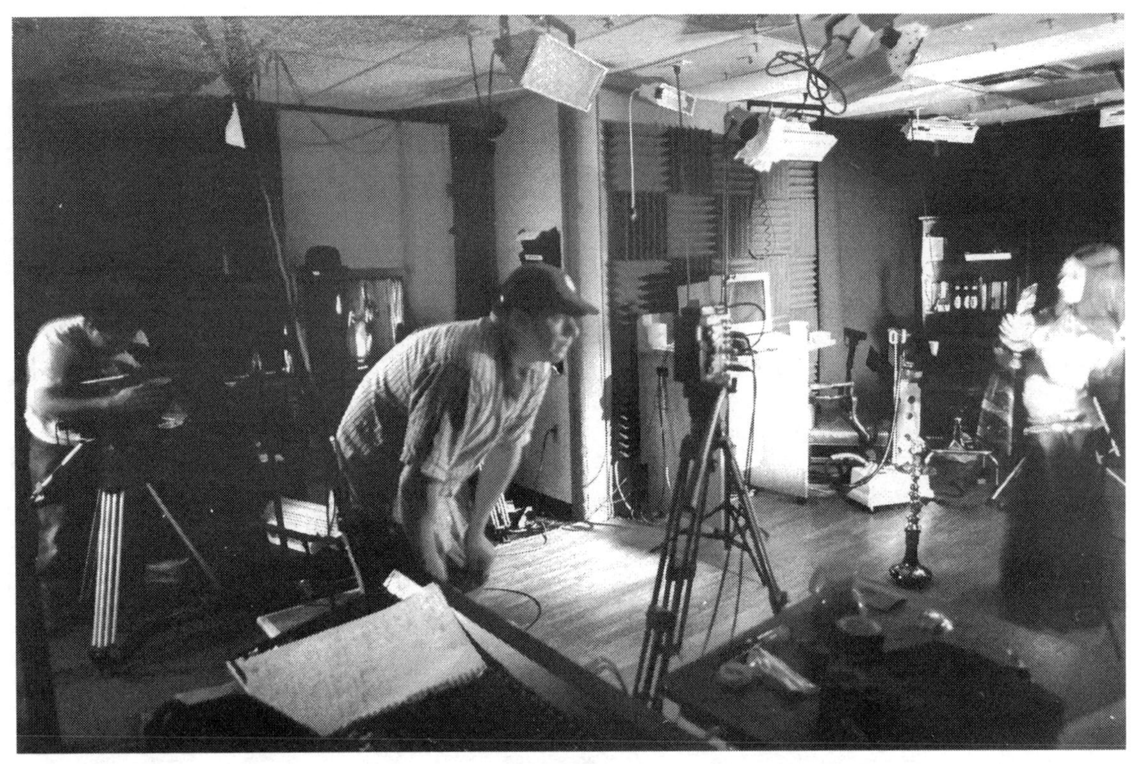

Filming Expo: Magic of the White City in 2004 in the old FromUSAlive space where we made The Game Room.

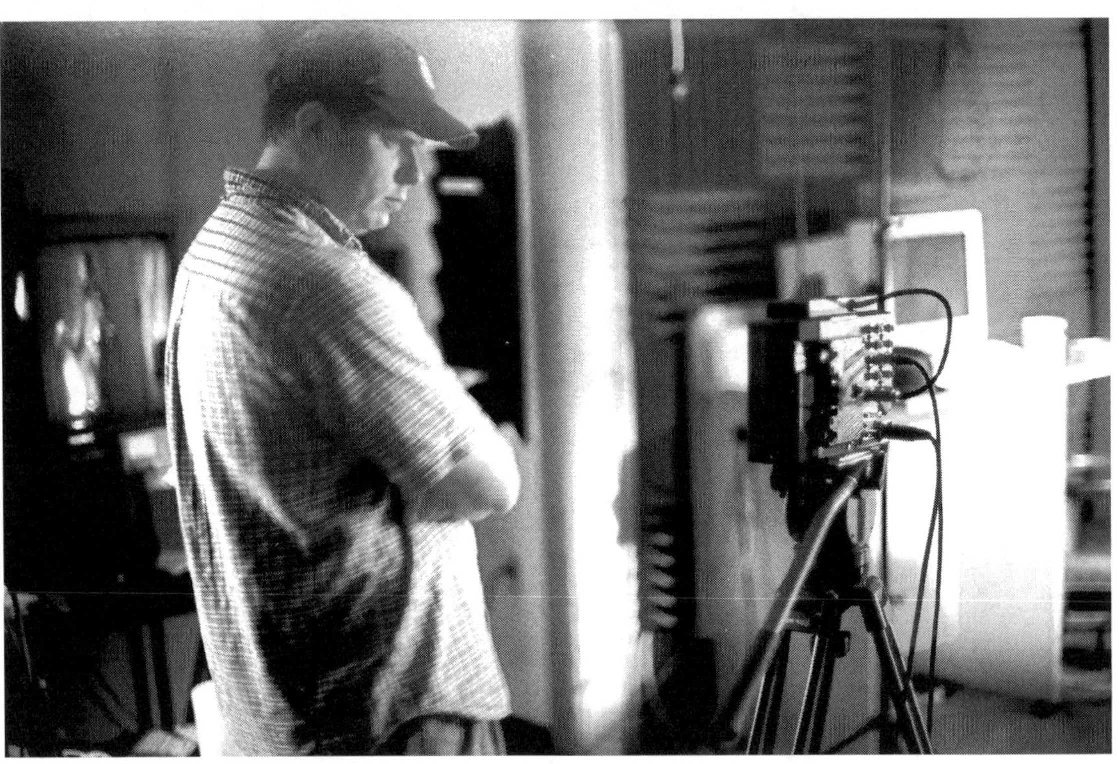

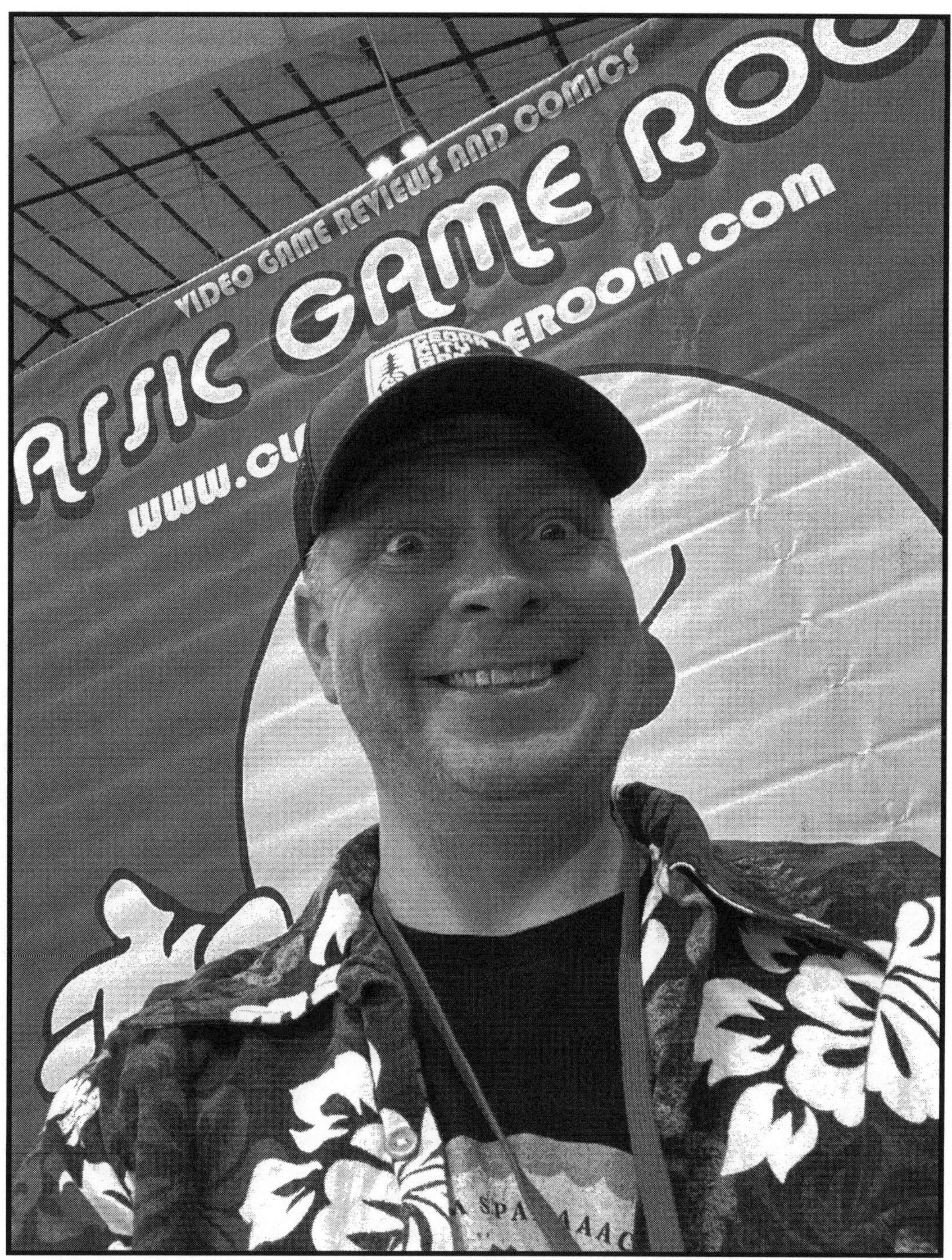

Mark at Music City Multicon in Tennessee (October, 2023.)

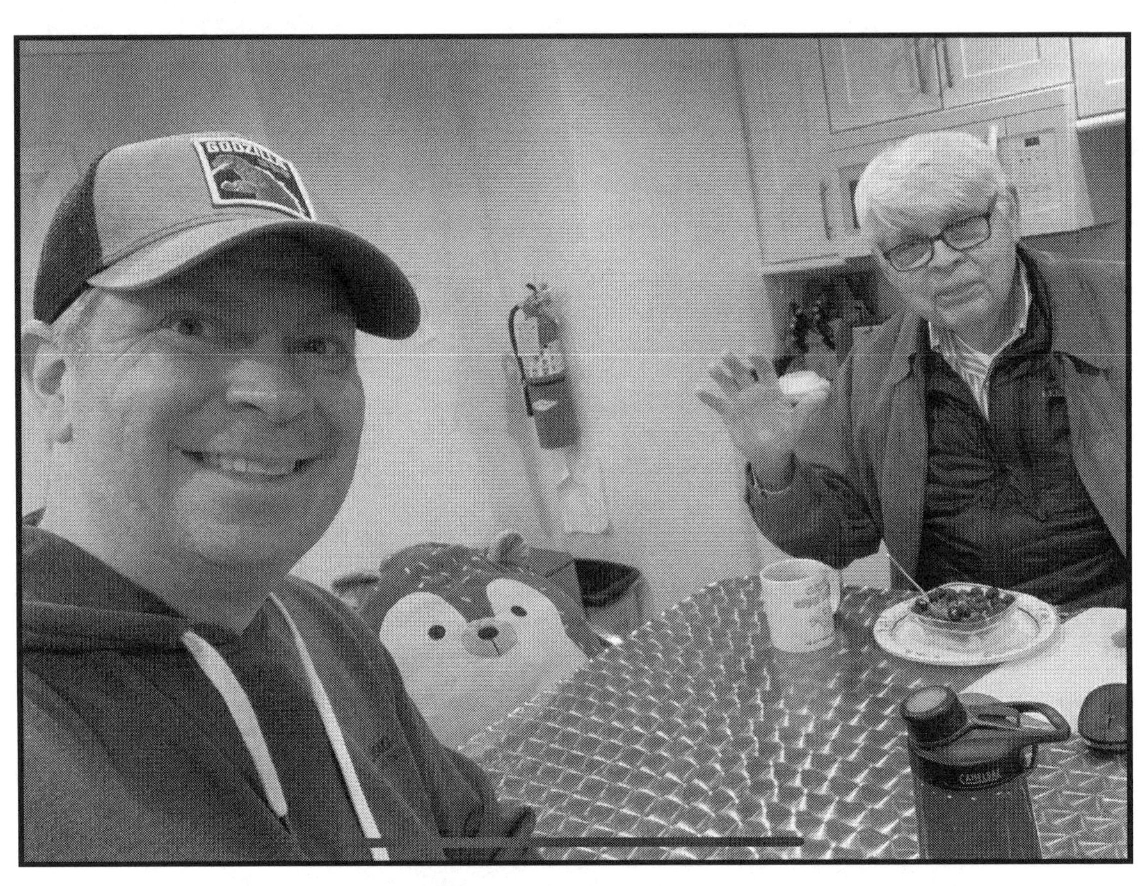

Mark and Michael Bussler circa 2023

CHAPTER 9
THE RISE AND FALL OF DVD

Our DVD business was established and chugging along by 2006-2007, but we needed more DVDs. We needed a LOT more DVDs. Specifically, we needed DVDs that didn't take me two years to make.

How about that Game Room thing? That was kinda fun.

Around this time the market quickly filled with documentaries "as told by" the celebrity of the hour, and our catalog filled up with mediocre history documentaries that we licensed from outside producers which I cleaned up and tweaked before release. The path forward with in-house productions was questionable because they just took too damn long, and we needed to churn out stuff faster.

In this time, our World War 1 project was moving along sluggishly, and nobody was happy about that.

The only other project that I could propose which wouldn't cost much money or take a lot of time to make was a documentary about The Game Room. In fact, it had no budget at all since the shows were already shot and for the most part, already edited.

I think I proposed The Game Room DVD as a way to

fill the gap in between my releases since WW1 was running behind and I didn't have anything else planned, and maybe we could sell a few Game Room copies.

We changed the name to Classic Game Room for the DVD. It was old, you know? Classic. (And classy)

Beneath the surface, there were rumblings about The Game Room. It wasn't as forgotten as I thought it was and from time to time someone would ask about it or email us if we still made it. I did a talk for Horses of Gettysburg in 2006, and some people showed up for The Game Room.

It was like... hey, I did something back then. Maybe there's something there. I certainly didn't think that I would ever do it again. I frequently hear from angry, entitled YouTube cultists that I made Game Room to get rich and famous at the expense of real gamers, but as you can probably see, the show just kinda happened. Sure, that would have been awesome if it was true, but how about we just sell a couple of DVDs to keep our in-house production operation going for another year?

I spent a few days in 2006 digging through storage collecting old Game Room tapes. I digitized them, loaded the footage onto the Expo: Magic of the White City editing system, and had some good chuckles. It was better than I remembered.

We had all kinds of pro recording gear in our tiny studio by then, so I filmed some talking-head inserts recounting my experience on The Game Room and chopped up the video lickety-split. We had digitized some totally obscure 1960s Japanese engineering film (on 16mm film!) years earlier for an instructional video. I edited it in with the Game Room footage and mixed it to silly music. That was that. It was a quick job, barely cost anything, and it didn't sell well at first.

We had a hard time explaining to review outlets what The Game Room was. The video nerds reviewing DVDs had never heard of it, and they didn't get the low budget appeal or the concept of Internet game reviews.

At roughly the same time that I was making The Game Room DVD (2006-2007 era), I also begged and pleaded to get my Westinghouse film project funded. A film about George Westinghouse was a bit more credible, and it did get funded. I piggy-backed some Game Room footage onto the Westinghouse budget and used the same cameras.

Funny story about the CGR DVD. If you look at the back of the packaging it says "Happy Orbit" in addition to Inecom. Well, Happy Orbit was going to be our low-budget comedy imprint.

Now, this was not my idea (this was my dad's idea, and one that I still make fun of.) He secured the rights to some comedy DVDs that were, in my opinion, NOT funny. But, at the time, we were looking to publish anything that we could, but we didn't want this goofy stuff mucking up sales of our credible history DVDs. So, there it is. Happy Orbit (more like Unhappy Orbit.)

The Classic Game Room DVD was sold for 15 years until I finally ran out of inventory in 2024. When all was said and done, the Classic Game Room DVD was a huge success! Someday, I might even reprint it (on Laser Disc.)

But I digress. Back in 2007, the DVD format was getting a bit long in the tooth and the review outlets were getting more excited about HD-DVD and Blu-Ray, both of which would have cost a fortune to produce. I found myself trapped in this weird period of time after DVD but before streaming, it's hard to remember that now.

In retrospect, Westinghouse might be my favorite of my documentary films. It was my idea, I wrote it and I worked closely with Ed Reise and the Westinghouse Museum to make it. It's a solid, well-made, no bullshit film.

I think I started the concept in 2007 to produce a medium-budget film about George Westinghouse and his accomplishments, many of which took place in and around Pittsburgh. By this point, I knew exactly what I was doing, and the film came in on budget and without incident. Everything turned out great. Sales were mediocre.

Once again, we ran into review outlets who were less than excited, though what reviews it did get were all good. We had a premiere at the Heinz History Center in Pittsburgh to roaring applause in 2008.

It's a good film and I'm proud of it. I shot Westinghouse in high definition, so we talked about releasing an HD version on Blu-Ray, but that never materialized because the licensing costs were astronomical.

At that time, I had also been working on a documentary film about the 1939 New York World's Fair but found that budget cut completely.

If there had been doubts before, the writing was on the wall for my documentary career for sure. We stopped in-house production after making Westinghouse.

My wife and I enjoyed our time in Pittsburgh, and we were thinking about starting a family, and that's not the kind of thing you want to do with an unstable artsy job that's about to end. A couple of my college buddies had been through grad school by then and were already into their second careers, which seemed like the most responsible choice. I started to investigate post graduate programs with a concentration in finance, even though I didn't want to do that at all.

Art careers are bizarre because you climb a ladder to the top, but if anything happens, you don't fall down one or two rungs. You slide all the way down the ladder to the bottom. That's where I saw myself headed if I stayed in filmmaking.

In 2007, in addition to making my last in-house film, I had a long list of projects to wrap up because we still had dozens of smaller DVD jobs about obscure crap to finish. We needed to complete them, deliver them to vendors, review outlets, and keep our DVD catalog growing.

You take this stuff for granted when making Internet videos, but each DVD job required a fair amount of money to produce. These were physical discs with artwork, and marketing programs, and they required shipping. We couldn't make them fast enough or cheap enough to keep up with the glut of new DVD content flooding the marketplace which all seemed to be "As Told by Morgan Freeman." How many films did he narrate!?

My job for those films was cleanup, marketing guidance, and some design work. None of them would set the world on fire. It was depressing, because we wanted another Expo, but couldn't budget it given the decline in DVD interest and the complete dud of World War 1 American Legacy.

In those days, a Blu-Ray project required, at a minimum, something like $20,000 to get off the ground. So we stuck to DVD.

"I'm like yo. Nobody's gonna buy this crappy comedy with an actor that nobody has ever heard of, or that documentary on county fairs, or that one about train stations." And no one did. They're probably still sitting in a warehouse somewhere.

Hold up. What's this thing called YouTube?

When was the first time you heard of YouTube? For me it was 2006-ish. I don't remember the exact moment. Somewhere there in between MySpace and Friendster and AOL was YouTube. They were a video site, that's all I knew.

However, upon closer inspection, it was like "hey, that's kinda what we were trying to do seven years ago except now people can upload stuff from their digital cameras."

That was about the extent of my excitement though, because our business was physical media and frankly, we had some bigger issues to deal with like marketing. People weren't buying our new DVDs because we couldn't get them into the review sites.

Oh... hey, can we use that YouTube thing for marketing?

We started to post videos on YouTube in 2007 to market our DVD catalog. That was easy.... it was too easy.

I posted a few videos of Stella (the Viral Dog!) and Edit-Station 1 who had a persona even way back then. One of my Edit-Station 1 videos ended up on the front page (or at least it was the front of a category) of this brand new thing called YouTube.

I was like "Hey, look, I got 70,000 views of that broken computer in my office! Awesome!"

That first wave of social media, which wasn't called social media, just quietly emerged. It was neat at the time.

MySpace looked like a cluttered poorly designed mess of garbage, and I don't think I ever even saw Friendster. But YouTube looked good.

A few of us in the Inecom office thought the YouTube concept was pretty interesting, and that it might open up some opportunities for our DVD business which was slowing down as Blu-Ray and Morgan Freeman pummeled it.

That's when I started to upload some Classic Game Room videos in 2007 to market the Classic Game Room DVD. People watched them and were like "Hey, I remember this show!" The DVDs started to sell.

A few of us got the relationship right away. People were watching YouTube, and they went out and bought the DVDs. A few other people in our outfit were not at all convinced because this whole "free website and free videos" thing was just inconceivable.

Internally, in the parent company, nobody wanted to relive the FromUSAlive era. Any thoughts of making a new show with a budget were stamped out quickly because, God forbid, there might be fun again.

Also, to be fair, new Game Rooms were not on the horizon because I was a professional filmmaker making a film about George Westinghouse at the time. I wasn't about to get back into comedy. I assumed it was just a one and done kind of experience.

Our DVD company had meeting after meeting about YouTube though, and somehow (I have no idea how), we ended up signing on with them as one of the first media partners. The short version of the story is that because we were a real company with a real EIN number and real products with real people like Gene Wilder, that we got in on the professional level and could earn ad revenue. That's my takeaway, anyway.

Not just anyone could do this in 2007.

Suddenly, the old Game Room videos started to earn some pennies which immediately leapfrogged them ahead of our lowest-performing DVDs.

Since I had the old tapes dug out and mostly digitized

from the DVD production, I just started uploading stuff to YouTube and watched it grow. I'm not sure if anyone else was paying close attention, but I saw the monthly earnings go from $10 to $20 and $50 or whatever it was. It wasn't much, but these were earnings that we didn't have to ship and fulfill. They just magically happened.

I'm thinking that if we can earn one hundred bucks a month on old Game Room episodes new ones could do much better. The comments way back then were encouraging, and I tried to convince my dad and the businesspeople around me.

Picture the scene if you will...

"Hey, businesspeople, I'm the boss's 33-year-old son, and I think that I should be playing video games for money on this website you've never heard of for $50 in ad revenue!"

So much eye rolling.

I joke a little bit, but not much. Everyone internally could see the growth and agreed that something was happening there, but the numbers were so small that nobody took it too seriously. It was still a drop in the bucket compared to our DVDs. This was a gamble that nobody was willing to take, so I just did it in my spare time.

By the end of 2007, heading into 2008, all of my filmmaking aspirations were on the way out, but I didn't mind messing around with our video cameras and the editing system to see if there was any way to make a new Game Room just to see what might happen.

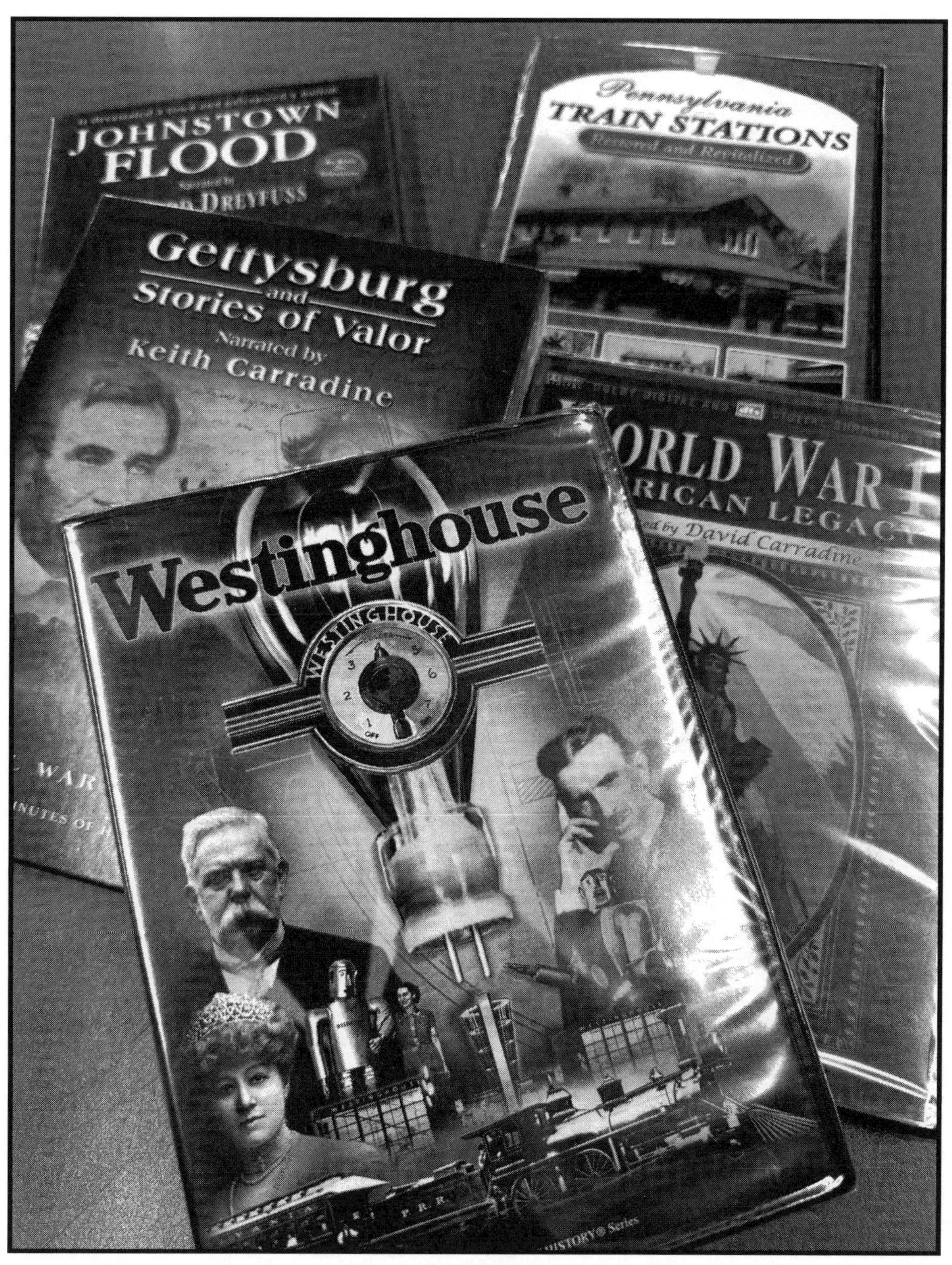

Inecom DVDs (2003-2008)

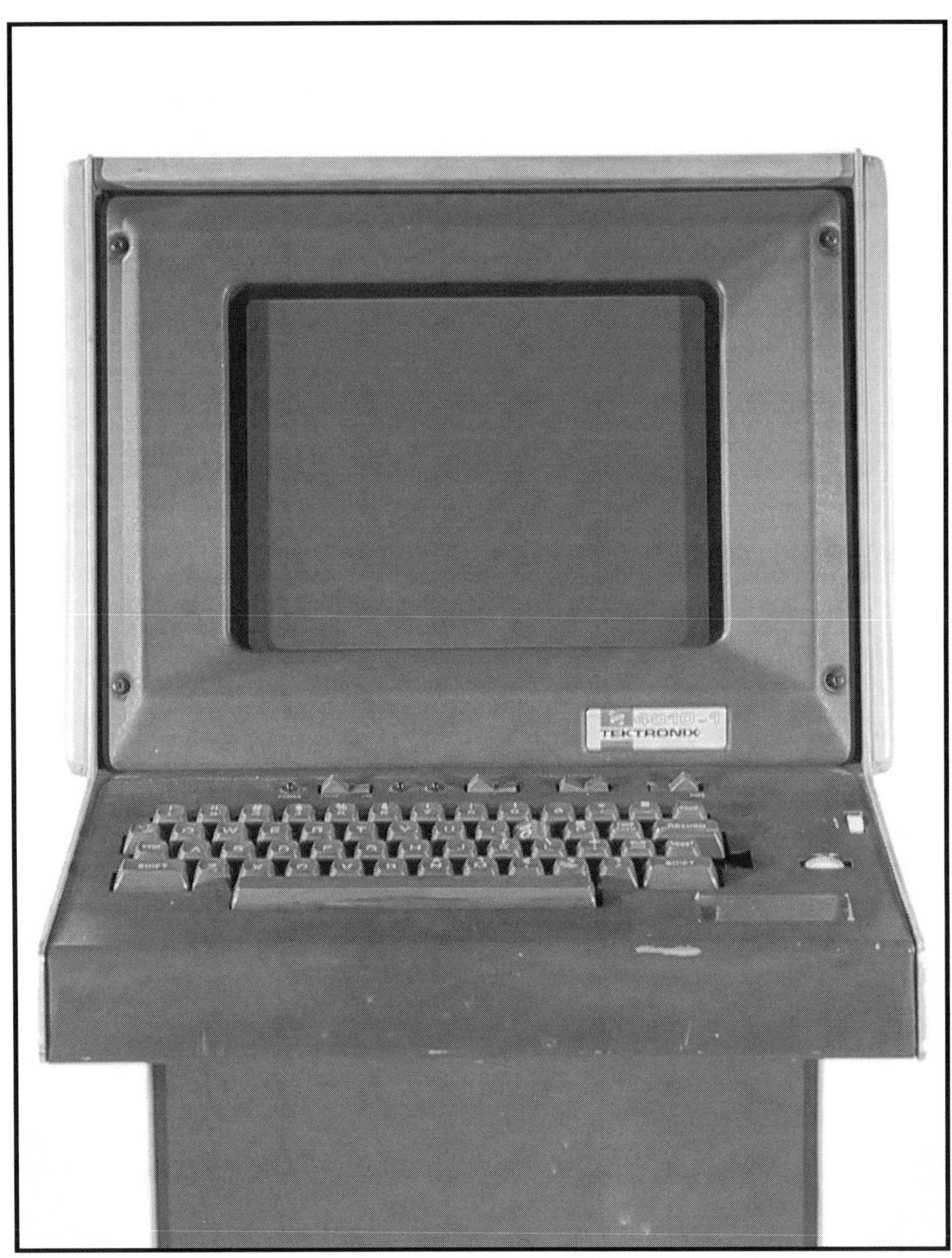

The real Edit-Station 1 (2017.)

CHAPTER 10
YOUTUBE

In early 2008 I was looking into the next phase of my life and accepted that my filmmaking days were over. It's not that I didn't want to make more films, but I knew that the risk of spending a full year or two researching and making a documentary hung entirely on the chance that a DVD review website would cover it positively. It wasn't a risk worth taking.

While researching post-graduate programs and planning to apply, I wrapped up our in-house projects and finished our remaining, unfinished low-budget DVDs. While doing that, I messed around with YouTube stuff because whatever, nobody was paying much attention and the Game Room stuff played well to an audience hungry for video game content.

In January and February of 2008, I shot some new Classic Game Room stuff and tried to find a format that worked. The original show was two people, and that was cool because we bounced stuff off each other. This time around it was just me and a bunch of computers and microphones.

Using our old gear from the '90s, I recorded some narration tracks about video games and made an experimental review of Halo 3. None of it was funny in the same way that the original Game Room episodes were funny, though. It was different and I wasn't totally comfortable with it.

I thought about getting Dave on board with some remote video shots, but the logistics were complicated and the cost too high. We weren't kids going to bars at 2 am anymore or playing Dreamcast together over the weekend. Recreating that would have been expensive and not nearly as authentic. Besides, nobody was going to give me a dime to produce a video game review show on YouTube. Nobody was going to go out of their way to stop me either, since it was basically marketing for our products.

So, I changed recording tactics and made the Zaxxon Atari 2600 review with more of a deadpan, straight forward delivery just to get it done.

I called it Classic Game Room HD because I assumed that, if it worked, the show would eventually be produced in high definition (which it was later that year.) The joke is that the HD stood for Heavy Duty.

The voice recording on that video is awful. "Monotone Mark" wasn't specifically my objective with the first Classic Game Room HD review, but I knew that if I tried to force it to be funny it would not be funny. So, I didn't try to make the early Classic Game Room HD reviews funny. I made them like mini-documentaries and watched what happened.

One must remember that in 2008, nobody else on the planet was reviewing Zaxxon for the Atari 2600. I had a good two year window where I was usually the first person reviewing some kind of old-ass obscure game on YouTube because this just wasn't a thing back then.

I recorded the early 2008 crop of Classic Game Room

videos in my basement by playing Atari 2600 and recording the gameplay on a VCR. The first Classic Game Room HD videos were recorded on VHS tapes left over from unused Inecom tape stock before the DVD explosion.

Why VHS? Classic Game Room HD emerged from an idle documentary production company.

We had a room full of high definition documentary editing and recording gear, but nothing to use it for since we canceled all in-house productions. This was all top-shelf pro gear and hilariously, we didn't have anything that could record an Atari 2600.

My workaround was to record Atari 2600 gameplay footage onto VHS tapes using coax (you know, with the old Radio Shack adapter.) Then I took the VHS tapes to work where I ran them via composite through our DVC Pro decks that converted the signal into digital coax which was one of the only formats our editing system breakout board would accept at the time.

Imagine Pac-Man on Atari running through a $20 Radio Shack VCR passed through $50,000 worth of high-end documentary gear just to get to your screen on YouTube. It was ridiculous, but I could move at light speed and shotgun out Atari reviews because we had a lifetime supply of VHS tapes and empty drive space for 2008.

The Classic Game Room Atari 2600 Zaxxon review went live on YouTube on February 11, 2008, nearly nine years after the original series debut. It wasn't an overnight success, but I recall the feedback being good.

It's hard to remember that in 2008, this wasn't a common thing and the "creator economy" did not exist. While the Zaxxon review and other early CGR reviews may not be very entertaining, they are credible little documentaries about these classic old school games. Classic Game Room always had a documentary foundation.

I repeated the process over the next few weeks in early 2008 by playing through my collection of Atari games. I'd work all day on depressing low budget DVDs, mess around with Game Room over lunch, work on other stuff, go home, plan for another career, and then unwind by playing Atari games into a VCR.

Eventually, I started to work some Sega Genesis, NES, and even Xbox 360 games into the mix. I began recording some stuff directly onto Betacam SP, which was a major pain in the ass because I had to lug this 50-pound rack-mount deck out of the office building to my home, and then from my garage down the steps into my basement. At least I was getting a workout.

Views on YouTube slowly began to rise and so did advertising revenue. Our small Inecom team was actually pretty excited about this, but it didn't look good inside our larger company. If it looked bad that the boss's son was seen "playing movie director", it looked really bad that the boss's son was seen playing video games in the office during work hours. Suddenly, people started paying attention, but that wasn't a good thing.

There was slow growth on YouTube, and Classic Game Room wasn't interfering with much, and the DVDs sold a little bit more than they did, so I converted the documentary setup into more of a professional recording setup for Classic Game Room. You've seen this in some old videos. I hooked the game systems directly into the Betacam SPs and the microphones hung over the computers. Technically, I knew exactly what needed to be done and did it without spending a company dime. Once again, this was before the "creator economy" and hundreds of USB microphones and HDMI recording options.

The reports of gunfire, laughing, and screaming sounds emanating from my office were not appreciated. For the first time, Inecom seemed to be at odds with my dad who liked growth, but he also liked peace and calm.

"Is Mark finishing up these DVD projects or is he just playing video games?" I was doing both, but it certainly didn't look like it. I remember getting dirty looks one time I was wheeling Edit-Station 1 around and making computer talky noises. This new Inecom thing was starting to resemble that old Internet TV channel. The next thing you know there's gonna be girls walking around in miniskirts again and a minibar....

I knew it looked bad, but I also started to see real potential since the numbers were going up at an accelerated rate, certainly much faster than DVDs about local farming conventions. Additionally, I started to find my voice for Classic Game Room as a one-person show.

Expanded over months, the growth charts looked incredible, and if they continued then Classic Game Room would be a thing worth paying attention to. I tried to talk my dad into splitting off the production company. He shot that idea down immediately. He was probably right because our primary business was selling DVDs, and we were good at that. Boxes of DVDs don't just make, market, pack, and ship themselves to gift shops, which was our main outlet at that point.

Additionally, as silly as this may sound, our Let's Dance Salsa series continued to kick ass on DVD. But, without a big hit like Expo: Magic of the White City, Inecom wasn't growing either. And if the DVD market continued to slide and review outlets wanted only Blu-Ray then the future was not rosy.

It took most of 2008 for anyone to see what I saw in

the beginning; solid growth that practically doubled every month without the marketing and shipping expenses. Prior to YouTube, this just did not exist and it's easy to understand why people didn't catch on. We made a show, kinda for free (but not really,) and people just tagged along and watched each episode.

And to be fair, without that complete high-end professional studio just sitting there, mostly vacant, this would not have happened at all in this way. This is how I made hundreds of videos in the early days (even though YouTube viewers later said I didn't give them enough and that I didn't work hard enough for them.)

So, you know how kids today turn on their smartphones and make 4K videos for free? Yeah, this is the shit I had to go through to get Classic Game Room off the ground. Everyone, including my dad, my wife, my coworkers, and my friends, thought I was absolutely crazy.

I'm jumping up and down and screaming "you need to draw the growth lines out ***without*** marketing and raw material expenses! That's why this is different!!"

The middle of 2008 was tense as things around the office started to change, and the economy was showing signs of something. DVD sales continued to slide as the competing high definition formats took over. Worst of all, the boss's son was playing video games and pretending to feed beers into a broken computer terminal in clear view of professional employees (it did *look* crazy.)

I had to have a serious talk with my dad about where this was heading and let him know I was looking into going to school and maybe continuing Classic Game Room on my own, but at the same time knowing I had a good job and a family on the way and that I was totally trapped. I didn't want to waste my time designing covers and menus for low budget DVDs that people would never buy because Blu-Ray was clearly where that business was headed.

In the movies people just throw caution to the wind and make these big, dramatic life changes, but in real life I had other people to worry about.

We almost stopped the Game Room stuff right then and there for the simple fact that it was the least worst option to deal with. He was smart enough to see what I saw though, so we swept it under the rug and just added it into the Inecom mix on the down low.

The prospect of keeping my video entertainment career was exciting so I slowed down my grad school research, which was causing a good deal of stress because I didn't want to do that either. This was all a lot more carefree and fun when I was 24!

So, I moved most of the Classic Game Room production into my basement away from prying eyes because it was an embarrassment. Doubling business every month was an embarrassment... go figure.

Anyway, the previous owners of our house must have had an in-law suite with a tiny kitchenette in the basement. It was weird and we didn't use it, so I adopted that space and turned it into a filming location.

That crappy little kitchen counter with the seashell print is famous the world over for Classic Game Room hardware reviews (I believe it no longer exists.)

My father had some other stuff going on that I didn't even know about. He sold his business and retired. Then he spun the in-house production company off on its own and we barely skipped a beat and kept on running in late 2008 with the same crew and our DVD catalog.

Our small team, who seemed excited, went with Inecom and my emerging YouTube concept. I put together a long overdue business plan. In 2009 we moved the office space and inventory into Guardian Storage lockers while recording and narration remained in my basement.

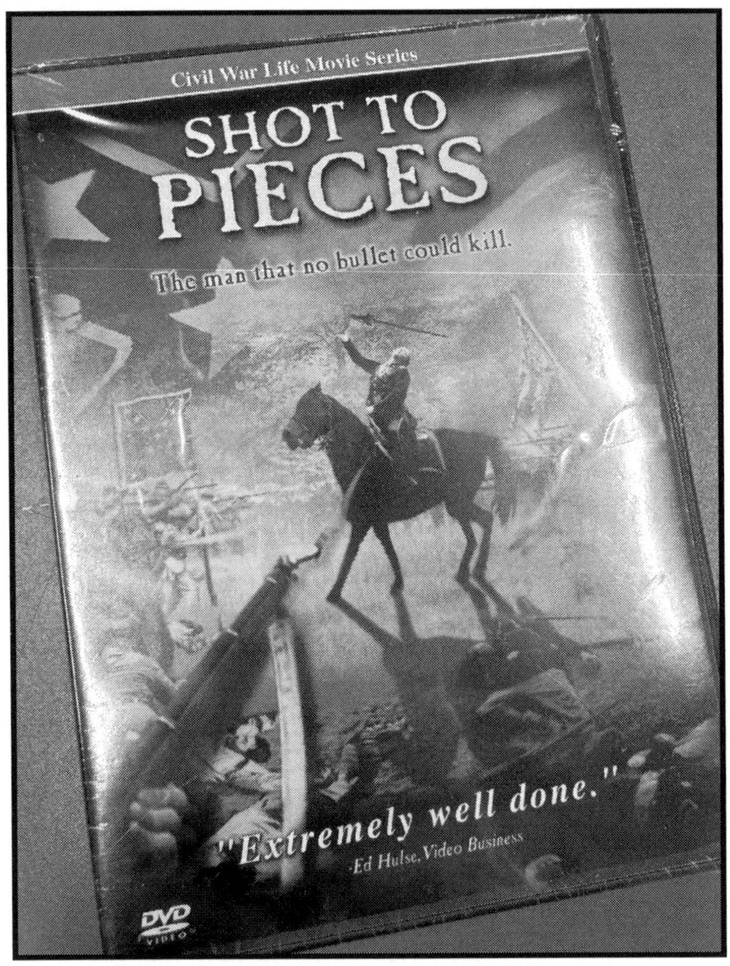

Shot to Pieces (2002.)

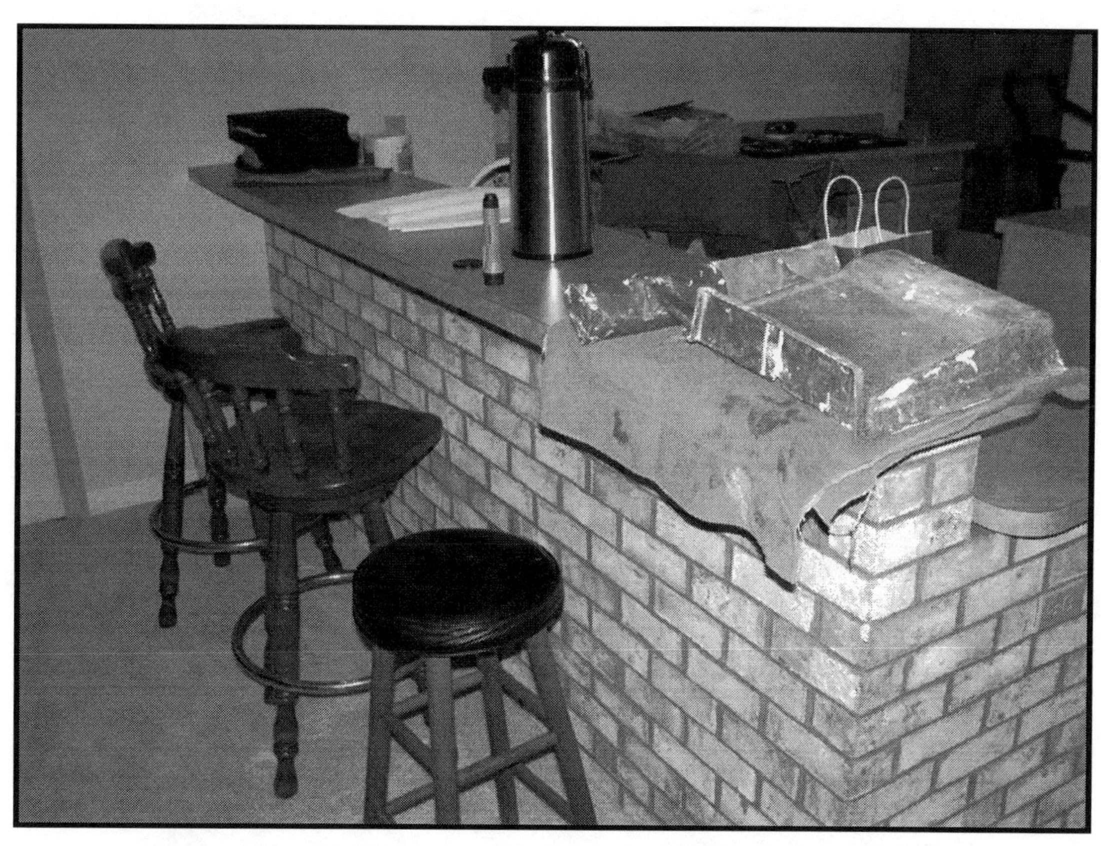

Our old downstairs kitchenette "bar" and recording space circa 2005.

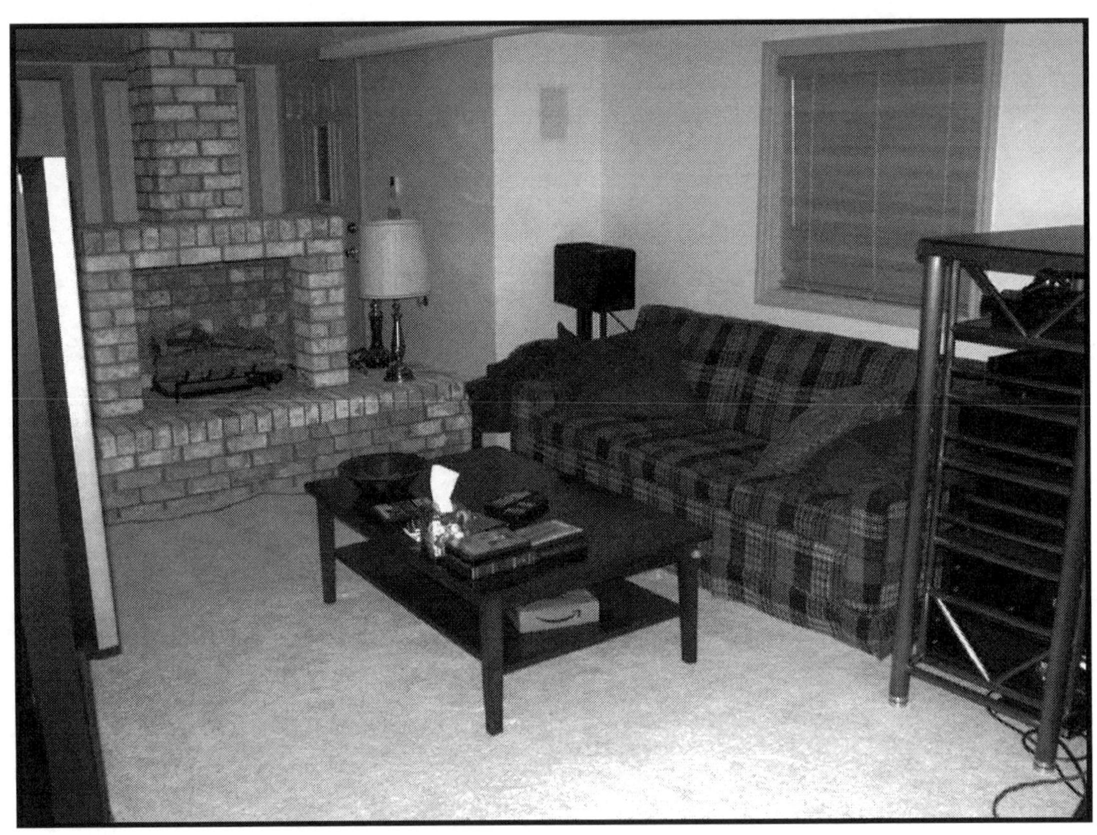

Before Classic Game Room over-ran my old basement, circa 2005.
The picnic table desk went behind the fire place we never used.

CHAPTER 11
IT'S RAINING SUCCESS AND FREE COFFEE

The best thing about working out of a Guardian Storage locker is the free coffee. They always had coffee on tap.

2009 was before the era of temporary office space for tech companies, in our area at least. Using my old Bucknell business templates, I drew up a five-year plan using the YouTube growth numbers, existing DVD sales, and a plan to seriously compete in the rapidly growing video game journalism industry.

If we had a poster of IGN we could have taped it to a dart board, because that's who we were gunning for. Whenever anyone mentioned game reviews, IGN was always the first thing that came up. But what were they doing that was so special? Their reviews were nothing more than watered-down marketing gibberish and half-assed bullshit number ratings. I dubbed them "corporate reviews."

Corporate Reviews and Propaganda.
C.R.A.P.

I have no idea what their offices looked like, but Classic Game Room brought you authentic game reviews from storage lockers.

Storage lockers?

Yes, storage lockers. Like the kind of lockers that movie bad guys store severed heads and drugs in but without the severed heads and drugs. You can store other things in them like couches, too.

It sounds weird, but storage lockers allowed us to be flexible and grow our business quickly (they were literally the equivalent of temporary office space which wasn't a thing, yet.)

We weren't the only people doing this. A lot of mobile IT companies had setups in lockers, and built temporary workshops and whatnot. We were probably the only people who moved desks and phones into storage lockers, but these were heated and well-lit lockers. It was nice, as far as living in storage lockers goes. And the free coffee was always hot.

This was a great time in my life. I can't imagine anything ever getting better than the end of 2008 and into 2009 when I moved my small recording setup into my basement. We had young kids and I got to see them grow up. Views went bonkers.

All that boss's son bullshit that plagued me for years went away because this thing was my idea. Classic Game Room was my business plan and it was doing great.

It was like living the dream. I woke up every morning, grabbed coffee, trundled down to the basement and recorded Classic Game Room. Stella the Wonderdog was thrilled to have me home all the time and often slept by my feet as I worked on CGR.

My best recordings were always done early when the hot coffee opened up my vocal cords. Back in 2009, people actually cared about quality, and they noticed.

And remember, in my mind, this was just the next

evolution of a big-budget documentary. I wasn't in this business to be a fucking bullshit influencer working for likes and attention. I was a producer. This is literally lost on everyone now that YouTube is synonymous with "influencers" and "content creators". What cost us probably hundreds of thousands of dollars to get off the ground would now cost an 8-year-old nothing on an iPhone.

It didn't matter if I was making Expo: Magic of the White City or Classic Game Room, it was a production that I loved to create. Those grad school plans faded away and I dug in and planned to compete against IGN.

I didn't think to take any good pictures, but I built a tiny recording setup into a little basement hallway next to my game room that led to a side door that would open and let in the breeze. For roughly six years I recorded the show in that confined space. I drilled monitors into a plastic picnic table and re-purposed the editing system and hard drive arrays from the Westinghouse documentary project.

My AV rack filled with game consoles and sat about twelve feet away next to a couch. I ran component video cables behind the couch, along the side of the room into the computer for fast and efficient recording. People wonder how I was able to make so many reviews back in the day. I made a lot because I built this streamlined workflow and, in the early days, the videos were simpler and more straightforward.

Most people making YouTube videos in the early days didn't have 16 terabytes of hard drives packed away in their basements.

Compared to the documentary business, this was a piece of cake. We didn't have to beg DVD review websites to review our DVDs or manage packaging runs and fulfillment. And because it was growing, that meant it was working and worth spending a lot of time on.

This is a good time to mention that CGR earned more in 2009 with a handful of videos than it does now with over 15,000 videos. The advertising rates were much better in the early days when people watched things on desktop PCs without ad-blockers.

You couldn't do any of this today. The depressed ad rates, combined with ad-blocker and a trillion videos and short-form content killed this entire business model for professionals.

These days you must yell and be extreme and pray for an A.I. algorithm to notice you. Back then, we just plowed through everyone with banks of hard drives, Blast Processing, and free coffee.

So, basically, I was left alone to grow Classic Game Room and spend 100% of my professional time on it. Nobody cared what I did at all so long as it kept growing. My dad still owned Inecom and had his way of running it, but he was happy that everyone else was happy and for a while, at least, the future looked bright.

In 2009 our experienced marketing team hooked up with big-name game companies so that we could get new games in fast and score big hits with big videos. Game publishers liked us immediately because our reviews got a lot of attention and we were professionals, having come from the DVD side. We made fast friends at the PR firms for companies like Activision, Sega, Electronic Arts, Sony, Atlus, Ubisoft, and more.

Every single day was growth. Back in the early days of YouTube, they had a page which listed the top channels and biggest hitting videos. Classic Game Room was often featured on that page right next to brands like Top Gear and Sesame Street!

We grew so quickly that I had to do a double take at the quarterly earnings which continued to double, and double again, and double again.

The DVD business became a chore and in late 2009 my dad wanted to sell it off to cover our startup costs. I vehemently objected but gave in instantly because he was right. Who was the guy who got to record game reviews in slippers every day? This guy. I had no room to complain about anything. DVDs paid for CGR (but I kept the rights to the CGR DVD.)

Had I known that my films would have a life on Amazon Prime a few years later I might have fought him harder, but we were too caught up in YouTube and didn't see streaming becoming the thing that it would eventually become. In hindsight, that was a mistake, but probably not a very big one. Streaming revenue is pretty awful, and we had some pretty big startup costs to cover back then.

I don't lose any sleep over it. If you want to watch Westinghouse or Expo: Magic of the White City, go watch them now that you've learned all the juicy behind-the-scenes details!

It was never my plan to "host" the show past 2009 or so because I was already too old to be a "game reviewer". My objective was to get it started and treat Classic Game Room like a brand, and then hire hosts to continue the shows under the spirit of the brand.

The 2008 and 2009-era is where I refined the one-man voice of Classic Game Room and got into a recording rhythm. The CGR style was to be "Chill, low-key, kinda funny, but not too obnoxious." My vibe was the relaxed vibe of revisiting old games or checking out new ones and showing off how they played. Keep it smooth, baby.

It was no more complicated than that.

Nowadays, in 2024, YouTube viewers expect me to make apology videos for running a company, going to college, and using crowdfunding. Now, you can't have a chill vibe about anything because FAME is all that counts. In retrospect, I can't believe how obsolete this "relaxed" approach was, but in the context of this story it's important to point out that Classic Game Room was the antithesis of modern extremist Internet content.

You can't run in the race for very long without facing competition, and we hit our first big challenges at some point in 2009 or 2010 when we saw our biggest competitors like IGN, Machinima, and upstarts like Mahola starting to do what we were doing. And they were doing it faster and with talking heads on screen.

IGN, in particular, quickly ramped up Internet video game coverage with new shows boasting high production values, muscular guys with big necks, attractive girls with expensive haircuts, and bigger budgets. We were all like "Ohhhh shit, we gotta step up our game."

I was the Classic Game Room show, the entire thing. I made every part of it, but there were only so many videos that I could record and edit as a one person show. Our growth seemed to be tied to my output, which is to say that I needed to make more videos faster. If IGN could churn out five a day or whatever they were doing, we needed to keep up somehow. This was a problem because I could only play so many games.

After exhausting my familiar collection of Atari and Sega Genesis games, I started to dig into new games that

I'd never played before and that took time. Lots of time, especially when viewers were demanding bigger games and proof that I beat them (which I rarely did because I had no time and I'm not all that good at video games.)

I'm pretty quick with production. But, once I started to dig into bigger modern games like Fallout 3, output slowed down. I turned to hardware reviews to offset the recording time, which did quite well.

Was I the first guy making controller and accessory reviews on the Internet? Probably not, but I was among the first people who aimed a camera at a controller and talked about it. I had no idea that anyone would actually ***watch*** that.

Hardware reviews would become some of Classic Game Room's most popular reviews early on. I went to the game store and bought piles of cheap controllers, wires, and memory cards with the intent of making videos out of them! I didn't actually need 50 Sega Genesis controllers, I just sort of ended up with them...

FUN FACT:

Remember how the DVD business grew out of our Internet TV business, and then the sale of the DVD business funded the Classic Game Room YouTube expansion?

Those random piles of Sega Genesis controllers would go on to help fund my print business which in turn paid for the book that you're reading right now.

Back to 2009.

Professionally, what I needed to do was step aside from hosting Classic Game Room and take on a producer role, but viewers seemed to enjoy my delivery. This was a surprise to me, and probably to everyone because I'm not that charismatic. I'm weird and artsy and techy and can quote Star Wars at will, but I'm not a good host. Why people enjoyed my hosting is still a mystery, and it caused a bit of struggle because it prevented me from really focusing on producing.

What we needed in late 2009 was more game reviewing power. Our plan evolved from just me in a basement into expanding the Classic Game Room format with new shows. My format would serve as guidance. We were great at marketing and distribution, but our team did not have experience in studio management.

Also, the moment I would talk about stepping away from hosting to producing, videos like Ben 10 Alien Force on the Wii would blow up and I'd have no reason to ever consider not hosting. (in hindsight I should have stepped away regardless.)

Those early big videos caused some long-term headaches.

Before they were called viral videos, we had videos hitting tens of millions of views. And they were random. Remember, we're professionals and rely on data, and we couldn't figure this data out for anything.

Mario Kart videos did well, and lot of the Wii stuff was getting big hits. When that Ben 10 video blew the roof off with 55,000,000 views, I found myself in a position where I couldn't replace myself even if I wanted to (and, I did kinda want to.)

A dream job seems great until you realize it's consuming your entire life, and you can never, ever keep up with it... and dreams always end.

By 2010 I wanted to slow down, and hoped I could step into more of a producer role. The daily production schedule was starting to take a toll, so I tried to stagger my schedule with a few big games, a bunch of small ones, and some quickie controller reviews that took no time to make. It was always about volume because we never knew which video might bring in those Ben 10 numbers.

What most people don't realize about this kind of job is that it's my job to make it look fun, but it isn't always fun. Once it starts to turn into work, the fun suffers. I loved it, and I enjoyed making videos every day and seeing them do well, but I also knew that we had to expand and create more shows, or we'd lose to the pretty people with spray tans on the West Coast.

I knew damn well that those other shows had a deep bench of California production resources that we did not have in Pittsburgh. On the flip side, we had a relatively low cost of operations by comparison. But that didn't mean much if we couldn't compete at all.

We decided to look for more production help. But where does one go to find someone who wants to be a video game reviewer? And how much time could I really spend on training another host or reviewer when another one of my recent Transformers game reviews hit 20,000,000 views?

To complicate matters, the stigma is that Mark is just this unemployed goofball making video game reviews and netting straight profit off millions of views. As you can see, that's not at all how this was. These views paid a lot, but we burned through all that in startup costs.

Any mention of this being a business always turned off viewers. "Mark is just a chill guy playing games in his basement." Sure... maybe that's like 25% of the story.

We were a real business competing in a business that was about to get overrun by amateurs. We knew that, and understood that time was critical. We needed new shows and fast.

In 2010 we interviewed a bunch of people, maybe actors. Everyone wanted more or less the same thing though; to get famous on our dollar.

This was the first time I started to see that side of this business, which may come as a surprise to fans of the show. I wasn't in this for the fame, I was in this because it made good business sense and allowed me to continue my filmmaking career. The people we interviewed wanted fame, fame, and more fame.

We shot a few pilots here and there. None were good. The "host" would just say thanks and leave and start their own YouTube channel after seeing how we did it. Then they'd shit on me on Twitter and make fun of us.

We made it look easy, and as you can see by now, that's part of the appeal. It IS easy to make a video.

For the most part, back in the day, we had a strict no-on-screen policy because shooting live footage of a person on screen with a camera cost more money and took more time than straight narration. This is why my shows were, largely, narration-over-gameplay. Occasionally I went on screen, but I didn't see a direct relationship to higher views, so I did it sparingly.

"But everyone is on-screen now, that's how influencers work!"

It wasn't like that in 2009.

Fast forward to 2024 when your smartphone is literally made to shoot selfie videos with perfect color balance and audio. Back in the day, filming a person on set required microphones, a camera, lighting, tape digitization, and post production.

But all the people we interviewed wanted to be on screen because they wanted to be famous like Mark. We cobbled together some cheap sets, but they were always just that, cheap. They weren't going to compete against IGN.

And I hated this "but Mark got on screen" whining crap we got from some prospects. Hey, I've been at this for 15 years. You just walked in the door. Pay your fucking dues.

I started to develop a heavy handed producer approach.

You always hear people online complaining about dictatorial directors and producers, well, there's a reason for that. People will literally gut you to have a slice of your fame. I took no shit as a producer and that didn't win me any friends.

It's funny how the tables turned because my dad and the business crew were suddenly the nice and forgiving ones. "They seem nice!"

"They have no idea what they're doing when it comes to filmmaking!" I'm flailing my arms like Bender.

It took a bunch of tries and cost a fair amount of time, but in mid-2010 we started to roll out videos with hosts who weren't me.

I remember that fans were super confused because people always viewed a YouTube channel as a YOUTUBE CHANNEL. There can be nothing on this channel except what people expect on this channel! I never understood that. The fact is, I never watched a lot of YouTube.

To this day, I still don't get this obsession with a YouTube channel. It's a worthless piece of shit that you don't own which can be shut down at any time by YouTube, why is this so important to people?

We hired Derek in 2010 who endured a hail of bullets for his first several videos as viewers trashed his work because he wasn't me, which I didn't think was fair at all. YouTube viewers are a fickle bunch.

Our solution was to create a spin-off channel called

CGR Undertow, as maybe a reference to understudy or something. In hindsight, this was a long-term mistake because it complicated messaging. It split up our brands which was a bad idea, but we didn't have tools to easily segregate content, though I'm not sure why we needed to.

Derek was the first consistent host, and to Derek's credit, he really cared about the video games and journalism. He had some background in journalism writing, and he's an easy-going guy who we all got along with.

However, nobody watched Undertow, and it was immediately losing money. And we had no idea what to do. (To this day, the Undertow channel exists, and people continue to send hate mail and complain that I won't give it to the community for free. I mean... really? We paid for it. We paid a lot to make it. And it has never, in 15 years, turned a profit. The sense of the worthlessness of production costs these days is mind-boggling. By this logic, Disney owes me the Star Wars rights because I enjoy Star Wars.)

Anyway... how was IGN able to churn out this rotating cast of hosts reading basic boiler plate over teleprompters and get away with it? We were so confused. Again, in hindsight, I can see ways that we could have better incorporated new shows into our existing "channel", but that's irrelevant now (and it would have all ended the same way.)

Our competitor, Machinima was blasting out thousands of shows. Our other competitors didn't seem to have trouble hiring the next attractive person who would have a million Twitter followers and fans out the wazoo. We tried the same thing, but nobody liked our news shows, and we really struggled to find anyone with connections to the industry. I guess that's where the West Coast operations had the advantage, they were right next to the game industry and YouTube.

I can remember meetings where we interviewed new "talent" and they would have, literally, no idea about how to make or produce a show. The business team thought it was all nice, and I'm like "This business is a fucking meat grinder. We aren't doing a good job at this at all."

We sucked at running a studio operation and I have no patience for directing hosts because in the end, I know they hate me because I'm the guy in their way when they want to get famous.

Even though Classic Game Room was bringing in some huge views, and the growth continued, it was all on my back and I don't think anyone, including me, liked that. Entertainment is all about growth, all the time, and we really needed big new shows to pick up the torch, and we never got there.

This business is all about momentum. When you lose your momentum, you're fucked.

Undertow struggled, our CGR news shows bombed, the other spinoffs barely got off the ground, my CGR interview shows tanked, and most of the pilots never even made it into editing. We had a hard time hiring writers for the website. But my Transformers reviews brought in millions of views. My hardware reviews brought in millions of views. Activision wanted me to review their next game.

Be careful what you wish for, it might just come true.

While 2010 and 2011 were good years overall, and the peak of our viewership and output, we didn't know how to grow the company on a website that we didn't own. Even way back then, it was clear that YouTube was going to become a problem because as YouTube grew, so did the number of people who could post content there (without any experience or expensive hardware.)

Soon enough, IGN and Machinima weren't our biggest competitors. It was reaction videos, top 10 videos, viral videos, and videos from amateurs who tapped into the community aspect of YouTube.

Suddenly, the narration-over-video Classic Game Room format was old and tired. But it continued to grow.

From the production standpoint, and the game review standpoint, the 2010-era was fantastic and fun. The UPS truck would roll up every day and drop off new big-time AAA games from major publishers for Xbox 360 and PS3. I'd rip into them, play the games, chop up edits, record narration, and post them to a growing audience eager to hear what I had to say.

A lot of these games were good, and some were awful. I tried to review things from the standpoint of "who is this game for?" Classic Game Room was a real review show, in contrast to the attention-seeking influencer trash that you have now. I could have gone off about how terrible Call of Duty whatever is, but instead, I approached it from the perspective of somebody who likes Call of Duty-style games. The publishers liked that approach too.

Also, I got pretty good at "narration on the fly" and quickly learned the ins and outs of these games. Classic Game Room was always unscripted, and I think the serious fans enjoyed that loose and kind-of abstract approach to reviewing (while the YouTube cultists eventually demanded Wikipedia levels of research and proof that I beat each game.)

Most of these games never even had endings because it

was the dawn of the ENDLESS-ONLINE-GAME-WITH-MICRO-TRANSACTIONS. I called it years ago, but nobody listened.... the seductive allure of free games....

I can't even remember what my favorite games were from those years because the entire thing blends together. One day I'm playing Dark Souls, and the next day it's Cloudy with a Chance of Meatballs followed by Call of Duty Ghosts and then a racing game. The iPhone games started to slip into the schedule and viewers HATED them, even though they would get more views than Dark Souls or the newest God of War.... I'm telling you this business never made any sense.

Classic Game Room really was the cure for the corporate review. Never did I regurgitate marketing messages or give number ratings (real ones, at least :)

At that time YouTube had competitors, most of them are gone now. But back then, we uploaded CGR videos to a variety of Internet video companies because nobody thought that YouTube could be a monopoly forever. We uploaded to places like Revver, Blip, Dailymotion, Vidme, Facebook, even AOL. There were some other ones, too.

Nothing even came close to the Classic Game Room channel on YouTube though, which I think was called IncomCompany at the time because we couldn't figure out how to change it.

The Undertow concept chugged along and gained some steam, but it also cost a lot of money to produce. At one point, after our fledgling studio system was in place in our storage lockers, we had around eight or ten people rotating through and making game reviews. We were uploading to other websites and marketing on Facebook and Twitter. We had gameplay channels and even a channel devoted to nothing but game trailers, but growth was slowing down, and expenses were climbing.

At one point someone shouted at me that "Mark just thinks he's God!", and I'm like... "well I did invent this, and I get 99% of the views. So, I don't know... maybe do your job?"

I started to grow some producer fangs because I could see it starting to go backwards. But unlike the professional filmmaking days, anytime someone got upset with me, they'd be crying about it like a bitch on Twitter.

I flew out West and went to E3 in 2010 and 2011 and did everything I could to cover it from top to bottom. I remember the first year we didn't really understand how big it was, and overbooked my schedule. I was running from one end of this giant trade show to the other and back again for meetings and demonstrations. It was like sprinting a marathon! I'd show up for talks breathing heavily covered in sweat.

I shot video footage with a Canon Powershot and a Flip Video camera and edited it at night while chillin' with some beers at the hotel bar. Then I'd upload them to YouTube on a laptop. This was pretty futuristic at the time. The days before the iPhone could do it all were more interesting.

E3 was a blast, but like a lot of other cool things from back in those days, it couldn't survive the live streaming and influencers who were about to change the business for everyone. E3 shut down in 2024. Machinima is long gone, and IGN still sucks.

As this story enters 2012, keep in mind that my business plan was not just to grow the Classic Game Room show, but to grow our company into a legitimate video game journalism brand and website. I'll be the first admit, that I vastly underestimated what we needed to do to compete in the "games journalism industry", but also, I never saw the rise of the viral video and instant no-talent celebrity.

Our growth was massive until it wasn't.

We were one doubling away from turning our Inecom game review network into a big business. All it would have taken was one more doubling.

To this day, my friends and viewers and people who heard about the brand think this whole thing was a fucking joke. Like... "how did you actually think that making game reviews would work?"

We were just one year away from turning Classic Game Room into a serious, profitable, journalism business until every door slammed shut in our face at the exact same time.

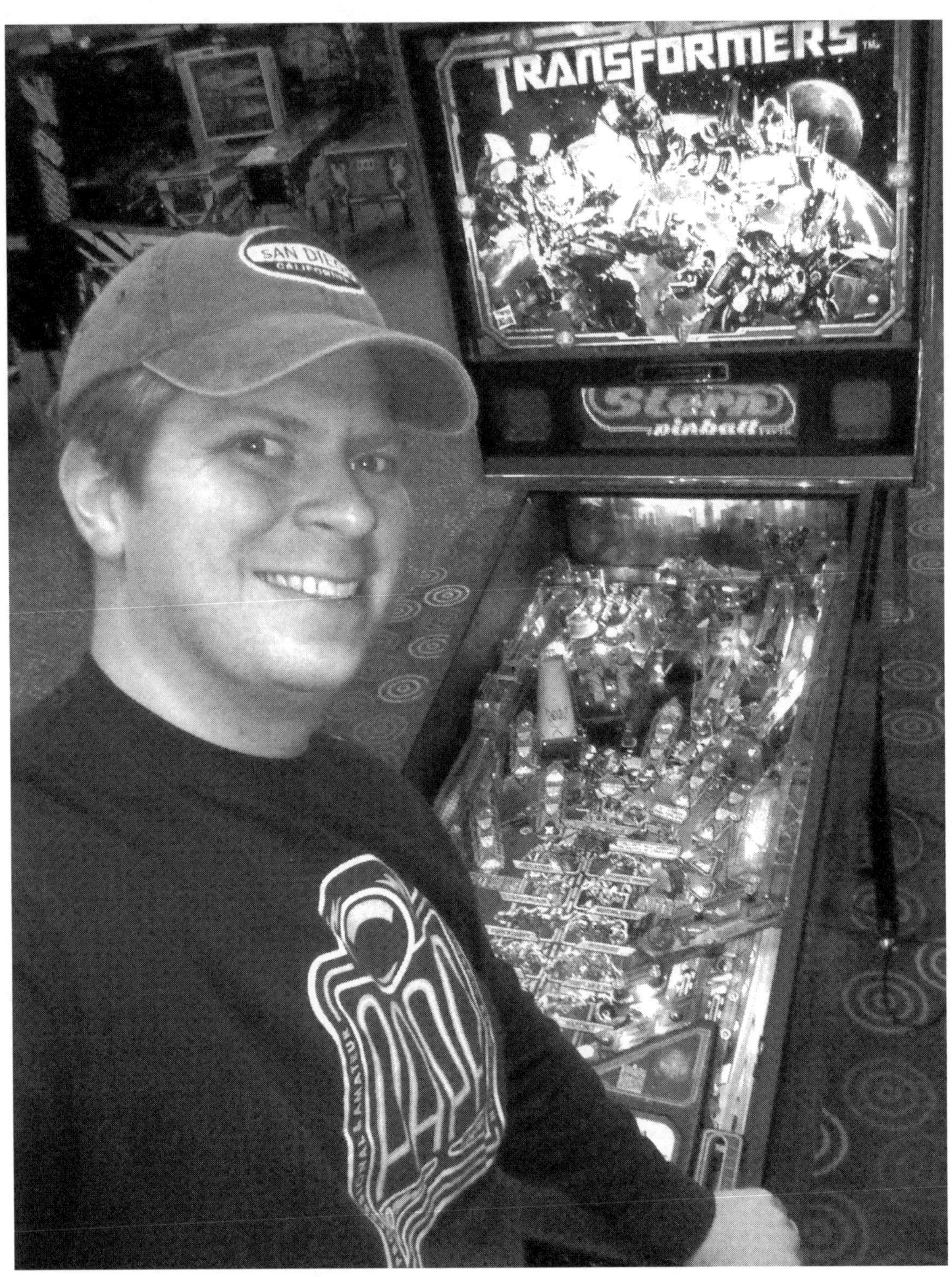

Mark filming Transformers pinball at PAPA in 2012.

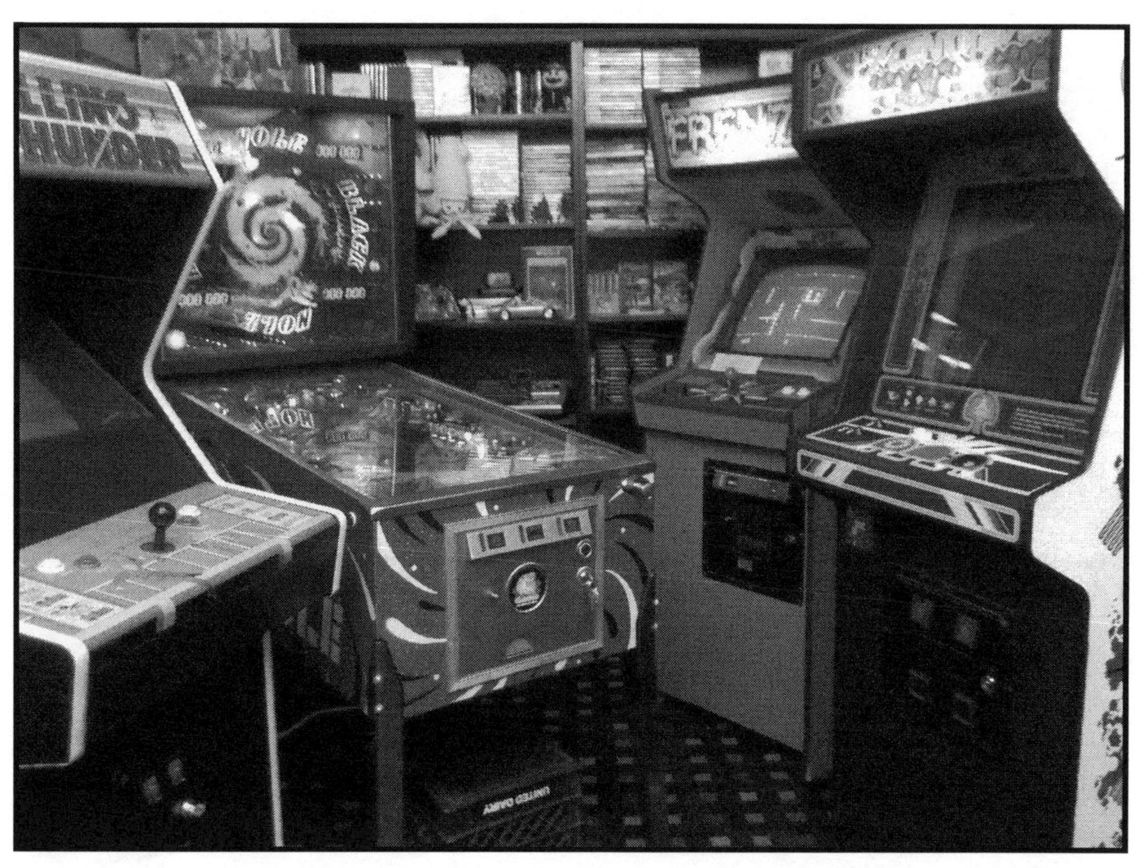

Classic Game Room set in “storage” on March 20, 2012.

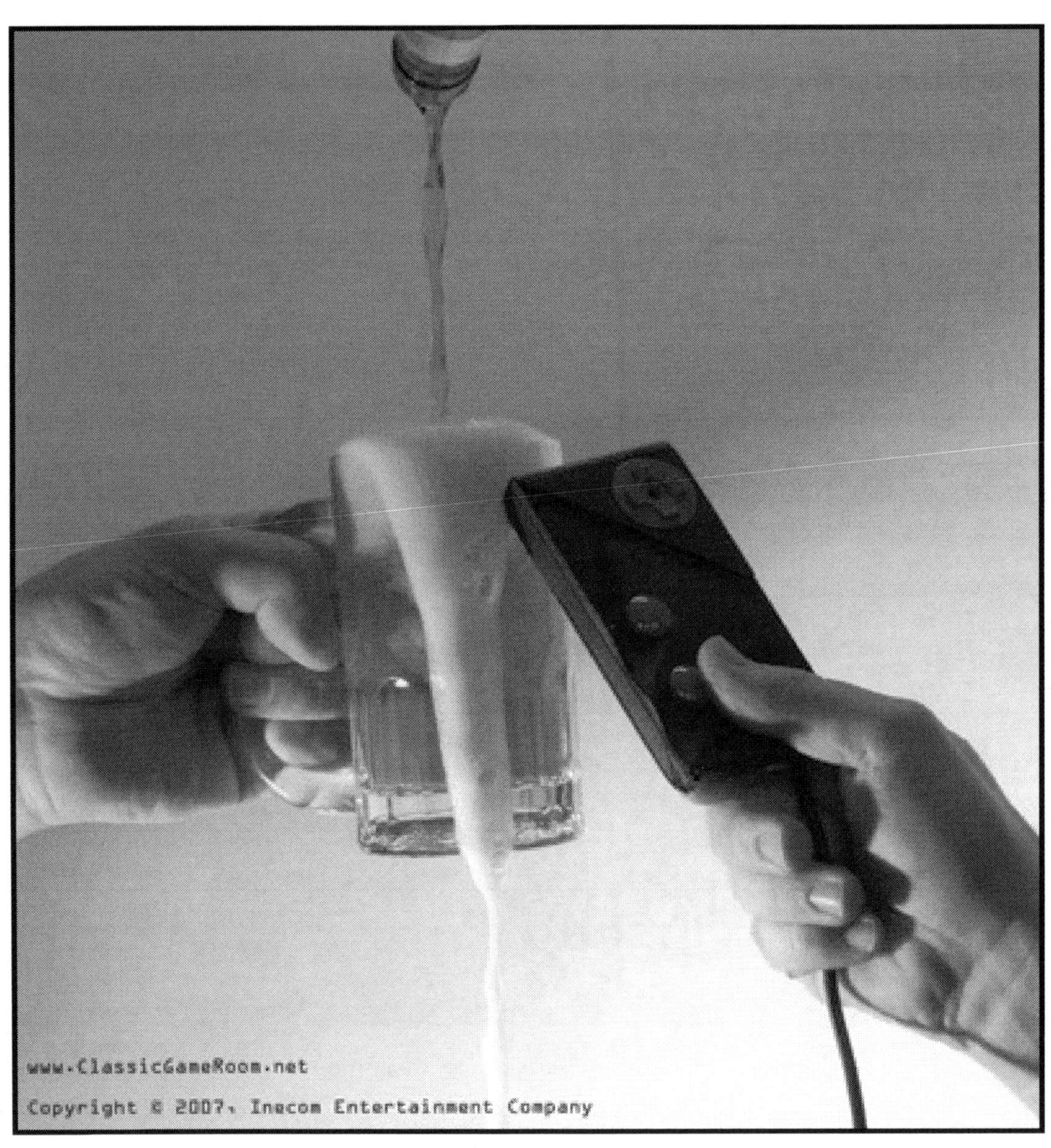

Photoshoot for the 2007 DVD.

CHAPTER 12
TRUXTON, EDF, VECTREX, BIRD WEEK!

You never know what's going to strike a chord with the audience. Some Classic Game Room reviews just seemed to turn into their own things. Why? I have no idea.

2009's review of Truxton wasn't a breakout success. I thought it was clever to start the video by digging through an old crate of vinyl and pulling out a copy of Truxton, the band! Believe it or not, at the time, I wasn't familiar with Truxton. It wasn't a game I owned back in the day and I just thought it was another vertical scrolling spaceship-kinda game like Fire Shark or Twin Hawk.

What caught my eye was the title and packaging artwork, so I immediately associated it with an 80s hair metal band and wrote a funny song about it.

Spaceships of red, blue, and green
You can hear the alien ladies scream
We want Truxton!
Ahhhhhhh!!!!!

Admittedly, it's one of my best written songs, at least from the lyrical standpoint. The music and singing are awful, but that's what I had to work with back then. Maybe I'll redo it now that I have way better instruments.

At the time, YouTube viewers seemed to really enjoy the clever spirit of Classic Game Room, and that review just popped off screen with Edit-Station 1 playing guitar along with the Truxton gameplay.

I don't think the review is anything special beyond that, but after a few weeks on YouTube, maybe it was a few months, people started making their own videos to the song and I thought that was awesome. You can bet it came as a surprise when I saw a kid playing my silly Truxton song on guitar!

For whatever reason, that particular running gag stuck with the show and I will be forever associated with Truxton. I'm totally fine with that because I like Truxton, I think it's a cool game, I met the developers and they're awesome, and I think Truxton is a good work of art.

TRUXTON
TRUXTON
ROCKING THE UNIVERSE APART!

Earth Defense Force is another one of those games that just seemed tailor made for a Classic Game Room review. I first reviewed Earth Defense Force 2017 on Xbox 360 and did little more than repeat the absurd dialog from the game and mocked the guy's inability to flex his knees when jumping.

"Do you like death? Then die!"

The writing is hilarious, and it's a super-fun game too. I reviewed pretty much every other EDF game over the years and really enjoy them. Every time you blow up space bees you gotta shout "EDF, EDF, EDF!!!!!"

Back in the early days of 2009 and 2010, viewers loved the Vectrex reviews and over time Classic Game Room became associated with the Vectrex,

Obviously, I think this is great because I love the Vectrex.

I bought a Vectrex in 2009 after getting really into retro gaming as CGR took off. The Vectrex is an amazing 1982-era vector-graphics based game system, and I had never even seen one before! My Vectrex came with a stack of games for less than $200.

It totally struck a chord because most other people had also never seen a Vectrex before, and maybe people appreciate it, maybe they don't, but it was really hard to film back in 2009. The Vectrex runs at a really odd frame rate and it flickers and I had to speed our camera way up and sometimes try to de-interlace the footage. It was a nightmare to shoot the Vectrex but wow, did it look cool!!

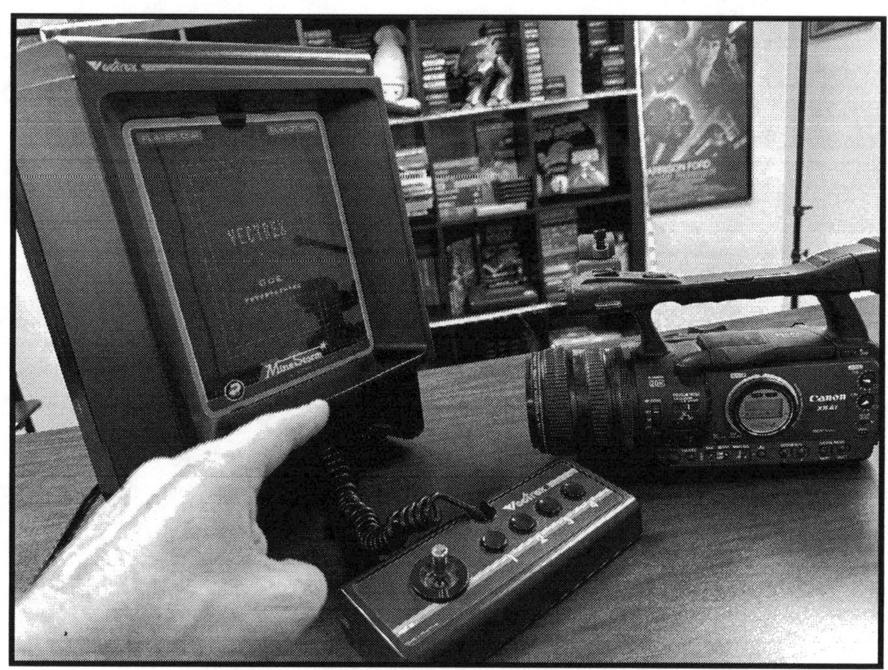

Filming this Vectrex with that camera was a challenge!

Over the show's run, I reviewed most of the Vectrex catalog and a variety of accessories like the 3-D Imager. There's nothing like the Vectrex, and one of my fondest memories about making Classic Game Room is sharing my discovery of its awesomeness with the audience.

Sadly, I had to part with most of my Vectrex collection in the Great Purge to fund my print business, but I kept the game console which has one of my favorite games built right into it; Minestorm!

It's always a great day to play Minestorm and shout EDF at the top of your lungs.

Or, you could also shout Lighthouse!

Why Lighthouse? I have no idea, but many of you will no doubt get the reference before I even say the name of the game. Bird Week!

BIRD WEEK BIRD WEEK BIRD WEEK

If my memory is correct here, I think I recorded the Bird Week narration in the office on the day (or within days) of us learning that Classic Game Room would be shutting down for good in 2015, so the recording is straight-up unhinged to say the least.

Bird Week is like Defender with birds. It's a classic Famicom game that's a lot of fun, but for whatever reason, maybe because the world was collapsing around me, I just went bonkers on the recording and it clearly resonates with viewers. Those were my favorite kinds of reviews, the ones where I felt free to do whatever. I guess I had nothing else to lose that day since it was all ending.

I don't do many shows or conventions, but when I do, I always get to sign some copies of Truxton and Bird Week.

LIGHTHOUSE!

Speaking of crazy videos, how about VIRAL DOG. As one friend put it, "it's funny that you called it Viral Dog, yet it never went viral." Sad, but true.

In the early days of YouTube, dogs and cats were hot. Many a dog or cat video went viral, and I tried to make fun of that and get a viral video at the same time. It didn't go viral, but it is memorable and a lot of fun. I even shot one called Viral Dog Reacts to Viral Dog!

Stella was a monster from Hell and an awful animal in every way. She almost burned down our house, she ate an entire family of live moles, and she once shit herself and then wiped the poop all over our furniture. She lived a long and happy life until 2021.

THE DOG IS VIRAL!

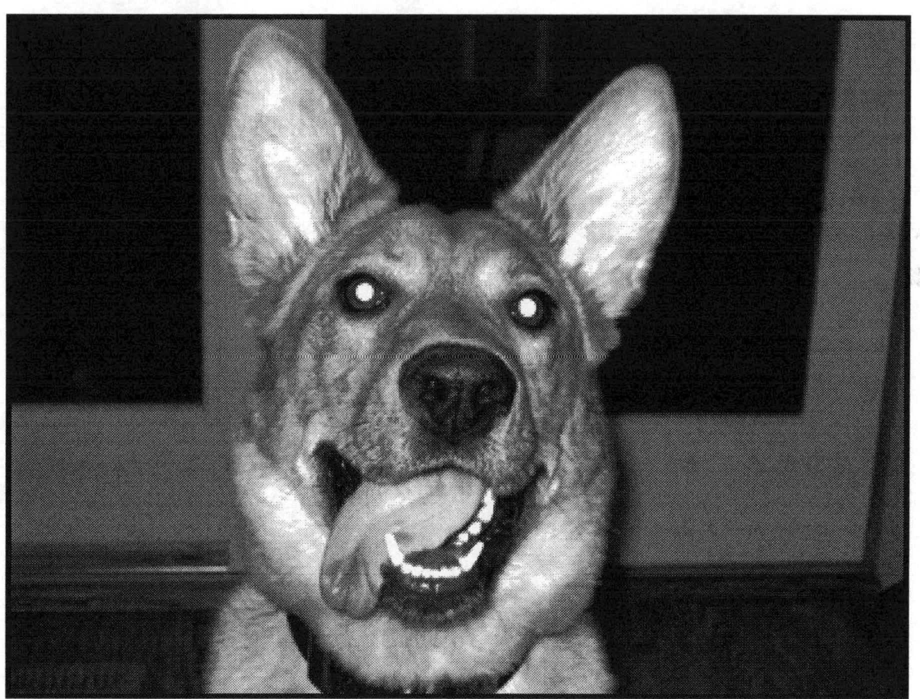

Stella circa 2008. She's probably thinking about what to break next.

One thing I haven't covered yet is my favorite videos! Gosh, there's so many to choose from. By my estimates, I made roughly 4,000 game reviews between 1999 and 2024. And, I should add, I did the editing, recording, and narration on every single one of those.

It's hard to not have fond memories of the 2000-era Game Rooms. We were kids then, and I had so much fun filming those with Dave. When I watch them now it's like I'm looking at a completely different person on the screen (which is true, I'm not like that at all anymore... well, maybe a little bit.)

The Seaman review was off the rails funny because how could it not be. It was called freakin' Seaman, and it was voiced by Leonard Nimoy, AND WE COULD KILL IT. Lewd and inappropriate yes, but also fucking hilarious.

X-Men for the Sega Genesis was great because we had all the time in the world back then (it seemed) and filmed that in the back yard of the company building. Who can ever forget the greatest X-Men of all, The Lush and Pottymouth?

The Real Game Room is a triumph of filmmaking. Lawrence of Arabia blows compared to The Real Game Room. Did Lawrence ever cry in a bathroom about his private time or play Alien for the Atari 2600? No. My point is made. We were on fire in that video.

Sega GT was tons of fun. There's nothing bad about playing Sega Dreamcast and then lighting toy cars on fire in the parking lot. And obviously, People Hunt.

I also have fond memories of recording stuff like Maken X, Tokyo Xtreme Racer, Omega Boost, and the magnificent Chu Chu Rocket (MOUSE MANIA!) Those were all good. There's just no way to capture that time of life again and I really like our top shelf Game Rooms.

The 2008-2009 era was also a lot fun because things were still new, it was like a new lease on life for my film career, and I saved my job by playing Atari. What's not to love about that? I don't like the Zaxxon review for Atari 2600, but I really like the Zaxxon review for Atari 2600.

Specifically, as I'm writing this, I can't remember too many others that stand out. I have fond memories like waves, I remember the eras.

The Atari-on-VHS era was great. I also really liked that period when I got back into collecting and discovered gems like M.U.S.H.A., Truxton, and Fire Shark. I'm not sure they're the best reviews, but they're good memories.

I really enjoyed the Vectrex and Magnavox 2 eras as well because I was discovering those game systems for the first time, as were many of the viewers. Since I didn't grow up with either, it was tons of fun to play their unique catalogs for the first time and (usually) be the first to make reviews on the games.

As I'm sitting here writing this, I think it's weird that some of the best Classic Game Room videos came out of the worst time for the business in the years 2013-2015. As you'll read shortly, everything fell apart in that time, but I had all the toys in the world with which to make good videos. I had access to every game system ever made, an arcade, a slow-moving cherrypicker, and bottomless production resources. The Truxton arcade review came out in that period, as did Barney's Hide and Seek Game, The R-Zone, Necronomicon, the Hyper Neo-Geo 64, the Game Boy Printer, all the Famicom Disk System stuff, the Game Boy Micro, and countless more.

Classic Game Room 2085 will always have a place in my heart because it's what the show was meant to be, and of course, the foul-mouthed Magnavox Odyssey Voice.

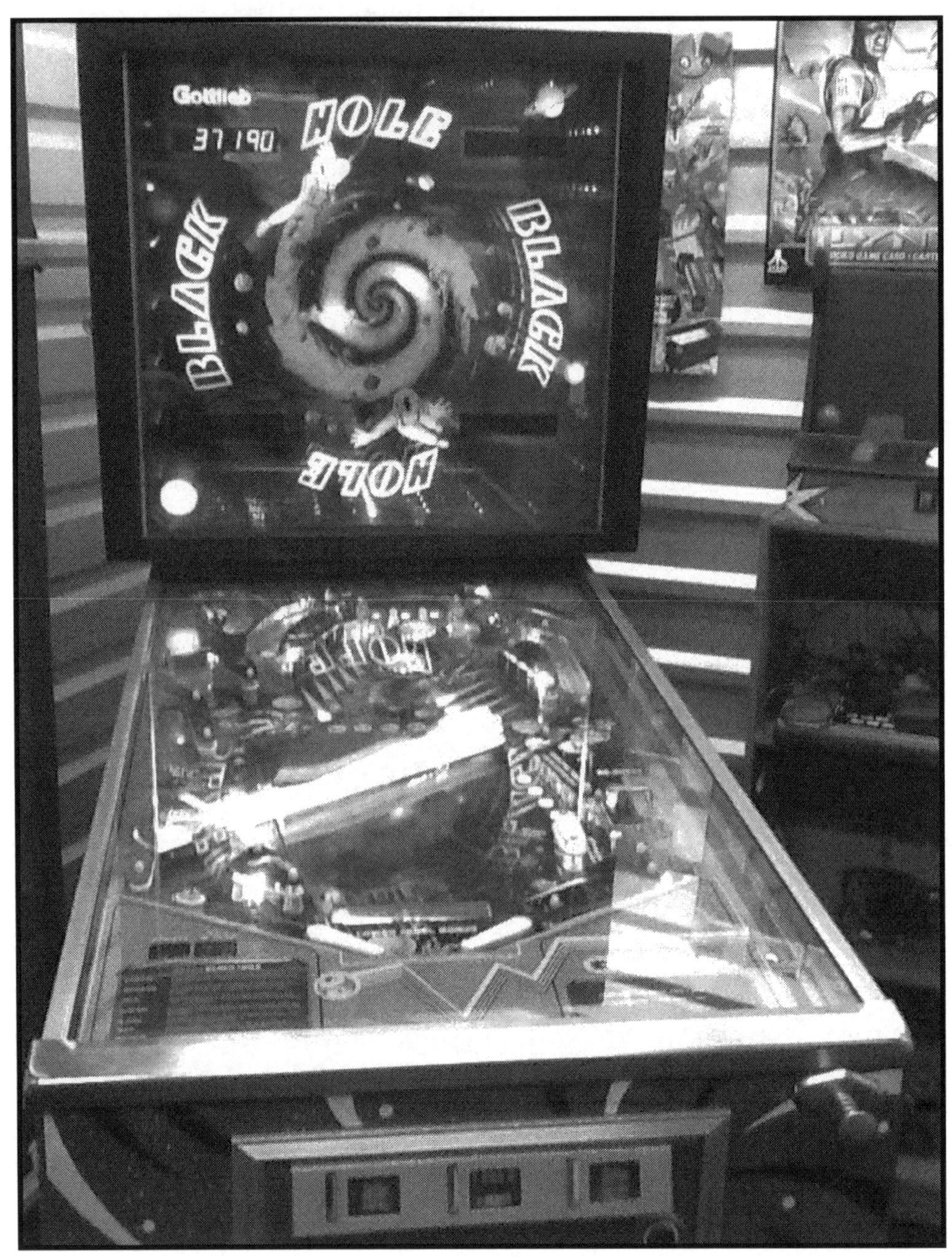

Black Hole pinball in the storage locker circa 2012.

CHAPTER 13
STORM CLOUDS ON THE HORIZON

2011 and 2012 were fun years and we made lots of great videos. Loads of viewers discovered our shows in that era, but YouTube was changing. Viewers wanted more than just narration, they wanted to see someone on screen. They also needed constant interaction.

The original Game Room from 1999 had people on screen, and I think people really liked that, even if the production values were terrible. However, we also had a bigger studio back in those days and the videos, adjusting for production time, probably cost a lot more to make. But, agreed, there's nothing like having some likable people on screen talking to the crowd. That's always a winning formula.

I'm a fan of assembly-line production, and my narration-over-editing style was faster to produce, easier to manage, less expensive, and it still brought in big views. But the views were not nearly as big as the emerging crop of new YouTube stars. These new stars were blowing our hard work to bits, and all they did was talk on screen.

I gave in to demand and started to shoot video segments on screen, but it didn't really increase views. It just increased the cost of production and slowed everything down.

Viewers thought we were all having fun, and I think they enjoyed the team atmosphere we had with our spin-offs and Undertow, but viewership peaked at the end of 2011. Once views started to go backwards, warning flags went up everywhere (and it never turned around.)

I saw the problem right away, and the problem was clickbait. Clickbait gamed the YouTube advertising engine. As far as I'm concerned, clickbait ruined the entire Internet.

YOU WON'T BELIEVE WHAT SHE SAID WHEN.....

Sigh.

In 2012, I had a hard time explaining to my team why the icon for the video was more important than the actual video. They said "But we need to make good videos or else fans will be upset."

"Yes, but people don't know if it's a good video if they don't click on it."

"So, what do we do?"

"I have no idea."

We didn't know how to keep the quality of our content high while also competing against cheaply-produced clickbait videos and the rising crop of Internet stars. I never fully understood why people preferred obviously half-assed ranking videos and reaction videos to our genuine journalism, but that's probably because I still saw the show as a documentary.

My dad wanted to sell the channel to one of the larger competitors in 2012, I objected. I probably should have just let him, it would have saved me a lot of headaches over the next couple years. I think the companies who were interested in buying us out are all out of business by now.

If you think we had it rough entering the clickbait era, just imagine what our competitors with big-budget shows and real studio overhead went through. At least we knew how to run stuff cheap and scrappy from a storage locker.

But what of fun!? It was fun. We weren't making up the fun on screen, it was a good time. But good times don't pay the bills, and in retrospect, I look back on this 2012-era and second guess a lot of the decisions that I made. We never envisioned a future where YouTube would be the sole monopoly ruling over the entire Internet video business. That's not how any other business worked until YouTube and Facebook took over everything.

As a group, we were frustrated because we knew we made good shows, and we knew we made honest content. But viewers were flocking to clickbait and reaction videos. And, we didn't see a way to compete in the clickbait reaction video business. That's not what we did.

What we were good at was producing quality videos and selling stuff. But, in order to sell things, we needed a website. In order to get a good website in 2012 we needed programmers. To hire programmers, we had to move out of storage lockers because nobody wants to show up for an interview held in the back of a storage locker.

"But we have free coffee."

Come on, storage lockers are funny! We weren't actually going to murder you and put your severed head in a jar, that would count as an insurance liability. But, do kindly stand on the plastic when you walk into the storage locker....

At our peak, I think we had about four or five storage lockers on the ground floor, three of them were used for recording. Customers would walk in with boxes of books, clothing, and furniture and gawk at us playing Call of Duty and screaming like crazy people.

If we slammed one of the big blue rolling storage locker doors they'd set off the alarms all over the building. We did that a lot, as it turns out.

SLAM!

WEEEEOOOOOWWWWWEEEEEEOOOOOOWEEEEEEOOOOOOOOOO!!!!!

There was no soundproofing, so gunfire and explosions echoed down the hallway all day. It had a college dorm-like atmosphere that I really enjoyed.

I bought a bunch of arcade games and Black Hole pinball and built a small set out random shelving and pieces of old furniture. Some of the early videos from that time showed the bare metal storage room walls. I joked it was underwater and called it A.L.F.A.R.

Aquatic Laboratory For Awesome Reviews.

Eventually, that turned into the Intergalactic Space Arcade after I installed a few more games like Centipede, Rolling Thunder and the Neo Geo.

Black Hole pinball taunted innocent people walking by with "Do you dare enter the black hole!"

Considering that my whole 2012-era set was built inside a fairly tiny storage locker, I thought the studio segments looked and sounded pretty good.

These are also the years, 2009-2012, when I experimented with what would eventually become the hot trend a decade later; Shorts & TikToks!

Years before TikTok, I saw that short videos were far

less expensive to produce and earned more or less the same amount of money as the big ones. The number of clicks is what mattered, and who cared if the video was about video games or toy cars?

For the most part, I could get away with whatever in those years because people liked me (I didn't have to make any hard decisions yet.) My kids were young and I had a lot of my old Star Wars figures, Transformers, and G.I. Joes unboxed and laying about, so I filmed them.

The CGR Garage and CGR Toys channels were born! As with Undertow, we tried to segregate the channels so the "gamers" wouldn't be inconvenienced with videos showing up in their inbox like Thomas the Tank Engine. They hated that. "Unsubscribed!"

Our toy reviews, in particular, performed better than the Classic Game Room videos when taking production time into account. I couldn't make enough of them fast enough, but I also needed to prioritize Classic Game Room because it was the breadwinner.

We tried hiring people to review cars and toys but, like the early days of expanding our CGR videos, anyone who could do it wanted to do it on their own and YouTube's easy self-publishing allowed them to do that.

Regardless, we made some great toy reviews in those years. The little car reviews are also fun and quirky. Years later, those kinds of die-cast and collectible figure videos would prove to be extremely popular on short form sites like TikTok. Once again, we were ahead of our time.

At some point, during those years, I ended up with every video game console imaginable, but no time to enjoy any of them. That's the curse of a dream job. But the stuff rolled in from fans around the world and we thought it was a good way to engage the audience.

The first thing that anyone sent to the show was a sleeve filled with Sega Saturn games. Then a very generous fan sent a Neo-Geo CD game console, and I always did my best to give a shout out and thank them. I never expected anyone to send anything, and I certainly didn't expect to receive expensive game consoles and rare video games.

Once we started giving shout outs to fans for sending stuff to the show, the floodgates opened and we were drowned in game donations.

It's a strange phenomenon when the overall hits are going backward, but enthusiasm about the show is increasing. That was also 2012. Viewers were ecstatic, or so it seemed, to get a videos from our growing empire of shows every day

We were also drowning in a nonstop supply of PR copies that included every bad game based on a summer blockbuster movie. I think they released like 10 versions of one of the Transformers games on Xbox 360, Wii, Nintendo DS, PS3, PSP and whatever else at the time. Lego, Rango, Shrek, Monsters vs. Aliens, Captain America, Kung Fu Panda, you name it. We had countless movie games in our schedule, and they were the games that got the views. But not the games that subscribers liked... it's funny how it always worked out like that.

We were swamped, but it was so freakin' cool to have a growing video game museum. But where could we put a video game museum, and what do we do about interviewing programmers who are distrustful of a company working out of storage lockers?

"Welcome to your interview. Don't mind the alarms going off and the people wheeling couches down the hall."

Programming was my dad's jam, and he was always

working on that stuff in addition to his other experiments and inventions. He was excited about the growth of our YouTube channels, but he also saw the risk of making videos for a very fickle audience on one platform which was unpredictable.

We needed to get off YouTube as an exclusive platform.

In 2011, I started to film videos at the Professional and Amateur Pinball Association, or PAPA. Maybe you've seen their logo on the CGR videos filmed at their location. I forget how I first met them, but PAPA, based out of Carnegie just outside Pittsburgh, was the biggest collection of rare pinball machines that you've ever seen.

The owner gave me permission to film in return for thank yous and publicity. I befriended his team and Mark, who ran the operation, and basically got permission to film there whenever I wanted.

I think their business dated back to the early dot-com days, I'm not sure. However it happened, this collection was incredible, and it was meticulously cared for. PAPA had a dedicated team who maintained the machines and also ran tournaments which brought in people from all over the world to our city. I loved it all.

The Classic Game Room pinball videos are among my favorite videos even though nobody watched them (in the grand scheme of things.)

It was more fun to film pinball machines and physically interact with them than to just record gameplay and talk over video edits. Pinball reviews provided an endless, non-stop supply of goofy one-liners and sight gags, combined with some totally rad pinball machine action.

One of things I really liked best about PAPA was their arcade atmosphere and how cool it made the videos look.

Shooting in a studio is very rigid. Shooting in an arcade surrounded by games and pinball was way more awesome. I like that the pinball reviews and arcade game reviews made the videos feel like an arcade experience. To me, that was pure CGR.

We we rapidly growing tired of storage lockers, alarms, and failed interviews. My dad was looking for any excuse to relocate our company and get into real estate so he could have more room to expand his experiments, start new businesses, and store his classic car collection.

It's never just one company with my dad, it's always two or three. He'll never retire. EVER. He wanted to grow the website and use it for multiple businesses and increase his programming staff so that he could design software again. He already had people interested in leasing office space.

Real estate was pretty recessed at the time after the 2008 financial collapse and nobody, I mean nobody, wanted a building in a shitty office park. He scooped up a dilapidated warehouse, which continues to serve as the CGR print publishing warehouse to this day. But long before that, it was going to be a video game museum, arcade, and studio space for our empire of Classic Game Room shows.

We spent a few months here and there ripping out the floors and fixing the place up. It's a huge space, though not as big as PAPA was (their warehouse was ginormous.)

I moved my small collection of arcade games into our empty warehouse and started to assemble a set, but then realized that it was SO BIG that filming was infinitely more challenging than I imagined. PAPA was filled with games, thousands of games. I owned about twelve. I couldn't afford to buy a couple hundred more, so I did my best to round out the set with Ikea book cases, posters, TVs and game consoles.

We bought an El Camino and spent some quality father and son time tinkering with it and driving around. The 'Camino made a great set piece and looked perfectly at home parked next to a Pac-Man machine and Millipede.

I'm like "This is what CGR is all about. 1980s arcade games, El Caminos, a disco ball, and beer posters."

Nothing could have been cooler. I started to film on the new epic arcade set. I couldn't wait to blow viewers' minds with this collection of sweet disco awesome-sauce.

Views dropped.

Was it the El Camino's fault? Was it Pac-Man's fault? No, it was my fault for not reading the changing demographics on YouTube.

When CGR started on YouTube way back in 2008, the majority of the audience was tech savvy, nerdy, and actively looking for niche market games. These were people who figured out how to watch YouTube in the days when YouTube was an obscurity.

By 2013, YouTube was mainstream, and the audience was much younger, less nerdy, less educated, and into popular games like Minecraft and Skyrim. They gave no shits about an El Camino or an aging host obsessed with Airwolf.

The audience in 2013 wanted to watch a show with someone they could relate to. Someone wearing a headset and yelling about things. Someone in a gaming chair live streaming Call of Duty or whatever. Someone just like them.

2013 was the year that being "just like them" was far

more important than being an experienced documentary producer. 2013 is the year that being a "show" didn't matter. Being a part of the YouTube community is what mattered, and that had nothing to do with producing a show.

The 40-year-old college educated guy surrounded by thousands of dollars of arcade games and a classic car was literally the opposite of what the mainstream YouTube audience wanted. Devoted fans of the show loved it, but the growing younger audience couldn't possibly care less about production values and loathed this crappy old show which wasn't "just like them."

For the first time I could see that my age was going to be a problem, but that was just the beginning of what would ultimately turn into a nightmare.

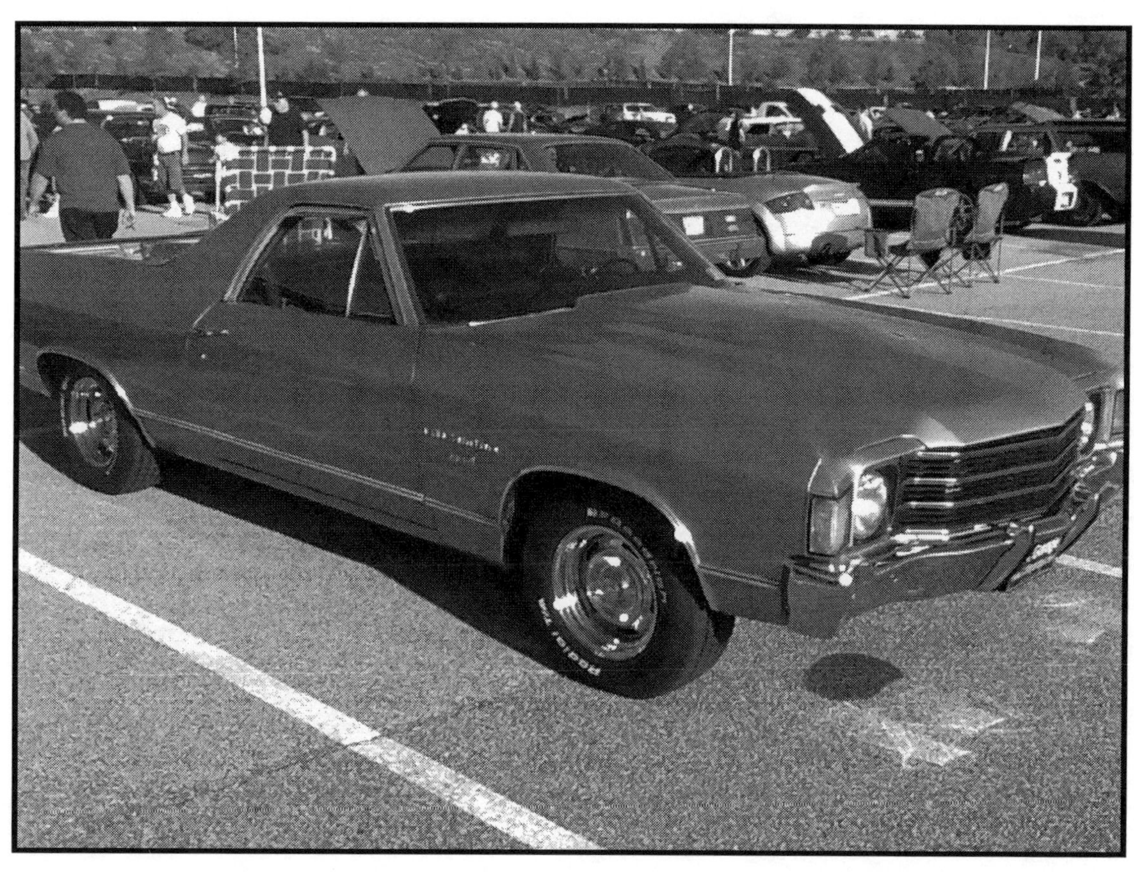

CGR El Camino at a car show in 2012.

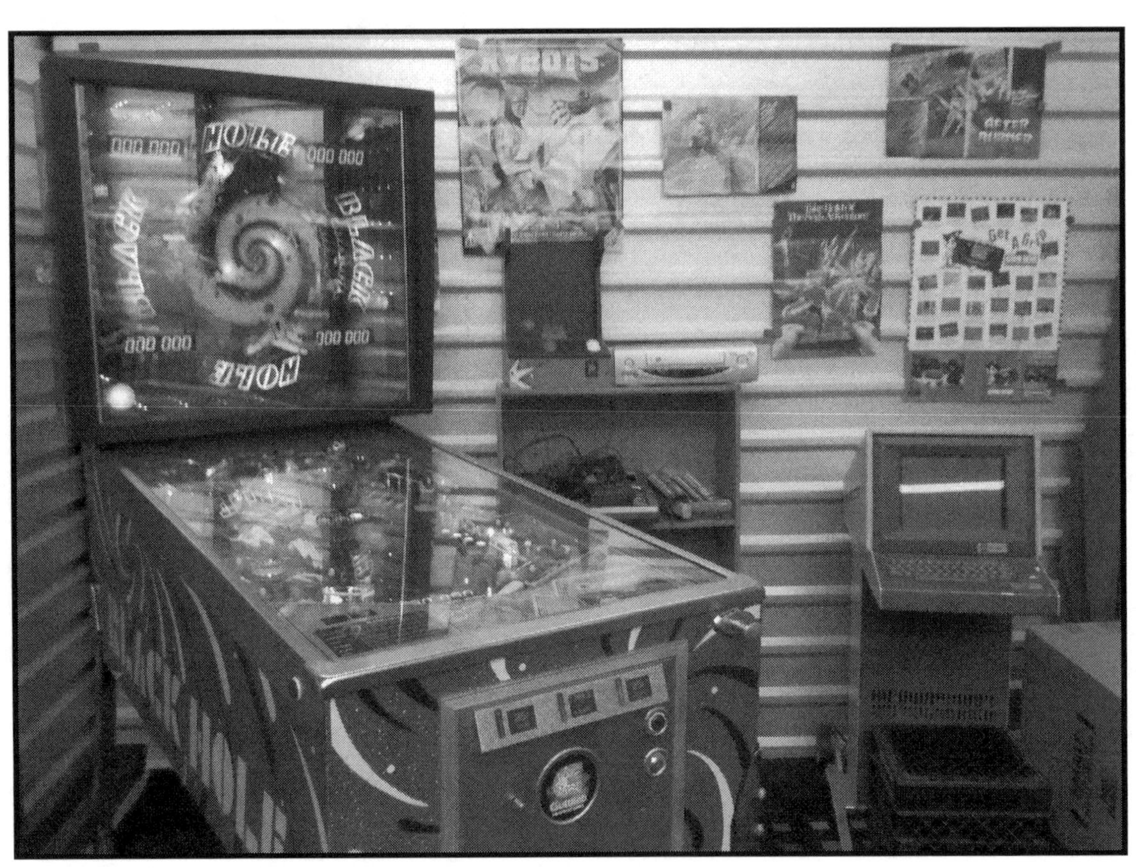

Classic Game Room set on February 7, 2012.

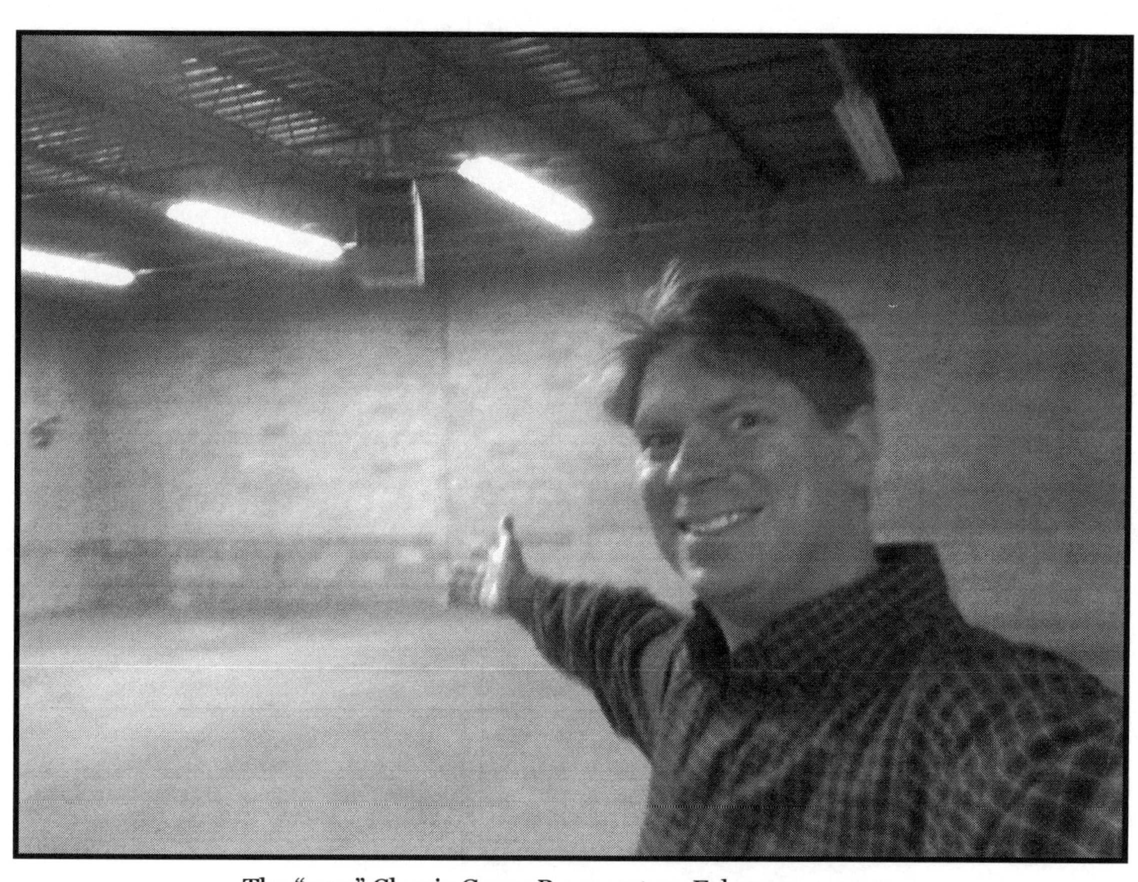

The “new” Classic Game Room set on February 4, 2013.

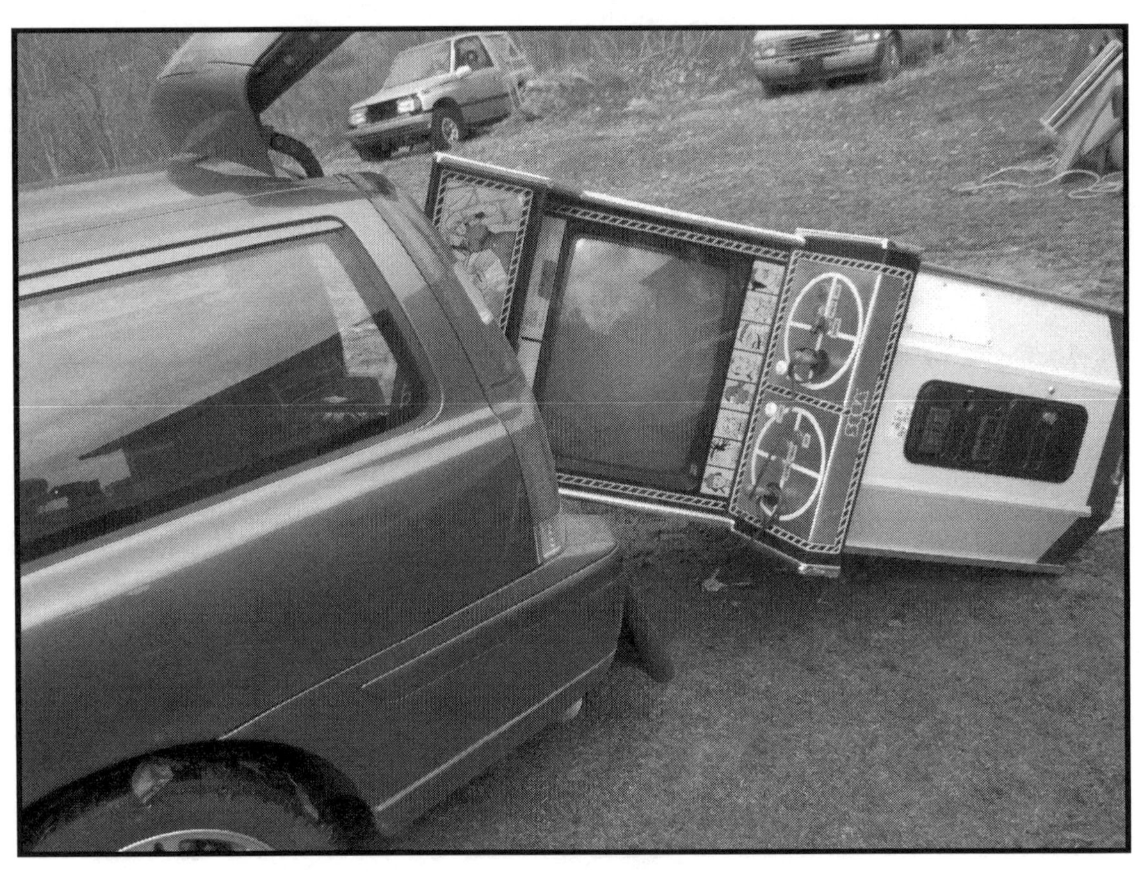

Failed attempt at loading the Virtua Fighter cabinet into the back of a Volvo.

CHAPTER 14
WARNING, WARNING, HUGE ENEMY APPROACHING

Making Classic Game Room was always fun because I love producing a show. This is very important to clarify. I love producing a *show*. But, by 2013, it was becoming clear that the classic "show" concept was obsolete. What I called "producing" was becoming something called "content creation."

> Classic Game Room entered 2013 like a lion. Classic Game Room left 2013 like a lion kneecapped in four knees and bashed over the head with a shovel.

The early days on YouTube were different because viewers were excited about everything because it was all new. Nobody cared too much about how we did it, just that it was there.

These days, the moment a video hits YouTube, it's classified as free garbage and completely disposable. Viewers watch it for free, so they assume it was free to make. They are very concerned about how it is there, and whether or not it deserves their viewership. This changing attitude crept in without us paying enough attention to it.

I viewed our shows as being unique, well-made, and of value. Imagine an old guy with an old guy hat screaming and waving a cane around at kids on his lawn. “You dang kids!! Back in my day, we would’ve killed to watch a show about arcade games with an El Camino on screen!”

Kids watching YouTube need to relate to the host. The power of a charismatic host confidently talking into a camera is absolute. It has nothing at all to do with “producing”. It’s about being likable.

This was all becoming evident in 2013, but we had a company to run and employees to employ. You can’t just change directions on a whim when you have employees.

None of us, me included, knew how to produce this amateur content that looked like it wasn’t produced by professionals. So, we continued to do what we knew how to do and tried to get our growth back.

We were all optimistic in early 2013 as we moved our growing company, piece by piece into a new building. Classic Game Room studios rented space in our overlord’s newly refurbished warehouse and several offices for editing. Other rooms were left empty to rent or turn into new businesses.

I spent a few months refining the CGR set. I built and lit the arcade, and designed new spaces for recording the Undertow shows. Undertow got a spiffy new editing suite and room for lots of recording hi-jinks. Surely, the audience would grow because we put more into the shows, right?

Our respectable building made hiring programmers easier, and we embarked on a sizable website plan to tie all of our shows together with product sales, advertising, and our museum collection.

Writers posted articles every day and the concept started to show some potential, albeit slowly.

We had a huge plan in the works to host our videos on the Classic Game Room website so that people could enjoy them without the clutter of YouTube. (We always hated the fact that after a Classic Game Room video ended, YouTube would go and drop you into somebody else's video. We paid to get you there and we want to keep your attention!)

In early 2013, things could have gone any direction. Just imagine what our warehouse space would look like with rows of arcade games, cars, and 1,000 Sega Genesis game consoles. It was so close,; we were almost there. You have no idea how close we were.

We could open up Classic Game Room for tours, parties, shows, and even have a gift shop filled with swag like t-shirts and flamethrowers. Classic Game Room could be a destination because we could do it, and we had a huge YouTube channel that reached millions of people!

We had real plans to make a real museum and gift shop. When videos are getting millions of views, one can do that.

But, as you might expect, none of this stuff came cheap and running a company isn't free (despite that fact that gurus on YouTube tell you otherwise.) There was a lot riding on my "show" and my constant being-on-all-the-time performance.

The new space was a lot of fun, but yanking the recording process out of my basement slowed things down. I'm a big fan of assembly line production and I get flustered without it. When I removed that from my workflow, everything just ground to a crawl.

By 2013, I had this shit down to a science!

I'd play a game, preferably a short game because I had to get a bazillion videos made (I hated RPGs for this reason.) Depending on the game, I'd play it as much as I thought I needed to in order to figure out what the was about and who it was for. I'd throw the edit and narration together and BOOM.

This was the classic formula dating back to 1999.

Obviously, good games were more fun to play and review. But sometimes games were so bad that they made the best reviews based on the fact that they were awful. There are loads of NES games and garbage from the 16-bit era that fit into that category. An awful Sega Genesis game like Barney's Hide and Seek game made for the funniest game review.

Don't even get me started on the R-Zone and the Game.com, they were comedy gold.

I didn't read the room, though. The devoted fanbase loved our videos, no matter what we did. The funnier and wackier the video, the better. However, the mainstream YouTube audience moved on completely.

They wanted live-streaming, angry videos, ranking videos, and eventually, Wikipedia-sized dissertations about the video game spanning two or three hours with endless detail and critical analysis. Who has time to make that?

Who has time?

Let me tell you who has time. Other people not running a business. And they could do it better than I could.

Sure, CGR videos looked cooler in the new space with more room to film and goof off with stuff, but the cost of each video also went up. I could wave beer glasses around and make R-Zone jokes, but we were stuck in the mud, and I knew it. YouTube's monopoly was not going away, in fact, they were becoming the sole source of distribution for ALL video content online.

I couldn't believe it. We were going to be flattened by kids yelling at each other about Nintendo game rankings.

Nobody could believe it.

"If we make better shows, people will appreciate them."

No, it doesn't work like that. We had to escape YouTube, but had anyone ever done that? This stuff was still all so new.

As I'm writing this in 2024, various "channels" have tried to move their large audiences from YouTube into a pay-per-view or subscriber models on their own platforms. Every time, their YouTube audience tears them to pieces and turns on them.

There is no escape. YouTube has you addicted and brainwashed. They know they have all the free content, and you want it. And you deserve it.

To defy YouTube is to defy God.

We wanted to distribute Classic Game Room beyond YouTube and its growing mess of clickbait and Minecraft let's plays that none of us knew how to make. If we could just, somehow, anyhow, get the show onto another platform where WE controlled the ecosystem, then Classic Game Room would thrive.

We had the muscle to do it, but would the audience enjoy our shows on our platform?

By mid-2013 our website was nearly complete, but we didn't launch it yet. We still had a few bugs to work out.

It was sometime that summer when I woke up to an inbox filled with YouTube copyright violations or whatever they called them at the time. Like, dozens of them, maybe hundreds. It was a lot, and it didn't look good. Nor did it make much sense.

Twitter was blowing up out about it, and I remember one jackass saying "Har har, I'll bet Classic Game Room is freaking out right now!" It's nice to see the compassion from an audience who received free content from us the past several years.

Upon further inspection, it looked like YouTube put some kind of automated music copyright sniffer into place which demonetized videos that contained music that belonged to someone else. So.... that was basically every video that we made.

Mentally, I was kind of prepared for this, but not practically.

Now, I'd like to point out that playing music from the game in a piece of journalism is completely legal. We didn't break any laws or do anything wrong, but YouTube's automated system didn't see it that way. Did IGN have this same trouble? We were so confused.

Music copyright theft was a growing problem, that much I understood. And I could see why YouTube would take action against people uploading music in videos that they didn't own, but Classic Game Room is journalism. Also, we were one of their oldest partners.

Surely YouTube would help us out.

Hahahahahahahaha.

We contacted them, but YouTube was not at all helpful. The days when YouTube would speak to us like we were actual people were long gone. Some of our contacts at companies like Konami and Capcom helped out and reversed these claims on their end, which they didn't even know about. Nintendo ignored us. All our Mario Kart review revenue was obliterated overnight (we used to make a pretty penny on Mario Kart reviews.)

It finally happened. Our reliance on YouTube as the sole point of distribution punched us in the nose.

I called it! But suddenly, this was all my fault for not fixing it ahead of time. It's not like I didn't try, but nobody ever watched anything on any other platform, ever!

For years, we knew this was coming and tried like hell to diversify away from them, but YouTube is all that anyone wanted. YouTube is the only platform that viewers would accept. YouTube is where we earned 99% of our revenue. Without YouTube, none of this would have existed anyway.

What a mess.

It's now more than a decade later as I'm writing this, but if I could go back in time to tell 2013 Mark something, it's to pack it up and move on.

But, ohhhh no, 2013 Mark was stubborn. Also, we had employees. And office space. And bills to pay.

With a pencil and paper, I started to run numbers incorporating the loss of ad revenue across all of our biggest videos. In short, we were probably going to lose about half of our advertising over the remainder of the year.

Well, that sucks.

"Hey Mark, when's the next video game review on YouTube?"

Never?

If making bigger and better videos didn't work, Undertow was stuck in the mud and not growing and costing a fortune to produce, and not enough people were buying t-shirts to keep the ship afloat, then what else was there?

Conveniently, we just wrapped up our new and fancy website to host game reviews.

> "Fuck this shit, let's finally move to our own website."
>
> Oh yeah. Screw you YouTube, Classic Game Room is coming to town. Fear our mighty El Camino and low budget website!

I'm laughing about it now. We knew we couldn't compete head on against Google-backed YouTube and companies like Facebook, so we made our website very silly. Users could make codenames inspired by G.I. Joe action figure cards. Instead of liking videos, users could give them beers.

"Cheers!" was better than "Thumbs up."

I made some videos about it. I think people swore at me and called me names because all anyone wanted was YouTube, and we defied YouTube. We used DailyMotion to host our videos. In mid-2013 we discontinued YouTube uploads, and it almost worked for a few minutes. People were shocked because I guess nobody had ever done this before.

It's amazing how important all of this stuff became overnight. People really cared about YouTube, like a lot. This kind of passion about one shitty company was never a thing before the Internet.

Within a few days, our website was up and running and the launch got off to a good start. At first, fans thought it was pretty neat and watched our daily video uploads on ClassicGameRoom.com. They could leave comments in our pro-CGR space and sign up to made codenames. Finally, we had people in our own ecosystem. We could even market t-shirts and beer glasses to them with our own ads on our very own website. This is literally what we wanted to do all along, to make videos, but control our distribution.

It wasn't a crazy idea.... For 1999.

Fast forward to 2024 when I am running this *exact* concept, and it *does* work. But the tradeoff is that I lost 99.99% of my YouTube viewership. However, in 2024 all of my business comes from other stuff.

From time to time I look back at this period and wonder what we could have done differently. Every timeline ends in the same way though (it's like Loki.)

Had we changed this or that, or cut this channel, or made Top 10s, or whatever; A.I. and TikTok would put it all out of business over the next decade anyway.

Our 2013 website plan actually *was* the future of Classic Game Room, but we couldn't afford to scale the site with the catastrophic drop in viewership.

In 2013, the tech giants were unstoppable, and America hadn't seen monopolies like this since the Railroad companies of the 1800s (anti-trust laws apparently don't apply to tech companies) A handful of mega-corporations suddenly owned everything online and it was deemed the "flattening of the Internet."

Remember those DVD review websites we tried so hard to impress back in 2007? Yeah, they all fell before the might of YouTube and Facebook. Writers for those sites are now competing against screaming teenagers on YouTube and TikTok who "review" by typing A.I. prompts into Chat GPT.

The flattening of the Internet flattened the Internet

from millions of websites down to two or three.

Classic Game Room was far from the only company struggling with this rapid change, but as one who lived through it, I can assure you that it was maddening.

Eventually, viewers who watched the show on our website got bored and went back to YouTube because YouTube has a trillion videos and works better because they has a trillion dollars to spend on programming. We had one programmer and tried to recreate Facebook on the cheap. It wasn't bad, and we should have stuck with it, but that would have required more external financing (like the 2000-era website.)

Whenever I see someone complain about how shitty YouTube is in 2024, I'd like to remind them that they made it that way by refusing to watch stuff on other platforms. Yes, I sound like an asshole, but I'm also right. Just imagine if you had other options that aren't TikTok.

2013 is also the year that smartphones went mainstream. Only a company like YouTube and Facebook could afford to make an app that worked properly. What chance did the rest of us have?

To this day, I still get a lot of flak from idiots looking to stir up drama about our move away from YouTube, but it was the only move that I could make other than shutting Classic Game Room down, which nobody wanted to do, because we had all been so fortunate to do it in the first place.

Unfortunately, after the expensive website and move into our new office space, this setback was starting to really impact the bottom line of Inecom.

2013 ended in a bloodbath.

But, rather than pulling the plug, we went back to what we were good at. Making things and selling them.

We spent more time building our presence on Amazon and Ebay. We hooked up with other sales outlets and I designed t-shirts, wristbands, drink coasters, stickers, glassware, and anything else I could slap the Classic Game Room logo onto.

Classic Game Room the flamethrower? If only I could have found a vendor....

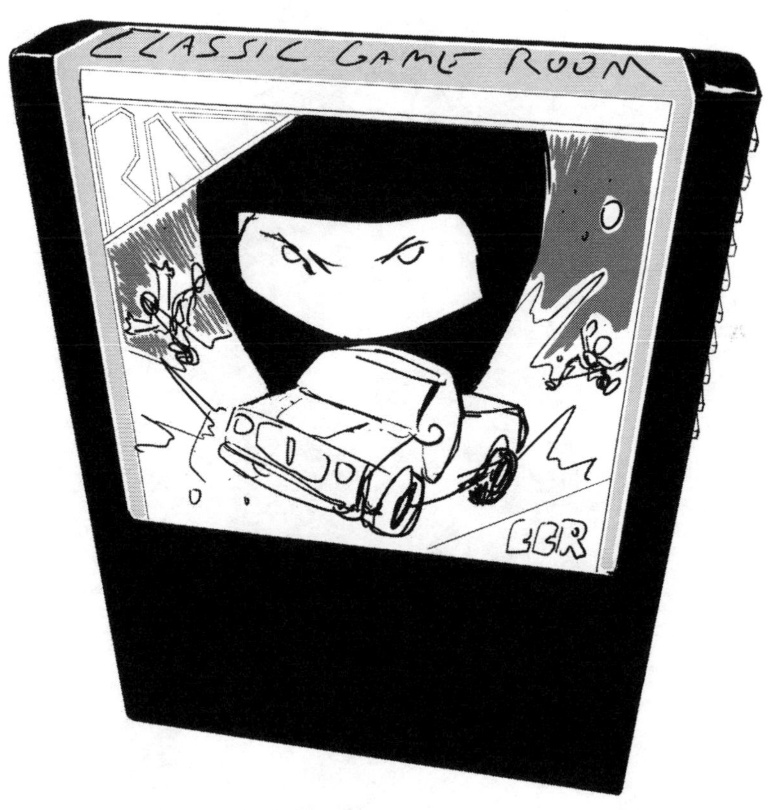

Classic Game Room shirt design concept.

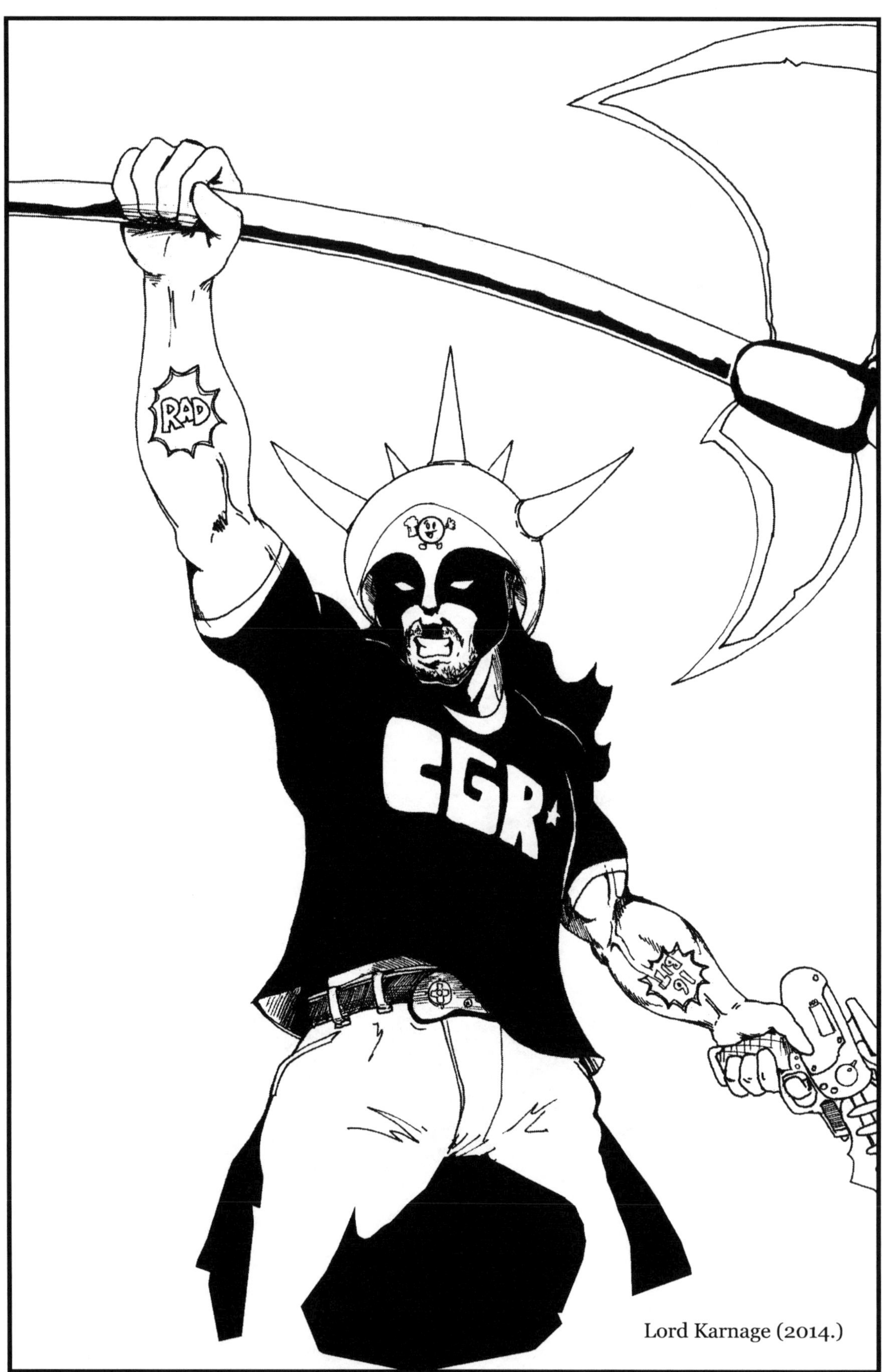

Lord Karnage (2014.)

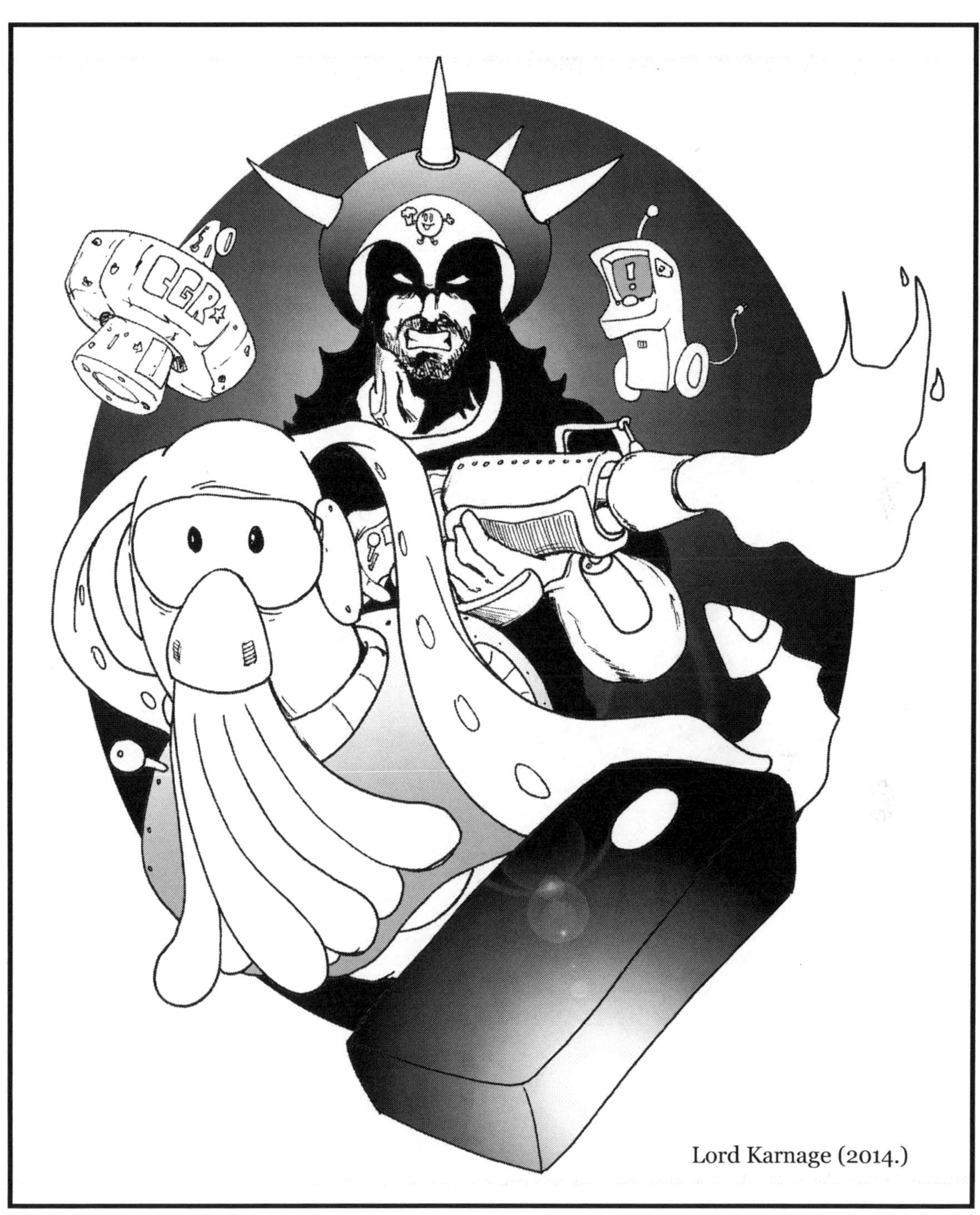

Lord Karnage (2014.)

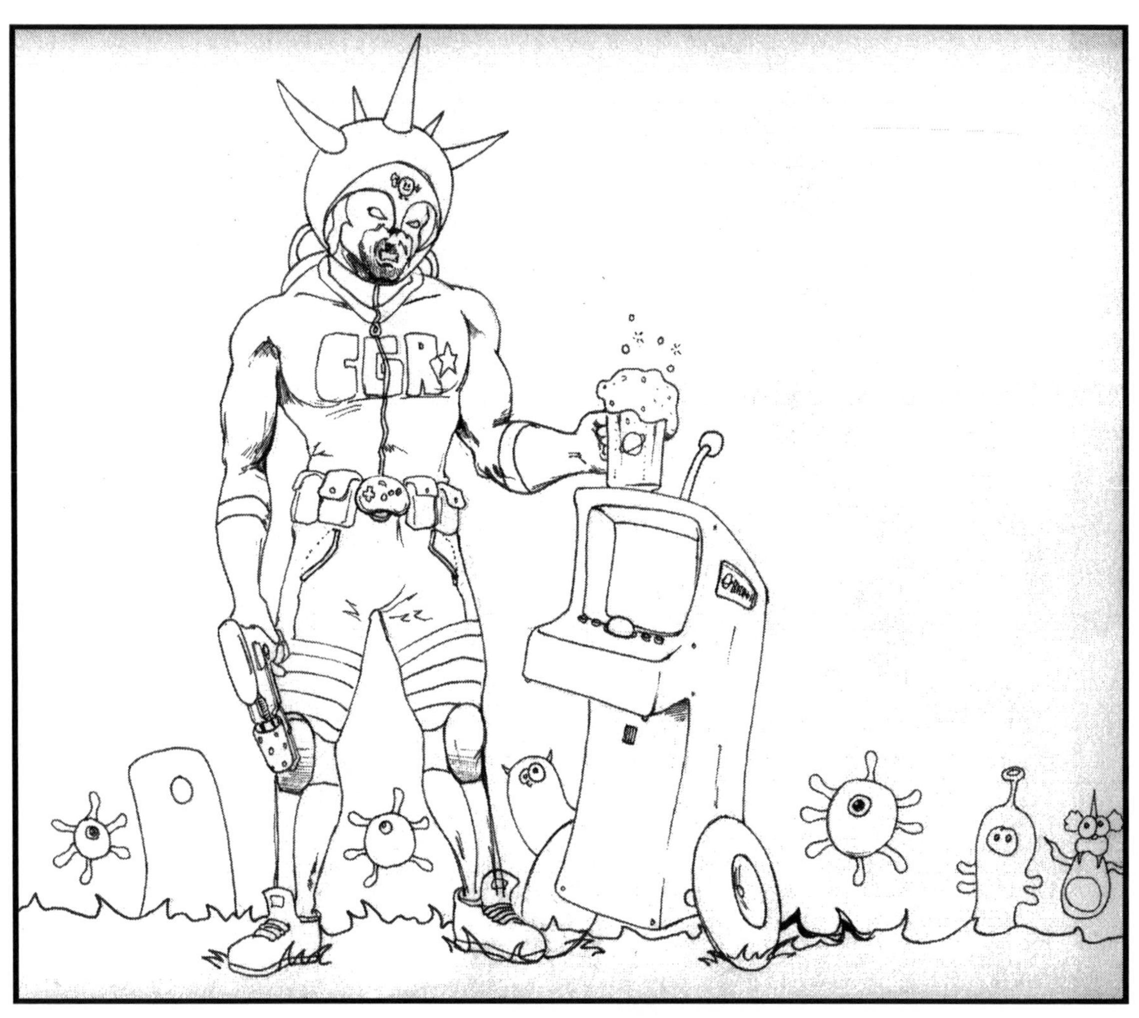

Pen and ink drawing of Lord Karnage and Edit-Station 1 from 2014

CHAPTER 15
ALL HAIL LORD KARNAGE

Our website kind of worked. People enjoyed it, but it wasn't enough to support the whole business. We lost half of our audience overnight because we defied YouTube. YouTube convinced an entire generation that they were the only game in town (for the record, I remember a time when we were perfectly happy without them.)

When we "left" YouTube, we personally insulted and inconvenienced thousands of people who stopped watching out of spite. Too bad they never took the time to realize we were literally bleeding money out the ass and going out of business while giving them free videos that year.

The loss of advertising revenue from our YouTube channels was crippling, and we needed some of it back. Annoyingly I had to produce content for YouTube again, even though I really did not want to. We desperately needed it for marketing because our Twitter and Facebook presence wasn't worth shit, despite the fact we worked pretty hard on that too.

We defied YouTube and we lost. We would have lost if we didn't defy them just the same. The real damage came from the loss of revenue earned by our biggest videos. The videos that brought in the big bucks like Transformers and Ben 10 and Mario Kart week after week were gone, and no new reviews ever replaced them. As I'm writing this a decade later, I can tell that since 2013, I haven't produced a single successful Internet video. Not one. Nothing ever went viral again after 2013.

Basically the ad model for the show was screwed because our videos, collectively, didn't get the viewership needed. Our overhead grew higher than it should have, and we were unable to react and successfully adapt to new trends. Additionally, YouTube's younger audience didn't care for our arcade games and groovy disco ball.

Most of the audience saw this whole YouTube conflict as a personal offense and stopped watching, so if there was any one thing which killed Classic Game Room's Internet success it was probably that. The audience wanted drama, apology videos, and apparently, justice because we were mean to a multi-billion dollar company that profits from people opening boxes on camera.

We should have shut Classic Game Room down, but my dad kept it afloat. If you enjoyed any of our videos from 2014-2015 you should thank him, because I wanted to trim our production budgets with a chainsaw. He didn't want to see anyone get upset and made sure that we had what we needed as a business to face this new challenge and succeed.

My dad doesn't like quitting, but I don't like losing. We butted heads over the direction of the business and agreed to concentrate on higher-quality content and better physical product sales.

However, we knew damn well that just making Classic Game Room videos for YouTube was not the answer. Product sales were the only future for Classic Game Room, and we had experience with that.

I have no proof of this, and it's likely just a conspiracy theory, but I think YouTube blacklisted our channel after I tried to direct people to our website because it never worked the same again. The "channel" is simply broken, and it has been since 2013.

By late 2013 entering 2014, we were down but not out. Classic Game Room allocated more time to making things like t-shirts and glassware, which always sold reasonably well. I learned to use Kickstarter and launched a comic book based on my absurd alter-ego, Lord Karnage.

Wait, where did Lord Karnage come from, anyway?

Way back in 2010 or 2011, I don't even remember, I made up a goofy character and named him Lord Karnage for a Tiger Woods golf game review on the Wii. It was funny and at some point I started working it into videos as a running joke.

Later on, for what reason I don't know, we couldn't rename the YouTube channel ClassicGameRoom, but I could name it Lord Karnage.

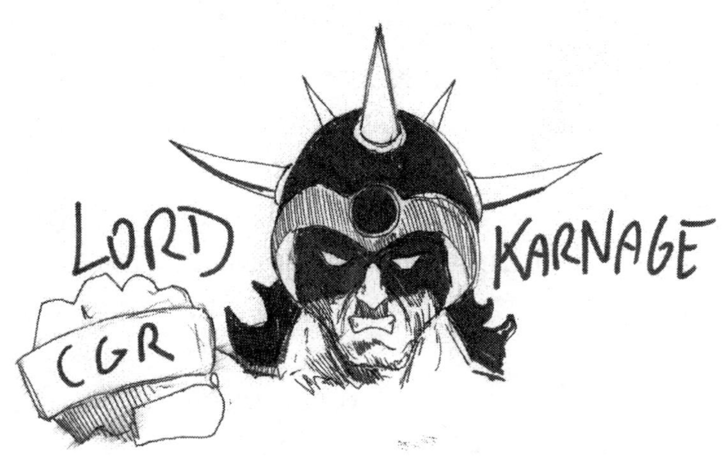

One of the first drawings of Lord Karnage (maybe the first)

Suddenly, I became Lord Karnage. That was not the intent! (I never liked that people thought I was calling myself Lord Karnage because it belittled the hard work that went into producing Classic Game Room. It made it seem like a joke. I dunno, maybe it was a cool name though.)

Lord Karnage the comic book would be my first successful Kickstarter campaign, the first of many. We sold a bunch of them in 2014, but we still had a long way to go to get our company back on track.

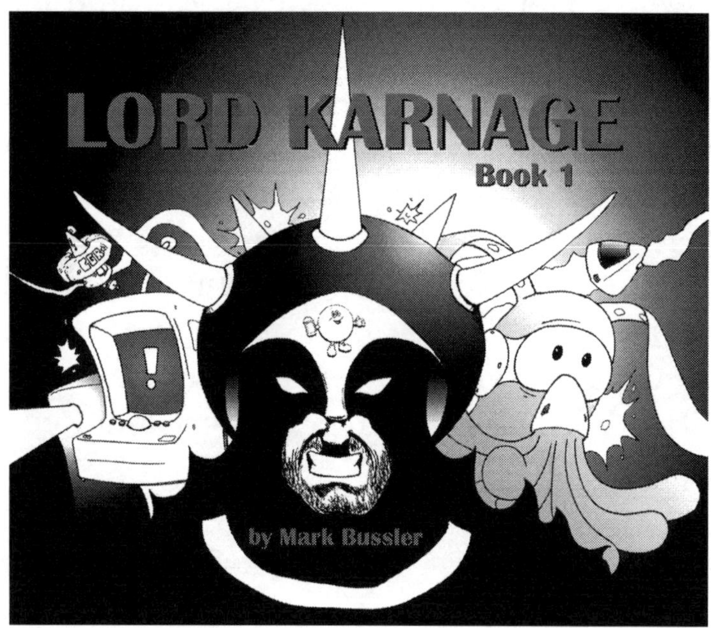

Let's talk about Lord Karnage!

Though I tend to credit Ethel the Cyborg Ninja with launching my publishing business in 2017 (with her reprint on Amazon,) the honor really belongs to Lord Karnage from 2014.

It was sometime in 2012 or 2013 when I went into a school function for my kids and tried to draw a picture on the blackboard only to realize that my drawing skills had become very, very rusty.

Drawing is like weightlifting. You need to keep at it and practice or else you lose it. I wasn't happy with this at all, and decided to get back into drawing.

After the Lord Karnage gag became a thing on the show, I thought it would be fun to give the guy a face and draw some pictures. I made a few videos. Around that time, I went to a local business leaders meeting and one of the guys was explaining how his company used Kickstarter. I took notes.

2014 was a weird year for our business, because I think we were all pretty optimistic about the website and made good videos that year after the dust settled from our struggle with YouTube (for a short time,) but we needed new products and pronto.

So, I embarked on a comic book that summer called Lord Karnage Book 1! It is an absurd book, and the art is very raw compared to what I'm doing now, but the story and characters are hilarious.

Classic Game Room beams a negative review of Ocarina of Time into space and pisses off an alien race of Cosmic Death Bricks who attack Earth. Lord Karnage shouts and screams, Edit-Station 1 banters, clone Marks die, and Space Gar gets the power to Black Hole Vortex (which is a huge plot point in 2024's Ethel the Cyborg Ninja 3.)

We even get to meet Heyzoos the Coked-Up Chicken in comic book form for the first time!

The Lord Karnage Kickstarter was a huge success for a comic book coming out of nowhere. I drew the entire thing using pencil, pen and paper, and at one point had all of the pages spread across my dining room as I finished them and lined them up to make sure the book made sense. It took forever and would be my last pen-on-paper-exclusive book. I moved to digital drawing on a Wacom later that year for

Ethel the Cyborg Ninja.

So, for those of you who enjoy my comics, graphic novels, and my art in general, check out Lord Karnage Book 1 (or the reprint called Lord Karnage 1.5.) It's a lot of fun and I'm very proud of it.

Spirits were a good bit higher after Lord Karnage. People liked it, we successfully filled the orders, and it brought in a few bucks which proved that we had the moxie to succeed.

In addition to our new books, we sold posters, new shirts, and grew our business on Amazon and Ebay. Product sales picked up, but not enough to cover the rapidly declining ad revenue.

Shows like Undertow, which required three people to make, bled the in-house production company to death (it was like a repeat of 2007 but worse.) The team making the show was mad at me for not promoting it more, but my show was also going down the drain. I'm not sure people saw that we went down the SAME drain.

Fans shouted "Give us more! Give us more!"

But nobody watched any of it.

Videos never reached subscribers.

Competing channels hated us and loved to see us suffer.

The in-house team was frustrated.

We were all so confused. Nobody could digest the fact that people said they liked our videos but refused to watch them because of forces beyond our control. CGR desperately needed to get away from the toxic cesspool of YouTube so that it could grow again.

After the success of Lord Karnage, in 2014 I launched a Kickstarter for The Best of Classic Game Room and we knocked it out of the park. We put out a sweet 4-disc set as the "Laser Hyper Vision Album Set" which included a Blu-Ray and full-size, color insert. We didn't get it out the door until 2015, but happy 15th anniversary CGR!

We ran Kickstarters for a CGR Undertow DVD and even another comic book called Ethel the Cyborg Ninja. The Classic Game Room marketing engine was running full speed ahead. We were good at that.

But we were not real gamers.

We were sell-out businesspeople.

The Kickstarters turned off a lot of viewers (on top of the YouTube debacle) because we marketed them nonstop, which is what you have to do to sell physical products.

Views crashed even lower in 2014 and 2015.

I did a talk at a con in 2015 and had to fake it, to a pretty large audience, that "everything was awesome" because everything was definitely not awesome.

Behind the scenes, my father was not happy with the situation. He saw that we all worked hard and tried, so he wasn't upset in that respect, but I know he knew our business model was screwed.

Remember that the entire reason I sold people on the YouTube concept in the first place was growth without the hassle of production, overhead, marketing, shipping, and fulfillment. Now we were right back in that business and growth would have required a LOT of additional money. Our DVDs, Blu-Rays, shirts, and comics weren't selling well enough to support a half dozen employees.

Every day we'd clean out an inbox filled with complaints from YouTube viewers. It wears on you and you start to resent them.

I mean, I'm sitting there reading this shit like "Fuck you. You got free videos and now you're complaining about it? Why should we ever give you anything free again?”

Nobody on the business and finance side was happy. I felt like I was wasting my time and goofing off playing video games. It was no longer fun to play video games and even less fun to talk about them.

Our website fizzled out with the drop in users who went back to YouTube. Our long term plans to stick with our network of shows collapsed with the rapid plunge in viewership.

When I learned that anyone and everyone involved in funding this struggling company was done with it, I couldn’t argue. It was devastating and I got sick for a few days because I did everything that I could possibly do and the damn thing still failed. This wasn’t just a one-person hobby channel. We ran like a business because that’s how it started in 2008.

Undertow was the first to go because it never, once, ever made a profit. The team worked hard to make good reviews, but it took like three people to make them, and relatively speaking, nobody ever watched it. People seem to fondly remember Undertow and a lot of viewers sent us nasty messages about canceling it, but nobody on YouTube would ever watch it.

Everyone was upset, of course they were. This should have worked. On paper, this worked. We set the Undertow team up a great studio space with training, new computers, every game console in the world, free games, and a professionally managed YouTube channel, but it couldn’t compete against reaction videos and angry reviews.

I remember meetings where I was trying to explain that Angry Video Game Nerd just got 3 million hits on his recent video. PewDiePie is getting like three times that, and our recent Undertow review that took three people two days to make, got 2,000 views. That's like $20 in advertising revenue. And it didn't move product.

I've seen some of the old team from that decade make fun of me on Reddit and on podcasts. Pro tip, if you ever want to get hired again, maybe don't make fun of the guy who runs the company on Reddit.

Since then, several other popular "networks" have burned to the ground. I watched as former "creators" and employees took to Twitter and YouTube to trash owners and fellow employees. Hey, this business sucks. Looking for drama by picking fights online doesn't make it any better for you or anyone else. If you want to blame someone, delete your YouTube app.

I had a good time working with Derek and Brandon in particular, they were there the longest. I loved our three-way dynamic in the few videos that we filmed. Derek was always down for whatever (like being clubbed to death by a Game.com,) and Brandon's dry sense of humor was good to bounce things off. Few people could act alongside Heyzoos. I wish we could've done more with it but alas, we were basically thrown off the platform.

We closed the rest of the company down, piece by piece at the end of 2015. Everyone was taken care of. The last thing we did as a business was to fulfill the Kickstarter orders for Ethel the Cyborg Ninja in December of that year (I talk more about the Ethel book and Heyzoos in the Ethel the Cyborg Ninja Databook 2024.)

At the end of 2015, I was going to be the last to go after shutting everything down and figuring out where the hell to store my museum collection that was never fully cataloged along with 20 arcade games. Nobody was left to even help carry the boxes into storage.

I packed games into wine boxes without labels and wheeled them on a dolly into the pits of despair while viewers sent hate mail complaining that we shut down their favorite shows they weren't watching.

Did YouTube not accurately count our views?

The thing is... who can say? Were they being honest with their reporting? Technically, they don't have to. I'll just throw that out there...

For every channel that went down in flames over the decade like Classic Game Room, a thousand more popped up in their place. There is some logic if YouTube chose to prune the old-timers.

The For Sale sign went up on the warehouse at the end of 2015.

Better reviews didn't work.

More reviews didn't work.

Change didn't work.

Different channels didn't work, nothing worked. We had a good team of people, and we just couldn't get anything going.

Nothing worked because everyone in the world could be a star on their smartphone. You can't compete against that with professional, heavily-edited content.

We couldn't engineer videos that went viral, and we couldn't pretend to be kids with headsets. The original concept of narrated intelligent game reviews was so tired.

In late 2015 I announced that we'd be closing the channels and would finally put the whole damn business out of its misery.

I scrambled to find another job and quickly organized

and set up some plans to continue and monetize some of my comic strip projects like Disco 8-Track and Ethel. After looking over the financial realities of jumping into the comic industry with no publishing reach, I almost threw up. Within weeks, I would be going from a million views a day down to zero, and with no income.

When you fall off the art ladder, you fall all the way down and land on your ass. That grad school plan started to look like an option again, except this time I was a lot older, with kids, and not at all happy about that.

My family was furious with me. YouTube viewers sent hate mail and mocked me in videos. "Mark is the laziest YouTuber!" They screamed. "He isn't even trying."

I turned 40 years old watching my creation and years of hard work burn to the ground.

Then, Patreon emailed me.

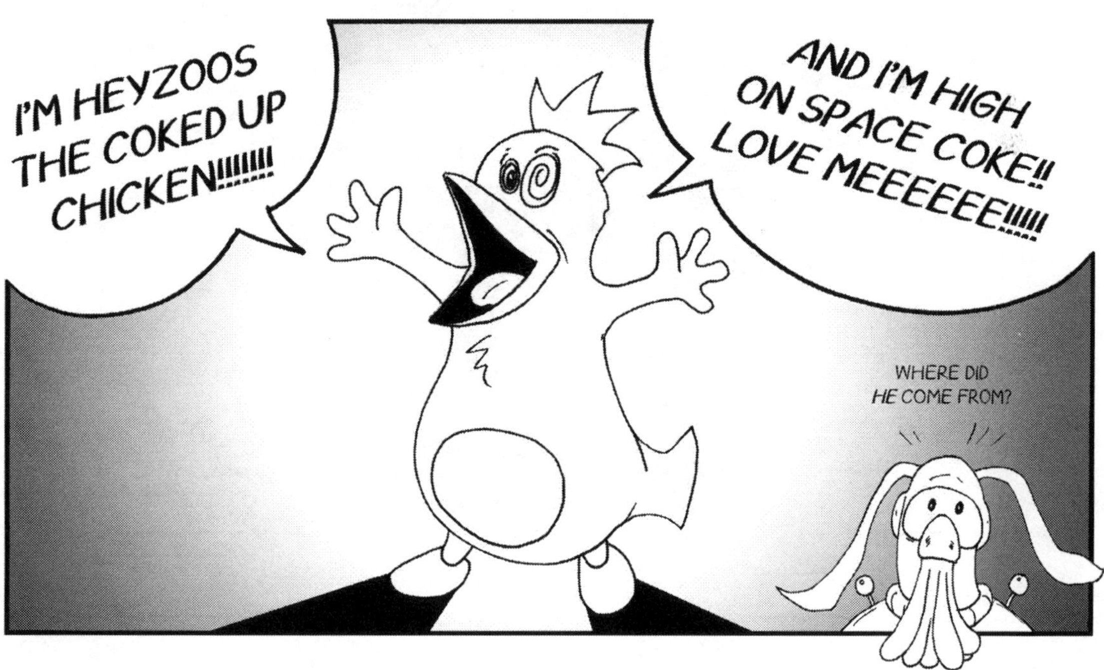

First print appearance of Heyzoos the Coked-Up Chicken in Lord Karnage Book 1 (2014.)

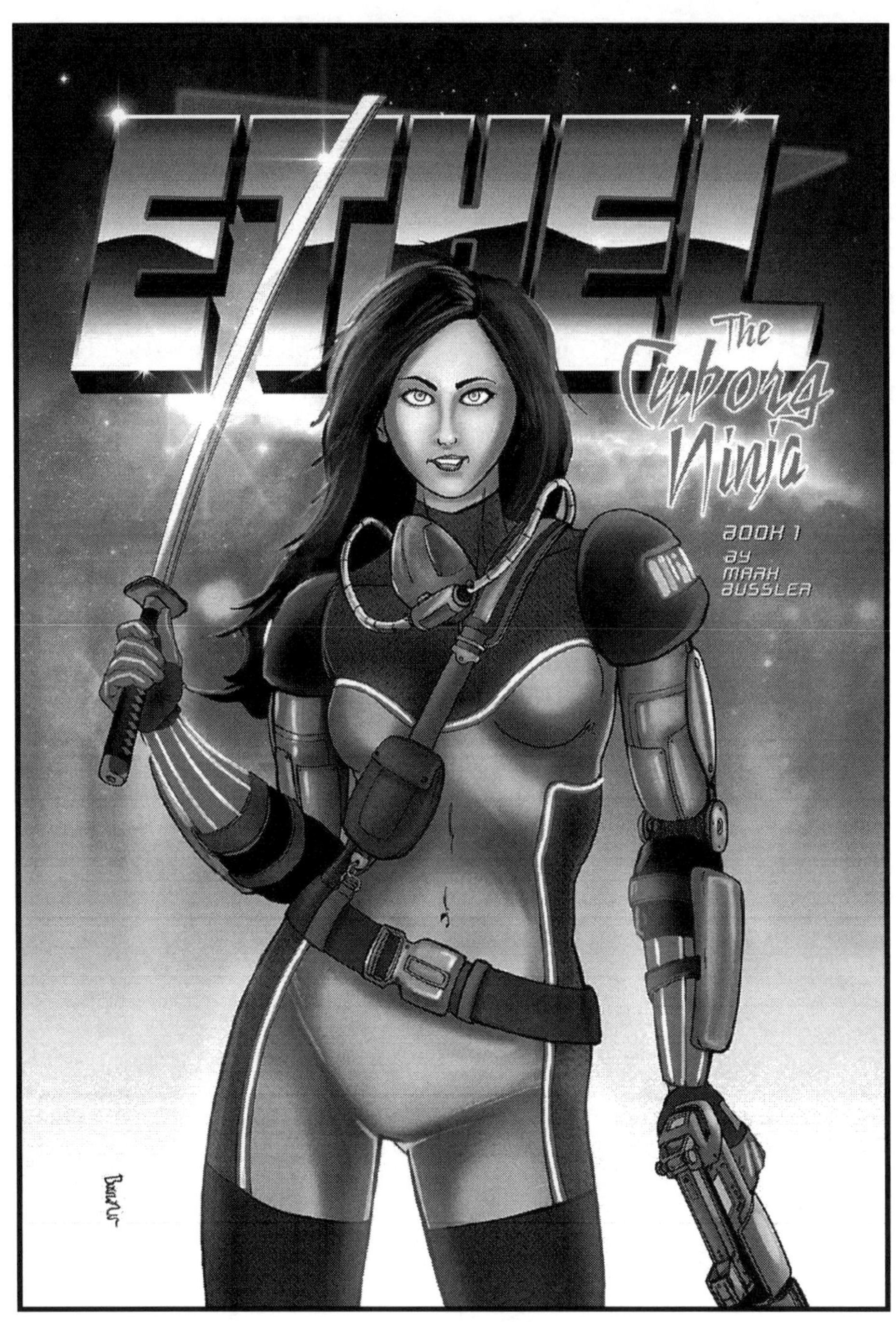

Ethel the Cyborg Ninja Book 1 from 2015.

CHAPTER 16
A NEW HOPE

I'm surprised that I even saw the email from Patreon because I'm a pro at ignoring emails.

They said they saw my "shutting down CGR video" and could be of use. Patreon was brand new in 2015, and I'd heard the name a few times but didn't think much about it. Patreon was like Kickstarter but for YouTube shows (maybe?)

Patreon billed themselves as "recurrent crowdfunding" or something like that. I called them up and it seemed like the perfect solution, especially considering that I was about to be unemployed at the end of the year and didn't have time to put together any good job prospects (because, you know, lots of people in Pittsburgh were totally looking to hire a 40-year-old video game reviewer with obsolete DVD authoring experience.)

After a few phone calls with Patreon, I began to understand their concept and saw that they understood the challenge of running a professional business with unreliable Internet advertising revenue (surely, I wasn't the only person dealing with this.) In my mind, it sounded like Kickstarter, and Kickstarter had always worked well for my projects up to that point.

I didn't specify why, but I offered to buy out Inecom from my dad. He was happy to be rid of it but also suspicious as hell. I know he thought I was going to make a mess out of it.

Someone should make a movie called **In 2016 I Bought My Very Own Failing Company**! It was like adopting a puppy. A puppy with a shitload of overhead, boxes that needed to be moved, technical problems, insurance bills, a broken brand, an expensive website, and a completely useless money-losing YouTube channel.

The prophesy from Dilbert had finally come true. The boss's son sunk the company.

Take it back a few weeks....

At the very end of 2015, after talking with Patreon, I whipped up a new business plan and calculated what Inecom would need to support operations, my job, insurance, electricity, family and all that kind of real-life stuff that nobody ever thinks about when watching free YouTube videos (remember, if they're free to watch, they're free to make, or so they say....)

After my Kickstarter experiences, I had a pretty good idea of what to do (in a broad sense) and was confident it would work well enough to get the business back on its feet so that I could untangle the mess.

I want to clarify this. **There was a MESS to untangle**. A huge-ass mess. Getting it funded to untangle the mess was job one.

On January 7th, 2016, I launched a Patreon video and announcement for the Classic Game Room Patreon. Fans could subscribe at different tiers and pay to keep the show going without ads. Considering the channel had about 475,000 subscribers I expected about 10,000-40,000 people to jump on the Patreon for a couple bucks a month, which would have totally saved the show and my company.

What actually happened is that about 1,500 people jumped on the Patreon at higher tiers than expected.

Hooray, the show was saved! Sort of, I hadn't calculated for the fact that fewer Patrons at a higher rate would lead to faster depreciation and totally screw up my business plan.

Nor did I plan for the massive revolt against Patreon, because, for the most part, people seemed to like Kickstarter. But they hated Patreon. They DESPISED Patreon because suddenly, even though the show was still free, some element of Classic Game Room was PAYWALLED.

So, let's talk about the term Paywalled. Paywalled is a term used by entitled idiots to describe something of value that they want but refuse to pay for. For example, nobody ever whines about a Big Mag being Paywalled, or a PlayStation 5. But a YouTube show SHOULD BE FREE.

Suddenly, viewers had to pay for something that was once free even though it was still free, but there were parts of it that maybe weren't free. Paywalling!! But not even... oh my God.... This is why you can't have nice things.

Once you're known for giving away free things, that's hard to get away from, in fact, it's impossible. Lunch may not be free, but YouTube videos sure as hell are.

But, the first few weeks of Inecom on its own (and back in a basement) were great and it looked like Patreon might pull it off.

In the early days of 2016 Classic Game Room, and by extension, Inecom, got a huge shot in the arm and a chance to fight space bees again. Classic Game Room resumed operations, but this time without a fancy website and expensive product operation.

The first thing I did was slash all expenses by 90-95%. It would take me a while as a one-person company to move out of the studio and close the sets and sell the editing computers. So, while I was in the process of shutting down the on-screen space I continued filming. I loathed that I had to continue on YouTube. Posting every video was like knifing myself in the foot, but I had to do it.

YouTube. Never have I seen a company change its initial vision so thoroughly and get away with it. What was once a cool and creative space to post videos and "broadcast yourself" devolved into a mess of attention-seeking copycat clone garbage, but their fans gobbled up all of it.

How are you all enjoying those YouTube Shorts? Those are great. They're really tops.

Anyway, my expensive, custom website went down in flames because I couldn't afford to hire anyone to program it, and I didn't have time to learn. Bang! Years of hard work vaporized in an instant.

Personally, my dad and I were fine, but professionally I think we were happy to be done with each other. He had plans for his businesses that didn't involve me and that was just fine. The building was about to be sold. Good riddance. I never wanted to see it again.

Even now, as I'm writing this, the sense of frustration was overwhelming. Why on earth did people prefer conspiracy theories about school shootings to my videos? What's wrong with our world that it came to this...? Like I said earlier in the book, in the FromUSAlive days, the best content did the best. Was Classic Game Room, a pioneer in the field, not the best? Or at least good? Or maybe not just a complete piece of shit? Angry people making racist hate videos got more hits... that's what it came to.... but why?

I soldiered on, but my relationship with Classic Game Room was strained to say the least. I loved producing a show, but man, I fucking hated YouTube with the burning fury of a thousand suns. You're not supposed to get emotional in business, though.

My dad thought I was making a mistake by trying to stay in entertainment, but from my perspective, I just needed to untangle the mess and rethink my strategy. For years I had wanted to get back into publishing things like Blu-Rays and shirts, but I just wasn't sure how.

I hated the entertainment business, I still do. I did not want to stay in entertainment, but I saw the marketing benefit of being out in front with a show that people liked.

My company needed to be rebuilt from the ground up without all the bullshit overhead and money-losing spinoff shows. Inecom 2.0 would be built like a fucking tank.

CGR moved back into my basement and I shot it with a smartphone and GoPro like everyone else. Without studio space, offices, spin-offs, and the money-hemorrhaging website, Inecom's footprint became much smaller and more manageable. The cost savings were apparent overnight and actually worked out really well.

Like they said in my business classes. "Run it lean and mean." How about that? I must have taken a few notes after all... in between the drawings of 40s and guns.

There was a bunch of other boring business stuff to deal with, but for the most part, shrinking the company and restructuring it put the train back on the rails.

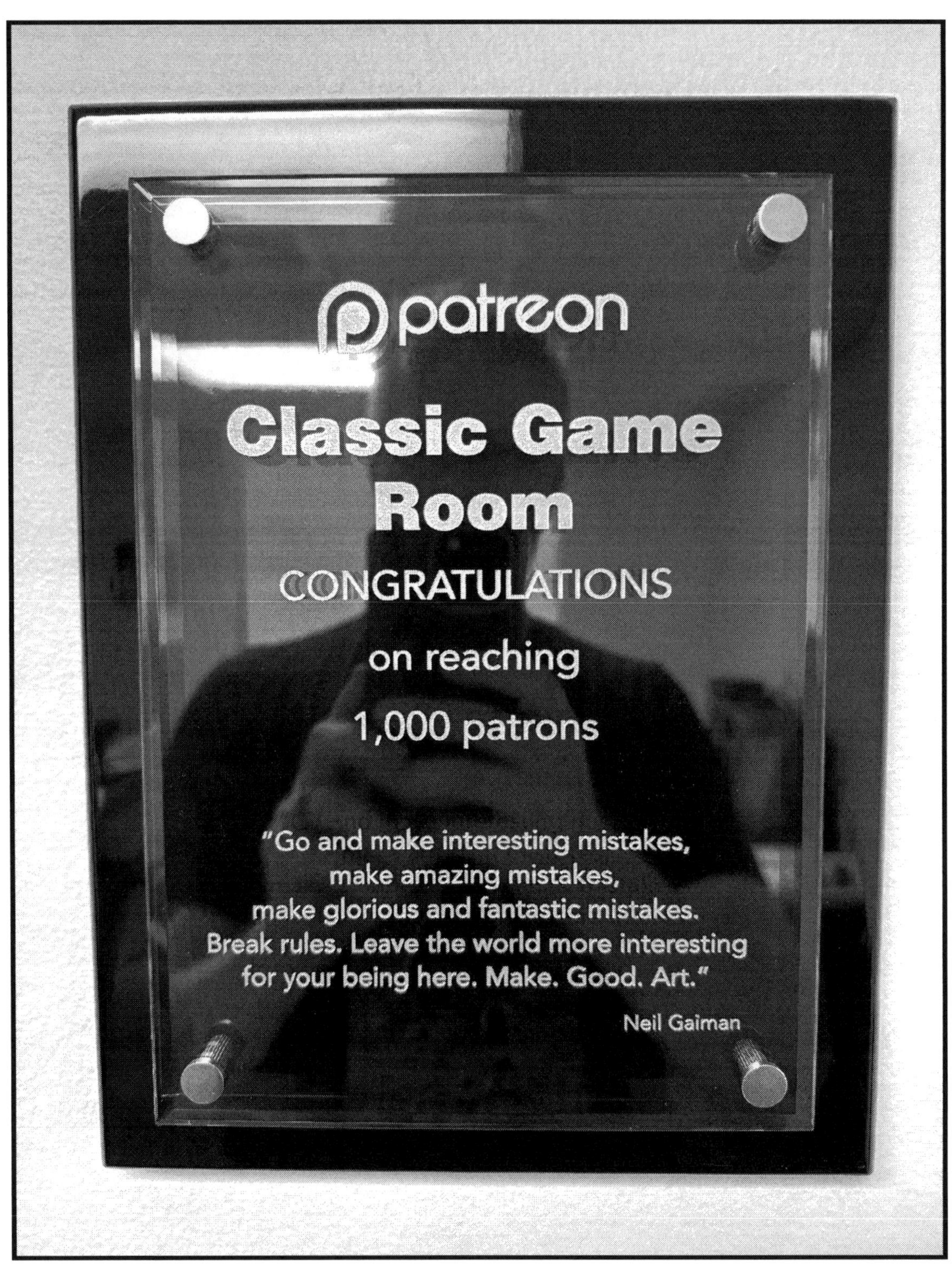

They do not send a plaque when you lose 1000 patrons.

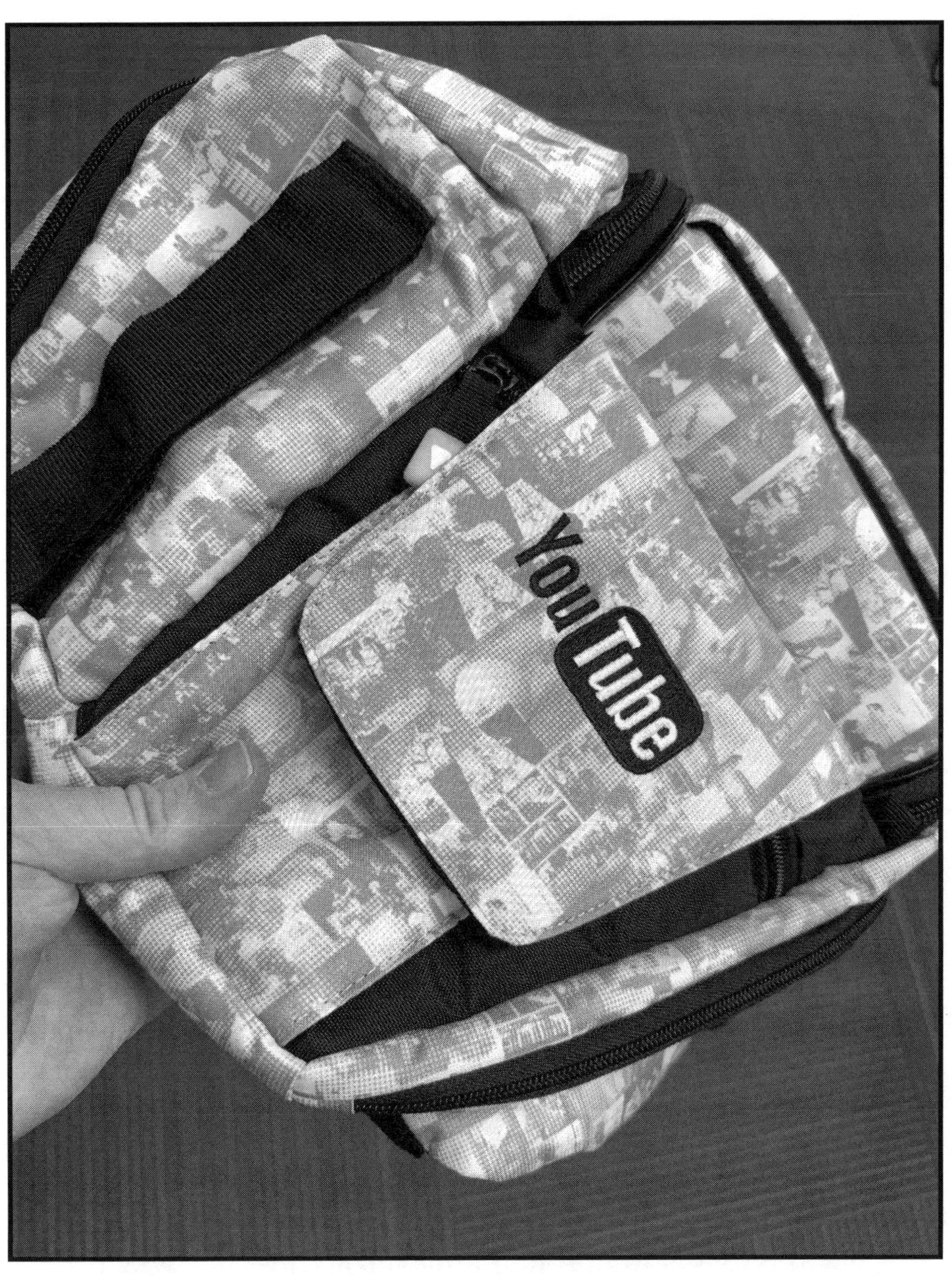

We never got a plaque, but YouTube sent us a camera bag in 2011-ish!

My arcade games went into storage along with boxes and boxes and boxes and even more boxes of video games and controllers. Let me tell you, I had a lot of games stuffed into boxes (I still do.)

2016 was around-the-clock work, but also a lot of fun because the Patreon was doing well enough to justify spending all of my time on Classic Game Room. And because the company was a one-man operation, I could adapt to the rapidly changing YouTube scene without fear of freaking out employees and owners who didn't like erratic changes.

I tightened the operation and cleared out inventory. But one does not just bounce back from an 80-90% drop in revenue. It was very stressful, but still better than being unemployed.

I didn't see the long term problem with Patreon until after the first few months. The problem (the big problem) is that it went backward. Patrons and earnings declined every single month. After that first explosion of backers, it was perpetually in a constant slide backward.

A lot of people jumped in at first to keep it running, but then couldn't afford to keep paying every month after that. As I had it explained to me, and from what I calculated, I assumed that people would pay two bucks a month to watch CGR without ads. More people were into paying ten or twenty dollars a month, but only for a few months. And some generous backers paid a whole lot more than that, and as one of them told me "I can't do this for long, so you'd better figure this out fast."

The show ran pretty smoothly for most of 2016, but I couldn't sell Patreon to YouTube viewers for anything. The mere mention of Patreon was like a swear word. So, not only did Classic Game Room defy YouTube, but now it's asking for money to continue defying YouTube.

After the first month, I never had a single month of growth with Patreon.

I'm a marketing guy, so I did my traditional marketing things like putting Patreon ads in front of videos and promoting it on the socials. Holy shit, people hated that. People were like "why am I paying for this show when there are other game review shows out there that are real!?"

So, if I can't sell Patreon, and it turns viewers off, and they leave, then they won't join Patreon, and I've lost viewers, and now ads and crowdfunding are tanking... All signs point to ZERO which means going out of business. Again.

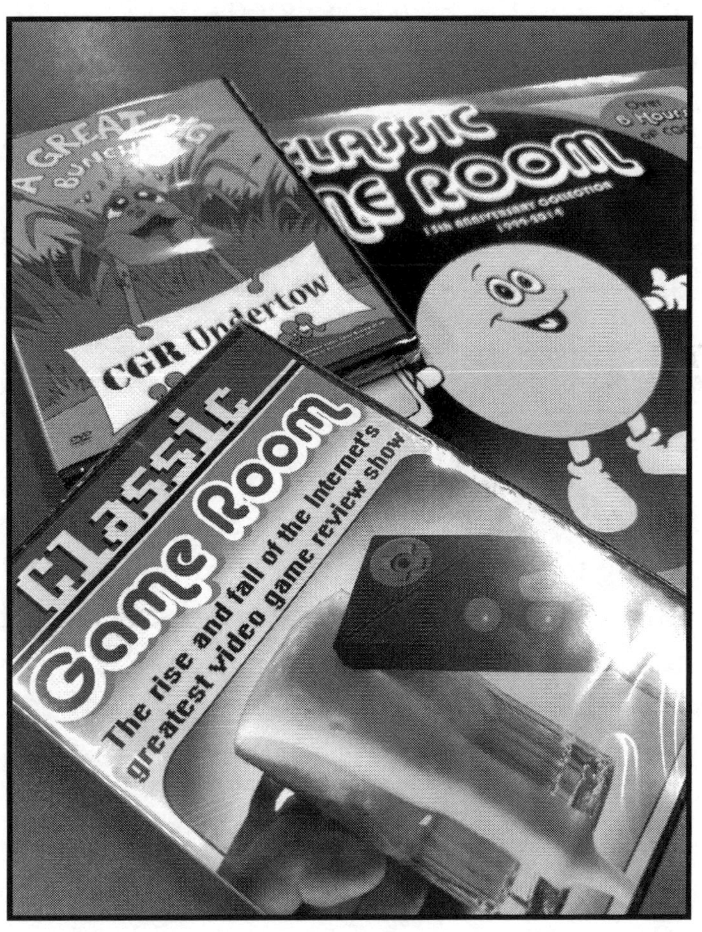

Classic Game Room DVDs and Blu-Ray from 2007 and 2015.

This is where my huge pivot into publishing started.

My dad thought I was crazy. My friends thought I was nuts. My family was annoyed that I didn't have a finance job like my college peers. Viewers were mad about... well, they were mad about everything.

"What you need to do is make an apology video and get back in the game." - viewer email

What I wanted to do was turn the company into a profitable product sales business, aka, publishing.

I had some time to figure it out but not much. Maybe a few months. The Patreon struggled, and I quickly became exhausted, but it was work and I had to do the work to keep the ship afloat until I could build a new ship.

The downside to working alone is that I immediately over-extended myself. I juggled a lot of projects and a YouTube channel with 410,000 subscribers (I lost about 60,000 subscribers over Patreon).

The Patreon-era was brutal. I drew roughly 30 custom digital drawings a month for high-tier backers, I drew a comic strip, and worked on a comic book. I recorded ring tones and made a podcast. I was playing games constantly and recording footage and editing. I hung in there through 2016 in good spirits, but saw the Patreon drop by about 50% come December of that year, which was not good. The YouTube views continued to plunge. The videos near the end of 2016 were only getting maybe 5,000 views a video. That's a big drop from millions.

Other YouTubers, including some of my friends who I admire, made it look easy, and maybe stuff worked out great for them. But damn, my work just got thrashed. Obviously, I couldn't keep making videos with a 50% drop in revenue year to year.

The problems with recurrent crowdfunding are many, but the big one is that you're easily replaced by someone who isn't using recurrent crowdfunding. Other YouTubers work for free, and that makes them more likable in the age when anyone can do it.

So, not only did lose my paid subscribers over time, but I also lost my remaining YouTube audience.

I was never able to successfully manage a YouTube show while simultaneously growing a real business. I don't know why, but free YouTube videos and a publishing company are like oil and water.

Going back to that "Did YouTube blacklist the channel?" thing, even with 400,000 subscribers, new videos in the 2017-era only got about 2,000 views each. So, not only did Patreon turn people off, but new people weren't coming in to watch the free videos in the first place.

People always have a long list of things that I should have done, but videos getting 2,000 views and dropping is no cause for investment. The show did better in February of 2008 when nobody could even watch YouTube on their U.S. Robotics modems via America Online.

Even though 2016 ended strongly with good videos and the CGR Supreme collection on Kickstarter, I could see that if I stuck with YouTube and video game reviews that I'd be out of business by 2018. The numbers don't lie.

I drew up a new business plan in the early days of 2017 planning for the complete and inevitable collapse of the CGR Patreon and the YouTube channel.

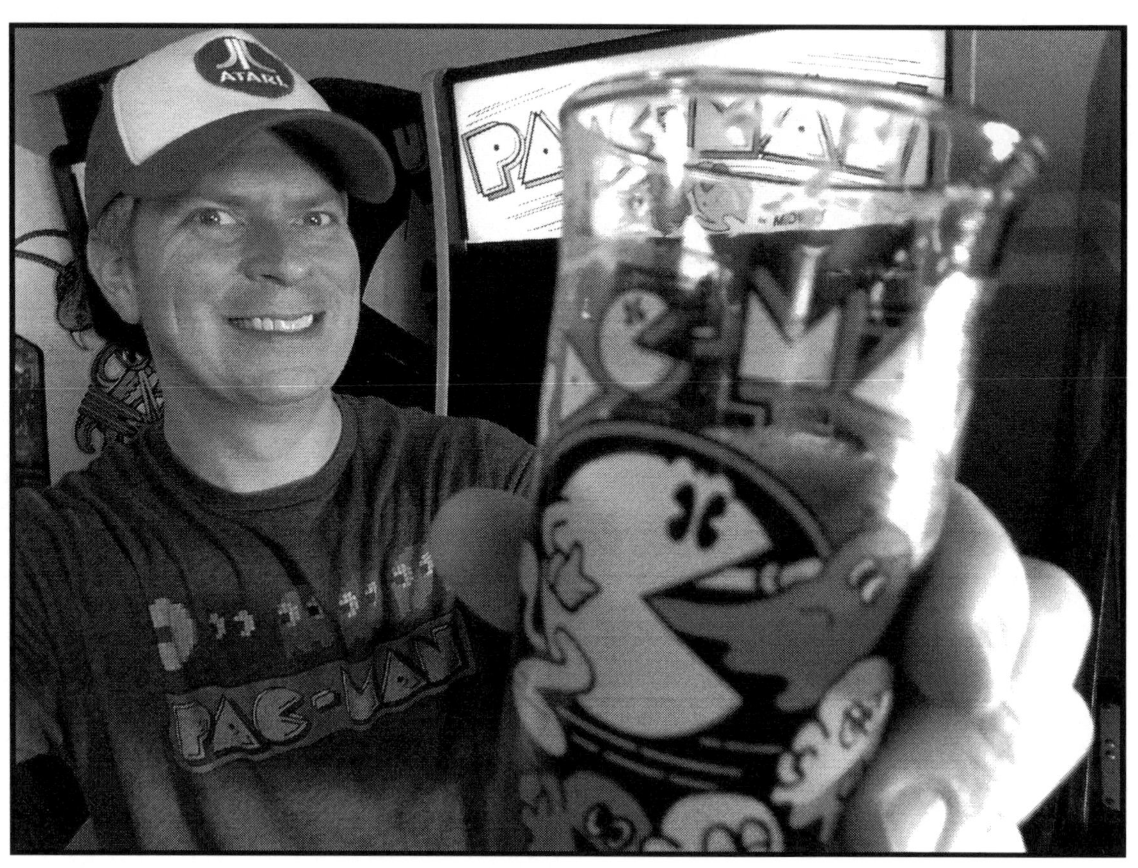

Mark and Pac-Man circa 2017.

CHAPTER 17
THE KOBAYASHI MARU

In early 2017 I was still producing daily, or at least mostly-daily Classic Game Room reviews, but views were awful. Instead of trying to fix the video game review show, which was clearly on the way down, and the Patreon which was dropping double digit percentages month-to-month, 2017 is the year I righted the ship by pivoting away from free gaming content entirely.

What would Captain Kirk do?

It's the Kobayashi Maru scenario. Kirk would win the no-win scenario by reprogramming the computer.

"You mean he cheated."

Screw you, David! Kirk's solution works. And you die in the next movie, so shut up.

"I don't like to lose." Kirk says while munching an apple loudly in front of everyone like a boss.

Years earlier, I launched Lord Karnage the comic book. One of the versions was a hardcover edition, another version was released as a digital book on Amazon, but I didn't think much of it. Digital book sales never amounted to a lot, so I forgot it was even there. But it was there, earning a few bucks.

In early 2017 I did a deep dig through all of my numbers. I scoured every sales outlet that I still had in place from the old days and added up all the fractions of pennies. Kindle caught my eye as a place where I could grow content outside of the poisoned disease-infested worthless shitpile of YouTube. Lord Karnage didn't sell particularly well on Amazon, but it sold a little bit without me having to do much, and it wasn't YouTube.

Ah-ha!

A few of my friends wrote books and they turned me on to some new things that Amazon was doing with Kindle, so I jumped on that ASAP.

2015's Ethel the Cyborg Ninja did well on Kickstarter and, in my opinion, it turned out great. It's a better book than Lord Karnage, and one that deserved more readers. But, more importantly, it was 100% complete and ready to publish when I needed a new book to publish with Amazon.

> Our plucky space heroine, a drunk chicken, and Edit-Station 1 changed my life forever.

Ethel the Cyborg Ninja would pave the way for CGR Publishing to eventually surpass Classic Game Room, but I didn't know that then.

I did some tinkering with the cover, resized the pages, and reprinted Ethel the Cyborg Ninja Book 1 in the spring of 2017. I did a bit of marketing and it sold.

That's all I needed to see. After Ethel, I put a plan in place to make about a half-dozen more books. These would be brand new books from the group up!

My first all-new 2017 print release was How to Make a Video Game Review Show that Doesn't Suck, which was a test piece for the Ultra Massive Video Game Console Guide series.

At the time, I continued to make YouTube and Patreon videos and tried to document this process, but the videos didn't do well, certainly not compared to the glory days. But, I think it did well enough to get this stuff off the ground.

Who's ready for some awesome photographs of video game consoles on the beach? Apparently a bunch of people, because The Ultra Massive Video Game Console Guide sold well upon its release in late 2017. I actually tried to launch it with a Kickstarter but met huge resistance from angry Facebook followers who claimed that I shouldn't be charging money for things.

Is everyone drinking the poisoned Kool-Aid?

I self-financed the first Ultra Massive book with a credit card.

Upon release, the Ultra Massive Video Game Console Guide sold like bonkers. I had a second one ready to go right behind it and would complete the third and fourth volumes in 2018. Even though the sales figures for the Ultra Massive series would be dwarfed by my upcoming World's Fair book series, they showed huge potential and really perked me up about the entire "running a company" thing after YouTube turned into a living hellscape.

Every time I logged into YouTube, I was greeted by people shouting at me about Patreon and canceling Undertow, which I didn't even do. (and who were these people who watched Undertow when the view counter showed nobody watching Undertow? I'm telling you.... This shit doesn't add up.)

Classic Game Room channel hits plummeted even further in 2017 as views sunk to an all-time low.

Subscribers were, apparently, never getting notified of new videos. You can have 400,000 subscribers, but if only .005% of them are active, you only have about 2,000 subscribers. So, my dumbass video game review show ended up getting roughly 1,000-2,000 views per video. Awesome. Glad I worked hard on it for a decade.

This is when the misinformation machine really started to kill the channel as well. I had Internet friends turn into enemies after getting radicalized by fake YouTube comments and Reddit posts. One guy accused me of writing a book about robots and space aliens as a metaphor for animal abuse. Someone who sent a lot of games to the show said I sold them all (I didn't.) One guy demanded I send a game back to him because his brother stole it from him 15 years earlier. Long-time viewers said I didn't open up about my personal struggles and stopped watching.

Some people just sent shitty drunk messages in the middle of the night about how I shouldn't be working for money. The show was supposed to be free.

Are you serious? Are you even reading what you type?

Apparently, I faked the show's launch in 1999.

I owed viewers an apology video for using Patreon.

Many people said Classic Game Room copied The Angry Video Game Nerd (I don't even know James, but damn, he hit the nail on the head with that Angry thing. No wonder his shows always did better.)

One of my major problems with expressing creativity on the Internet is that people have no patience, sympathy for, or understanding of failed ideas. In art and business, you're going to have more bad ideas than good ones; that's a fact. Bad ideas and failures are how one learns and then figures out some good ideas that lead to success.

Behind the scenes, it's easy to screw things up and learn from them. Publicly, however, when you're a known celebrity (even a D-list celebrity) it's another story. I've tried many things that led to "Look how desperate Mark is!" and "Look at Mark failing!" because people were so consumed by juvenile YouTube drama surrounding Classic Game Room that they couldn't possibly see that there was a bigger picture.

What would Kirk do? He'd teleport all of those morons into the Sarlaac Pit while quoting Dickens. "It was the best of times, it was the worst of times, and fuck you."

I'm a big experimenter when it comes to ideas, I learned this from my dad. I don't mind screwing up because I do it all the time. I've had several major fuckups turn into successful products in time.

I released a lot of things in 2018 that were nothing more than throwing darts at the wall and experimenting to get a diverse sampling of data.

My favorite colossal fuckup is Lord Karnage in the Valley of Moon Wolves. It was my first (and only) attempt at writing a fantasy novel just to see what would happen.

Lord Karnage in the Valley of Moon Wolves is a completely absurd sci-fi adventure starring my comic book characters Lord Karnage and Edit-Station 1. They get a cry for help from a distant planet, they show up, they kill everything, they befriend villagers, they kill more things, stuff blows up, there's a huge battle scene in a volcano, and everyone gets laid. Awesome.

It's half-baked at best and probably poorly written,

but I wanted to see if I could make the transition from comic book writer to novelist because drawing comic books takes forever. As I found out, the writing process and proofreading take even longer and I'm way better at drawing and copywriting than novel writing. It's a completely different skill set.

When I write comics, the action is depicted with storyboarding and pictures. When I write novels, I'm trying to weave a tale and use fancy words and for me to pull it off I'd need an editor and that would blow the budget up. So, in short, I'm not a good novelist.

Lord Karnage in the Valley of Moon Wolves was my first try at releasing a pre-order on Amazon, and also my last because I'm awful at deadlines (no surprise because I'm always juggling 20 projects.)

I ran behind, rushed it to the end, and released an incomplete version on Kindle which I assumed would auto-update with corrections made on release day. Assuming is a terrible ideas as I quickly learned. Most readers didn't get the full book. Maybe it updated eventually, but it was pretty bad anyway... so, basically, a colossal fuckup. I was a major asshole. Gunners Mate First Class Major Asshole!

But, the cover design was great and directly led to some of my best cover designs on other books which have gone on to sell many copies. I took a drawing and applied a certain retro vibe (as pictured on the next page.)

The Lord Karnage cover inspired a design style that I later used on Dante's Inferno, Paradise Lost, and Crusades. If Lord Karnage led to those books, then Lord Karnage deserves a giant huge-ass margarita or fifteen.

Lord Karnage won big-time, baby, but not in the way that anyone else on the planet saw. But I know that without trying it, I'd have never eliminated that as a bad idea and, I

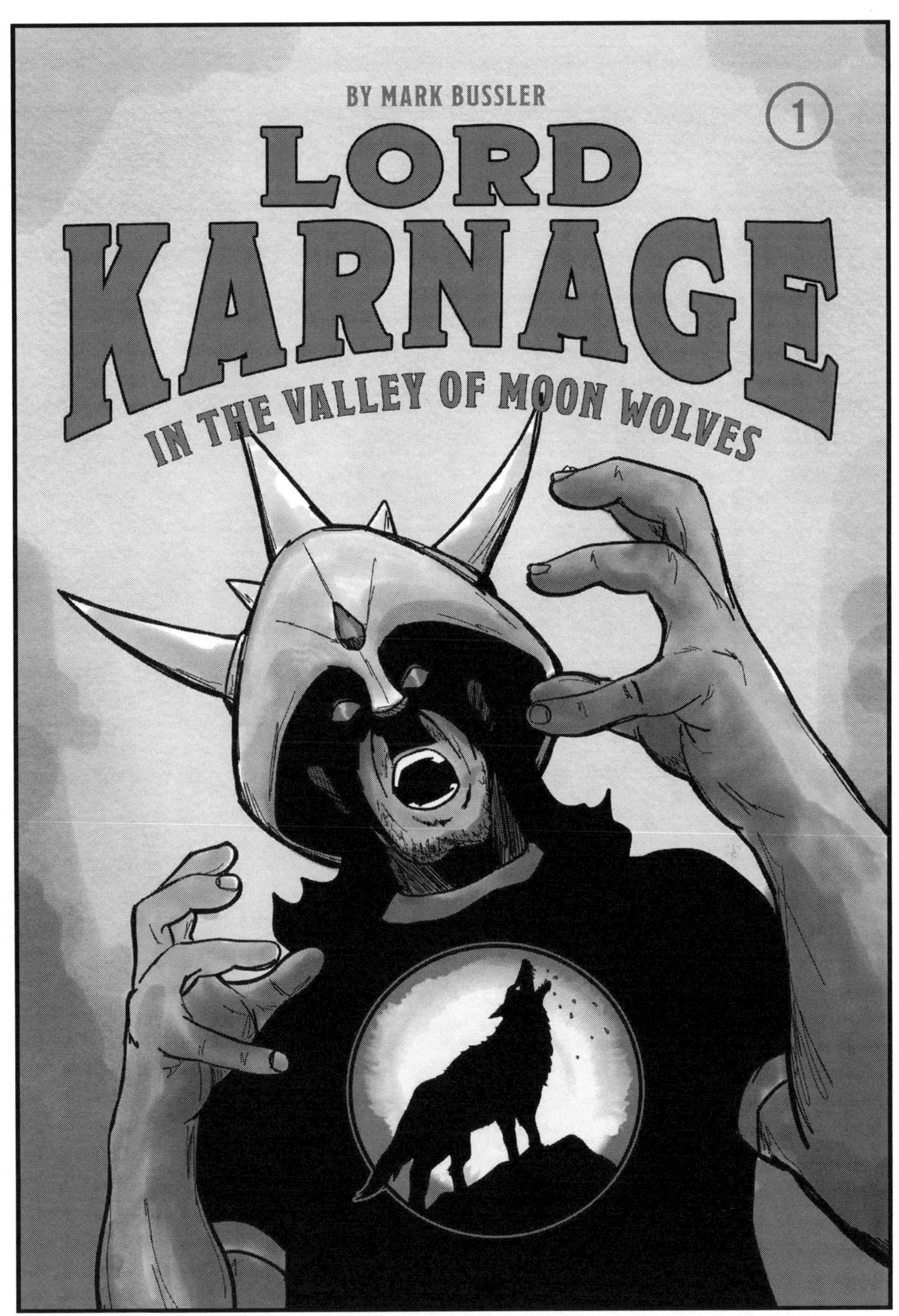

Lord Karnage in the Valley of Moon Wolves (2018.)

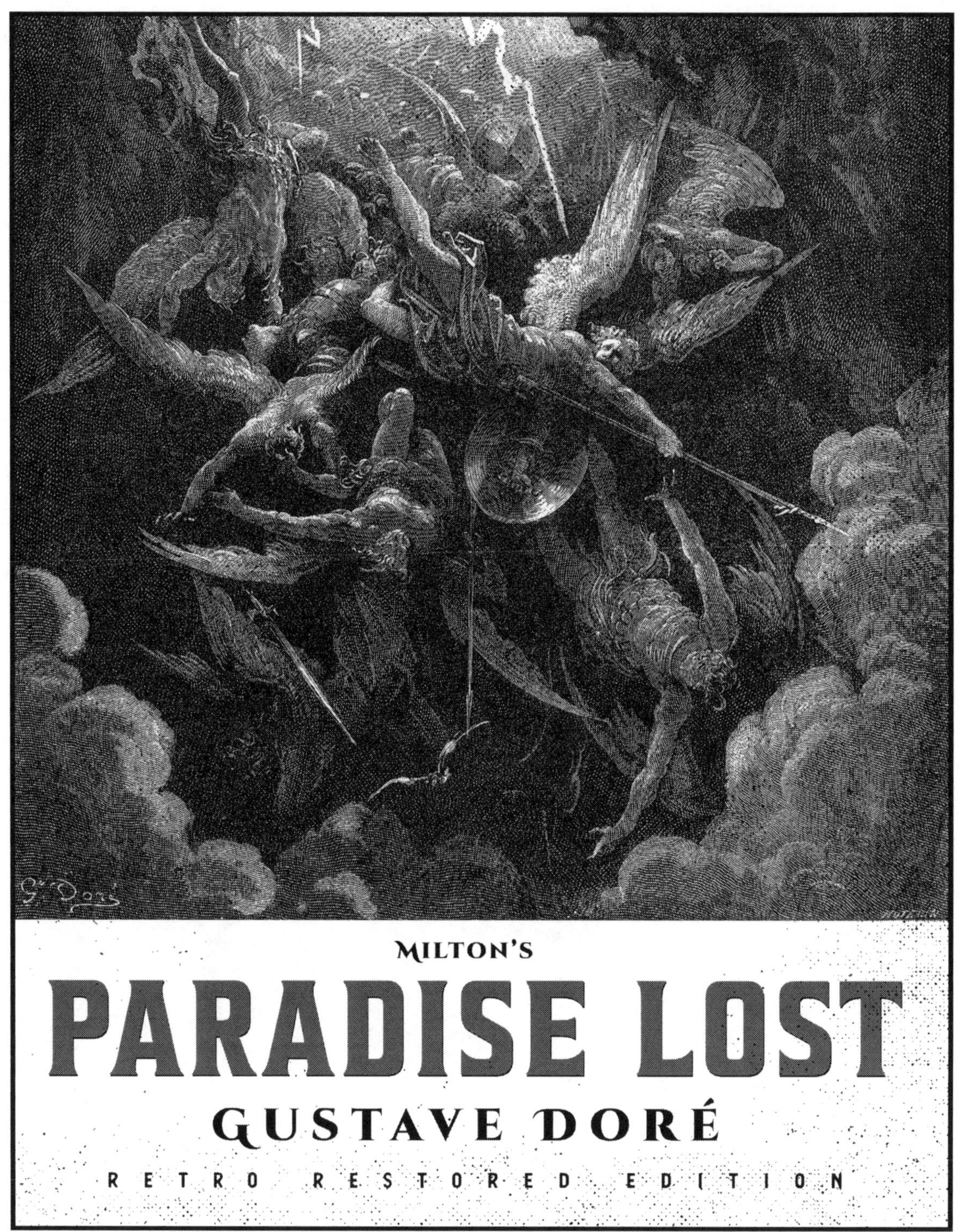

Milton's Paradise Lost: Gustave Doré Retro Restored Edition (2020.)

probably wouldn't have ever come up with that totally rad retro cover design concept.

After fits and starts the Amazon business kicked the shit out of my YouTube business that year, not that it took much effort.

But I still really liked product diversity, so I didn't want to just quit making Classic Game Room. Also because the entire business was called Classic Game Room. It's hard to just drop the thing you're known for. It's a cooler name than Inecom, too.

However, If I didn't pivot away from money-losing YouTube videos and a collapsing Patreon into something else, Inecom would be bankrupt regardless of what it was called. Production overhead was still wasting money.

It was not lost on me that while everyone else was focused on being the next big viral YouTube star, Amazon is over there just quietly taking over the entire planet.

There was this brief moment in time when it looked like Amazon might even compete with YouTube.

It is easy to forget that YouTube crushed or absorbed every one of its competitors including Dailymotion, Vidme, Vimeo, Revver, Blip, Yahoo, AOL, and whatever else. They wiped them all from the face of the earth. But Amazon was Amazon, and I watched what they were doing closely.

Amazon launched Amazon Video or whatever it was called as an alternative to YouTube. Users could post their own videos on Amazon Prime! It's laughable now, but in 2017, Amazon seemed like they might pull it off and I jumped on board.

I did this knowing that my YouTube career was already over, but before I liquidated my production company and canceled the show outright, my plan was to launch one final round of Classic Game Room as the biggest Classic Game Room.

Classic Game Room 2085.

One must remember that I had no interest in being a YouTube star. That wasn't even a thing in 2008. I like producing a show. I like filmmaking. Remember that documentary career that you read about 100 pages ago? That's what I most enjoyed. I enjoyed crafting a well-made piece of moving art.

I didn't think that launching a bigger-budget version of Classic Game Room on Amazon was a big deal, but apparently the Internet did.

"You can't do that!" One angry viewer shouted at me on Twitter. Were these comments left by YouTube employees? You know what lemmings are, right?

"Classic Game Room is doing something controversial!" another person screamed and swore at me.

Remember what Ron Maxwell said. It's the drama, not the content. It is the drama that matters, and how one deals with the struggle of being trapped and suffocated by YouTube.

If I had come out sadfishing with dramatic stories about heroin addiction and relationship drama people might have cared. But nobody gives a fuck when you're like "I'm fine. I'm just applying my business degree."

Thanks to whining and complaining, I couldn't market Classic Game Room 2085 on Twitter or Facebook. Any mention of it on YouTube was met with hate mail and nonsense.

It's a shame.

Classic Game Room 2085 was awesome. It's my favorite version of the show because I just didn't a flying fuck when making it. It was so much fun to produce. I would have LOVED to make it a full-time project.

In Classic Game Room 2085 I went to the future. I was verbally abused by a talking computer. I made original music and filmed it on a well-lit set that contained Pac-Man, ED-209, a disco ball, and Thexder. It looked and sounded like a proper TV show. CGR 2085 is what I always wanted the show to be and I'm very proud of it.

How did I make Classic Game Room 2085? Slowly and methodically as a one-person show.

Production started at the tail end of 2017. After renting a room for business operation and shipping again, I unpacked some of the old set pieces and shelving and bit by bit, crafted a new set.

You might recognize some of the stuff on-screen from the storage locker set, and even the set from the warehouse. I covered shelves with LED rope lights, game boxes, toys, and doodads. Two microphone stands and a drop-cloth bar strung between the arcade games held the spinning disco ball. It was actually a very small set, even smaller than the storage locker. But smaller sets are easier to light and mic (the old warehouse set sounded like crap by comparison!)

I used the show Top Gear as a template. The first several episodes start with the "here's what you can expect in today's episode!" and then dive into well-shot, silly segments about the Sega Genesis and Panasonic 3DO and whatnot. Instead of just doing voice-over-gameplay, I filmed studio segments and cut them up with my co-host for the series, Edit-Station 1.

Obviously I voiced Edit-Station 1 and used voice filters to make me sound like a computer. I thought this added some of the old-fashioned back-and-forth commentaries from the original 1999-2000 years, and it provided bumpers for editing since I filmed everything unscripted and eventually ran out of steam each take.

I filmed Classic Game Room 2085 on a Canon 1D with a manual lens for that big cinematic look. The audio gear was all top-notch, and I even bought a top-of-the-line Rode shotgun mic for the studio scenes that hung directly over me and out of sight. I created all original music for the series using Garage Band on iPad, and even included some behind the scenes making-of the music footage (the CGR 2085 music is another precursor to Omega Ronin.)

There was no crew. None at all, and I did all the editing, so I'm editing in my brain while filming. Before each shot, I'd focus the camera manually on my Atari hat hanging on a mic stand, and then slip in behind the desk before recording.

The lens had a narrow depth of field for that nice, soft background look. That was very, very difficult because I couldn't move around much or I'd be out of focus.

The audio recording was equally difficult, but eventually, I got it. Technically, CGR 2085 is the best the show ever was.

Classic Game Room 2085 got off to a slow start but was very well received by viewers. Unfortunately, Amazon only showed it in a few countries. I didn't know that right away, but YouTube viewers made sure to blame me for this and complained on Twitter and said I singled out their countries to block.

Think about that. I was accused of singling out Canada as a country to block. Use your brain... why would I do that?

Apparently CGR 2085 never aired in Canada or Australia, two of my biggest markets. I had no idea that they wouldn't fix this immediately, but since Amazon wasn't technically "free", they didn't. Behind the scenes, there are a bazillion tax and licensing issues with paid content distributed internationally. That's where YouTube really had them beat.

Yo kids. Listen up. Once you have success on YouTube and it goes away, you never get it back. I could have made The Empire Strikes Back and people would have said it was shit because I wanted money for it.

At one point I said that YouTube should be called Entitlementvision, and the joke went about as well as you might expect.

Classic Game Room 2085 did well enough for me to consider a Season 2, but the print business came from behind that year and flattened it. It wasn't even close.

By April of 2018, after only a few episodes, I had to push down the gas pedal on print which took the wind out of the CGR 2085 sails. I still managed to wrap up about 12 solid hours of Classic Game Room 2085 though, just enough to publish it all on Blu-Ray six years later (no, I didn't plan that in advance.)

CGR fans (the ones who could see it) loved it. Regardless, I had to shut down the studio and strip the set for parts to sell and fund the next iteration of Inecom.

Classic Game Room was cursed by this point, or so it seemed. It was pretty obvious that the mainstream audience would NEVER pay to watch anything. Additionally, the show's exclusion from international markets really didn't help. Game reviews were also totally obsolete and replaced by live streaming, influencers, and the big mega celebrities.

I canceled Game Room 2085 after about 22 episodes because it took too long time to produce, and I had other things to do.

"Classic Game Room 2085 was incredible! Why did you cancel it?" - Fan email.

Because I had no choice.

2018 was a rough year for Inecom. Transition into a print business was not easy, nor did it happen overnight. I was personally happier to face that struggle than to try dealing with Internet game reviews though, because people weren't yelling at me about books or crying about paywalling on Twitter.

Classic Game Room 2085 was a bit of a commercial dud and it lost money. So, it wasn't a cause for celebration. But it turned out good, so that's nice. Yay.

Holiday book sales were weaker than I expected that year, due in large part to a huge and immediate oversaturation of video game books on Amazon. I suspect that a few people may have been watching what I was doing, also I didn't really figure out the marketing side yet.

I had dozens of boxes filled with outdated Xbox 360 and Wii games collecting dust in storage, most of which were sent by marketing companies over the years for review. I sold off the old marketing copies as fast as I could list them on Ebay. Thank you Wii shovelware for helping to keep the company afloat when I needed it!

While I gutted the studio and condensed my print operation, I figured I'd try one more wackadoo approach just to see what would happen with video. I still saw some marketing potential in being relevant on social media (which was dumb.)

I tried to keep my toe in the game by chopping up the Classic Game Room format into little bite sized chunks and posting them on Instagram as CGR Infinity. I didn't see it clearly then, but short videos were the future. Still, viewers hated CGR Infinity when it dropped on New Year's Day in 2019.

I made 60 episodes and watched my inbox fill up with complaints about Patreon and Amazon and how terrible I was for being mean to YouTube. As it turns out, I'm a shitty awful human being.

Would things have turned out differently were it called Angry Game Room?

I had a few rough draft episodes of Classic Game Room 2085 Season 2 assembled and even collected a few game consoles that I never had before like the Bally Astrocade and Darth Vader Atari 2600.

In mid-2019, I quickly finished them and cut together a collection of reviews called CGR 20th to celebrate Classic Game Room's 20th, anniversary but declined to put it on Amazon because I didn't want to pay for captions, knowing full well that nobody would watch it there.

CGR 20th sold a few copies when I released it on Vimeo On-Demand and USB cards in 2019, which wasn't a big surprise considering its limited release. At least I finally got to film the Darth Vader Atari and Odyssey Voice before selling them along with the disco ball.

One positive, though, is that I got really good at managing an Ebay store. Inecom's Ebay business is massive nowadays.

Like 2018, 2019 was also a challenging business year with slow growth. I took a deep dive through the studio remnants. I ripped out cables and connectors and sold everything which wasn't necessary or bolted down, except donated things.

Even though some viewers lied and defamed me by claiming that I sold donated games and systems, they're all still languishing in boxes in storage.

I never felt it was cool to sell donated stuff. Sorry we couldn't get to it all, but if you've read this far into the book, I'm sure you understand.

I got a two-beer buzz selling the old video gear. It felt great. 1999-era XLR cables brought in ten bucks a pop which was ten dollars needed to make new books. All the RE-20s and the ancient Neumann were banged up but still worth something. I even sold the CGR editing system hard drives. Liquidating the studio worked and kept the business running, but I was starting to get nervous.

Restructuring Inecom took longer than expected and felt like wasting time at the time. There was only so much overhead I could eliminate. At some point, it needed to actually grow faster!

Building a business foundation from the ground up requires patience and commitment. It's boring, it's expensive, and it doesn't feel like moving forward. It's not a dramatic overnight success like you see on TV.

I'm not sure that the longtime fans of the show know this, but by the end of 2019, Classic Game Room had fully evolved into CGR Publishing with a catalog of 50-60 books and countless shirts on Amazon. There was growth, but it was nothing like those crazy days of 2009 and 2010.

The sales just hadn't caught up to production yet so it never felt successful even though it actually was.

I remember chatting with my dad one day who said,

"You look busy!"

"Yeah, but sales aren't there yet."

"You're building. Building is good. Keep building."

How'd he always know what to say?

The CGR Publishing imprint started to appear on books near the end of 2019 because, as I saw it, the name of the publishing company didn't matter. I kept it close to Classic Game Room in case I ever wanted to use the social media channels in the future.

It was tough.

The complete collapse of the video business exacerbated the situation. Overall video advertising earnings dropped 80-90% from the company's peak in 2012, and Patreon dried up. It was brutal, but still way more awesome than producing shitty videos for YouTube.

I ended up selling my Atari 5200, Colecovision, Magnavox Odyssey 2, a few Segas, some of my rare Atari games, my Saturn, and a bunch of spaceship shooters that I bought over the years like MUSHA, Truxton, Dodonpachi, and my Thunder Force games. People assumed this was a free fucking joke for me, but it was pretty serious.

The fact that Inecom didn't go out of business after losing roughly 90% of its video revenue in 10 years is remarkable.

CGR Publishing released an eclectic array of books in 2018 and 2019 as I tinkered with formats, concepts, and super old-school restoration work.

Some of the books turned out great like 1904 St. Louis World's Fair: The Louisiana Purchase Exposition in Photographs, The American Railway, and my How to Draw

Digital book.

All Hail the Vectrex came out in May of 2019, one of my favorites. You gotta love the Vectrex!

I released a few comics in those years including Ethel the Cyborg Ninja Issue #2 and a few of the Heyzoos the Coked-Up Chicken books.

Lord Karnage in the Valley of Moon Wolves is worth a quick read if you enjoy the Lord Karnage characters.

A year earlier in 2017 I tried making a kids' book called Surf Panda. The character would also appear in Manga Teacup Cherry Blossom (which is hilarious.) I also added a short story about Lord Karnage drinking a planet's margarita atmosphere into Lord Karnage 1.5 which is great. I'm biased, but Lord Karnage is awesome.

Rest assured, we'll see more of Lord Karnage. I just drew a bunch of pages with him for Ethel the Cyborg Ninja #3 (2024)!

UNSUBSCRIBED: How to Succeed When the Platform Fails also missed the mark because the last thing that "content creators" want to hear is that you won't be instantly famous and successful. That would be my last foray into instructional content about "creation," except for maybe this book.

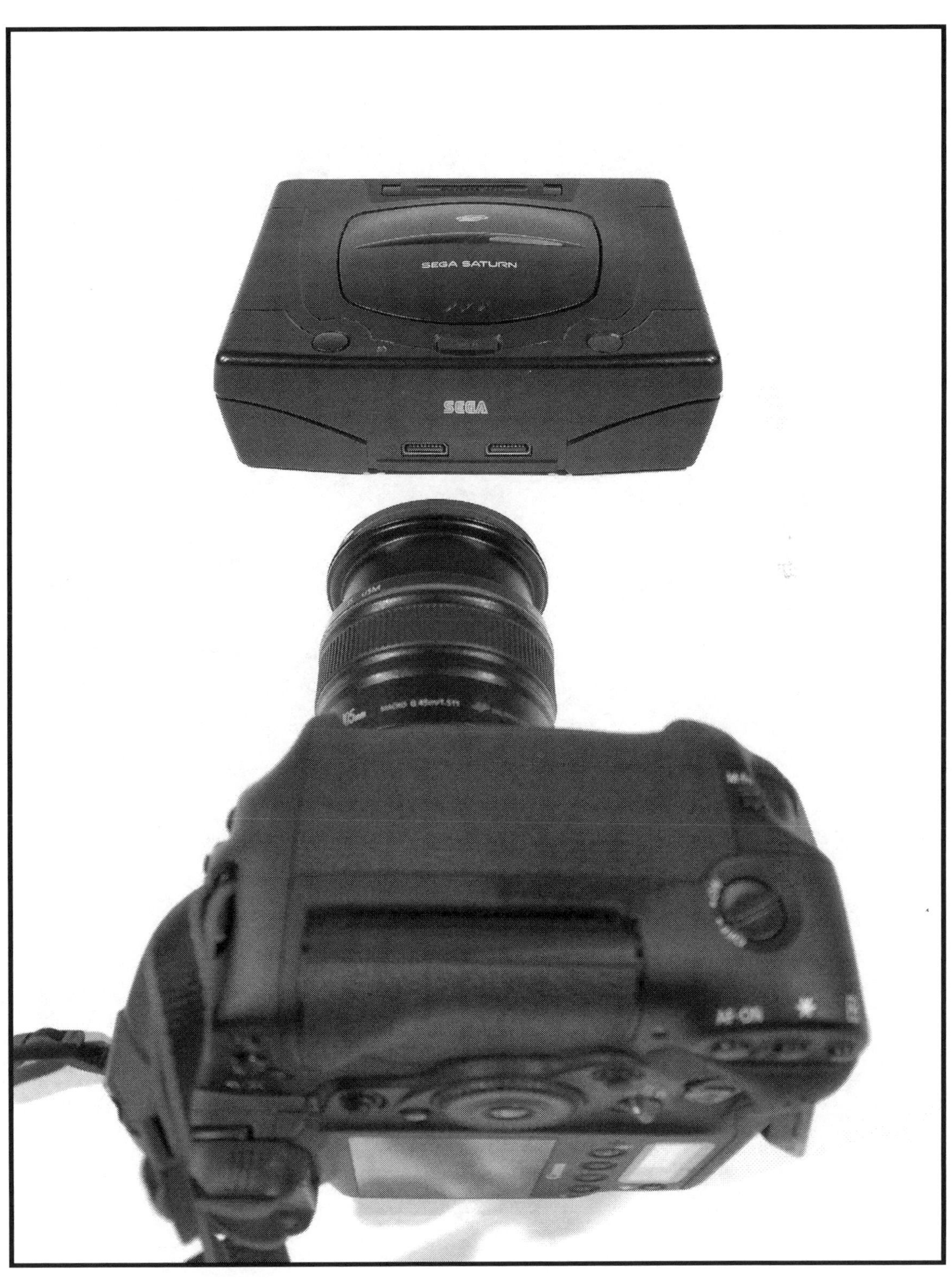

Ultra Massive Video Game Console Guide photography, 2017.

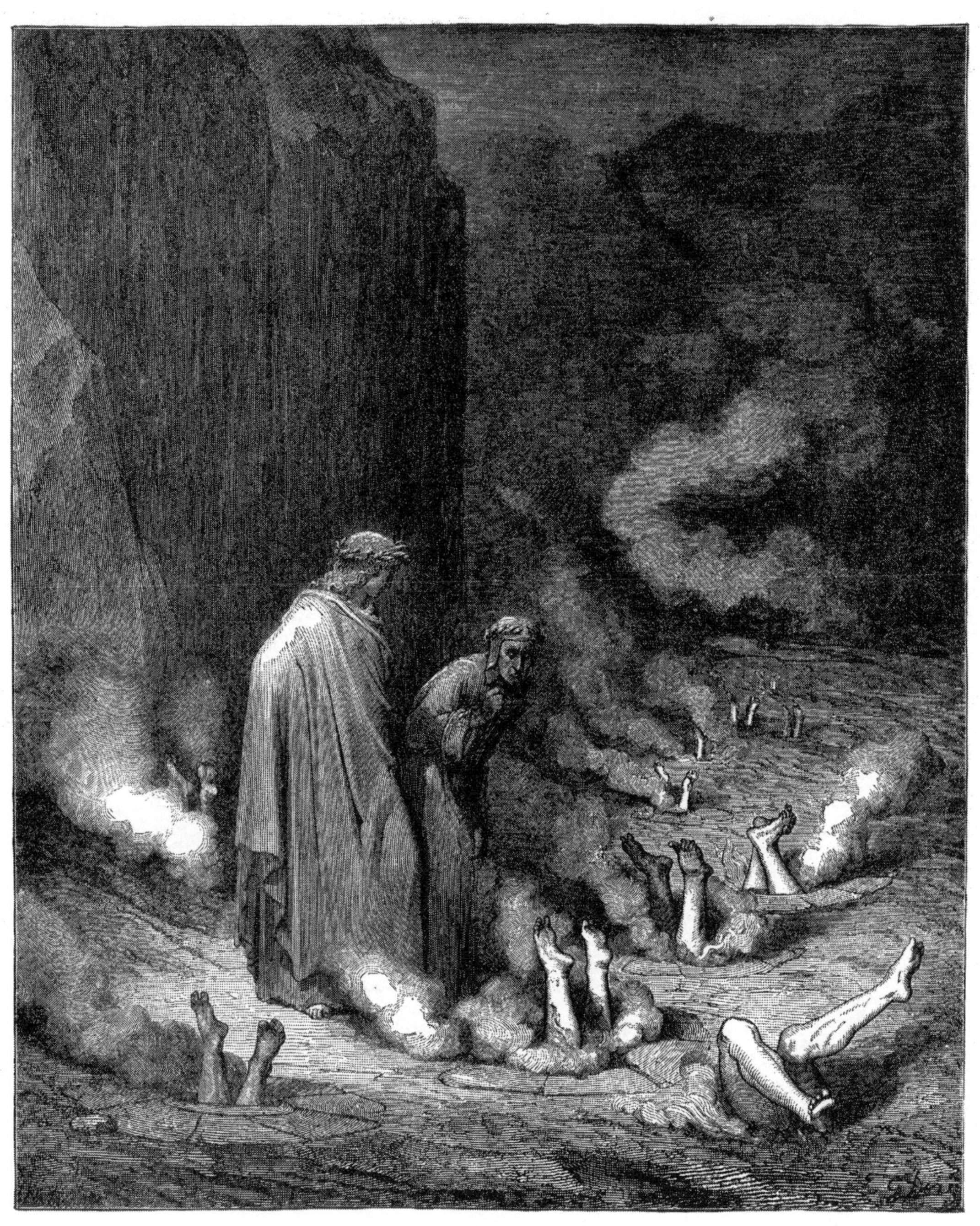

Look at these brainwashed fools watching reaction videos.
'Tis a sad state of affairs.

Canto XIX., lines 51, 52.

CHAPTER 18
DO SHEEP DREAM OF ELECTRIC ANDROIDS?

A reminder that 2020 is one year after the events in Blade Runner, and I would argue that Blade Runner's vision of the future is much better than the dystopian wasteland that we actually live in. At least the murderous replicants didn't have to endure countless influencers, a crumbling idiocrasy, and a global pandemic.

For the most part, I wrapped up video production in '19 but continued to tinker with some YouTube videos here and there because I needed some kind of marketing exposure, even if it was on my least favorite platform in the world. My lower-budget 80s Comics series had been chugging along since mid-2019, and serious fans enjoyed it a lot. The video game crowd hated it and made sure to do everything they could to let the world know how displeased they were that someone might be having fun without them.

It's not like I didn't know that 80s Comics wasn't as popular as Classic Game Room was in its heyday, it was just fun to make and I enjoy sharing my love of comic books with people. I shot 80s Comics on my smartphone and tried to keep the early videos under 60 seconds to post on Instagram and the emerging TikTok, but they always felt rushed at 60 seconds.

Eventually, I started to make them 2-3 minutes long,

which fit the format better. What was crazy to me is that my iPhone did a better job filming stuff in 2019 than a $20,000 TV camera did in 1999.

For years I had been messing around with the "Drawing with Lord Karnage" series. Additionally, I tinkered with some "behind the scenes" and even launched a few projects like Omega Ronin in 2019 as a drawing video.

The market for drawing instruction videos is, and was, as large as the video game market on YouTube. But the channel was sadly labeled as a VIDEO GAME ONLY channel, and every drawing video was also met with complaints that drove away potential subscribers and fans (not that the subscription thing worked anymore.)

At some point it became clear that I needed at least three people to manage a YouTube channel with 400,000 subscribers because I couldn't keep up with the endless complaints and comments and people demanding responses to comments and all the while, nobody is watching anything anyway.

In late 2019 I could see that art and print were going to be a big part of my future plans, and I tried to work that stuff into YouTube videos but it didn't work either.

This led to my least popular video of all time... a pen review! No videos ever got more complaints than my art supply reviews. I could have sewn live kittens into a fur coat and it would have been better received than a pencil review.

I mean.... wasn't it obvious? I was expanding into art projects, and stuff like pen and pencil reviews were actually quite large on YouTube. People will happily watch pen videos if they're into pens. And if people are watching pen videos, and a pen video takes me five minutes to make, then that pen video pays for, at least, some of the pen.

Once again, my inbox filled with complaints and hate mail and eventually, I just lost patience. It's not fun making videos only to see people complain about them.

I continued 80s Comics in 2020, but I loathed the entire video business at that point. It wasn't working well for marketing, it certainly wasn't earning any money, and I couldn't afford to hone my drawing videos into a better series because they always entered the arena of a gaming channel. Nor could I take the time to start over (people would have sniffed out the new channel and destroyed it too.)

Inecom weathered a tough 2019. I was very concerned about 2020, and that was before the pandemic! Even though the business foundation that I built was solid, it still had a long way to go. Sales remained sluggish because I wasted time on stuff like Unsubscribed and Lord Karnage in the Valley of Moon Wolves instead of books that actually sold. Every 2019 video was also a complete waste of time and money.

I didn't panic, but I wasn't running around cheering either because I knew I had to choose my projects better.

I started to scale back my storage space and finally began to sell my collection of arcade games, which was a punch in the gut. Selling arcade games is a royal pain in the ass, so it didn't go smoothly and (thankfully) I only parted with a few.

I'll never forget the day that I went to the gym in early 2020 and watched the news about this thing called Coronavirus that started in China, ravaged Italy, and appeared to be slowly approaching the U.S. I'm thinking, "It's not going to be long until this is in my house."

Trump lied and said everything was fine, which of course meant that everything was not fine. He later said to drink bleach.

Anyway, I went to get coffee one morning at the museum coffee shop in February of 2020, after Covid started to crawl across the U.S., and saw that nobody was there. It was like a ghost town (I did enjoy my coffee in peace.)

I think it was that same day in March when the World Health Organization declared Covid-19 a global pandemic that I moved a good chunk of my arcade games out the door. Was that the day Tom Hanks got Covid? For some reason, that made it seem really scary because if Tom Hanks could catch this thing, then so could you.

We got word that school would be closed. I went out and bought a case of beer and a few jars of peanut butter and prepared to hunker down through the apocalypse. One can survive on beer and peanut butter you know. Haven't you seen The Day After?

The early days of Covid were scary, and a lot of people forget this even though it outright killed over one million Americans. My kids went to virtual learning, which was a complete train wreck. Companies went remote work, and life as we knew it shut down. I'd take Stella for a walk around town and see nobody out and about. Nothing. No cars parked on the street, no commuters, nobody shopping at stores. April of 2020 was like a ghost town.

At that same time, we were told by social media that wearing masks violated our freedom or something like that. People took guns to state capitals and rioted for their freedom to not wear masks because Covid didn't exist. This was when I started to notice that not only was YouTube and social media awful because it was just awful, but it was also dangerous.

Since I didn't believe the bullshit I saw on social media, I wore my mask and stayed away from others as much as possible. I was already a work-from-home pro, and I rather liked the shutdown. Oddly enough, I embraced the hermit attitude and just went right back to business publishing books. My productivity increased because I had nothing else to do and found it easier to focus.

Also, no longer was I playing any video games and recording footage, that freed up a lot of time. For the most part, I also stopped posting anything on social media, which freed up that time (and put me in a better mood. It's amazing how bad social media is for one's well-being.)

So, while 2020 ravaged restaurants and businesses where in-person communications were required, those of us on the Internet went for a roller coaster ride.

Suddenly, my catalog of books kicked in, starting with my 1939 New York World's Fair book which sold to people in New York City who were trapped inside during the first deadly wave of Covid.

Unrelated to the pandemic, I also had about 40 book restorations in production from 2019 that just happened to land on Amazon in the spring of 2020. Overnight, my book catalog doubled. Business grew with it.

But, what about my Internet business? Ha, well let me tell you, people are terrible.

I had been trying to keep a small toe in the video business with my 80s Comics series on YouTube, which I thought was fun, especially as people were trapped inside during a pandemic. Nope. I got nothing but complaints and hate mail. Views remained below 1,000 per video. If new viewers showed up, they saw the complaining and left.

To this day, I hear that comic books killed my channel. They didn't, but now you don't get free comic book reviews on YouTube either. Why would I waste my time sharing my love of G.I. Joe with people who hate it?

I canceled 80s Comics and discontinued work on the YouTube channel for the next two years.

2020 went by in a blur, and I did my best to stay off the Internet and focused on work. I worked a lot. A whole lot. I wore a mask. I didn't drink bleach. I didn't go clubbing. It all blends together.

I launched my long-awaited Magnum Skywolf comic book into a vacuum in 2020. After years of development and stop-and-start drawing and writing, it just happened to come out in March 2020, right when the pandemic hit. I struggled to market it. That's the kind of book where I needed people to like me on YouTube to sell it.

My comic book projects took a long time to make, and I couldn't justify the expense without somehow monetizing my time with videos. I focused on non-fiction instead of comics.

By the end of 2020, book sales exploded. It was like living through the 2009 growth of CGR again. Any thought of ever getting back into video was a distant memory.

I don't even remember 2021 because it was more of the same. However, I do remember getting bored with living like a hermit and churning out books from my basement office every day.

That year I grew my hair down to my shoulders and started biking. While half my country rioted against vaccines because politicians and conservative media told them to, I did my best to get one early. It was super-fun to get vaccinated because it felt like I survived the end of days. I credit the long hair and my ability to quote Robocop at any time. Stay out of trouble. I did!

The fact is, I got kinda sick of my daily print routine by the end of 2021 and saw some marketing and advertising challenges on the horizon. For some reason, the shipping on my hardcover books from the printer slowed down and suffered a multi-week delay, and my clothing business was in shambles (Covid crushed my shirt business.)

A bunch of customers asked questions about it, and it occurred to me that I had no social media outreach anymore because I shut it all down. I had no way to communicate that books were shipping slower than usual, so hey, "order well ahead of the holidays!" T-Shirts also took eight weeks to print. These are the incidents that gave rise to Turbo Volcano and by extension, Omega Ronin.

In 2021 I paid a lot for advertising instead of wasting my time making YouTube videos.

I calculated that increasing my advertising expenses would cost the same as buying a bunch of electronic music gear and making Instagram posts. The music gear was actually a good bit cheaper and would retain its value. Therefore, I could try a new approach to marketing.

At the end of 2021, I started "Operation Turbo Volcano" to get back into the entertainment sphere for yuks and marketing exposure. I launched a podcast and started work distributing music to streaming services because why not. All your pennies are belong to Mark.

I was shocked to find that making music was a lot of fun and it reminded me of video editing in the good 'ole days of Classic Game Room. Before everything was awful and sad, making Classic Game Room was really fun! I missed the fun of making.

In early 2022, in addition to new books, I was composing new music under the artist name Turbo Volcano. The first two Turbo Volcano albums are an explosion of creativity after the 2020-2021 lockdown.

It is hard to explain to people how I did this, or why I even wanted to, but I find that making electronic music hits the exact same part of my brain that video editing does. It's the same thing to me. Also, I'm a total gearhead.

While I have no musical training, I do have a good sense of timing and a good ear, and plenty of experience DJing, so I just jumped into music production with both feet. It's like an art project to me.

As expected, music was impossible to market on Instagram and YouTube viewers hated it (though nobody was watching anything I made then anyway.) But, somehow, people discovered it, and Turbo Volcano slowly grew from nothing into a little blip on the radar.

Part of my plan was to use this music on commercials for Ebay and Amazon and whatnot, and while that never came to full fruition, the experience gained from getting tunes up on Spotify and Apple Music led to all kinds of crazy musical experiments.

Unlike the old days, when people would spend big money on physical albums, nowadays people stream music in the background from apps like Spotify. So, really, why not just make as much art as possible and let the market determine how good or bad it is?

I make songs like I edit videos. I compose, chop, polish, and release into the wild to never see again. I'm not planning to play any of them live, I'm not a live musician.

I'm an editor.

My Turbo Volcano experiment evolved into Omega Ronin, the one "band" I made which did turn into something.

I grew up in the 80s and listened to a lot of music. I love 80s pop music. It's a sound I know well, and I figured that instead of trying to make Turbo Volcano sound like 80s music, I'd make an 80s music band and call it Omega Ronin.

Why Omega Ronin? Back in 2019, when I was throwing pencils at the ceiling to come up with project ideas, I made a comic book concept called Omega Ronin because it sounded cool, and I could buy the URL OmegaRonin.com

I was pretty swamped at the time though, and couldn't get the project moving. I needed to focus on other things, so I paused work on the Omega Ronin comic book and moved on to other history projects instead. However, when I needed a cool band name in 2022 for my 80s group, I brought it back.

Omega Ronin is synthwave from the future of 1982!

What is synthwave? In short, synthwave is simple Cyberpunk-inspired songs played on Juno-style keyboard with a ton of reverb. A good starting point is to pick a key, make a few chord progressions and sequences, skin the tune with some delicious-sounding keyboards and viola, synthwave!

Omega Ronin's Halcyon Sunrise dropped in April 2022 and immediately started to pull in some streams from Spotify. The first four Omega Ronin albums are all straight up synthwave experimentation and snapshots in time of me working out the producing bugs.

Turbo Volcano was hard to classify, but Omega Ronin could at least be categorized, though I didn't stay in the predictable and expected synthwave genre for long.

Synthesizer music is, for the most part, about experimentation rather than musicianship. One can treat synthesizers like paintbrushes to paint sounds on a canvas. There's simply no right or wrong way to make electronic music, it's a much more creative platform than video.

In mid-2022, I worked on music a lot so that I could take a break from print for a little while and recharge. I tried mixing some tunes into Gran Turismo gameplay videos to see what would happen.

Being a rock star was not my intention. However, what I immediately liked about the music business was that the people who liked my tunes listened to all of them. It was very similar to my artwork in that respect. If people discovered Omega Ronin, they'd follow it, and stream each of the new albums. Nobody was expecting me to respond to comments or post apology videos about going to college. Music is way more awesome than video.

But music is nearly impossible to market. You can't get out there and say, "listen to this!" because nobody cares unless you're already famous. But what you can do is release your creations into the wild and take a grassroots approach to growing a new audience who discovers it on their own terms.

Also, it's fun. Primarily, it's fun. Honestly, you're not going to get rich making music any more than you will making YouTube videos these days. Streaming revenue across the board is in the dumpster. Don't become a musician to make money (they'll all tell you that.)

My publishing business footed the bill for Omega Ronin who, in return, provided some social media exposure but, more importantly, some small business growth and ideas. Omega Ronin was out there on TikTok, and Instagram, and even YouTube, and none of it worked great, but it was growing a little bit, which is of course more than I could say about Classic Game Room.

After making a bunch of Turbo Volcano and Omega Ronin albums, I started to take music production more seriously and pushed the envelope beyond what I ever thought was possible.

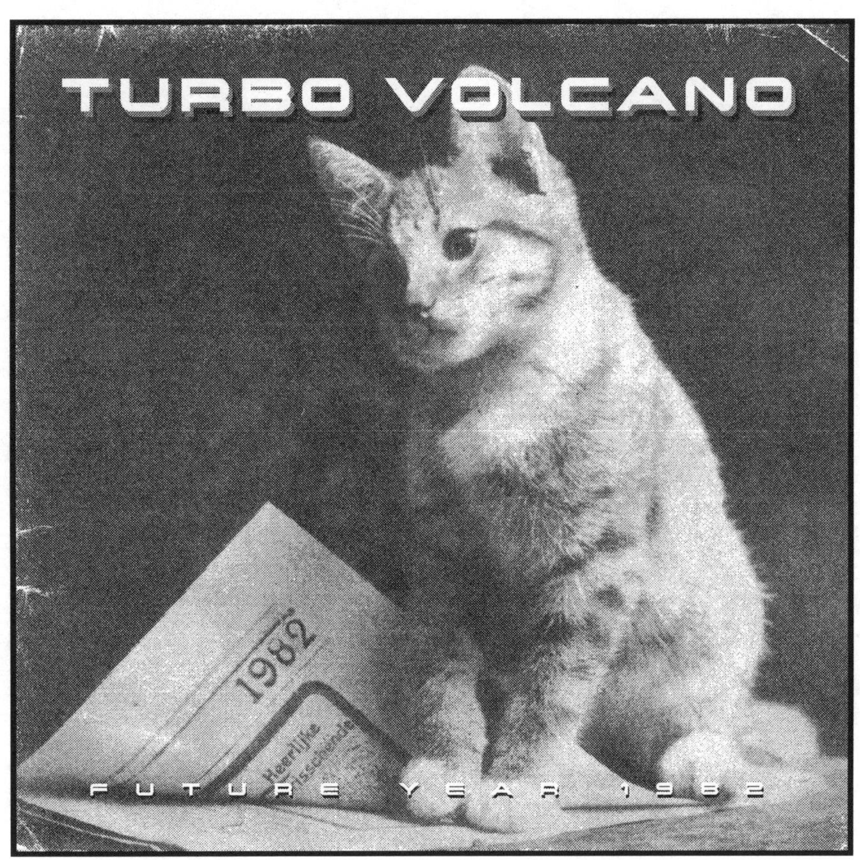

Turbo Volcano: Future Year 1982 (2022.)

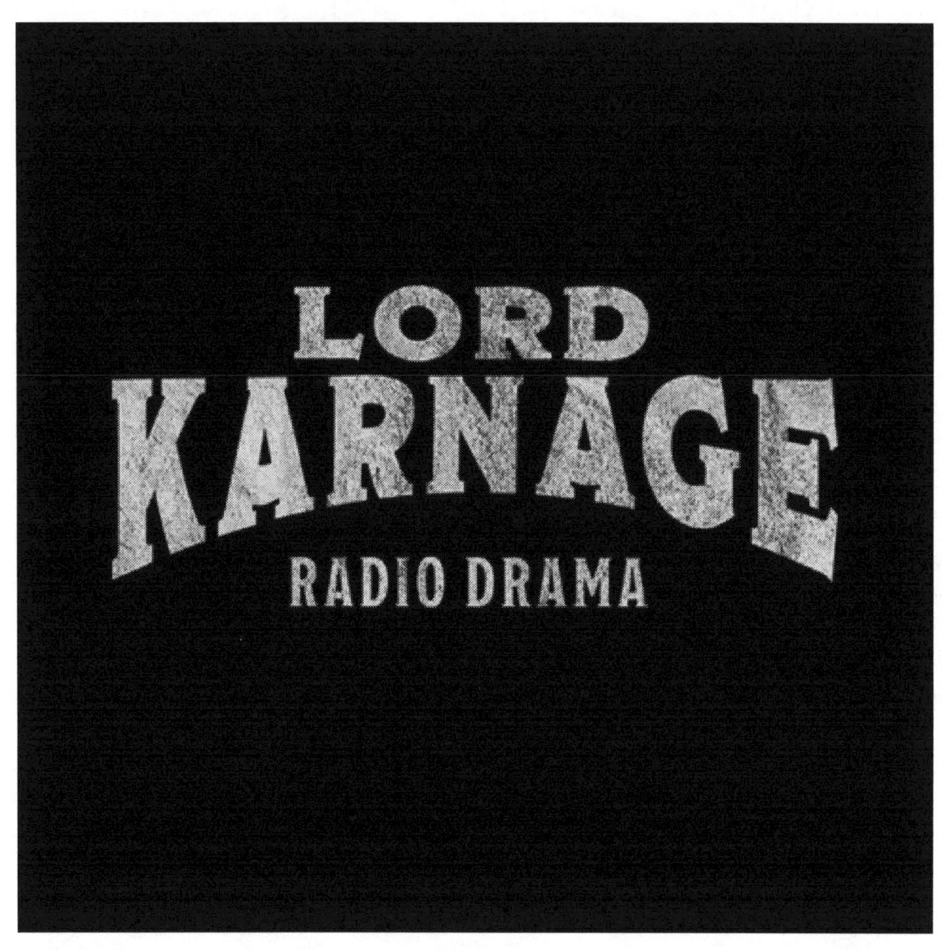
LORD
KARNAGE
RADIO DRAMA

CHAPTER 19
THE PODCASTS AND RADIO DRAMAS

LORD KARNAGE RADIO DRAMA

I love a good radio drama. I don't listen to any podcasts. Does that date me? Maybe. I'll take Orson Welles over Joe Rogan any day.

I released the Lord Karnage Radio Drama in 2018 to promote Lord Karnage in the Valley of Moon Wolves. Perhaps I am biased, but I think it's awesome. For whatever reason, I love doing wacky character voice work and had a great time talking like Lord Karnage, Edit-Station 1 and Wind Squid.

After releasing the Lord Karnage Radio Drama on YouTube, viewers, once again, complained and sent hate mail. I pulled it down and tried it elsewhere, but it didn't work on a website or podcast platform either.

Oh well. If you want a good laugh (or if you want to complain about something creative) you can find the Lord Karnage Radio Drama on CGR Supreme Volume 0.

CLASSIC GAME ROOM THE PODCAST

Podcasting is, for whatever reason, super popular. It's one of those things that I don't fully understand. Back in my day (get off my lawn!) we used to call it radio. But now it's podcasting. Like YouTube videos, there is no barrier to entry, so anything goes on a podcast.

I've tried various Classic Game Room podcasts over the years and usually (I'm 3 for 3) end up regretting that I took the time to do it at all. It's odd that people freak out the moment they hear me speak about something that isn't video games or Star Wars.

"Mark has an opinion on something!? Opinions and thinking are bad! Mark sucks!"

In the end, the only thing I tend to talk about is publishing or production issues. I can talk music mixing and comic books all day, but nobody wants to hear it.

OLD TIME KITCHEN

You don't know this, but I was very close to releasing a big show on YouTube and a podcast called "Old Time Kitchen." I say big because I was thinking about making a Classic Game Room 2085-sized professional production about old fashioned cooking.

In 2022, I worked on a series of antique cookbooks and called the project Old Time Kitchen. I even bought the URL and planned to film a cooking show! Can you imagine me wearing an 1890s getup with a bowler hat and mustache cooking antique meals in a black and white kitchen?

Think a semi-serious but also comedic cooking show with goofy old-time jazz music, film grain, and the occasional miniature showing a house burning to the ground.

I talked to a few locations about filming rights and specced out the gear and what it would cost in microphones, lighting, and cooking raw materials. It would have been, sadly, very expensive. Also, I'm not a good cook (which I thought would make it even funnier.)

The final decision came down to me thinking seriously about audience reaction and how this expensive show would play on YouTube. The old audience would probably hate it, and I could see younger Gen Z viewers not getting the joke at all.

So, before I spent a dime, I stopped looking into it and tabled the idea. I recorded a podcast about it, but also felt it wasn't what an audience would want.

A few music tracks were released for the series, and the books are in print. These are serious books, mind you, filled with serious 19th century recipes. Not for the casual cook.

But I'll leave you with an 1890s image of me wearing a mustache and setting myself on fire while cooking elk testicles with pine beer and fermented duck eggs. How awesome would that have been? Moose scrotum for the win.

CLASSIC GAME ROOM ADVENTURES

If you take a trip back to 2011, you'll find a time when I could make anything and people enjoyed it. Remember VU Ramblings and Classic Game Room Adventures?

I got bored talking games *every* day and tried to mix it up with some silly abstract recording concepts. VU Ramblings was just that, me rambling.

Classic Game Room Adventure is the series where Moon Wolves came from. I wrote a story and read it in each video, but each video ended with multiple choices like a Choose Your Own Adventure book.

Viewers at the time thought it was amusing, but it didn't win over many new fans. I ended up filming Ben 10 toy reviews instead because they got 10,000,000 views which was, you know, the business objective....

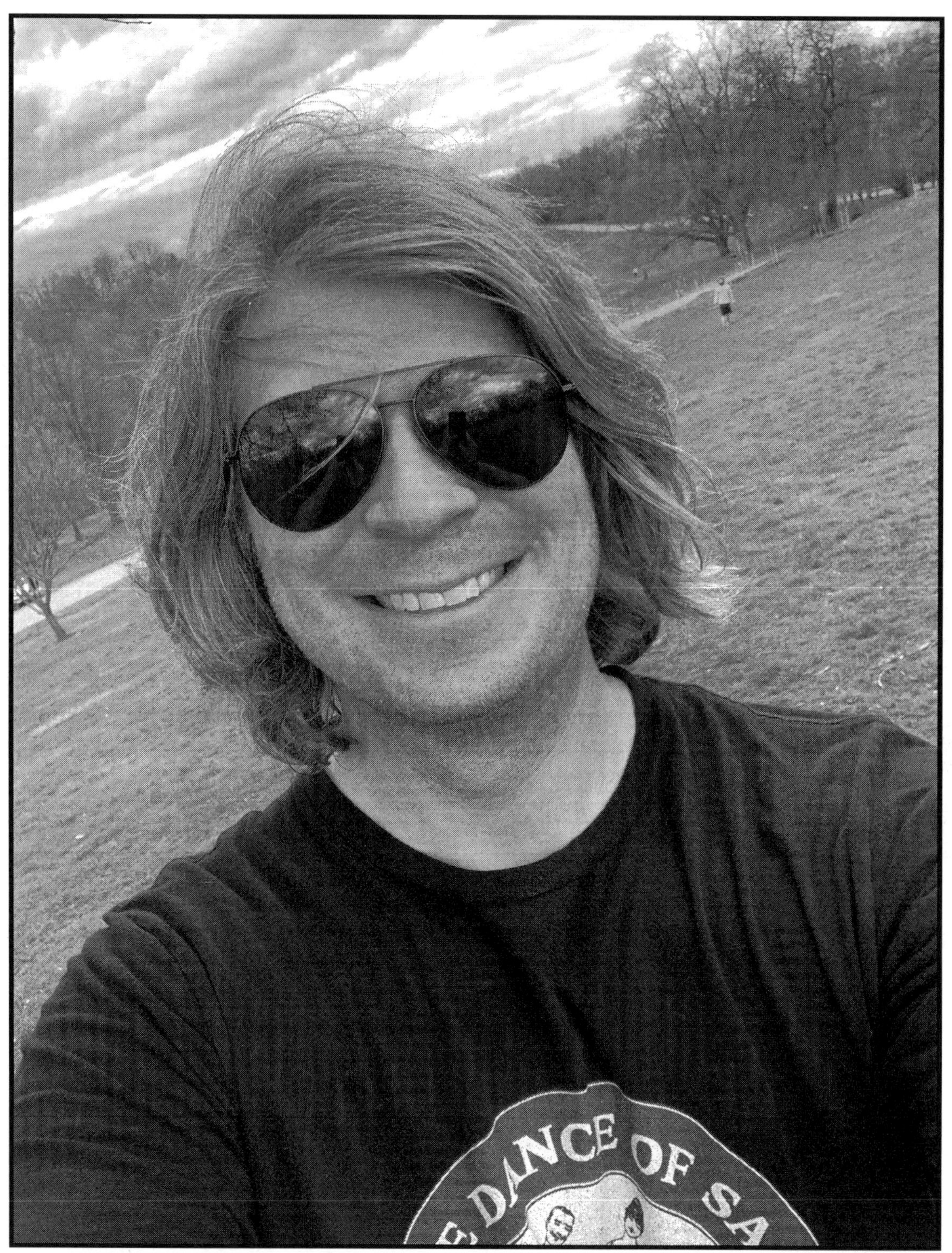

Pandemic Hair Mark from 2021.

CHAPTER 20
ONE LAST TRY

When 2022 came to a close I looked over all the numbers and was pleased to see another record sales year for CGR Publishing but frustrated that the marketing costs continued to climb. As more and more people got into self-publishing, the cost of selling each product grew. Pandemic-era layoffs led to a lot of work-from-home self-publishing startups.

There is only so much space on your screen, and companies like Amazon and Google know how to maximize paying for ad space in that limited real estate. It got competitive quickly. Only a handful of people were self-publishing books in 2017, but by 2022 it was much busier.

What to do? I could raise prices, but production costs behind the scenes climb right along with the marketing rate increases. I could spend more on marketing, but that ran the risk of eliminating all profits. By the end of year 2022, this was starting to turn into a serious battle for the retailer sites.

It reminded me of our DVD business back in 2006. We had good products back then, but we had to fight tooth and nail to market them.

Uh-oh... do you see where this is heading? What was my solution to selling the CGR DVD in 2007?

Fucking YouTube! (Screamed in the Dark Helmet voice... "I hate yogurt!")

Well, before I tried YouTube again, I tip-toed back into TikTok and Instagram.

I've since changed my tune on this, but in 2023 my approach was to get back into social media marketing with my new audio and video style thanks to Omega Ronin. Getting back into social media was about as much fun as eating a mouthful of sand, but it didn't cost much so what the hey...

By 2023, "free" social media marketing turned into pushing on a string. It's awful because they (the big companies) want you to pay to "boost your post." Followers hate advertising, and they hate marketing. The marketing posts never get any traction because nobody is excited about an advertisement, and the social media platform's A.I. sniffs out any advertising and squashes it because they want you to pay for it. So, in the end, it's a lot of work for nothing.

But it's better than nothing... maybe? That's the thing. Social media marketing sucks, but at least it's free and (maybe) better than nothing. There is always time associated with it and the time isn't free and there's 8 billion people doing it on their phones. That's the tradeoff.

In a very roundabout way, I started tinkering with TikTok and Instagram Reels and ended up digging some Classic Game Room stuff out of storage and it was kinda fun. I didn't end YouTube on a good note, and I loathed the idea of smiling on camera and getting social again, but I missed the technical stuff. Printing books and writing is cool, but I'm passionate about mixing and editing.

Even though there was a lot of complaining, people had also been asking for Classic Game Room to return for years, and maybe now that they saw how awful the rest of the video landscape had become, they might get into it. And maybe this would be the answer to my advertising dilemma.

However bad video was in 2017, it looked to be a billion times worse in 2023 with influencers, artificial intelligence, conspiracy theorists, gurus, racist podcasts, and every other clickbait piece of trash out there. Surely, people might acknowledge that a well-crafted show like Classic Game Room was worth watching.

Additionally, it occurred to me that 2023 was the 24th anniversary of the show, and 2024 would be the 25th anniversary! People would be so excited to see it again! Wow, Mark is so clever! He can count!

That's how Classic Game Room came back for a final season. This is the real reason, not the reason that YouTube gatekeepers made up. I couldn't care less about the fame, and the money wasn't there anyway. I brought the show back for marketing and because I thought I could sell Blu-Rays and glassware. Period. And if it had worked, it would have been a huge success.

So, as I saw it, I could spend a full year on a new batch of history books, or I could see about rebooting the show and trying to use it as my front-line marketing platform.

Keep in mind that by now, CGR Publishing (and Inecom, by extension) was bigger than "Classic Game Room" ever was.

But, I totally failed to see that nobody else saw that. They saw Classic Game Room as being big because it was well-known on YouTube and looked big, even though it wasn't big because the channel was broken.

Come on! It's the oldest Internet video game review show ever, and it celebrates 25 years in 2024! What perfect timing to launch a new product line. I totally thought that some people out there would spread the word and create some buzz. Maybe, for the first time since Agent 00400z, some big media outlets would pay attention.

The instant I started posting things the hate mail flooded in and the misinformation machine started up again. Suddenly, I heard from angry viewers that I betrayed them and they'd never watch it again no matter what I did. I guess that going out of business was very inconvenient for them.

My favorite conspiracy theory is the one where I was dying, and this was my cry for help. (I'm not dead yet! I'm feeling much better...)

Now, I didn't think an ad-supported YouTube show would work in 2023 because it didn't work before, and YouTube was more cluttered with gaming content, live streaming, and angry game reviews than ever. But I thought people might appreciate a breath of fresh air and some high production values, and a guy who knows his stuff.

However, none of this would mean squat unless I had new products to sell, which meant that I had to make a new Blu-Ray. Thankfully, Classic Game Room 2085 season 1 was perfect for Blu-Ray. This was all early spring, 2023.

Unlike the old reviews, Classic Game Room 2085 was professionally shot and would totally benefit from a Blu-Ray release. Additionally, its 12 hours of footage, combined with copious extras, could be evenly spread over four discs to make a terrific collector's set for new and old fans alike.

Also, people had been asking for it. A lot of viewers never got a chance to see it when it aired on Amazon five years earlier, so why the heck not?

Here we go.... Instead of digging into World's Fair research for another year, I set history books aside and went to work on making Classic Game Room 2085 Season 1 Blu-Rays. I even planned to shoot another season, Classic Game Room 2085 Season 2: The 25th Anniversary Blu-Ray set.

It took a few months to prepare, but I hatched a plan to use Kickstarter to fund not just season 1 Blu-Rays, but season 2 Blu-Rays and all related production expenses. It was expensive, but I had been getting some good feedback. After easing back into Instagram and TikTok, my marketing research showed that there was some demand and that, indeed, some viewers really missed the show.

I launched the Kickstarter for CGR 2085 Season 1&2 Blu-Rays in April and was immediately disappointed. There was an initial wave of people who LOVED it, but then it stalled and got stuck at 15% which meant that I needed to market it. So, I tried to market on Instagram, and ran into the familiar wall of angry gatekeepers who did their best to dissuade people from buying it.

The price was $80,000 to fund production of two Blu-Ray sets, and cover about six months of filming, new hardware, and post-production. It was a bargain, but I don't think that anyone else saw it that way.

I couldn't market the Season 1 and 2 Blu-Ray for shit because I struggled to message why I needed $80k to make a video game review show. Even at $80,000, it would have barely broken even. But, nobody gets this stuff anymore when smartphones do it for free... It was a dumb plan.

"Why should we give you money when so and so is doing it for free?"

It's... I mean, it's not really the same thing.... "CGR is like a giant TV show with a disco ball!"

So, I canceled the initial Kickstarter, which was free to do and didn't cost anyone a dime. No harm done. That's one of the good things about Kickstarter. Part of me thought I put the cart before the horse and needed to demonstrate what the show might look like. The other part of me instantly regretted doing it at all.

I retooled my plan and launched a much smaller Kickstarter to cover some of the costs required to make the Classic Game Room 2085 Season 1 Blu-Ray set and left it at that. Assuming that season 1 would get funded, I could then make Classic Game Room 2085 Season 2 for an end of year 2024 launch on my own dime.

To make a long story short, the Classic Game Room 2085 Season 1 Kickstarter made it easily and helped to cover about half of the manufacturing costs, which were extremely high for a four-Blu-Ray collector's set that runs 15 hours long. I slowly started work on Season 2 photography and reprinted the classic Classic Game Room beer glasses.

The glassware sold out immediately. CGR Glassware is the best glassware and everyone knows this.

But my Instagram marketing struggled, I lost followers, and TikTok wasn't growing at all, which left only one platform to spread the word.

YouTube.

Nobody on my end was happy about this (least of all, me,) but I tried it anyway.

In mid-2023 I decided to make a few YouTube reviews, cheap ones, but reviews nonetheless. The Ninja Golf review and Tempest 2000 dropped on YouTube over the summer of 2023 and were well received by viewers who seemed surprised to see them. They were throwbacks to the original series, and I had fun making them. They weren't too taxing on my schedule, considering I knew the games pretty well.

From there I tried a few other YouTube reviews like Flight Simulator and Diofield Chronicles; one game was free, and the other borrowed from the library. If I could keep costs low, and get people engaged in this show again, then maybe I could market the Blu-Rays. Glassware started to sell again, which was nice.

To be honest, I hadn't been playing games much at that point and had fun getting back into stuff like Diablo IV and Starfield. Viewers seemed to enjoy the reviews, but the numbers were TERRIBLE

How does a channel with 400,000 subscribers get 3,000 views on a video? Like... what's even happening?

Just show me some growth. Just a little bit. Anything. Anything but going backward.

I'll jump ahead a bit and say that between early 2023 and early 2024, Classic Game Room's viewership didn't grow at all. Not one bit. Across all platforms including YouTube, TikTok, and Instagram, CGR's viewership either stalled or went backward after months of hard work and video production. Thousands of dollars in production time vaporized overnight.

Glassware, t-shirts, and Blu-Rays helped to cover the loss. It'll turn a profit in the long run.

But what was supposed to be a more efficient use of social media to avoid paying a fortune in advertising expenses actually ended up being an even more expensive way of promoting a product for which there was, as it turns out, marginal interest.

Additionally, I found that the production times were far greater than I had expected. Each video took days to produce, not hours. Even the cheap, simple videos tied my production and business schedule into knots.

> "Atari Fanboy Mark is back and having a good time shooting cool stuff with an Atari 2600 and a few cans of Pabst Blue Ribbon. Meanwhile, there are stacks of book orders piling up and marketing copy sitting there unfinished collecting dust. Producer Mark is not pleased."

In the olden days, I had a marketing team doing the marketing, a business team doing the business, and a huge stockpile of gameplay saved up on hard drives. I had a routine and a rhythm.

By 2023 I was doing pretty much everything by myself or managing contractors. I had no stockpile of gameplay. No hard drives filled with footage. There were only so many nights I could stay up to 2 am and record something only to release it for 3,000 views on YouTube.

I got tired fast. And nobody was watching.

It's hard to get into a rhythm when it's not working.

Additionally, I was trying to plan filming for the CGR 2085 Season 2 Blu-Ray collection. And with no views and no growth on YouTube, what's the point of sinking time and money into CGR 2085 Season 2 when nobody is going to buy it? I can't even get people to watch it for free.

Well, I decided to see it through because I made the Season 1 Blu-Rays and the Blu-Rays are awesome. As a general rule, I don't have a problem selling a good product. I just need to tell people about it...

Let's mix it up and make some NOISE!
EDF! EDF! EDF!

Heading into '24 I planned to celebrate the show's 25th anniversary by putting a streamlined version of Classic Game Room 2085 Season 2 on YouTube and marketing the hell out of it on my socials to generate buzz. Like fighting space bees in a miniskirt, I knew it would face an uphill battle that required skill, finesse, and a jetpack.

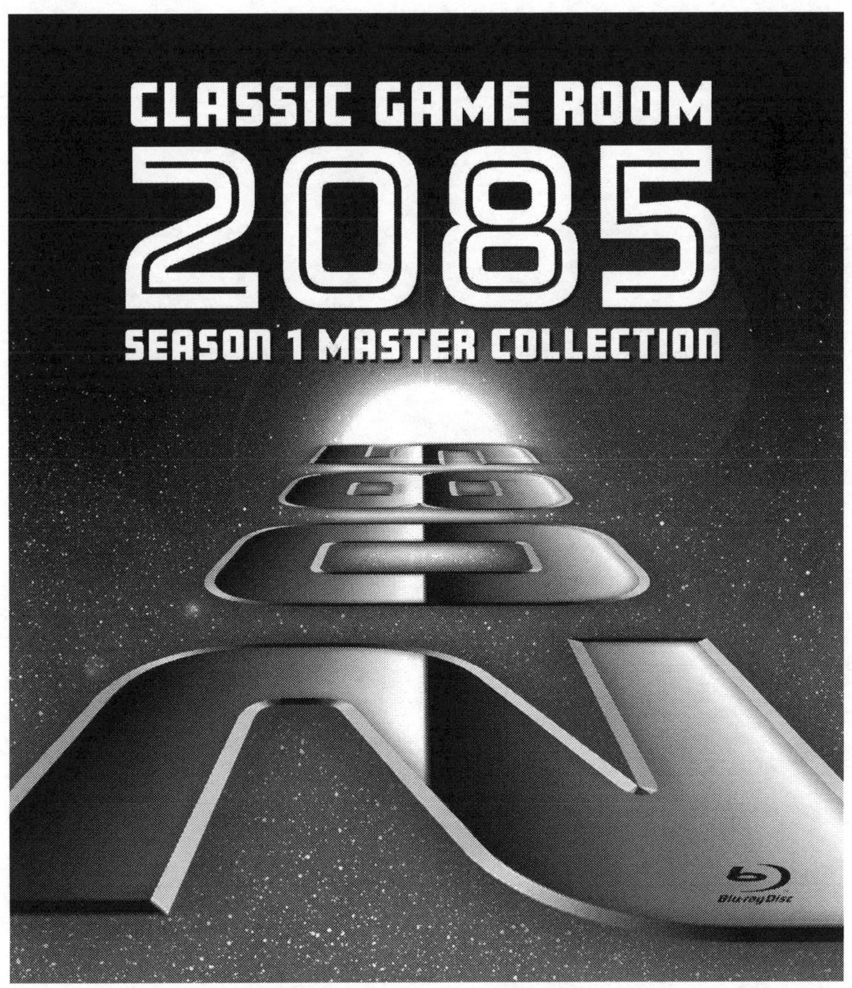

Classic Game Room 2085 Season 1 Blu-Ray from 2023.

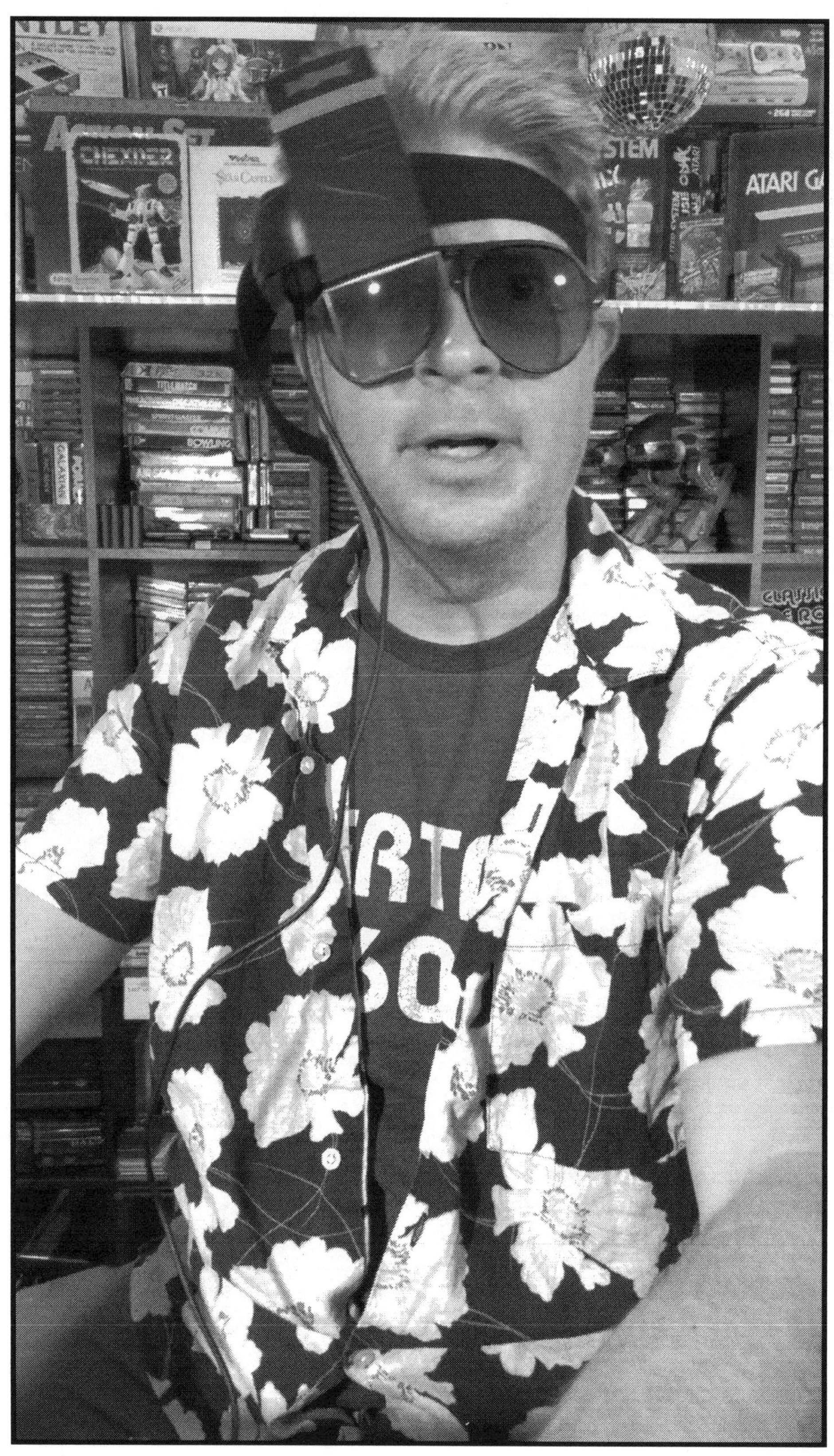

Mark on the CGR 2085 Season 2 set with the R-Zone (2023.)

CHAPTER 21
ENGAGE DISCO!

Let's back up a bit.

I ended 2023 by taking a few weeks in my warehouse space to unpack a few things in between shipping sessions. I bought a few gizmos for production and cobbled together a small set out of pieces from the old CGR 2085 set. I even bought new disco balls. The camera gear was left over from marketing videos, and while it wasn't nearly as good as my old Canon 1D, it was good enough.

In December 2023 I filmed a bunch of Classic Game Room 2085 Season 2 segments and started to edit them together with gameplay and music and was pleasantly surprised to see they turned out great! I was very happy with 2085 Season 2, even though I knew the studio needed some more work and that I'd have to buy another microphone for on-screen footage (which I held off on until I saw response.) I used my iPhone to record the studio audio.

Like CGR Infinity a few years earlier, I would launch Classic Game Room 2085 on YouTube on New Year's Eve when people would be ready to PARRRRTAY! A bad omen, I acknowledge, considering how poorly CGR Infinity did.

December 31. 6pm Eastern Standard Time. IT'S CGR 2085 TIME!!!

The first episode of Classic Game Room 2085 Season 2 dropped on YouTube. Then I went to bed.

The first episode was about the Evercade. It explained some of the CGR back story, received a good response from viewers, but had hardly any views after a week. Considering the time that I spent promoting it and marketing it, I was shocked to see it didn't even pass 8,000 views.

The next two episodes were also well received but faced declining viewership, the exact opposite of what needed to happen.

By the third episode of CGR 2085, which earned 4,000 views by its third week, I had to immediately rethink the entire plan.

This was on target to be my single worst product release since World War 1 American Legacy. The show that people said they wanted, on a channel with 400,000 subscribers, couldn't even hit 5,000 views for free. I totally misinterpreted the marketing data.

I stopped production instantly, canceled my plans to finish the studio, and slashed production times on the remaining videos by moving the live segments into my music studio which had a good microphone setup.

My family, friends, and marketing contractors are looking at me like "what the fuck are you doing playing game reviewer again?"

They weren't wrong. I'm sitting there holding my hands up in the air like "I swear to God, on paper, this should have worked."

Curses! Foiled again!

Now, I would be more upset about this were it not for the fact that 2023 was yet another record year for publishing, and that Omega Ronin had quadrupled in size behind the scenes and was generating a few bucks of sales and ad revenue without the crushing overhead that my video work faced. Additionally, new books were in development.

The complete collapse of Classic Game Room 2085 Season 2 didn't really affect much, but still.... really?

I mean, it's good to know for sure that either the channel was totally blacklisted, I suck ass at making videos, or that the market is so completely different than it ever was before... or all of the above.

Overall, the response from longtime fans was good, but again, where is everyone? Are they on Twitch or TikTok, or did they move on? Are they watching Pornhub instead of YouTube, or did they all grow up and have families and watch Disney+?

Once again, the data didn't add up. How were other people, making similar content getting thousands of times the viewership? My competitors were raking in millions of views, tens of millions! I'm bringing in less than 5,000. And low views mean fewer Blu-Ray sales than expected, even though glassware actually sold better than expected.

Cheers!

I'll happily take the shovel and put myself out to pasture, though.

Rather than losing any more money on it, I ended the show outright and tried to salvage the footage that I recorded by mixing it into smaller videos, and then some music videos, and lastly a podcast.

I even tried to ease the brand into the video game music business after few people showed interest in soundtracks, but the time required to set up a new marketing plan proved too expensive, and YouTube viewers, of course, wanted none of it (that plan evolved into comic book soundtracks, instead.)

Without a functioning YouTube "gaming" channel, I can't do anything in the gaming business. That's the end of it.

By 2024, I didn't have time to figure it out. It only took a few weeks to remind me that I had a print business to run, and that print business was much bigger than video.

As Captain Kirk said. "Know how everything on your starship works."

The same can be said about running a company.

Based on my 1999 narration-over-gameplay formula, Classic Game Room proved to be obsolete, time consuming to make, and too expensive to produce. I couldn't market it, and even the fans who loved it seemed frustrated that they couldn't get the word out either. Nobody cared.

Somewhere in there, I had the idea to release Classic Game Room as an endless live stream called the FOREVER STREAM. That was actually a good idea, so I'll pat myself on the back for that one.

But I couldn't justify the expense to hire someone to manage the comments field on YouTube which filled up with hate, complaints, racism, and misinformation that turned viewers and potential customers away.

I can't figure out how other people run their business on YouTube. It must cost a small fortune to constantly reply to everything, moderate every comments field, and get the word out to TikTok, Facebook, Instagram, X, and Twitch...

You know what...

I'll just stick to books and albums.

For what it's worth, unlike the 2017 era, the show's struggle to reach an audience didn't disrupt my company too much. A few viewers even sent tips (thank you, I do appreciate it!) But, alas, there's nothing I can do about YouTube. I can't make it work.

Even in the future, nothing works!

Especially in the future, nothing works!

If I can't market this thing on its 25th anniversary, then I can't market it at all. A few viewers were upset to see it slow down and stop, but most people didn't care. I'm not sure that I cared anymore, either. It was a bad idea.

The loss of time and money killed the fun that I had producing it. Thus, I canceled the second season Blu-Ray.

I stopped working on the new 25th anniversary designs. I canceled the few convention appearances I had set up to celebrate the show's 25th and cleansed my schedule of anything and everything tied to Classic Game Room.

I'll say this much. Watching Classic Game Room 2085 flop on YouTube, in addition to watching my work on TikTok and Instagram disappear into a void, helped me to re-focus on products that would succeed beyond the dystopia of Internet "content creation."

My dad and I still have lunch together regularly and chat about the good ole' days and what's going on now. Like me, he is also confused about why people seem entranced by an Internet monopoly instead of good, professional content. Then we change the conversation to mainframe computers and trains.

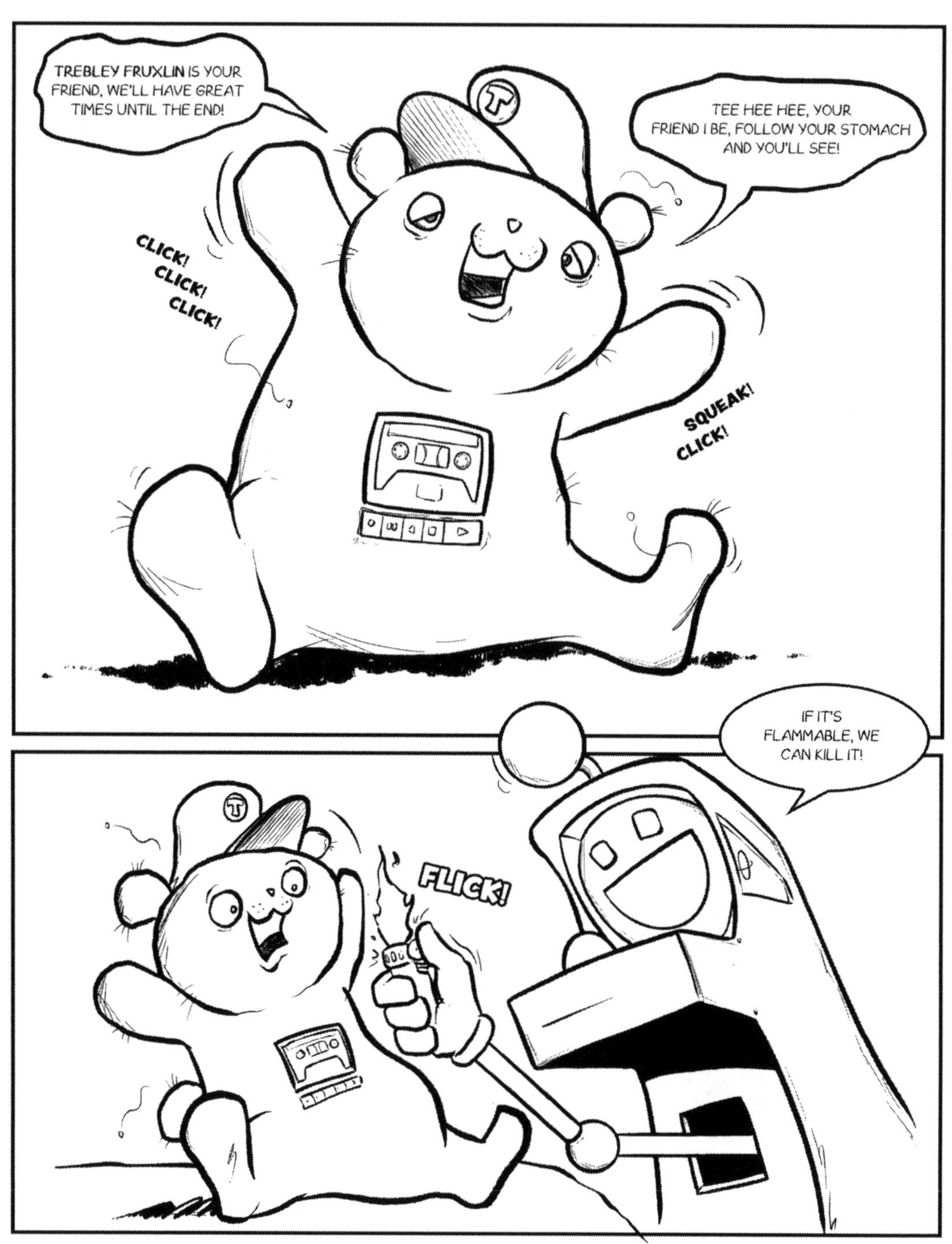

Trebley Fruxlin and Edit-Station 1 in Ethel the Cyborg Ninja #3 (2024.)

CHAPTER 22
RISE OF THE MACHINES

"Mark, I'd like to buy one of your books, but I don't like the way you treated YouTube."

- Fan email.

That's right. I was mean to the poor, multi-billion dollar company that spreads hate for profit. It's true.

Here we are in 2024 (as of this writing.) Is the game making good videos, or proving loyalty to a giant social media platform? I think you know the answer. I think we all know the answer, but what is the solution?

On my end, we discontinued posting videos on YouTube, deleted the app, and stopped uploading content to all of the of other social media sites. It has been a marketing challenge because we aren't reaching people.

But I told myself, and everyone I work with, this is the challenge I prefer. **We love this challenge**. If we figure out marketing without social media then we can keep that knowledge forever instead of being blocked, banned, blacklisted, rendered obsolete, or thrown off said shitty social media platforms.

Some people are great at it. Or so it seems... how much do they pay? Can you believe what you see? Are they even real human beings or computerized images?

In 1999 we had to spam forums, print stickers, make cold calls, pay for website ads, and run around screaming. You know what, that's a solution. There's a punk rock feeling to slapping stickers on phone poles.

I like that feeling.

I still run an email list like it's 1996 and it works better than 400,000 followers on YouTube. It doesn't work as well as being a successful influencer or Internet star, but I'm not going to block me from my own email list.

What does it take to succeed in social media? A completely different skill set than being an artist or writer.

Charisma helps. Being attractive helps, so does being persistent. Luck is also a huge factor.

You don't win battles with luck.

Also, do you know who is going to be really good at being charismatic, attractive, and persistent?

Artificial intelligence.

It's already there, but it's only going to get better at impersonating the lowest hanging fruit; easily stereotyped people saying what you want to hear.

PROMPT: Beautiful white woman with blonde hair and blue eyes talking about her fabulous weekend vacation in the Bahamas. Include pictures of her wearing a pink bikini.

PROMPT: 20-something gamer guy in black hoodie, wearing a white pro gamer headset and ballcap surrounded by blue LED lights talking about how awesome Call of Duty Ghosts is.

PROMPT: Angry middle-aged white guy with no neck and gray stubble in camo hat railing against liberals.

PROMPT: North Korean dictator talking about how missiles are on their way to the American West Coast right now.

Have fun, everyone!! Because with only two companies controlling all of the pipelines to your phone, this is what you're going to get. You'll get what they feed you. Suck it up.

With people asking A.I. "how do I make the most popular YouTube video?" you're going to have people, with literally no production skills or charisma of their own, competing against experienced professionals in the same space for the same pennies.

Professionals will get frustrated, but they'll stick with it because they have no choice. To do something else is to betray their YouTube audience. Before they go out of business though, they'll start using A.I. prompts, too.

It's already happening that way, and it has been for a while, but it's going to get even more absurd.

It didn't have to be like this, but it is. It is because most people who want to get famous will show fealty to their social media monopoly of choice to remain in good favor, because that's what matters to the audience that they're trying to impress.

"KAHHHNNNNNN!!!!!"

You've probably seen the trend through the latter half of my YouTube-era struggles, and it's like 95% not playing by YouTube's rules and not doing what was expected of me within the bullshit made-up laws of YouTube (and social media at large.)

When I started doing this stuff way back when, there was no "creator economy." Now, there is.

A creator economy is not necessarily a bad thing. The creator economy gives a lot of people a break that they might not have otherwise had.

But there are also no laws or legal protection for "creators" in the same way that there are for employees of actual companies. So, basically, you're on your own.

If you work at a fast food restaurant, they are required by law to treat you properly, not discriminate based on age, race, and sex, and give you certain rights and benefits. As a "content creator," you have none of that. So, basically, McDonald's has to do the right thing. YouTube does not because you aren't an employee even though you're called a "YouTuber."

You'll probably make more money at McDonald's too, because most people want to be YouTube stars and McDonald's has to pay more than they used to.

In conclusion: There is an entire (and growing) segment of the population working jobs with no employee protection, no insurance, and no good path forward beyond constant trying and persistence.

This segment of the population is competing against computers that can do it faster, better, and cheaper than they can to appease an audience who craves the most easily digestible bits of entertainment than they can watch in a 5-second window and then rapidly swipe away from.

But it gets worse. Let's talk about what I like to call "the theory of relativity," meaning, it's all relative.

So, you're an American and your YouTube channel or TikTok earns $100 a month. Ok, that's good extra spending cash, right? You can buy a copy of Call of Duty Ghosts, a cheap headset, and a few beers to enjoy over the weekend. Awesome.

You'll starve to death if that's your full-time job, though.

Now, let's say that you're from a third-world country that we, as Americans, can't even find on a map. There's a lot of them.

In that country, $100 is going to feed a family of ten for a month and probably put a roof over their head. Those people will murder you to get that $100. They'll work harder and smarter and more efficiently to get that $100.

For you, American, it's just another beer. Or maybe that's just me. The point is, it's all relative.

At this point, you've either thrown this book into the fire or you're nodding while staring pensively into a cup of herbal tea while New Order plays in the background (aging Gen Xers represent!)

I'd offer some suggestions, but since I'm a maybe somewhat liberal anti-Nazi middle-aged educated white guy who can quote Dolemite word-for-word, I'm everybody's asshole. Nobody wants to play with Mr. Bungle.

These social media platforms are worse than drugs. They get you hooked, they get you addicted, and they keep you coming back for more. It doesn't appear than anyone really likes them, so why do we keep using them? When is the last time you heard anyone (above the age of 12) say "Wow, I really like YouTube Shorts!"

Does that mean you shouldn't try to be a "content creator?" I'm not going to say it outright, but consider that you could also spend that time watching Dolemite so that you can quote it at parties, too.

"But I wanna get famous! Waaaaaa!"
- Edit-Station 1

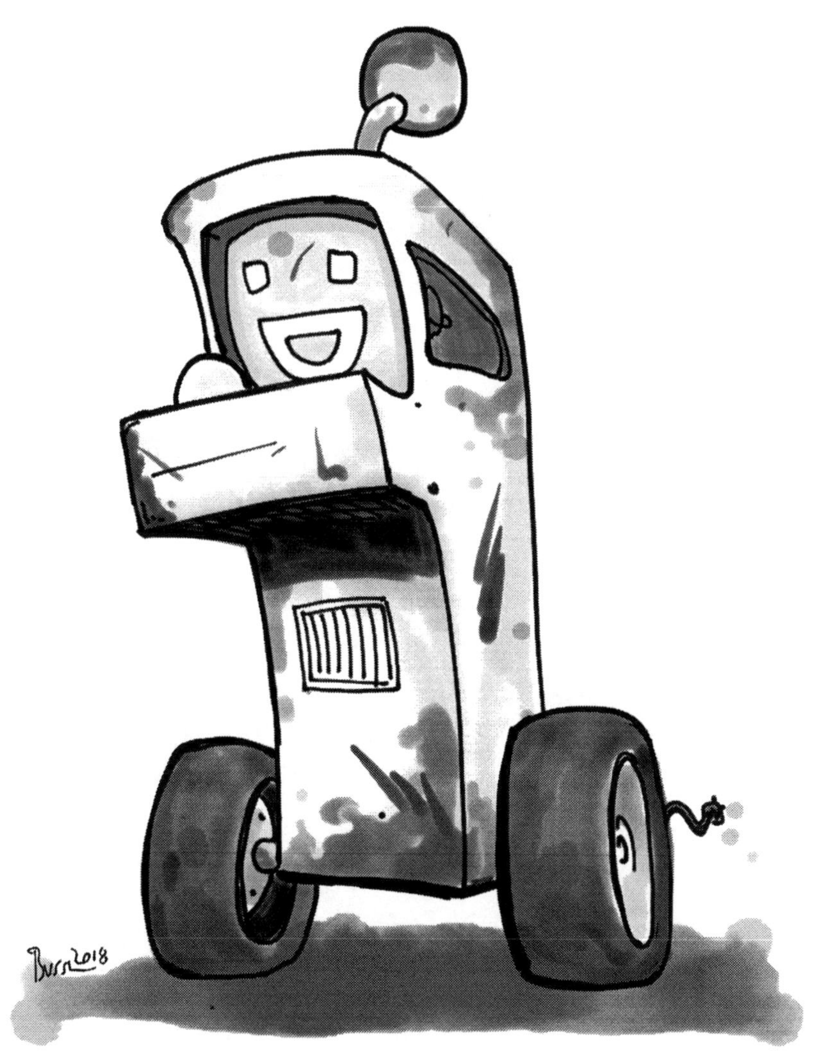

Edit-Station 1 from Lord Karnage in the Valley of Moon Wolves (2018)

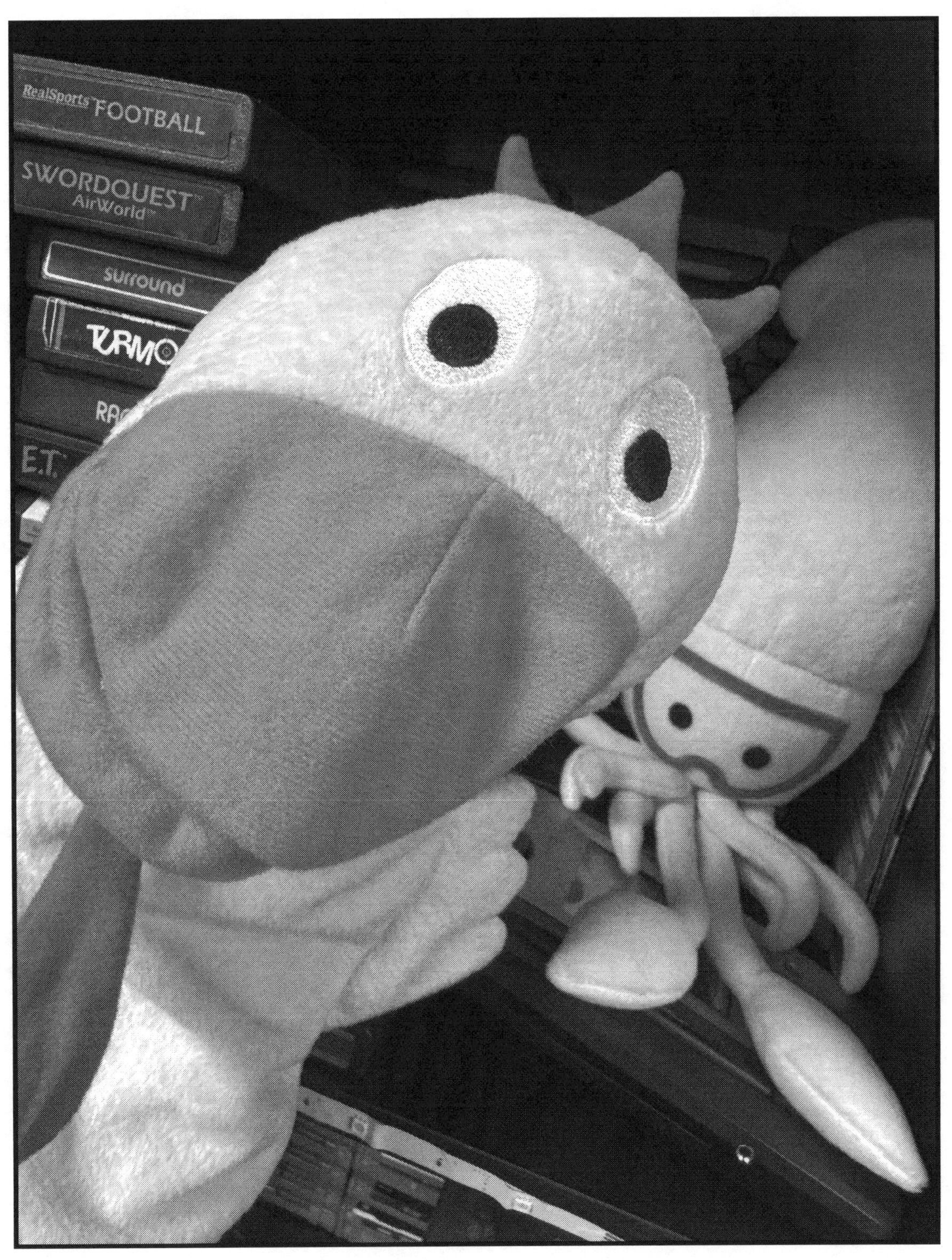

Heyzoos puppet and Wind Squid plushie on set in 2024.

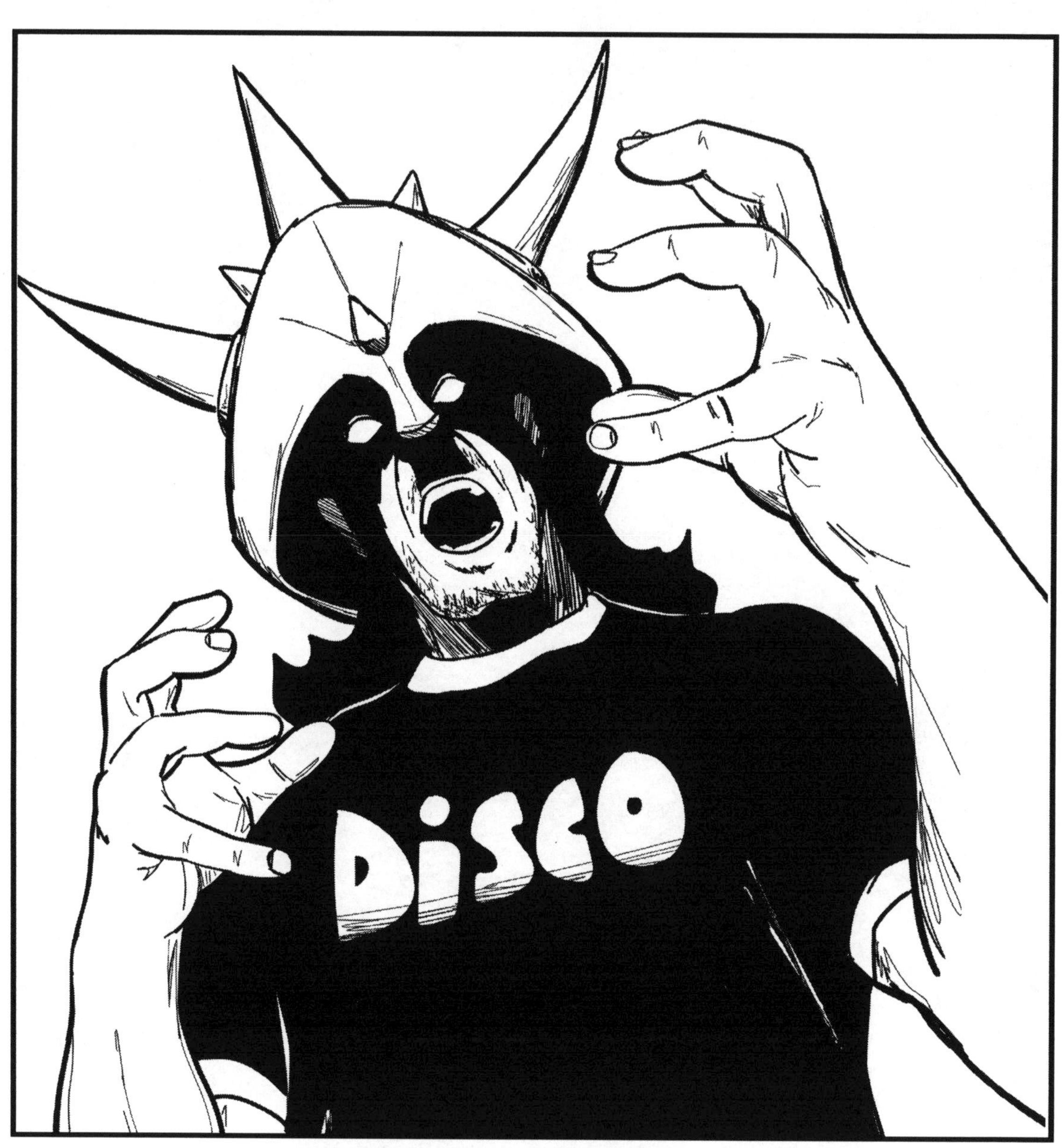

Lord Karnage (2018.)

CHAPTER 23
BACK TO WHERE IT BEGAN

I started writing this book with a 25th Anniversary celebration in my head. Not only would I tell the story of Classic Game Room and the olden days of FromUSAlive, but we could all collectively cheer as the show embarks on its next quarter century of reviews!

What actually happened is that I ended up clarifying a lot of stuff that has been bouncing around in my head for the past decade or so.

I learned a lot of stuff in business school that applies to what I've been through, and writing this book pulled it out of the cobwebs in my damaged brain, so I wrote it down.

Know Your Customers.

This one might seem obvious, but who are your customers? More specifically, who are my customers? Who *were* my customers?

One can always look at their YouTube demographics and whatever, but that's doesn't always answer the question. Let's break this down into three groups:

1. People who like video games.
2. People who like YouTube.
3. People who like Mark's Artwork.

This has changed over time, and I think it is best explained with some of those fancy Venn diagrams.

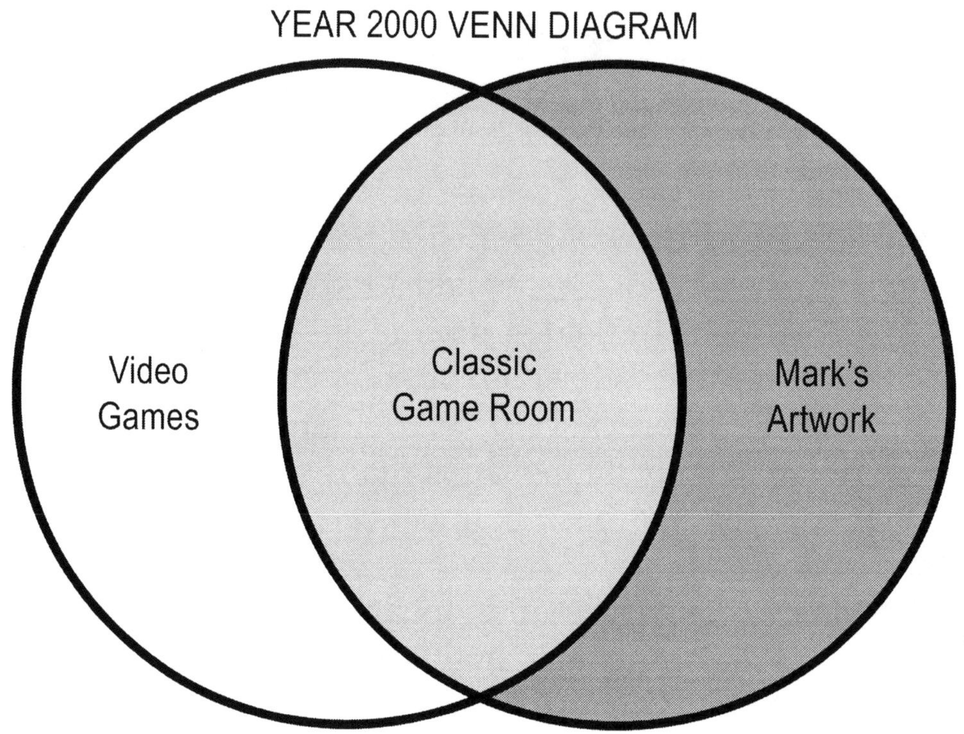

In the year 2000, there was no YouTube. People who discovered The Game Room were into video games, as represented by the left circle.

I'll draw another circle representing my artwork on the right, because I produced the show, and I also started to get known for my obnoxious and horrible comic book, Agent 0040oz.

In between "video games" and "Mark's artwork" were people who enjoyed Classic Game Room.

And in 2000, nobody cared if The Game Room was on FromUSAlive or any other website. That makes this Venn diagram very simple.

Let's fast-forward to the year 2010 when YouTube began to emerge as the most popular video platform.

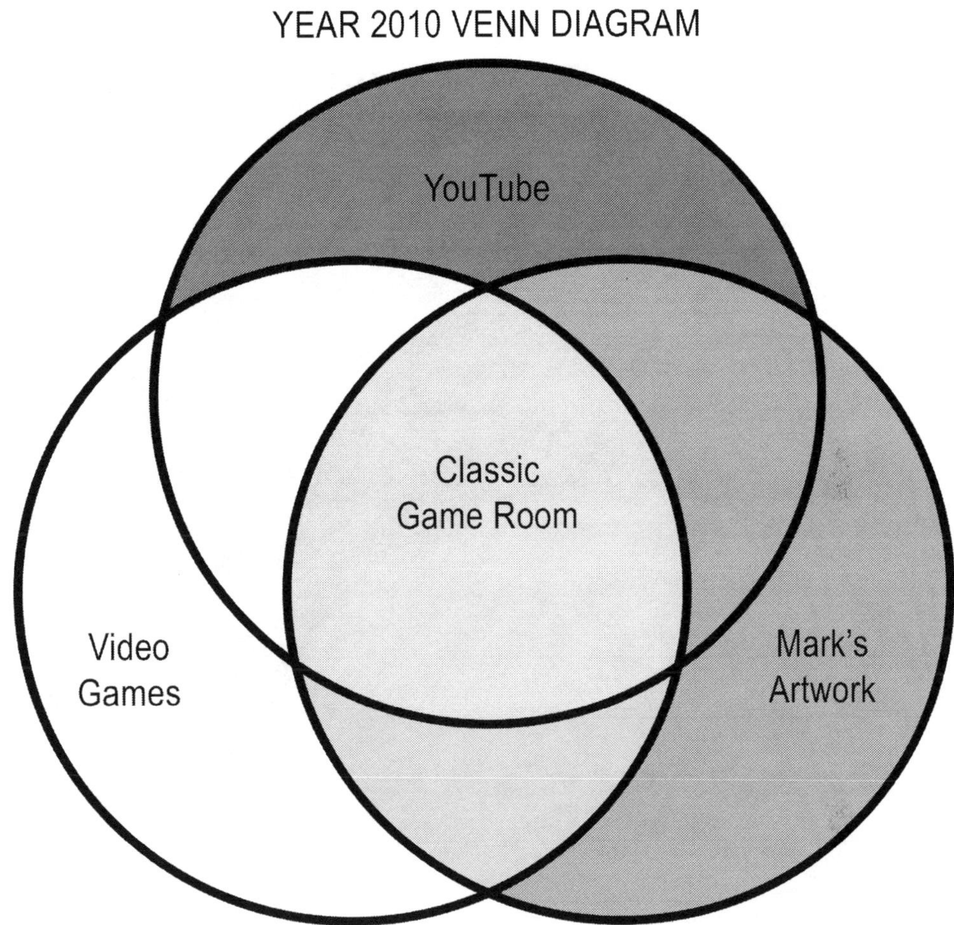

The diagram above shows that YouTube exploded as not just a platform upon which to host videos, but also a subject of interest itself. From my perspective, this is what 2010 looked like.

You dig?

So, in 2010 there were people who liked video games, people who liked my art, people who liked YouTube, and some cross section in the middle. This was probably the best year of perfect symbiotic harmony.

Fast-forward again to 2016 and you see that YouTube is not just an interest, but the dominant interest. This isn't drawn to scale, but you get the idea.

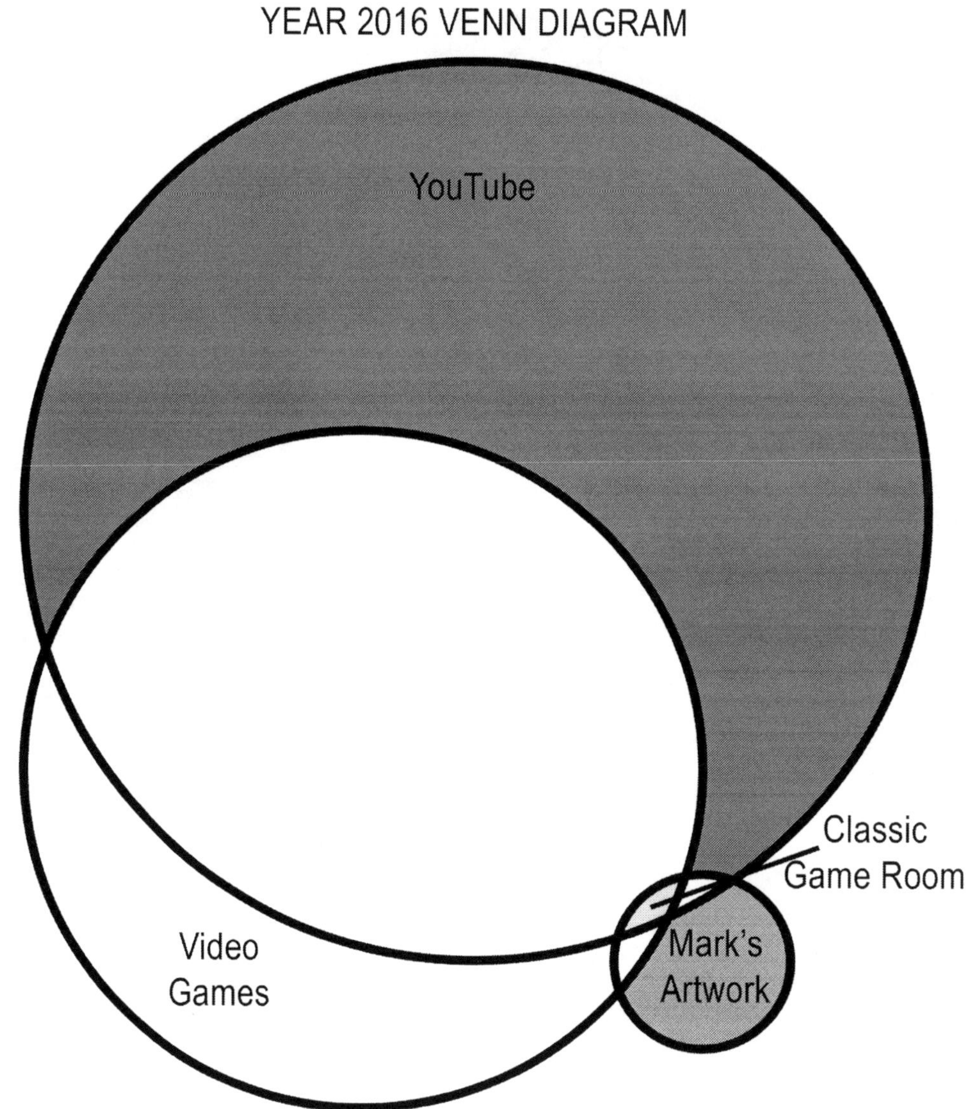

There are people who like games, and people who like my artwork, and Classic Game Room fans are in that little crossover space. But most people just like YouTube.

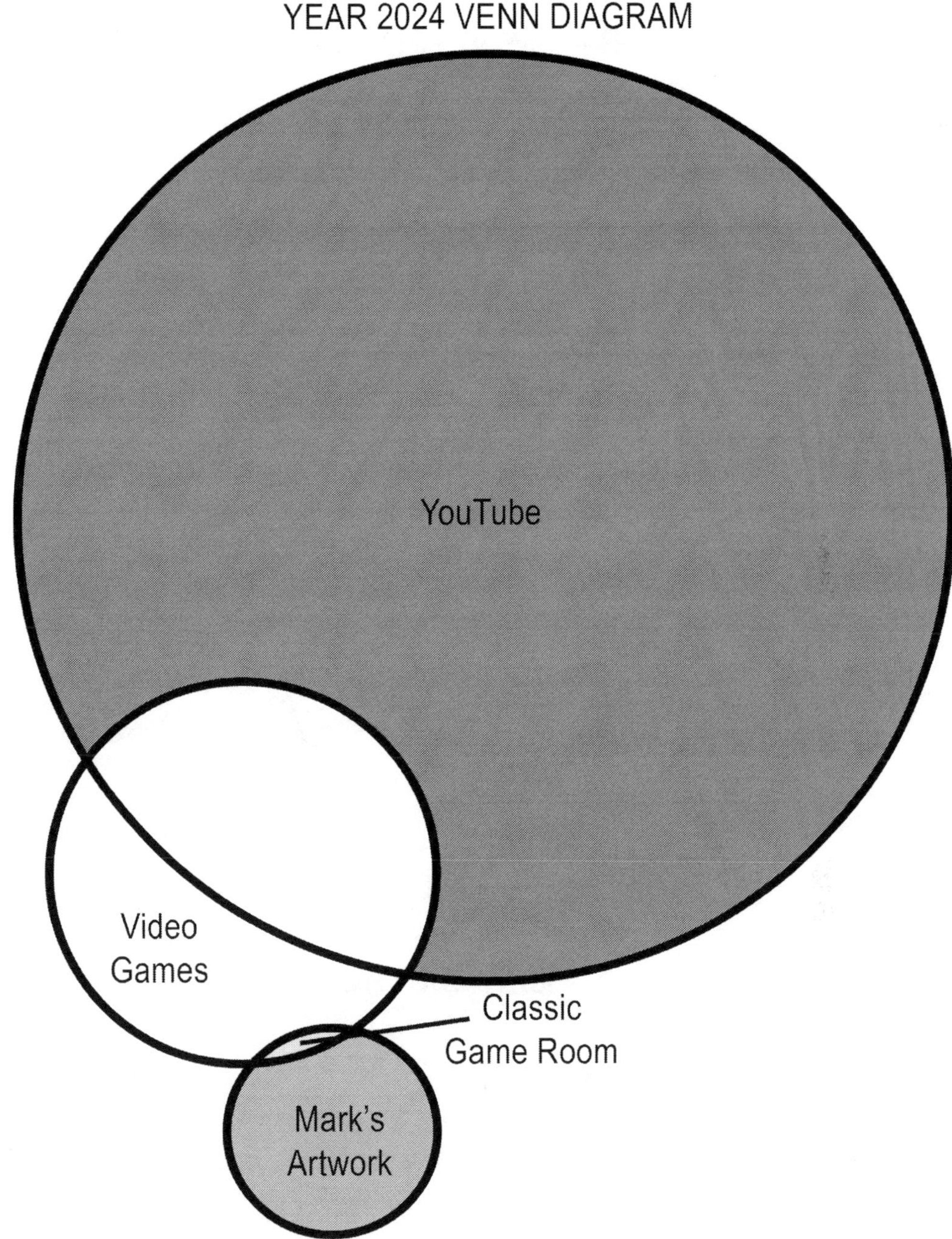

*Not to scale.

If anything came out of this book for me, it's this diagram. When I saw this it all clicked. This is the direction that I should be focusing on. My circle broke free!

By defying YouTube, I pissed off YouTube, the company and its devout flock. And YouTube, is by far, the biggest circle on that 2024 diagram (if it was drawn to scale it would be the size of the sun.)

Sooooo......

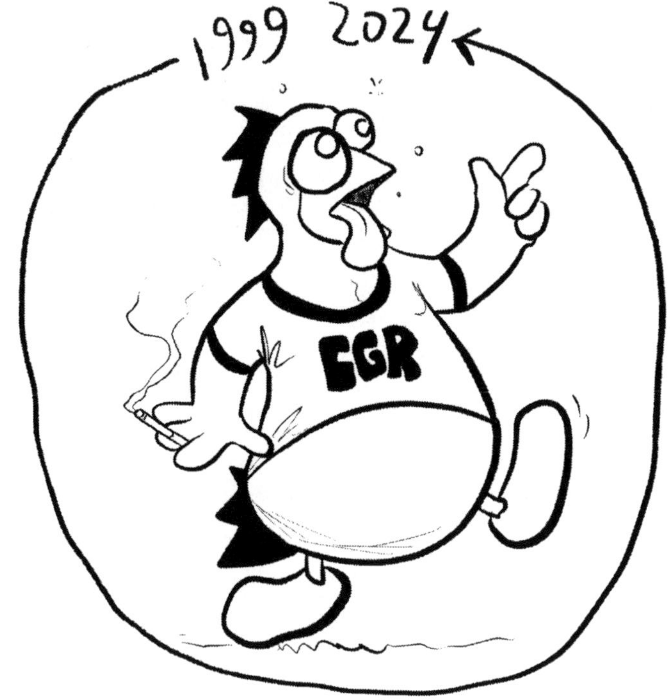

That was easy. It only took me 25 years to come around, full circle.

After 25 years of Classic Game Room, the show returned to where it all started because I identified the audience as people who like "Mark's Art." Period. There's no need to try and impose on the other two circles.

Is Classic Game Room over? No, in fact, I've been making new videos for my website. It's over on YouTube, which means that it will be over for most people because they've been misinformed that YouTube is all that matters, but it's not "over." I own it. I can do what I want with it.

Occasionally, you'll see some new Classic Game Room reviews on the CGR Publishing website. They'll probably be pinball and arcade videos because I'm not playing console games anymore (I don't have time to sit there and play console games.)

The good ole' classic Classic Game Room videos can continue ad-free on my clunky old-fashioned website provided that someone, somewhere, buys a couple shirts, books, and beer glasses every now and then.

I actually prefer that you watch them on my site, even without the ad revenue, because I don't want my work associated with YouTube anymore. They can have the influencers and the screaming, I'll take my hard work and keep it archived myself, thank you.

YouTube lost its way. It's sad. I don't want my art to be associated with their worthless hate-for-profit "content".

Business Plans Last Five Years

The other business school lesson that jumped out at me was the accuracy of the "5-year business plan." Business plans tend to last five years because if you don't get out ahead of your competitors within five years, you're screwed. That's right on the money.

I waited until the fall of 2024 to finish this book because I wanted to see if this is, in fact, the final direction of the company so that I could write a good ending.

Throughout 2024, while working on Omega Ronin, Ethel the Cyborg Ninja, and design work, I found my artistic voice again and remembered how much I enjoyed the "...and I say screw you!" attitude of college radio (and Star

Trek IV.)

My final foray into social media and modern "content creation" reminded me that I want nothing to do with it. It also helped to hone my vision for old-school products with lasting value.

Because of social media misinformation, short-form "swipe-away" content, and artificial intelligence, I decided to double down on my artwork and sink 100% of my production budget into real art instead of videos lumped into the "content creator" influencer category.

Social media is anything but social, let's be honest here. It's literally tearing the world to pieces by spreading misinformation and dividing us as people. Social media locks you in a bubble and feeds you exactly what you want to believe. It's tribalism. If you don't think that climate change is real, social media is there to reinforce your belief because the other tribe is wrong.

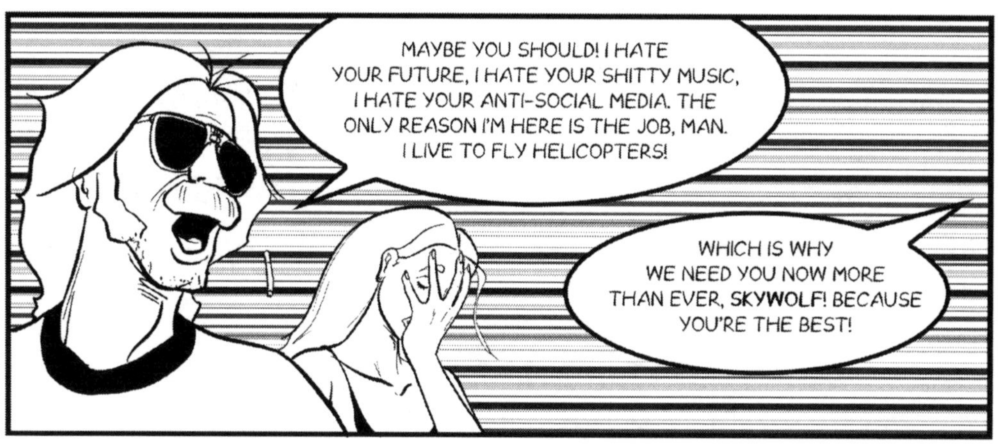

Magnum Skywolf (2020.)

They call it "content creation" because it doesn't matter what the content is just that someone (or something) makes it and posts it on social media. It could be a

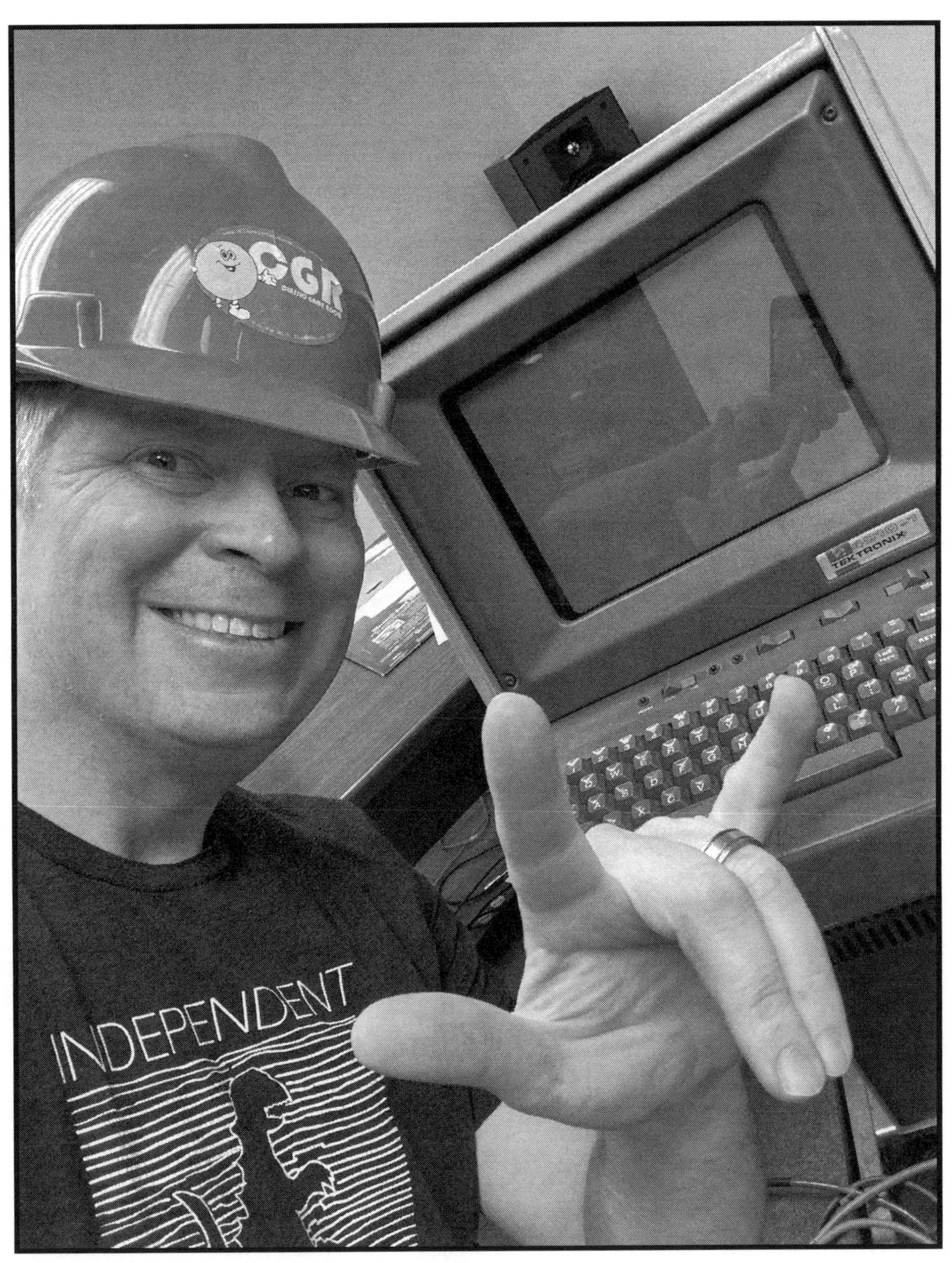

Mark Bussler and Edit-Station 1 (2024.)

kitten video. It could be an angry game review. It can be Nazi propaganda and hateful garbage. It's all lumped into the same bucket as "content."

"Content creators" are going to be the front line in the war against artificial intelligence and I'm betting on the machines to win that battle.

You know what machines can't do, though? They can't draw you a picture on a piece of paper.

What of the video game industry?

From the perspective of an outside observer, many of the same forces and consumer habits that wrecked quality online video content have also destroyed the video game industry. As I'm writing this in 2024, game companies are going out of business left and right and developer layoffs appear to be a daily thing.

It's the consolidation of everything into one or two things. Just as everyone watches only one or two video platforms, gamers play only Roblox and freemium games.

If you're spending all your time in Roblox, or GTA, or Minecraft, or whatever the hot BIG game is, you aren't playing the new quirky indie game. Or, more specifically, you aren't playing the new AAA game that someone spent a billion dollars making. Then it bombs, and the studio gets shut down, and gamers complain about it but don't change their habits.

Remember all of those amazing AAA action games and driving games with single-player campaigns from the PlayStation 2 and Xbox 360 eras? Gone. You'll never see another Red Faction or Time Splitters again thanks to game companies trying to predictably engineer the next hot multiplayer freemium shooter.

And what's next? A.I. generated games? You can bet if the mega-studios can save a buck, that's what you'll get. Especially if the players don't notice or care.

It doesn't really matter if the game is any good, what matters is that it's popular and always full of people (or A.I. bots that look and act like people.)

A high degree of engagement and community interaction is required for a modern game, which means that only a few really big companies can afford to compete in that realm. So, what you end up with is a few big games that are pretty much the same and engineered to be highly addictive.

It's the same thing with Internet videos. People say they want good videos, but then they watch the junk and complain that all anyone makes is junk. It's because you're watching the junk!

If consumers of media refuse to change their ways, then the two or three companies that control all of media sure as hell won't change theirs. If you want game companies to stop making season passes, then stop buying season passes.

What do game reviewers even review nowadays? I mean, you must have to Google what's hot, and then ask Chat GPT to write a script for you and then steal footage from someone's video. That sounds exhausting!

So, here we are.

Just as my website returned to its roots 25 years later, I have also returned to my original passion. Drawing.

I know that my audience is older and misses the pre-dystopian decades of the 1970s and 80s as much as I do, and they have money to spend and a desire for real physical content made by real-life human beings instead of A.I.-generated influencers with 12 fingers.

If you're going to be a professional artist these days, you'd damn well better create something unique and physical. Do something that a computer can't do better than you can.

Writing this book, while also successfully launching several graphic novels and a physical album, helped to clarify my vision and my artistic direction. I discovered that getting back into the Classic Game Room stuff was fun, but not productive. The Blu-Ray turned out great, as did the glassware, and the recent videos are good too. But the experience of trying to reconnect my little circle on that Venn diagram with the larger one was awful.

Omega Ronin and Ethel the Cyborg Ninja both celebrated successful Kickstarter campaigns, without social media marketing, and that shows the power of creating original art and delivering something of value to fans.

Inecom continues in Pittsburgh which has evolved into a vibrant and wonderful city filled with bike trails, breweries, arcades, and more! Y'nz better believe it.

Thank you to everyone who watched the show, reads my books, and jams to the music. LIGHTHOUSE! (original ending summer 2024... but then I kept going.)

Writing this book also reminded me that good 'ole Agent 0040oz was there from the beginning, shotgunning 40s and dropping bad one-liners. The world totally sucks now. Secret Agent James Brown may be the hero we need to light our darkest hour.

You just never know....

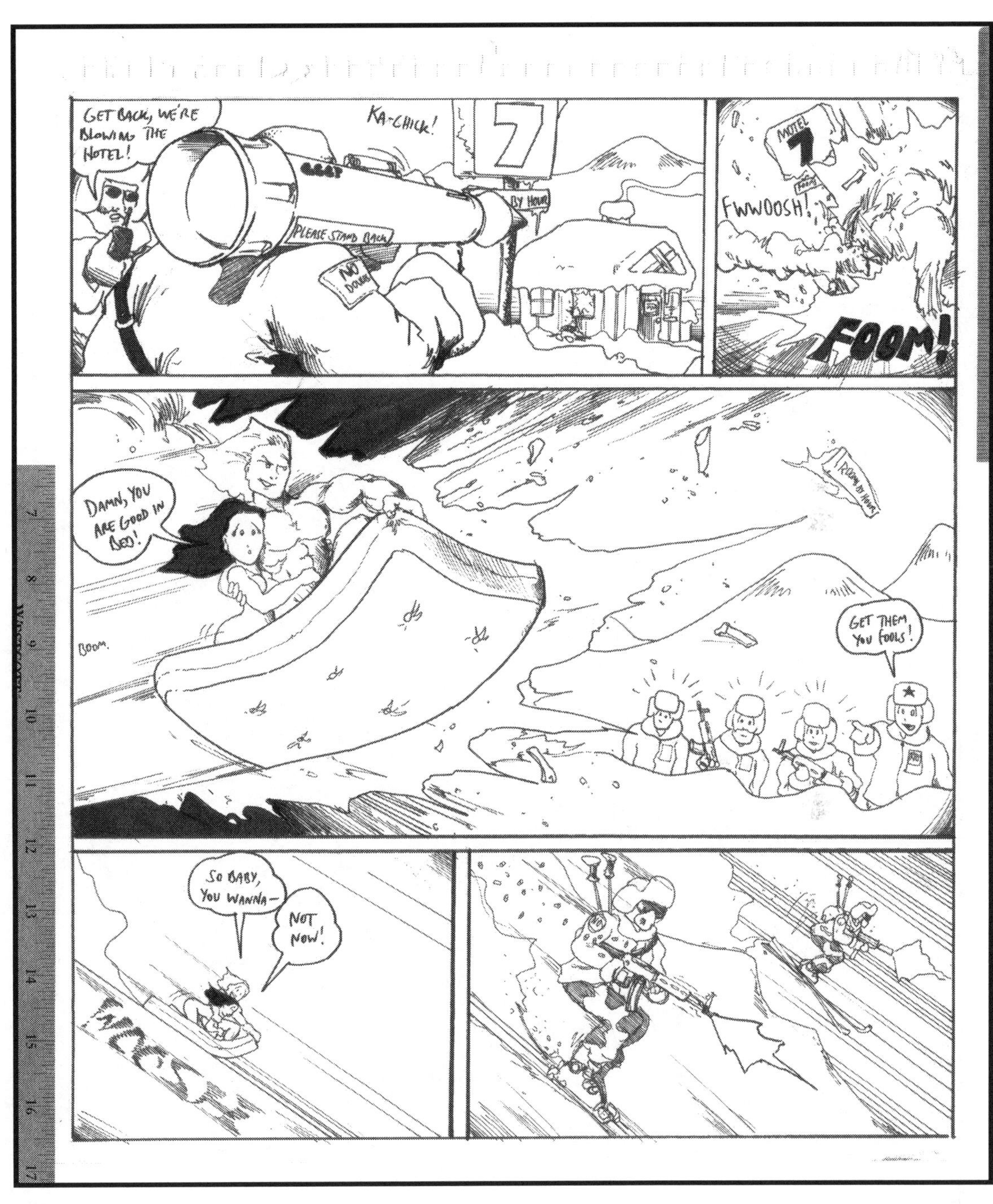

Original art for Agent 00400z (2000.)

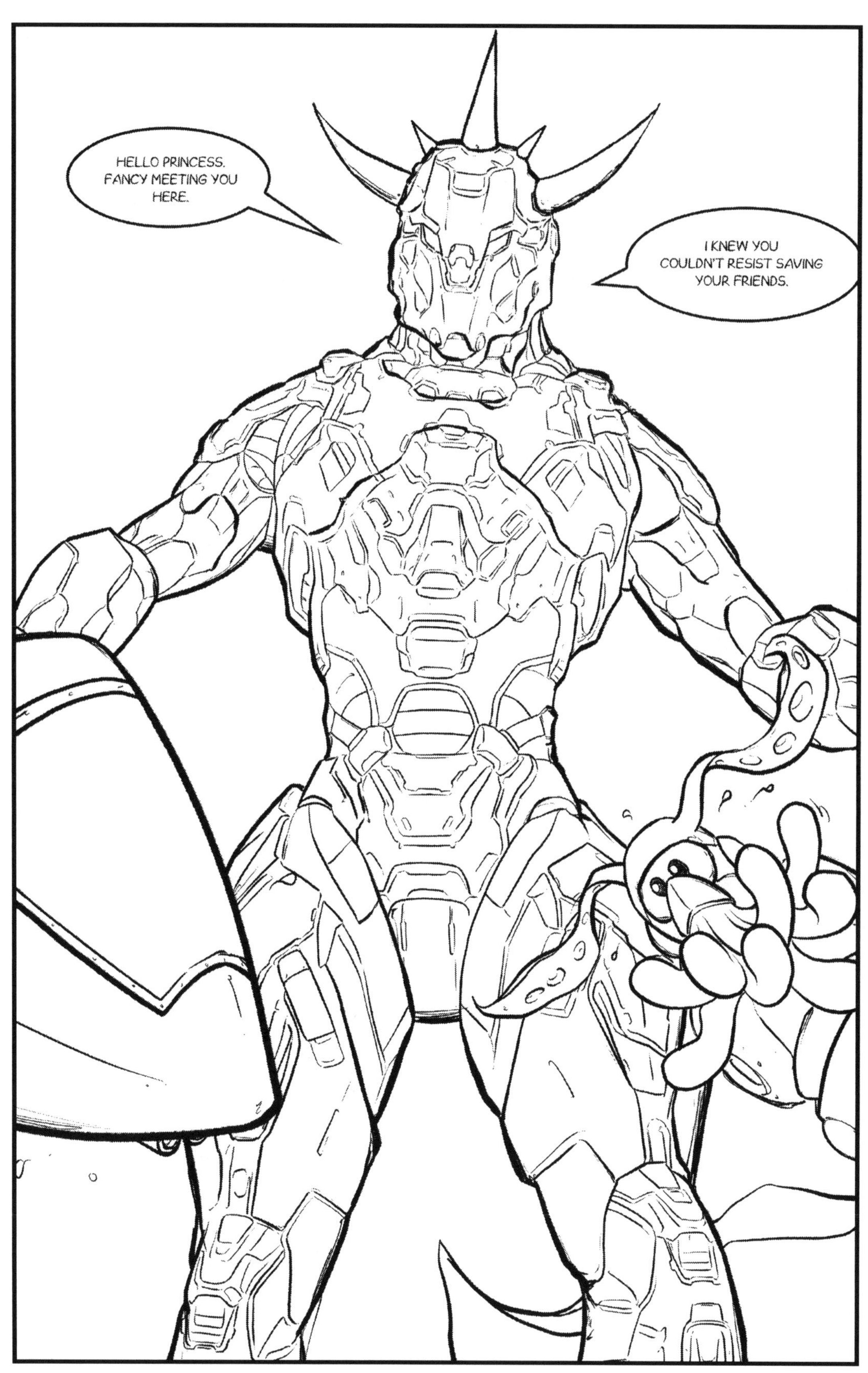

Evil Lord Karnage, Space Gar, and Wind Squid in Ethel the Cyborg Ninja #3 (2024).

CHAPTER 24
THE FUTURE OF ARTISTIC EXPRESSION ON THE INTERNET

I always thought it was interesting that, in his later years, my grandfather loved watching Francis the Talking Mule on VHS. When it comes to anthropomorphic talking quadrupeds, I side with Mr. Ed, but he grew up with Francis.

It was clearly comforting for him to watch something fun, familiar, and with a tie to the past that he could relate to.

My dad does the same thing and spends hours watching old movies on AMC that take him back.

I watch Magnum P.I. and Miami Vice. Not only do I enjoy the stories and characters, but I love seeing what things looked like back then. "Look at those old cars! Remember when people wore jackets like that? They're using a payphone instead of texting on their iPhone!"

What's the future of artistic expression on the Internet? I have no idea. It certainly won't be the same as in the past.

The rate of change is accelerating, that much is clear. If boomers find comfort in Rolling Stones albums and Woodstock nostalgia in the same way that Gen X soaks up MTV and Nirvana, what will Millennials do? What about Gen Z or Gen Alpha or whatever they call it?

"Remember when humans made YouTube videos instead of artificial intelligence farms?"

I already heard some of this in my later Classic Game Room seasons from fans who said "Remember the good old days of YouTube? They were so much better!"

I agree. They were better. So was 1984 Miami Vice. Nostalgia is a helluva drug.

So, what's next?

One can only theorize.

PROMPT: What's the next big thing on the Internet?
RESPONSE: Me! (Artificial Intelligence)

> If you truly have a desire to create art, and the Internet is the only way to reach a wide audience, and the Internet is controlled by two or three companies who randomize your chance for success, then perhaps the future of artistic expression on the Internet is not on the Internet.

People have been suckered into using social media, but it won't last forever. There's already a lot of pushback against it, and watching platforms like X (formerly known as Twitter!) burn to the ground, highlights the problems with building an audience on a service that you don't own.

This might sound crazy, but if you make art and go out of your way to NOT use social media, or YouTube, or TikTok, then you might get pretty good at finding workarounds. More likely, you'll probably figure out a good balancing act.

My approach to making comic books and music these days is to envision a finished product that can be sold physically to customers who enjoy my art and want to collect the real thing. I'm not saying that this is the right way to do it, but it's how I'm doing it in preparation for the eventual A.I. takeover of all social media art.

To be completely transparent here, I work in pencil, paper, and pen and ink. I also work with digital art.

When creating comic books like Omega Ronin and Ethel the Cyborg Ninja, I use computer animation, game engines, lightboxing, iPad, Photoshop, and every other digital tool that I can effectively use to tell my stories because I have to. This isn't the 1970s and I can't spend an entire year on one issue. I have to create dozens of issues.

But I can also still draw you a freakin' picture on a piece of paper. That right there is the future of artistic expression on the Internet.

My approach to music is somewhere in between physical art and music. I can't perform it live, because that's not how I work, but when you buy my record albums, you're getting a real, tangible piece of Mark Bussler artwork as a physical record (Omega Ronin is coming out on blue vinyl!)

Mark Bussler comic books are made for print. Ethel the Cyborg Ninja did better in 20 minutes on Kickstarter than all of Classic Game Room season 24 and season 25 did on YouTube, combined, over twelve months!

I've had months where Omega Ronin performed better on Bandcamp than 15,000 YouTube videos.

What do Omega Ronin and Ethel have in common? They are art, not "content".

Let the influencers have their influencing. Artists should stick to art. Therefore, the future of artistic expression on the Internet is up to you!

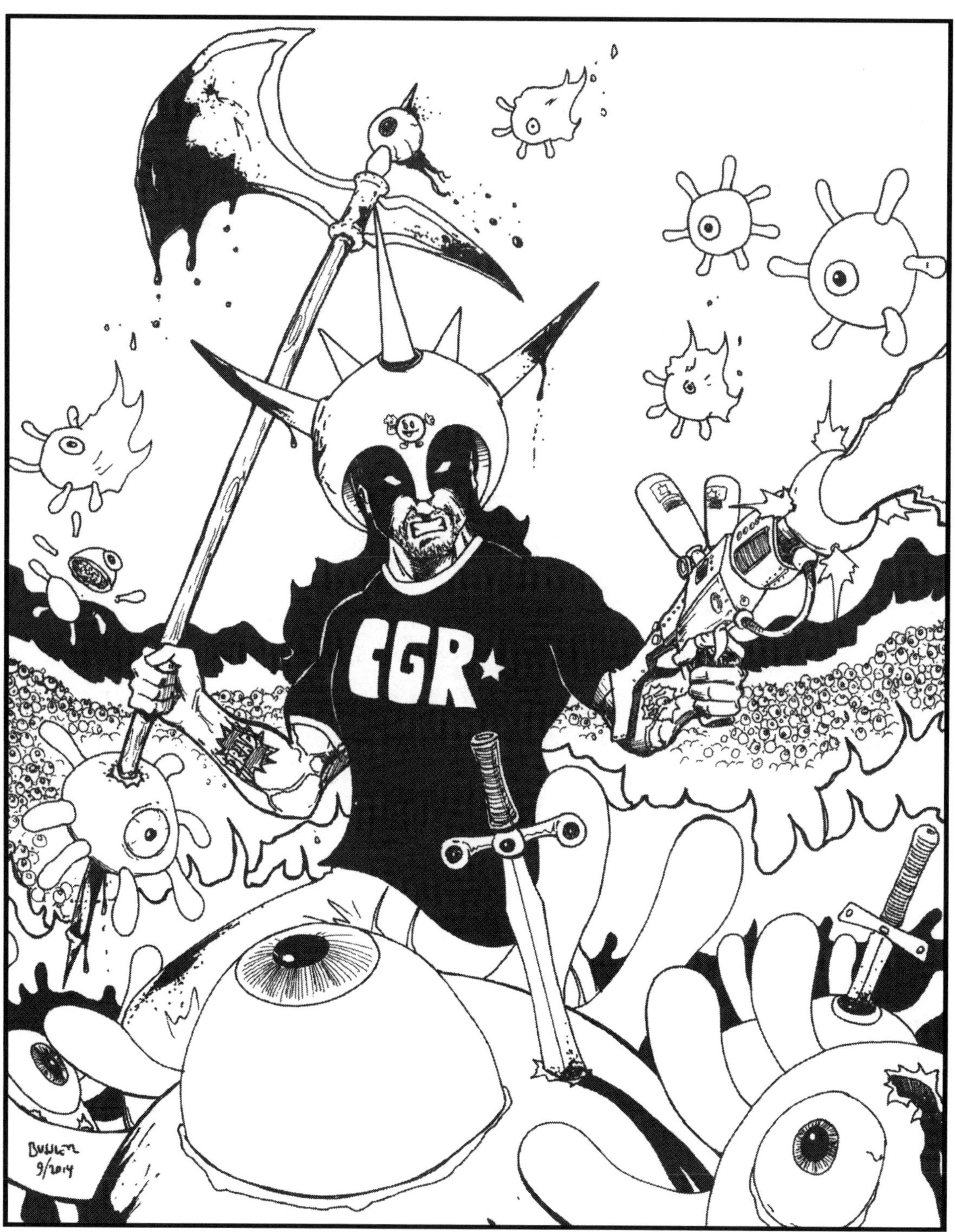

Lord Karnage (2014.)

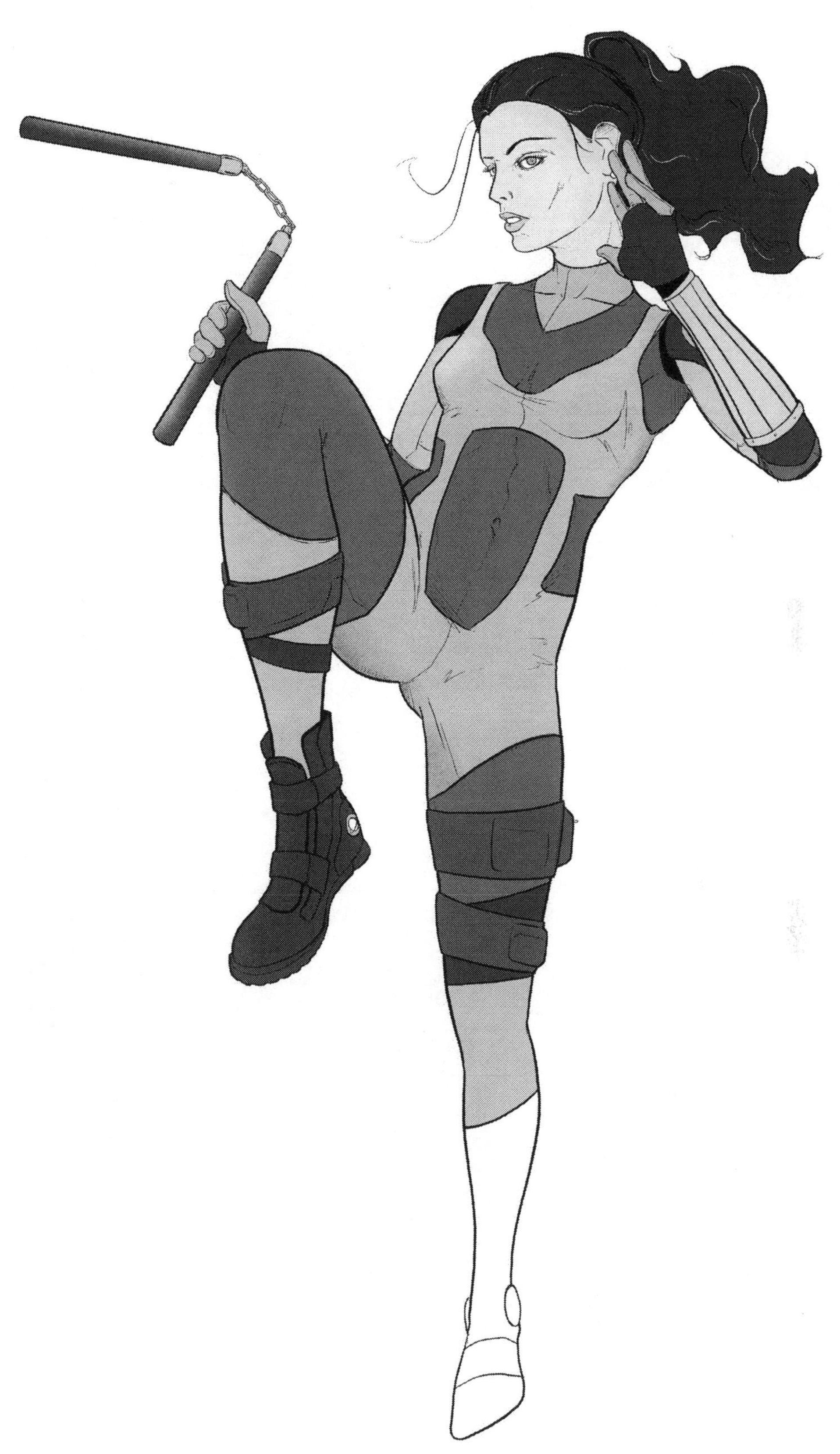

Ethel the Cyborg Ninja circa 2024.... with a missing boot!

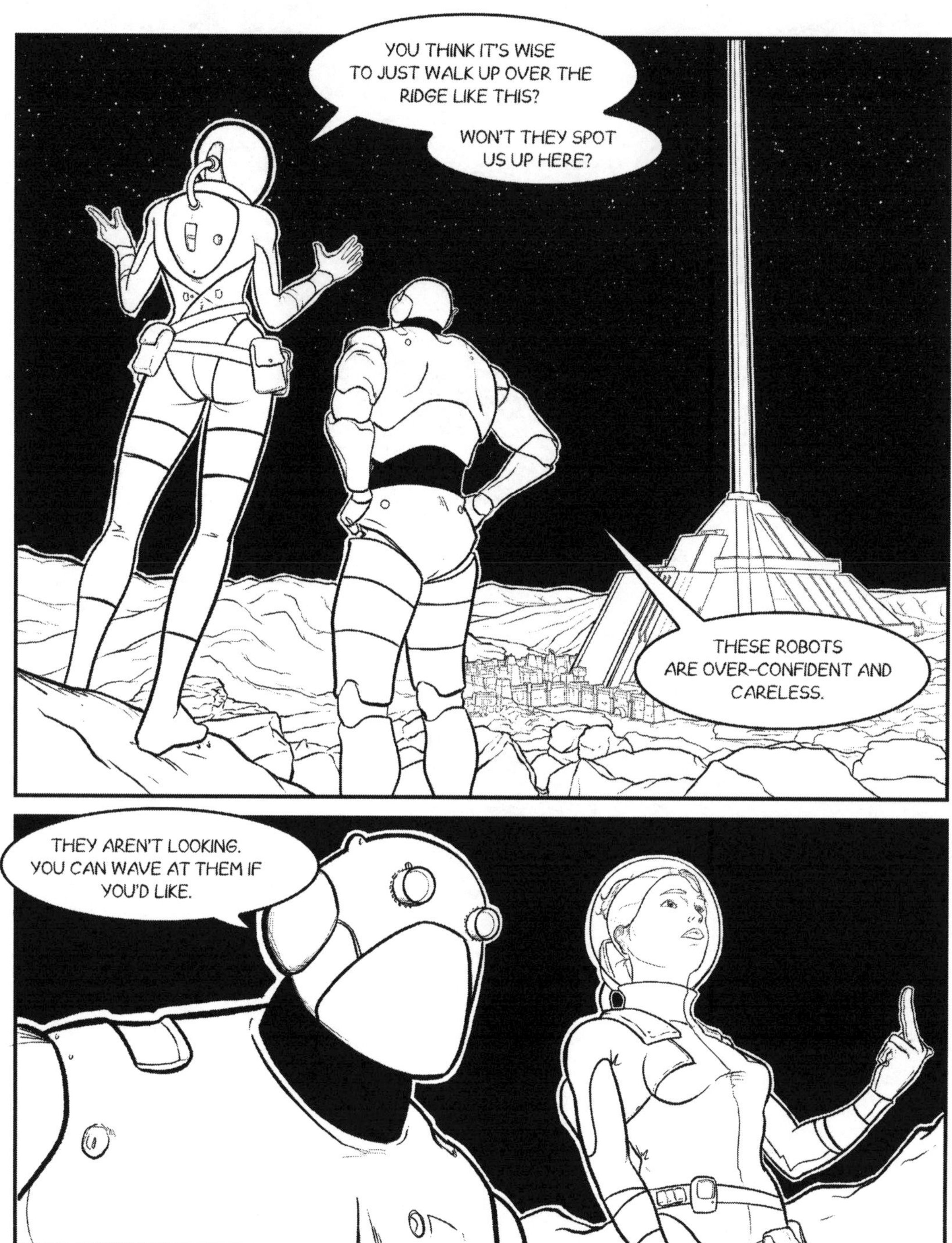

Omega Ronin Book 1 in production (2024.)

CHAPTER 25
ONE CRAZY JOURNEY

Thank you for reading my book! This has been a crazy journey that started the moment I first played Pac-Man and Atari 2600 way back when while Led Zeppelin and Van Halen played through the arcade speakers.

Classic Game Room, the show, has gone through ups and downs and ups and downs and I have absolutely no idea where it will go next.

Heading into this book, I assumed that I would have a clear vision of the show's next evolution, but I don't. It's possible that Classic Game Room will be tied to video game soundtracks in some way, it's possible that Classic Game Room will lead to more video game-themed books, or maybe the show will just periodically happen on the website from time to time when the mood strikes me.

Maybe there will be a future when people go "Man, I am really sick of these screaming game reviewers and A.I. generated shorts, I want to watch Classic Game Room again!" Classic Game Room could be the next Francis the Talking Mule. Clearly, I need to release it on VHS.

Classic Game Room always reminded me of the Kobayashi Maru scenario from Star Trek II. Kirk doesn't like to lose, and neither do I. His solution to defeating the unwinnable situation was to reprogram the computer.

My solution to defeating the unwinnable situation was to turn my company into something else. Thank you, Captain Kirk, for the inspiration!

Before I settled on the subtitle "The Past, Present, and Future of Artistic Expression on the Internet," this book was going to be called "History of Classic Game Room: The First 25 Years of Nonsense."

That implied that there would be another 25 years of nonsense. I'm totally down for another 25 years of nonsense, though, I'm not sure it will be Classic Game Room related.

But maybe it will. Who can say?

It has been quite an interesting journey from the summer of 1999 to the fall of 2024. This has been a career path that I certainly never expected (most of it didn't even exist when I graduated college in '98!)

Hopefully, fans of the series enjoyed a look behind the curtain. Maybe, those of you who want to be independent artists on the Internet got some ideas. Maybe you learned something from my mistakes. Maybe you've enjoyed my colossal not-give-a-fuck-itude towards artistic expression.

Perhaps there will be a sequel to this book in 25 years when I regale readers with the harrowing tale of Classic Game Room's evolution into a successful line of holographic barware from the future.

That sounds so dope.

Let's put it all this way. Now you've heard my story, when you read Omega Ronin, pay attention to the fact that the entire human race is murdered by A.I. robots because people are too consumed by watching social media videos to pay attention.

Collectively, humans turn into a bunch of idiots incapable of fighting off the murder robots so they go extinct.

Salvation only comes in the form of space mercenaries trained on 1980s music videos played from VHS tapes one million years in the future.

Honestly, I wouldn't have come up with that if I was having a good time making YouTube videos.

ENGAGE DISCO!!!

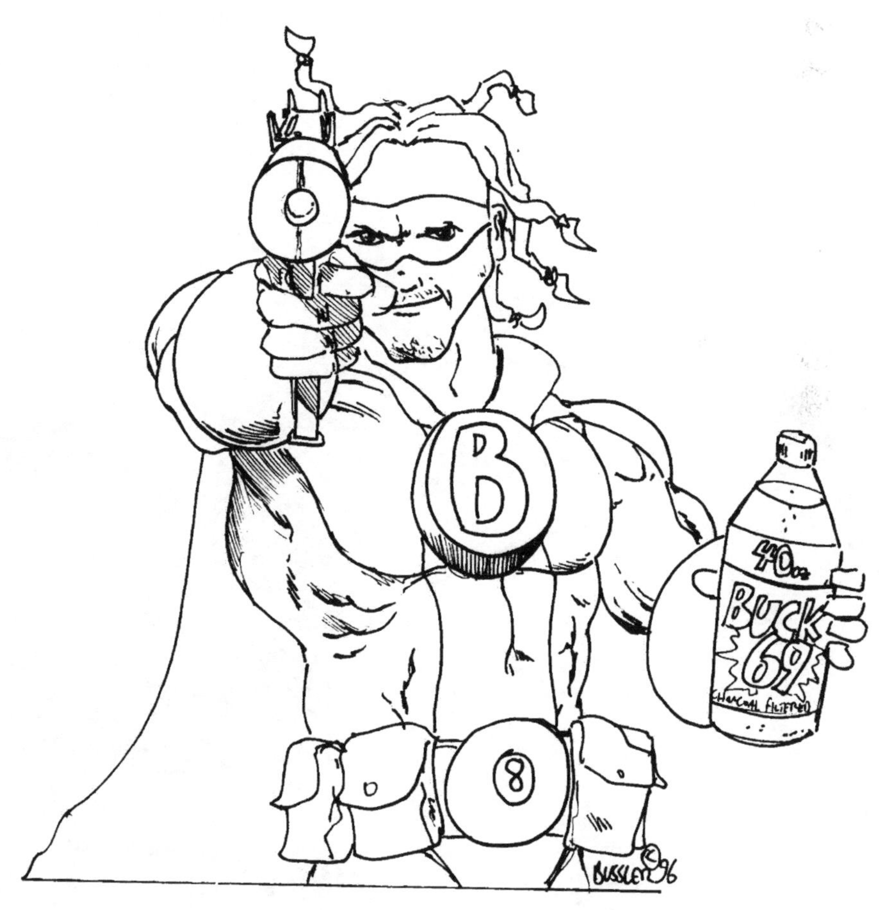

Captain Bucknell (1996.)

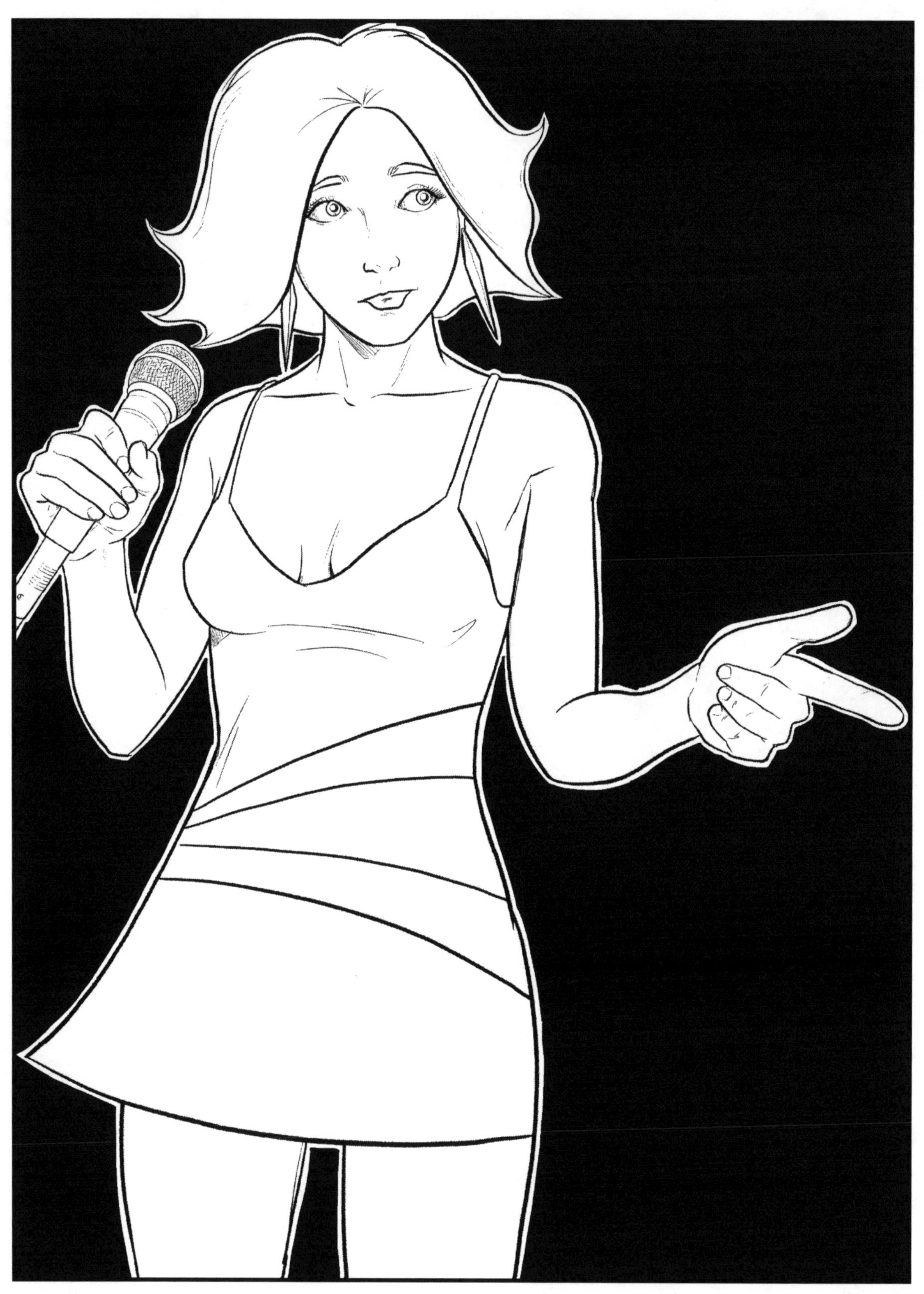

Cassandra from Omega Ronin Book 1 (2024.)

EPILOGUE

But wait, there's more! I started writing this book in January of 2024 and planned to wrap it up by mid-summer for my 25th anniversary convention tour. Since that never happened, I sat on the book for a bit longer to see how the rest of the year would unfold.

Over the summer, Omega Ronin the graphic novel, and the vinyl soundtrack were successfully funded on Kickstarter.

Additionally, Ethel the Cyborg Ninja Hardcover Trilogy Edition was successfully funded on Kickstarter.

As of this writing in the fall of 2024, both of those projects are in production and looking great. I did not use a social media marketing campaign, which allowed me to spend more time making and less time shouting into the wind.

I'm developing two new graphic novel series inspired by classic 1970s science fiction and fantasy adventures. I'm planning to release vinyl soundtracks for each of the books because I want readers to shut down their screens, turn off their phones, and lose themselves completely in the writing, art and music.

It was my experience with Classic Game Room that led to this because another thing that wasn't lost on me is that modern audiences multi-task everything; which is to say that they're streaming video while playing a game and listening to a podcast all at the same time.

The younger audience doesn't even want to sit through a movie anymore, they prefer their TikTok shorts. I don't get it, nor do I share their enthusiasm for short-form content, but my parents hated MTV and never understood it either. Things change.

My response to A.I., short-form videos, and multi-tasking media is to create something that doesn't fit into any of that, and Omega Ronin is the first release that embraces this "screw you, modern media!" attitude. The books are aimed at an older audience, or young people fed up with constant screen time who appreciate well-crafted stories and intricate line art. Besides, who else gives you books AND soundtracks? It's like a movie, but with more page turning.

Will it succeed? They're already off to a good start and I'm pleased. I'd rather focus on real art for the next several decades than try to keep up with changing consumer demands.

Where did artsy punk rock Mark come from??

I never cared much for punk rock music, but I always loved the attitude. Maybe you should know where this artistic inspiration comes from. Let's take it back, way back, back to 1979.

The air is thick with cigarette smoke that soaks into the wood-paneled walls and chunky avocado green shag carpet. The Star Wars radio drama plays on the radio because The Empire Strikes Back hasn't even been released yet.

That's how I remember it, at least. My sequence of

events may be off here because I was four. But, I definitely remember the tail end of 1979 because I remember flipping back and forth between the years on my dad's calendar hanging in his office. There was a train on it (of course there was, he loves trains.)

I have these weird memory flashes from that era like the one where a doctor put me under with a mask when I got tubes put in my ears. My mom said there's no way I could remember that because I was four, but I do remember.

One of the most vivid memories, relevant to this story, is that my dad took me to see The Empire Strikes Back. I think that was the first movie that I ever saw in the theater and HOLY SHIT it was AWESOME. It was so Lando.

Star Wars was everywhere in 1980. It was the single biggest cultural phenomenon that I've ever witnessed. I played with Star Wars figures, read Star Wars comics, and listened to Star Wars on the radio.

I'm an only child, so you can bet I spent a lot of time on the shag carpet playing with my Star Wars figures. I even wrote my own Star Wars stories (uh oh, now Disney will be coming after me... to offer a writing job because they were better than the swill you're making now!)

There's a reason my generation hates the modern Star Wars. Because it sucks. Also, because it can never recapture that powerful experience that shaped our formative years more than anything else.

I was Star Wars all the time, and that guided my viewing habits towards everything science fiction because sci-fi was hot back then.

My dad took me to Raiders, Star Trek II, E.T. (which I loathe) and we watched Buck Rogers in the 25th Century, Battlestar Galactica, and everything else sci-fi on TV.

That's why I love the 1970s and early 80s sci-fi disco aesthetic (that's so Buck Rogers.) Know that Wilma is on my mind every time I see a disco ball or a spaceship or.... And a.... well, Wilma is always on my mind. Let's just leave it at that.

Before kids scrolled mindlessly on their parent's iPhones, we made up our own adventures with Star Wars figures. I still live near the house where I grew up, and every time I walk by it, I point to a window and say... I'll quote my kids.

"Yeah, we know dad. You played with your Star Wars figures right there. You're repeating yourself."

I did! Specifically, the little metal ones because they fit perfectly well on the radiator below that window, and I could recreate the Hoth battle scenes (Disney take notes.... this is why people liked Star Wars.)

Grumpy Old Man Mark is in effect!

"Back in my day we had to use our imagination!"

It's true. Star Wars figures, and toys in general, are a great way to unlock creative play and storytelling. Also, back in the day, video games didn't show you every pore and hair follicle, you had to use your imagination when playing Atari 2600!

"You see that block there shooting blocks at the other block? That's the Millennium Falcon and it's fighting the Death Star! Wilma Deering is there, and she's wearing something tight and purple... dammit I get so carried away."

Apparently, the 1970s turned me into a pervy weirdo, but they also unlocked something creative in me, something that I still use to write ridiculous stories about space adventures and disco computers in the laser future.

Every time that you watch Classic Game Room 2085, or read Ethel the Cyborg Ninja and Lord Karnage, know that Edit-Station 1 is based on a real computer terminal that used to have a real job.

Here's the story. In the 1970s, after working at Westinghouse, my dad started a time-sharing company. (The joke is that you can't throw a rock in Pittsburgh without hitting an old white guy who worked for Westinghouse.)

Before personal computers, companies used mainframe computers because computers were super duper crazy expensive back then. People would access these mainframes using computer terminals, which did no local (personal) computing but connected via a modem. Thus, companies would share time on the mainframes.

Now, my dad is a self-made guy. He owned a mainframe, and I remember this mainframe. It was an IBM Prime computer (if I'm getting that right.) There were spinning tape drives, and cables and wires running everywhere. This would have been at the tail end of his time sharing days. I think it was about 1979 or so that he pivoted into engineering software.

His company was in the basement of an apartment complex in East Liberty, and I remember running up and down the hall and Edit-Station 1 was there in the hallway. Why was he in the hallway?

I also remember him hooked up to another computer and doing some computing. There were things on his green vector-graphics display. Important things!

He wasn't called Edit-Station 1 then. It (he) was a fully functional Tektronix 4010-1 terminal without a name or a persona or a fabulous science fiction comic book career or video stardom on Amazon.

If you want to get a good look at it, I did a bunch of closeup shots of its 2400 baud modem and little roller wheels for the Classic Game Room Feature Review of the Sega Genesis game, MUSHA.

The terminal doesn't have a mouse, but it does have spinning knobs that would move the cursor and of course, the break key is broken. There's also a rub key, because you never know when you might need to rub 1 out... you know, if you type the numeral 1 into the wrong place.

For whatever reason, that computer remained in the back room of my dad's company for the next 25 years until he started to sell the old mainframe stuff off and I was like "OH HELL NO!"

I adopted it, gave it a name, and now Edit-Station 1 is the greatest space asshole in the future of space.

Edit-Station 1 first appeared in 2007 on a YouTube video. That was back in my crazy experimentation days when making videos was fun and exciting!

Later, I started to draw him into comics and swapped out the keyboard for a Missile Command trak-ball because trak-balls are awesome, and the keyboard was a pain in the ass to draw.

His little wheels evolved into the big tires that he has today, and the antenna came from who knows where... all sentient computers need antennae.

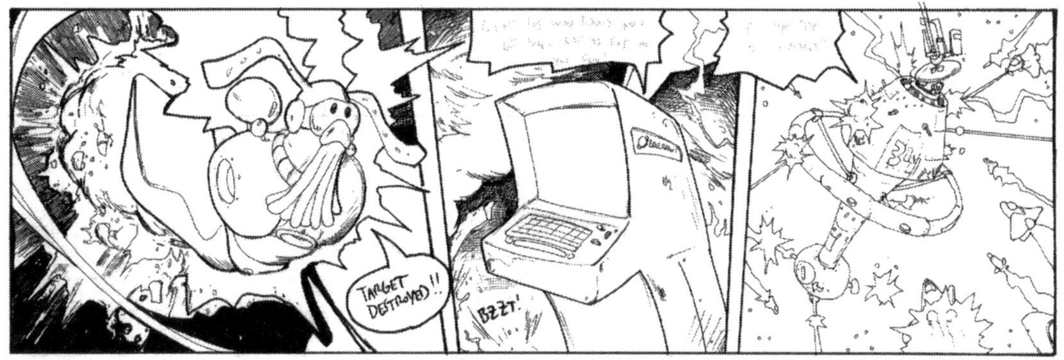

Early 2012-era drawing of Edit-Station 1 with a keyboard.

I drew a lot of comics in the early 1980s and became known in school as the kid who draws a lot. I also read a lot of comic books and watched a shit-ton of cartoons.

This was the 80s, this was the golden age of cartoons and action figures! We had an embarrassment of riches on TV back then.

He-Man, Voltron, G.I. Joe, Transformers, Go-Bots, Thundercats, Robotech, Galaxy Rangers, just to name a few. I watched all of them.

My favorite comic books from the era were G.I. Joe: A Real American Hero and Transformers. They were my favorites! I probably should credit George Lucas and Larry Hama (from G.I. Joe) with 90% of my personality. There's no problem that can't be solved by being a ninja in a top secret military outfit with a light saber.

The biggest challenge in 1986 was deciding whether or not I was going to watch Robotech or The Adventures of the Galaxy Rangers because they aired on TV at the same time on different channels. It was cruel and barbaric.

I loved comics. I loved movies and TV. Dad had a TV in his office and a VCR where I watched Conan the Barbarian for the first time. What is best in life? Conan on VHS.

A lot of the aesthetics that you see in my work like Ethel the Cyborg Ninja, and the moonbase laboratory in Omega Ronin, are based on my recollections of this time and place.

This is part of the reason that Star Wars fans like Andor. The designers of that series actually understand the 1970s aesthetics of computer terminals with the proper buttons and flashing doohickeys.

My father's company wasn't a huge success in the 1980s, but they still managed to send me to a private school which I detested with a juvenile fury that manifested itself in a variety of maybe not-so-good ways.

This was like Dead Poets Society-era private school with ties and a strict code of conduct. It was a miserable entitled boys club, and I hated it. I spent my time drawing violent comics and generally being an asshole. In 1989 I made sure to only wear my dad's old wardrobe of wide-bodied 1970s ties which were, in hindsight, amazing.

In addition to comic books, Star Wars, TV, and Wilma Deering, I found my other great love affair in video games.

I clearly remember the arcades because my dad and I would play pinball and video games like Pac-Man and Atari's Fire Truck at the mall. There was a great arcade at Monroeville Mall which was made famous by 1978's Dawn of the Dead. I remember when it even had an ice rink (that they later replaced with a food court.) Y'nz g'ahn d'ahn to Grah'n Ra'nd after skatin'?

We always had computers around the house, so I spent a great deal of time playing old school PC games throughout the 80s.

Though I played my friends' Ataris, I didn't get my own Atari until the Atari 2600 Jr. came out in 1986 or so. It was like Christmas! It might have actually been Christmas, I can't remember.

The price of the 2600 must have crashed and my mom bought it along with a stack of Atari 2600 games in white boxes (clearance?) Things weren't great with business then, and I'm really not sure how or why she did that. But, I loved that Atari 2600 (and I still do. It's the one I used on the show.)

Oddly enough, she picked up Swordquest Waterworld in that batch, which ended up being a rare game. I sold it in the 2018-era to help fund the book business, which paid off. Thank you Swordquest! (I always thought the Atari adventure games were overrated, to be honest...)

Shortly after the 2600 I also got an Atari 7800 ProSystem! Yes, I was one of five people in the United States who enjoyed being a professional gamer on Atari 7800!

This must have been 1987 or so, and I had a folding table set up in my parent's basement and I rocked Xevious, Pole Position II, Robotron 2084, Dig Dug, and Joust on Atari 7800 like it was my job because it would become my job two decades later.... go figure.

I remember that my friend down the street got a Nintendo Entertainment System. An NES! We played Super Mario Bros. and I thought, deep down, and I'm ashamed to admit this, I thought maybe I made a mistake asking for an Atari 7800.... but it was backward compatible with Atari 2600 and Yars' Revenge. The NES wasn't.

The NES is trash.

I mean, it wasn't. Actually it was pretty awesome. We played Metroid and Top Gun and I must have begged and pleaded something fierce to get an NES, which I did in 1988 or so. I don't remember how I got it exactly, but I had some great times with that NES playing Contra and Bionic Commando and Blaster Master.

Another friend was from, I think, the Philippines. His family had a Famicom which I think is where I first saw Bionic Commando. They also had a Betamax player (before the Internet, we never saw the Japanese stuff like the Famicom.) And he had Sectaurs. If you don't know what Sectaurs are, then your life is incomplete and worthless.

My NES lacked Blast Processing, though. I bought my Sega Genesis in 1989 at Ross Park Mall. Sega Fanboy Mark was born!

Altered Beast, Phantasy Star II, Herzog Zwei, Thunder Force II, the hits kept coming and coming! The power of 16-bits and stereo sound would pulse through my veins forever.

That Sega Genesis still works like a boss today and not only served as my main video game console all the way through high school, but also through Classic Game Room into 2024! It's likely you'll see it again. We're never parting.

I don't have any real personal attachment to the other game systems, but my Ataris and my Sega Genesis are family.

I played PlayStation through college and kicked ass in many a game of Virtua Fighter 2 on my friend's Sega Saturn. I think it was 2000 when I bought a PlayStation 2, which was an incredible game system. How many hours did I lose in Grand Theft Auto Vice City? All of them.

To make a long story short, I was really into video games, but they made the biggest impact on me when I was younger. I'd come home from school, and I just wasn't very happy. It's that time of life, and it sucks being a teen. My Sega Genesis was always there for me. Waiting, eagerly, to light up its red light and lift my spirits with high definition graphics and a volume slider. We'd rent stacks of Genesis games from the local Blockbuster.

I was able to channel a lot of those feelings and the overall sense of nostalgia during the 2008-2017 run of Classic Game Room. There isn't anything I'm typing here that I probably haven't said there in one form or another. One of my favorite parts of making the show in that period was exploring the vast catalog of games that I didn't even know existed. Games like Phantasy Star III were like $70 in 1990 money, so I didn't own very many.

In the Classic Game Room years, every week new games would come in from passionate viewers who wanted to see me play their favorites. It was a great part of the show. Everyone loved the map with pins identifying their locations (which I still have.) Sadly, there was no way to keep up with it. But, I really liked that. Who knew that games like Bird Week, Truxton and Mushihimesama Futari existed in the same universe?

Maybe there is another universe where people enjoyed CGR more than angry top 10 videos, and in that universe Mark is still playing through this massive collection and adding pins to the map!

In recent years, after building another company and doing lots of different things, I often find myself thinking about my college radio days.

I started as a DJ on my college radio station freshman year and discovered that it fit like a glove. Clearly, I was way into the MTV 80s music like Duran Duran and Van Halen, but I also got into 90s hard rock like White Zombie, Ministry, Soundgarden, Alice in Chains, Faith No More, and all the bands that you already know I like. Headbangers Ball was my jam, baby! That's where I found Mr. Zombie and Kyuss and so many other straight up bangers.

Well, in our little, tiny college radio station located in the ass basement of a science building or something, we had the vinyl graveyard. This was 1994, and nobody cared about vinyl. Nobody, except me.

You see, I had been scooping up cheap disco albums at a local record store for years and played them on my dad's stereo. I loved records! Before vinyl was retro cool, nobody wanted anything to do with it. You could get stacks of vinyl with a fiver in 1994 "What's wrong with you people? Who *doesn't* want KC and the Sunshine Band!?"

When I discovered this back room filled from floor to ceiling with copies of old Ministry, KMFDM, My Life with the Thrill Kill Kult, New Order, Joy Division, and all of the classic Wax Trax stuff that I never saw on MTV, my mind was blown. There was a bunch of classic rock crap in there too, but it was the less-mainstream 80s albums and early industrial stuff that made an impression. This was the coolest shit I'd ever seen (since that brand new Sega Genesis, at least.)

Over the years I ended up collecting most of my favorite albums on vinyl, and still play them to this day! My record player is sitting right behind me as I type this. I've been into movie soundtracks recently. I have at least 15 Ministry albums on vinyl by now.

There's something special about the tactile sensation of holding a record album that tapes, CDs, and certainly digital streaming services can never replace. It's like art, which is why I'm totally excited about pressing my first vinyl this fall.

As of this writing, Omega Ronin: Sirens, on blue vinyl, is still in production at the factory. It'll be here soon. Get ready to experience the sounds of future laser robots in hi-fi space-age stereo!

In one way or another Classic Game Room's ups and downs, and my comics, and thinking about my trip through time to write this book led to my vinyl and graphic novel experiment. It's funny how these things work out....

This has been a fairly truncated version of my life story, but when you read my stuff, now you know where it all came from.

...1970s mainframe computers, 1980s cartoons, a dusty room filled with records, and a certain someone special from the 25th century.

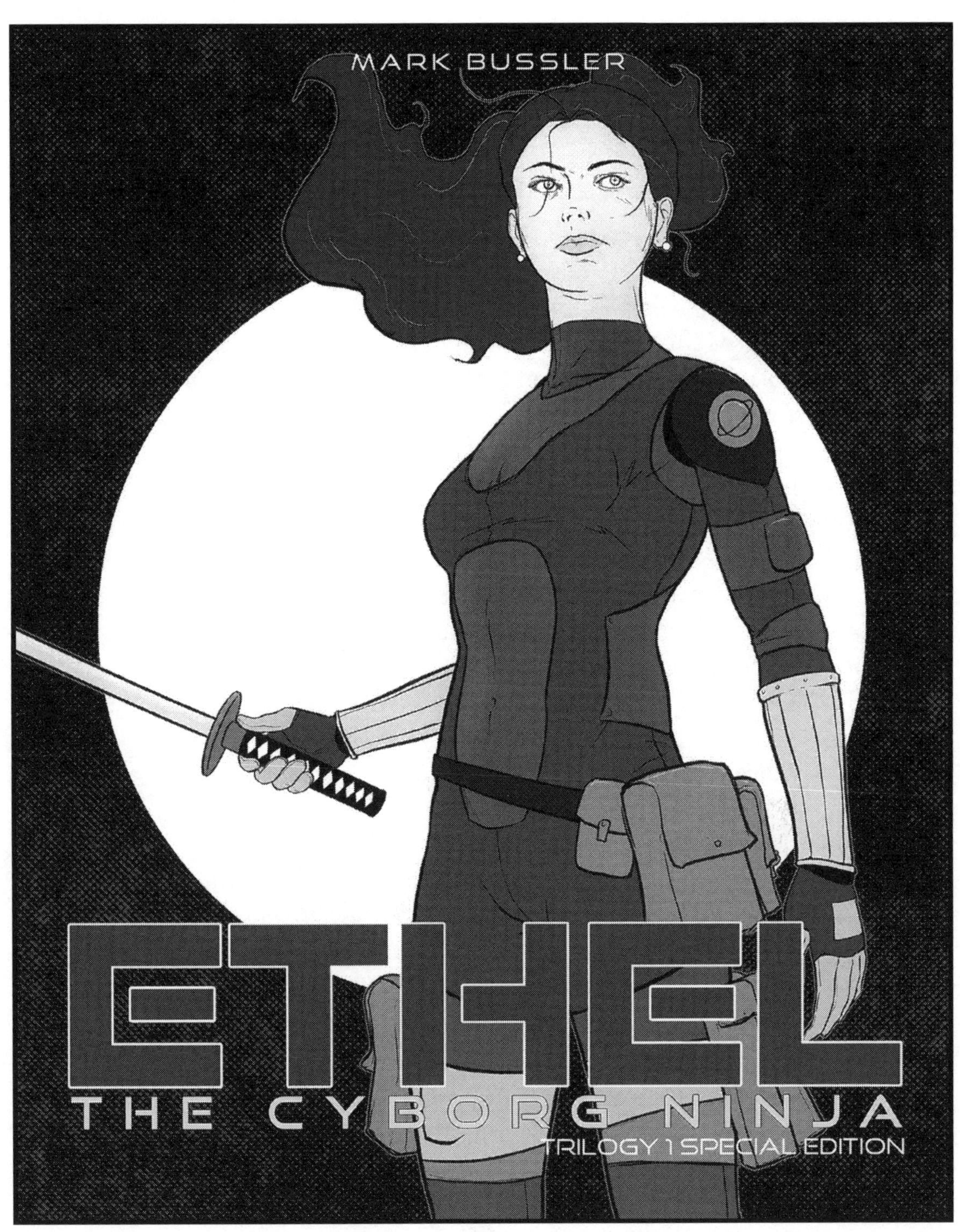

Ethel the Cyborg Ninja Trilogy 1 Spacial Edition (2024.)

COMPLETE LIST OF WORKS
BY MARK BUSSLER

1994-1995 - Bolfar: Hero of the 9th Moon (Bucknell Student Newspaper)
1995-1998 - Captain Bucknell (Bucknell Student Newspaper)
1998 - Mass Media (Bucknell Student Newspaper)
1999-2000 - The Game Room (FromUSAlive)
2000 - Agent 0400oz (FromUSAlive)
2001 - Civil War Minutes: Union (DVD)
2001 - Left for Dead (DVD)
2002 - Civil War Minutes: Confederate (DVD)
2002 - Shot to Pieces (DVD)
2003 - Johnstown Flood (DVD, PBS)
2004 - Gettysburg and Stories of Valor (DVD, PBS)
2005 - Expo: Magic of the White City (DVD, PBS)
2006 - Horses of Gettysburg (DVD, PBS)
2006 - World War 1 American Legacy (DVD)
2007 - Classic Game Room: The Rise and Fall of the Internet's Greatest Video Game Review Show (DVD)
2008 - Westinghouse (DVD)
2008 - Wind Squid (YouTube, Website, CGRpublishing.com)
2008-2024 - Classic Game Room (YouTube, CGRpublishing.com, Vimeo)
2014 - Lord Karnage Book 1 (Print)
2015 - The Best of Classic Game Room 15th Anniversary Collection (DVD, Blu-Ray)
2015 - Ethel the Cyborg Ninja Book 1 (Print)
2017 - How to Make a Video Game Review Show that Doesn't Suck (Print)
2017 - Lord Karnage 1.5 (Print)
2017 - Heyzoos the Coked-Up Chicken #1 (Print)
2017 - Retromegatrex #1: The Lost Art of Mark Bussler 1995-

2017 (Print)
2017 - Heyzoos the Coked-Up Chicken #2 (Print)
2017 - Old Timey Pictures with Silly Captions Volume 1 (Print)
2017 - Surf Panda (Print)
2017 - Ultra Massive Video Game Console Guide Volume 1 (Print)
2017 - Ultra Massive Video Game Console Guide Volume 2 (Print)
2017 - Pac-Man Collector's Guide: A Definitive Review (Print)
2017 - The White City of Color: 1893 World's Fair (Print)
2017 - The World's Fair of 1893 Ultra Massive Photographic Adventure Volume 1 (Print)
2017 - Classic Game Room Feature Review of MUSHA (CGRpublishing.com)
2018 - Classic Game Room 2085 Season 1 (Amazon Video, Blu-Ray, CGRpublishing.com)
2018 - The World's Fair of 1893 Ultra Massive Photographic Adventure Volume 2 (Print)
2018 - The World's Fair of 1893 Ultra Massive Photographic Adventure Volume 3 (Print)
2018 - Old Timey Pictures with Silly Captions Volume 2 (Print)
2018 - Manga Teacup Cherry Blossom (Print)
2018 - Ultra Massive Video Game Console Guide Volume 3 (Print)
2018 - Ultra Massive Sega Genesis Guide (Print)
2018 - Lord Karnage in the Valley of Moon Wolves (Print)
2018 - Unsubscribed! How to Succeed When the Platform Fails (Print)
2018 - Ultra Massive Video Game Controller Guide (Print)
2018 - Video Game Tome of Infinity Volume 1 (Print)
2018 - How to Draw Digital by Mark Bussler (Print)
2018 - Classic Game Room Feature Review of Herzog Zwei (CGR-publishing.com)
2018 - Classic Game Room Feature Review of Super Pac-Man (CGRpublishing.com)
2019 - Classic Game Room Infinity (Instagram, YouTube, Blu-

Ray)
2019 - Video Game Tome of Infinity Volume 2 (Print)
2019 - Heyzoos the Coked-Up Chicken #3 (Print)
2019 - Ethel the Cyborg Ninja #2
2019 - Classic Game Room 20TH (CGRpublishing.com)
2019 - All Hail the Vectrex: Ultimate Collector's Review Guide (Print)
2019 - 1904 St. Louis World's Fair: The Louisiana Purchase Exposition in Photographs (Print)
2019 - 1939 New York World's Fair: The World of Tomorrow in Photographs (Print)
2019 - Chicago 1933 World's Fair: A Century of Progress in Photographs (Print)
2019 - The Horrible Octopus (Webtoons, Print)
2019 - Amazing Ocean: Undersea Coloring Book for Adults (Print)
2019 - A Good Time at the 1939 New York World's Fair (CGR-publishing.com)
2019-2024 - 80s Comics (YouTube, TikTok, CGRpublishing.com)
2020 - Magnum Skywolf #1 (Print)
2020 - Robot Kitten Factory #1 (Print)
2020 - Old Timey Pictures with Silly Captions Volume 3 (Print)
2020 - 1939 New York World's Fair: The World of Tomorrow in Photographs Volume 2 (Print)
2020 - 1901 Buffalo World's Fair: The Pan-American Exposition in Photographs (Print)
2020 - Best of Gustave Doré Volume 1: Illustrations from History's Most Versatile Artist (Print)
2020 - Dante's Inferno: The Coloring Book (Print)
2021 - Best of Gustave Doré Volume 2: Illustrations from History's Most Versatile Artist (Print)
2021 - Classic Cars and Automobile Engineering Volume 1: Engine, Principles, Cylinders, Crankshafts, Carburetors, Clutches- (Print)
2021 - Classic Cars and Automobile Engineering Volume 2: Transmissions, Axles, Brakes, Wheels, Tires, Ford Car (Print)

2021 - Classic Cars and Automobile Engineering Volume 3: Motorcycles, Tractors, Shop Kinks, Welding, Questions and Answer (Print)
2021 - Classic Cars and Automobile Engineering Volume 4: Ignition, Starters, Generators, Batteries, Electrical Repairs (Print)
2021 - Classic Cars and Automobile Engineering Volume 5: Wiring Diagrams, Data Sheets, Questions and Answers (Print)
2021 - The Art of Ferdinand von Reznicek: Volume 1 (Print)
2021 - 1915 San Francisco World's Fair in Color: Grandeur of the Panama-Pacific Exposition (Print)
2021 - Robot Kitten Factory #2 (Print)
2021 - How to Draw Women's Eyes Inspired by Classic Illustrations Volume 1 (Print)
2022 - Retromegatrex Volume 2: The Art of Mark Bussler 2018-2022 (Print)
2022 - Turbo Volcano: Future Year 1982 (Music streaming)
2022 - Turbo Volcano: Supernova Robot Dungeon (Music streaming)
2022 - Turbo Volcano: Future Spa (Music Streaming)
2022- Turbo Volcano: She Wears Pink but Flies a Blue Lion (Music Streaming)
2022 - Turbo Volcano: No Champagne in the Volcano Room (Music Streaming)
2022 - Omega Ronin: Halcyon Sunrise (Music Streaming)
2022 - Omega Ronin: This Time It's Personal (Music Streaming)
2022 - Omega Ronin: Undercover Eyes (Music Streaming)
2022 - Omega Ronin: On the Line (Music Streaming)
2022 - Omega Ronin: Syntax Rhythm (Music Streaming)
2022 - Omega Ronin: Sky Warp (Music Streaming)
2022 - Omega Ronin: Touch the Mainframe (Music Streaming)
2022 - Omega Ronin: A New Hope Never Fades (Music Streaming)
2022 - Turbo Volcano: Ride the Lava (Music Streaming)
2022 - Turbo Volcano: Failure to Comply (Music Streaming)
2022 - When Our Antique Car Was Brand New and Lost Family Photographs of Classic Automobiles (Print)

2022 - When Trolleys Ruled the Earth: A Photographic History of Streetcars, Cable Cars, and Classic Trams (Print)
2022 - 1889 Paris World's Fair: The Exposition Universelle in Illustrations Volume 1 (Print)
2023 - 80s Comics: Ultimate 1980s Comic Book Review Guide – Volume 1 (Print)
2023 - Robot Kitten Factory #3 (Print)
2023 - Robot Kitten Factory Trilogy 1 Special Edition (Print)
2023 - Classic Trains and Railroad Engineering Volume 1: Antique Locomotive Operations Part 1
2023 - Classic Trains and Railroad Engineering Volume 1: Antique Locomotive Operations Part 2
2023 - Classic Trains and Railroad Engineering Volume 1: Antique Locomotive Operations Part 3
2023 - Classic Trains and Railroad Engineering Volume 1: Antique Locomotive Operations Part 4
2023 - Turbo Volcano: Covert Tiki Robot Maneuvers in Galaxy Tomorrow (Music Streaming)
2023 - Omega Ronin: Fourth Directive (Music Streaming)
2023 - Omega Ronin: Behind the Facade (Music Streaming)
2023 - Omega Ronin: Collision Course (Music Streaming)
2023 - Omega Ronin: Iron Metropolis (Music Streaming)
2023 - Omega Ronin: Cosmic Starfighter (Music Streaming)
2023 - 1889 Paris World's Fair: The Exposition Universelle in Illustrations Volume 2 (Print)
2024 - Omega Ronin: Mega Uniframe Super Hyper Armor (Music Streaming)
2024 - Omega Ronin: Beyond Nothing is Everything, Infinity Vice, Laser Groovy Getdown, Knight Eagle, Ranger 32X, Neutron Mindscape, Space Warr, First Class Ticket to Awesome, If the Universe is Expanding, What of Ghosts (*The Singles*) (Music Streaming)
2024 - Omega Ronin: Mission 1 Blade Horizon (Music Streaming)
2024 - Omega Ronin: Godforsaken Journey (Music Streaming)
2024 - Classic Game Room: Blast the Process (Music Streaming)

2024 - Classic Game Room: Never Stop Crushing (Music Streaming)
2024 - Classic Game Room: A Derelict Soundscape (Music Streaming)
2024 - Classic Game Room: Bottom Shelf Behind the Bar Beneath the Ray Gun (Music Streaming)
2024 - History of Classic Game Room: The Past, Present, and Future of Artistic Expression on the Internet (Print)
2024 - Omega Ronin Book 1 (Print)
2024 - Omega Ronin Art Book (Print)
2024 - Ethel the Cyborg Ninja #3 (Print)
2024 - Ethel the Cyborg Ninja Hardcover Trilogy Edition (Print)
2024 - Ethel the Cyborg Ninja Databook (Print)
2024 - Omega Ronin: The Documentary (CGRpublishing.com)
2024 - Omega Ronin: Sirens (Vinyl, Music streaming)
Soundtrack to Omega Ronin Book 1

Planned for Future Year 2025
2025 - Omega Ronin Book 2
2025 - Ethel the Cyborg Ninja #4
2025 - Heyzoos the Coked-Up Chicken #4
2025 - [Untitled Barbarian Series]
2025 - [Untitled Giant Monster Series]
2025 - Magnum Skywolf [Reboot]
2025 - Agent 00400z: A View to Another Octopus Tomorrow that Never Dies

CLASSIC GAME ROOM
GALLERY

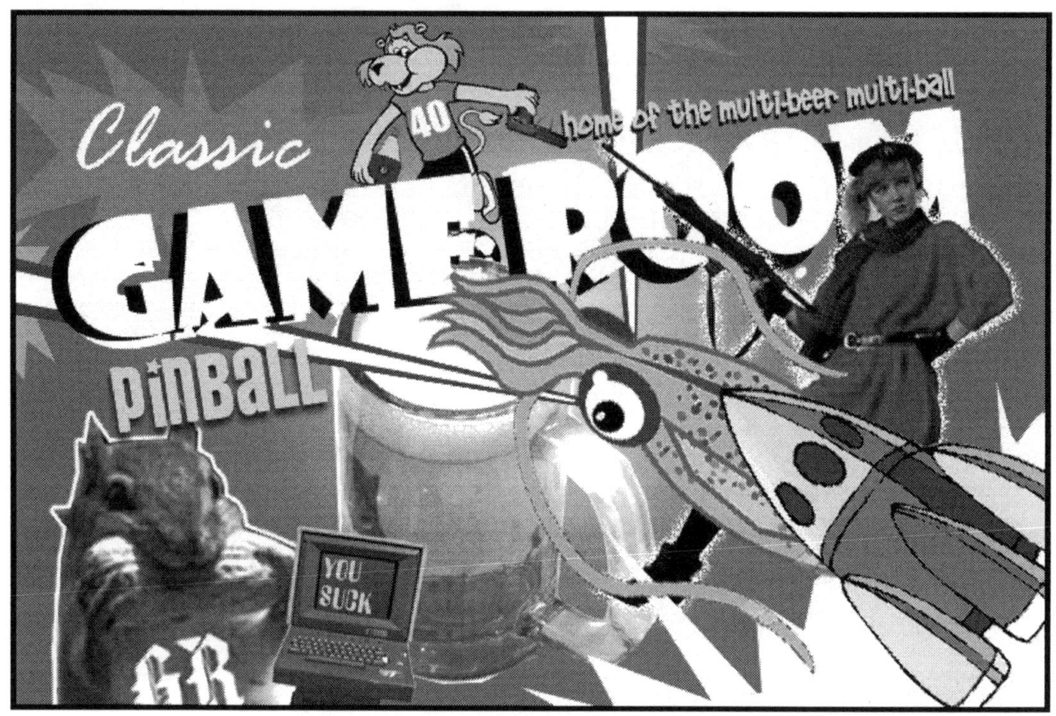

Will we ever get Classic Game Room TM the Pinball Machine?

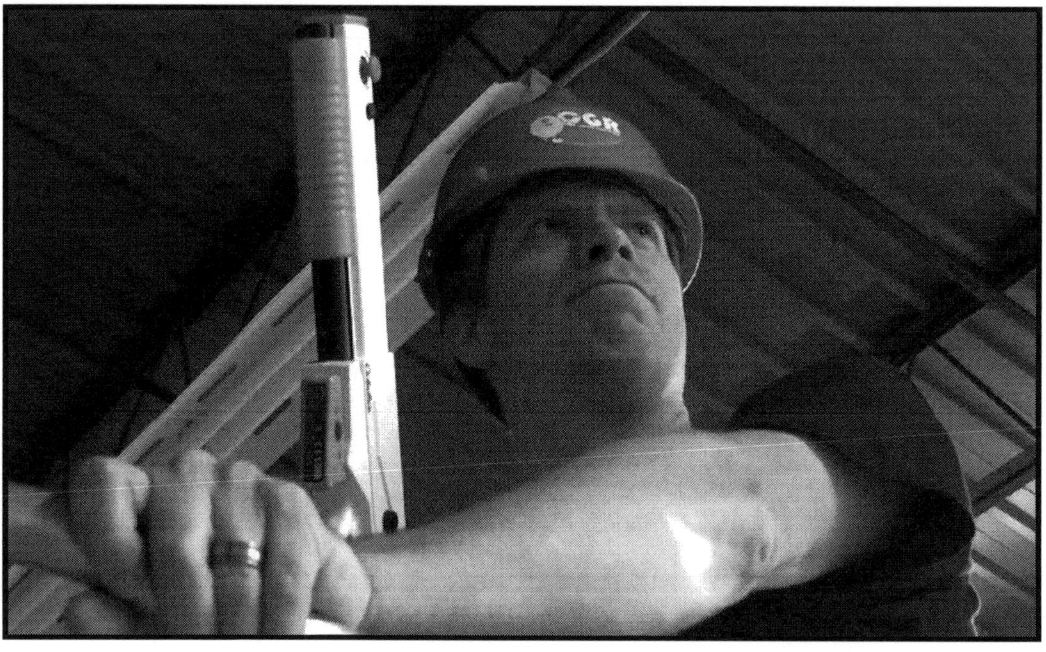

Mark hunting Space Crickets in a cherrypicker.

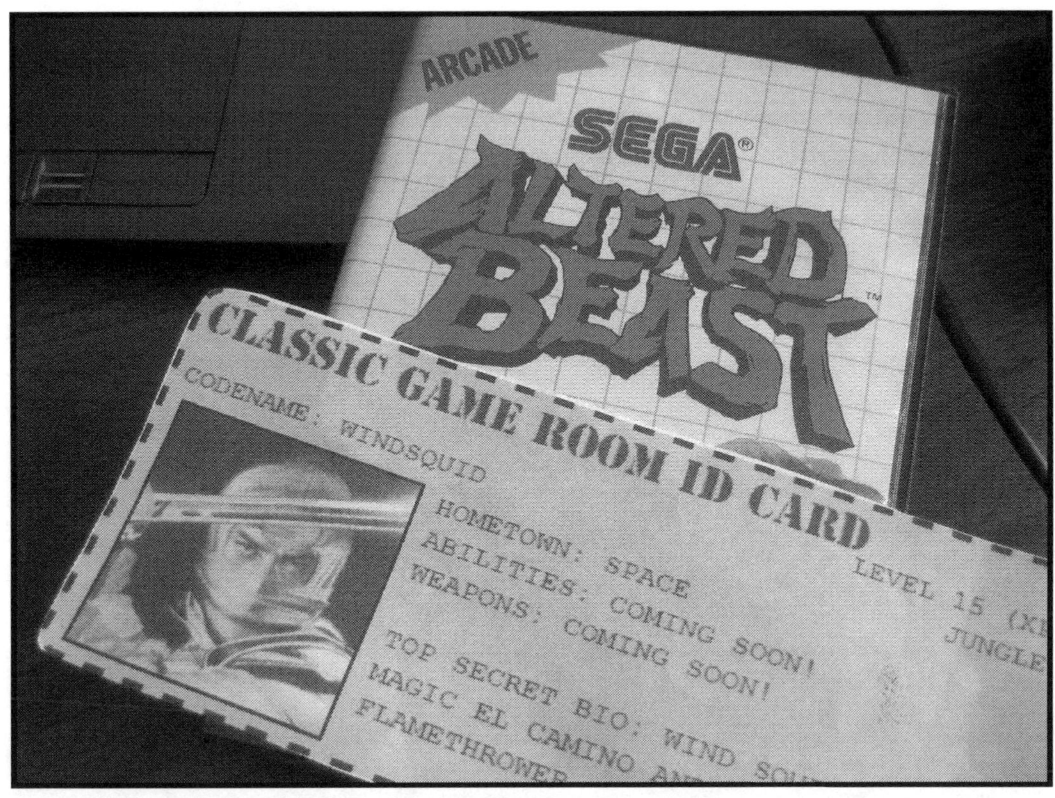

A Classic Game Room ID Card from the 2013-era website.

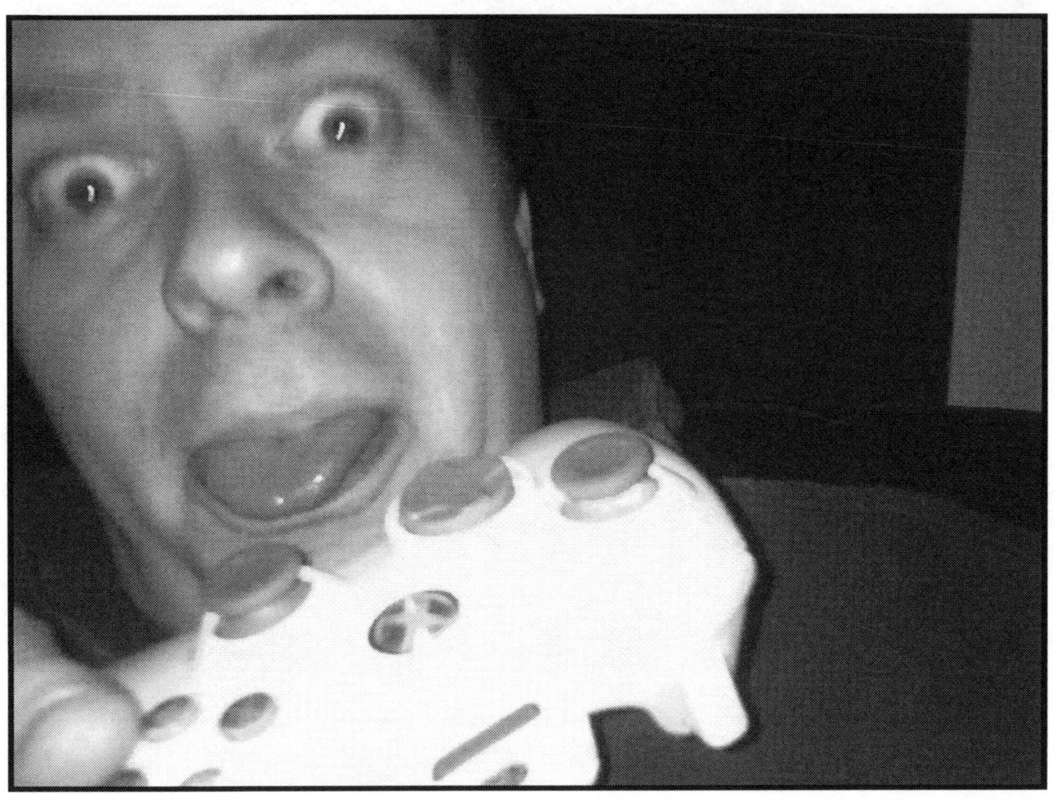

2007. I don't have any idea what's happening here.

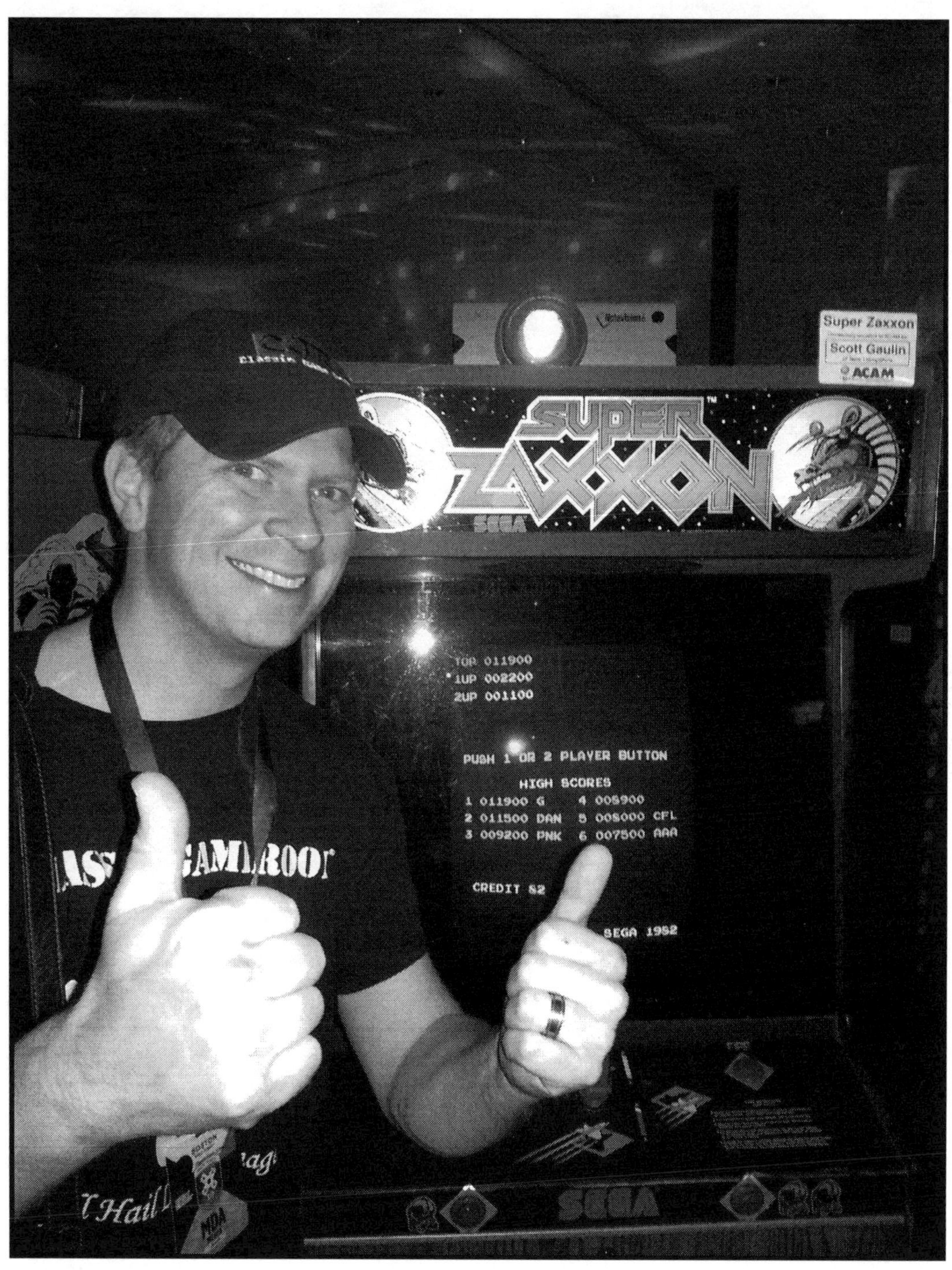

Mark at PAX in 2014.

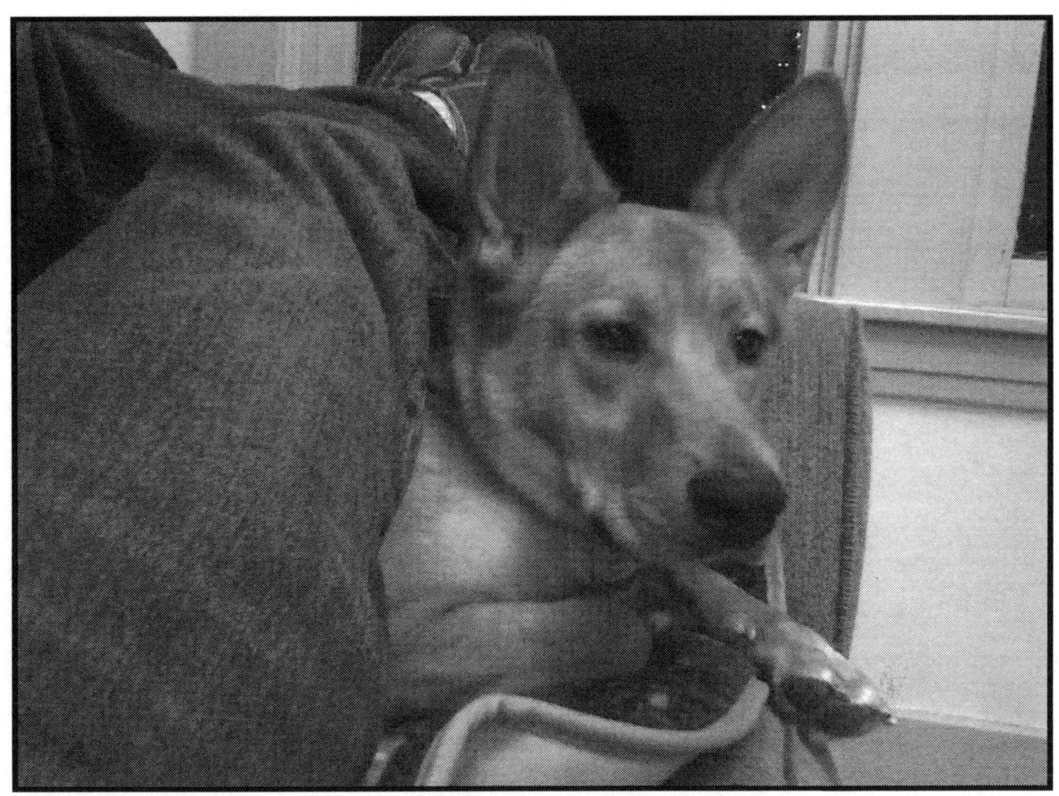

Viral Dog in 2008.

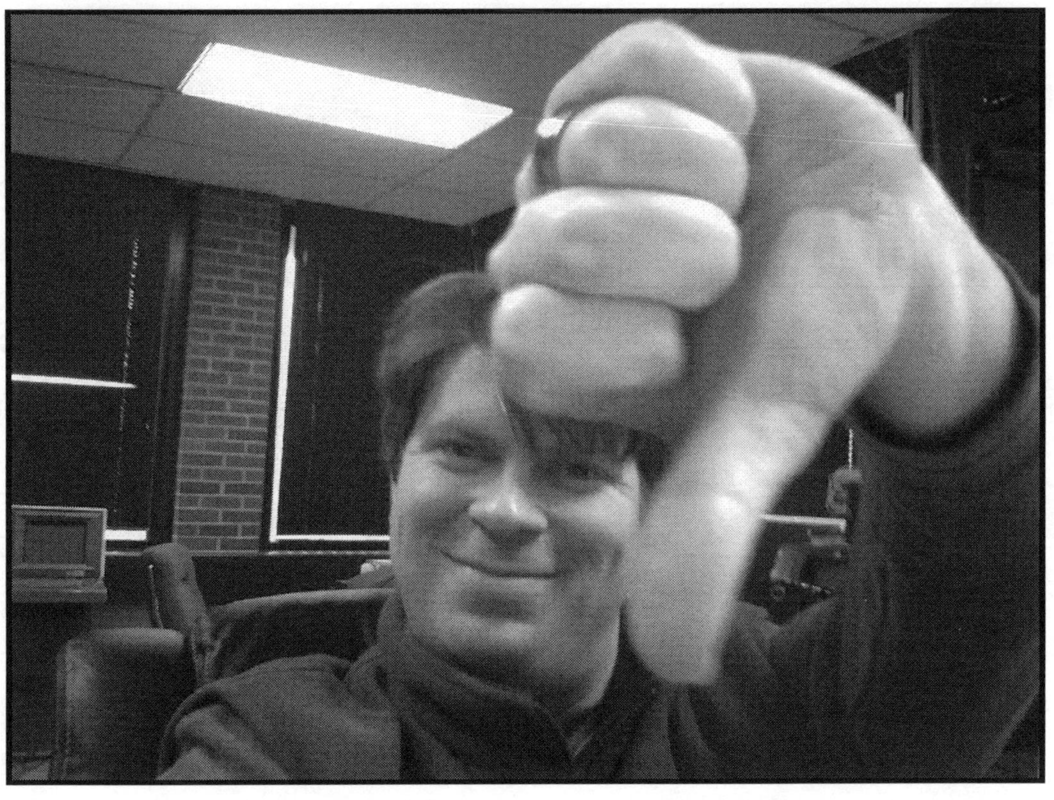

Inecom office in 2007. Edit-Station 1 in background.

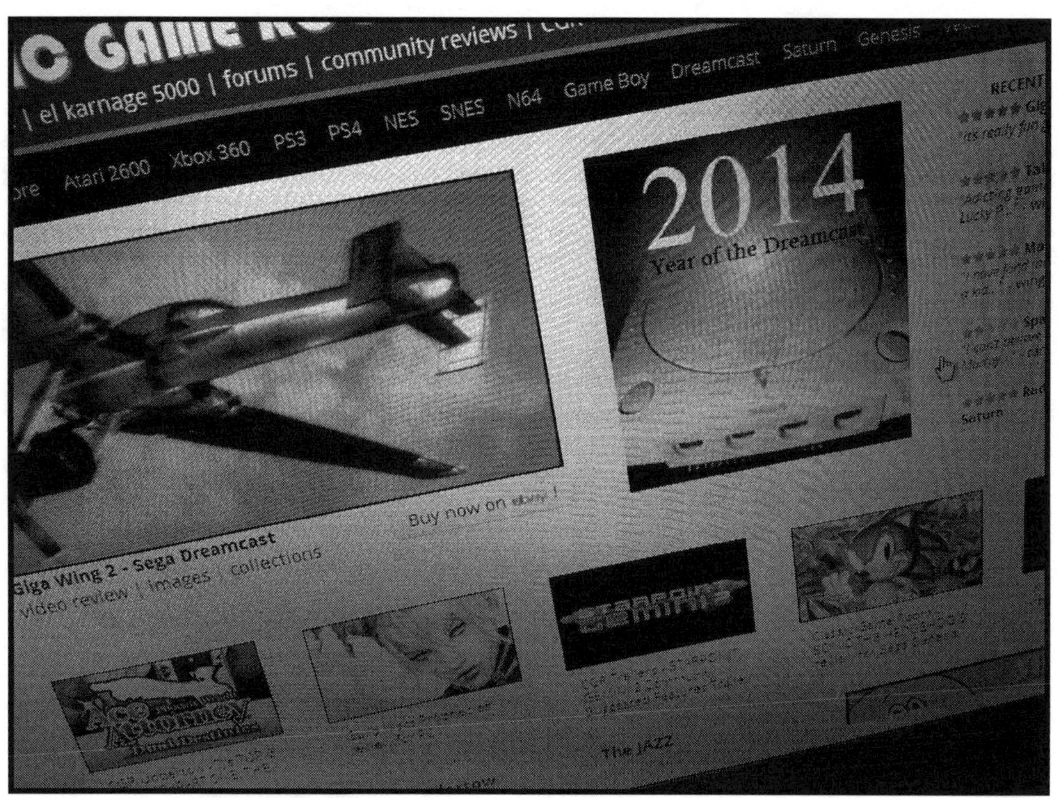

Classic Game Room website in 2014.

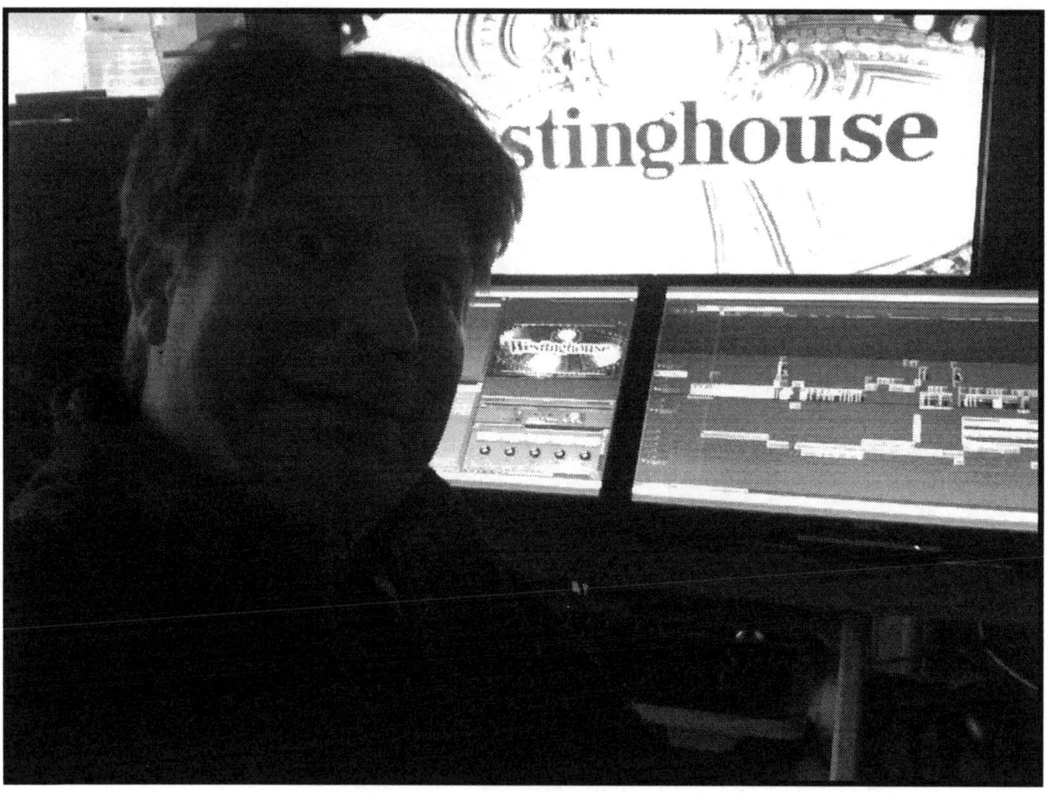

Mark editing Westinghouse in 2007.

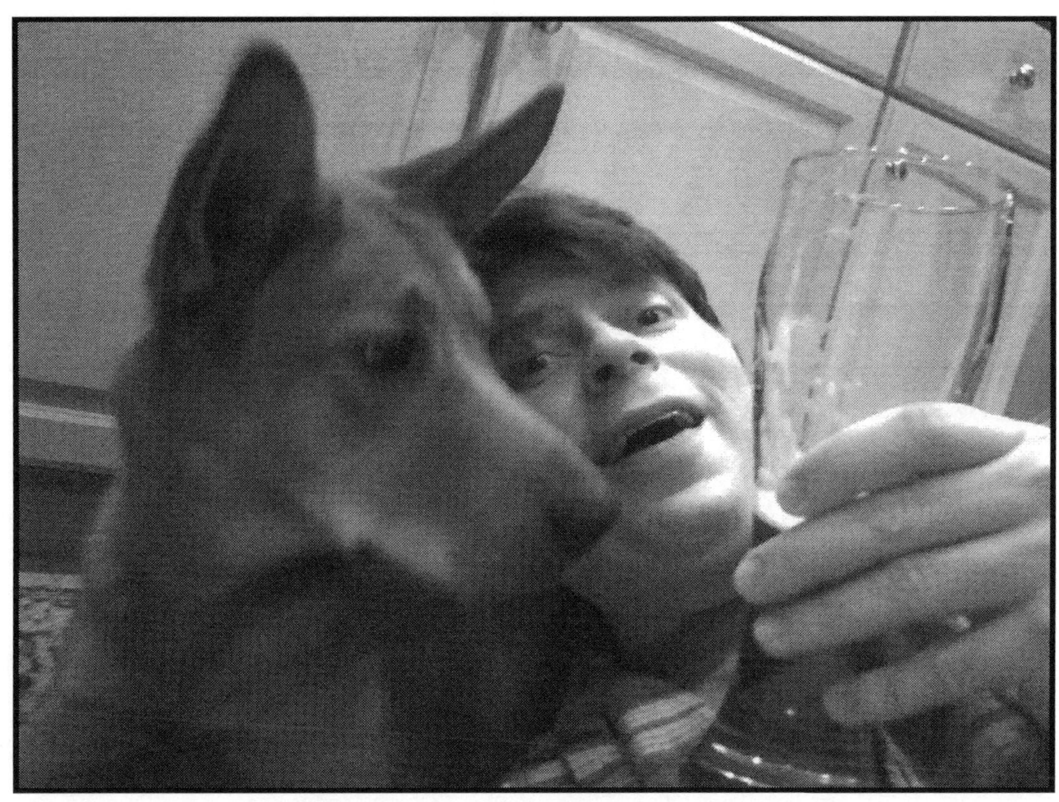

Two best friends forever (2007.)

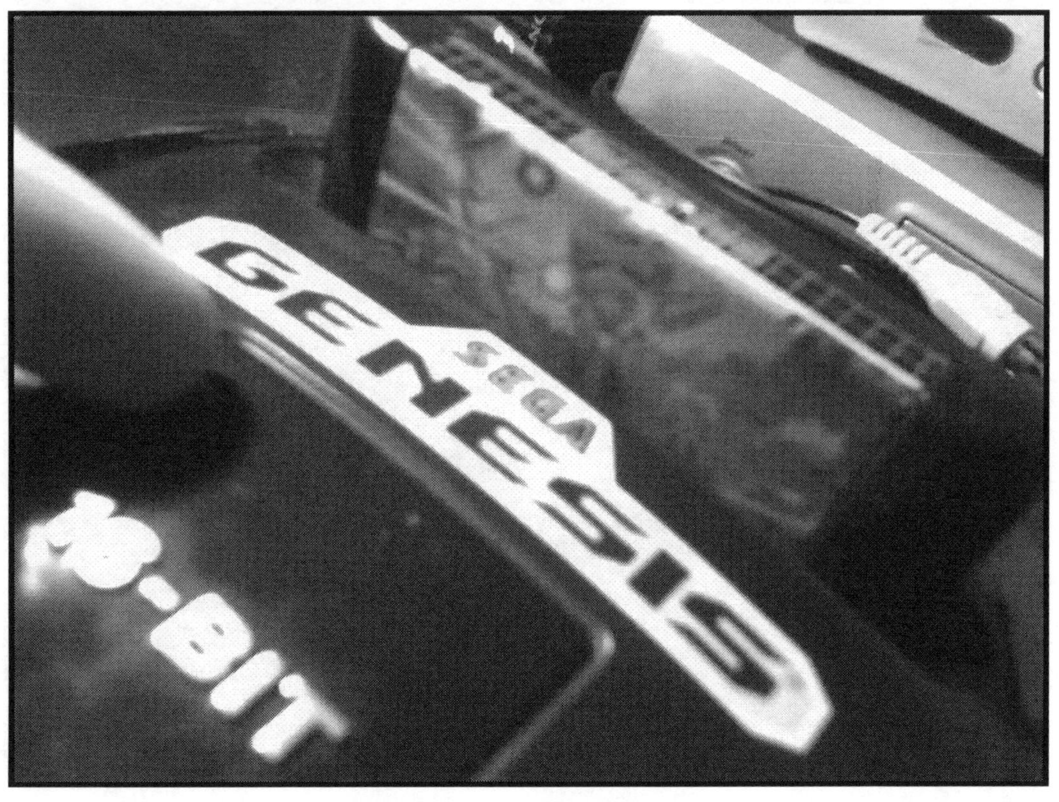

Blast Processing! (circa 2008)

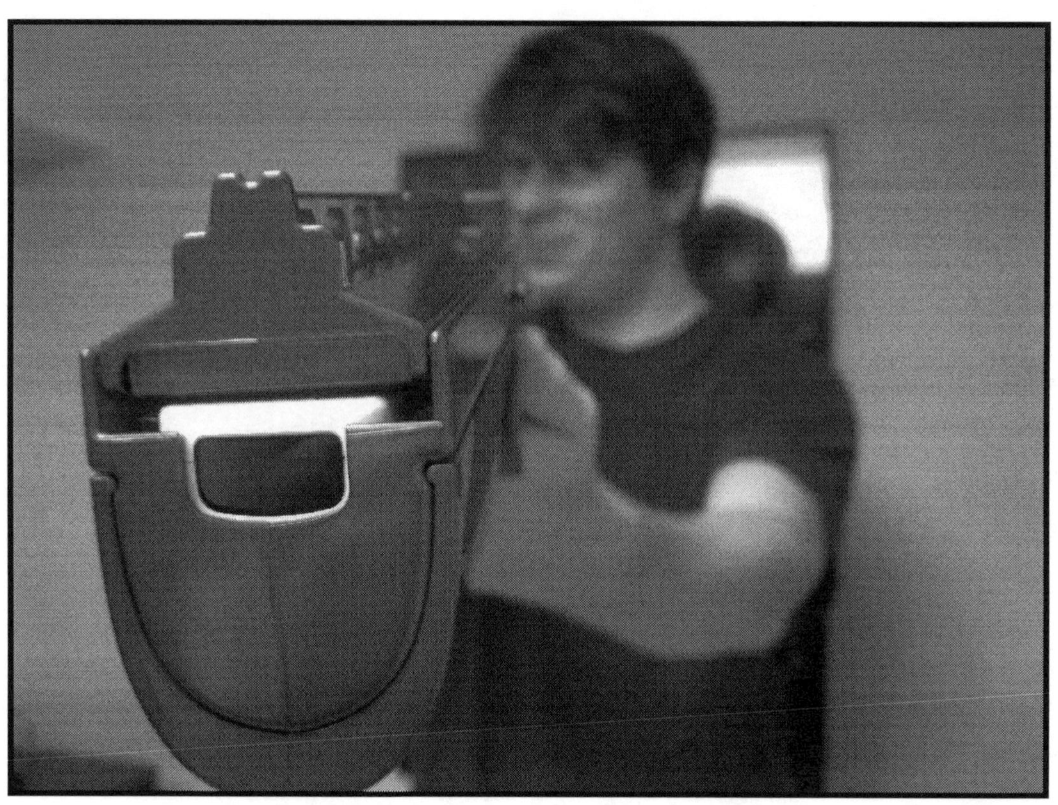

Mark armed and not-so-dangerous in 2014.

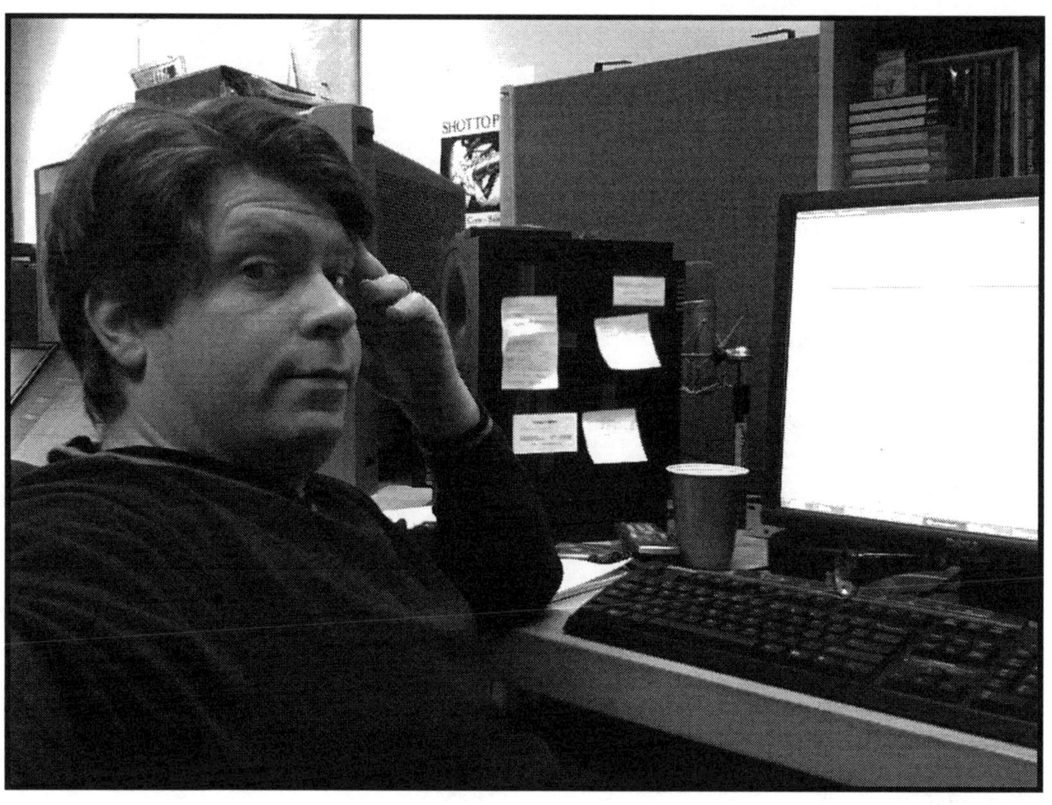

Inecom in 2007.

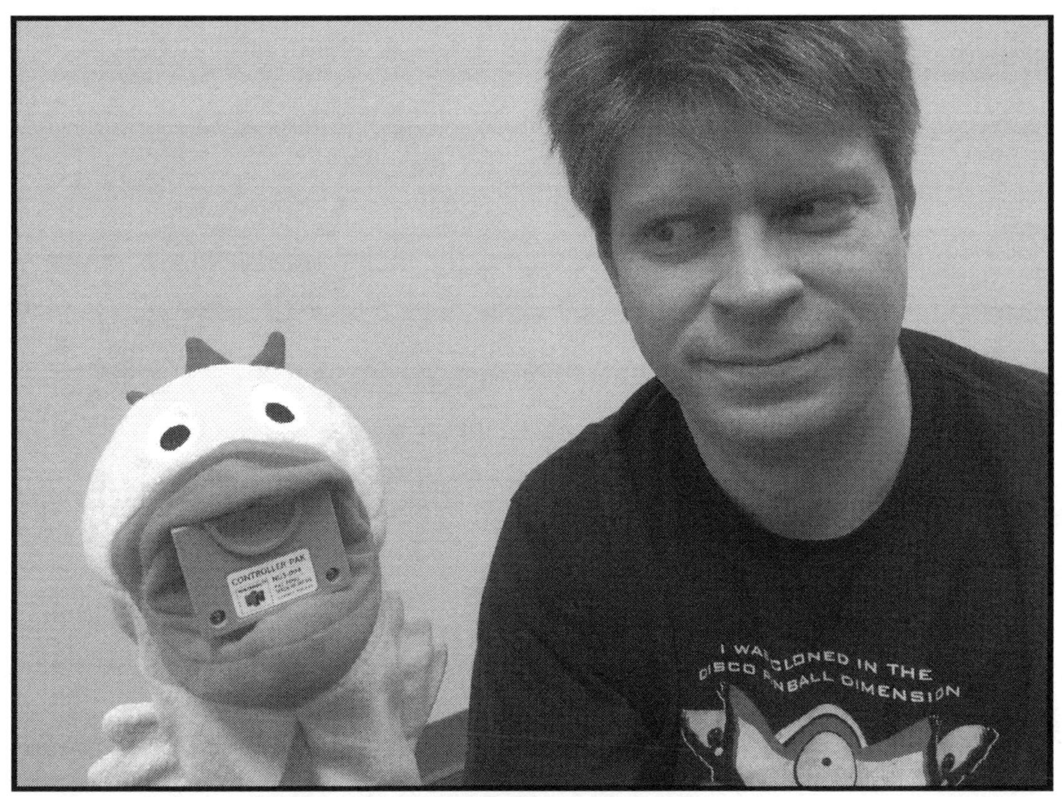

Mark and Heyzoos (2014.)

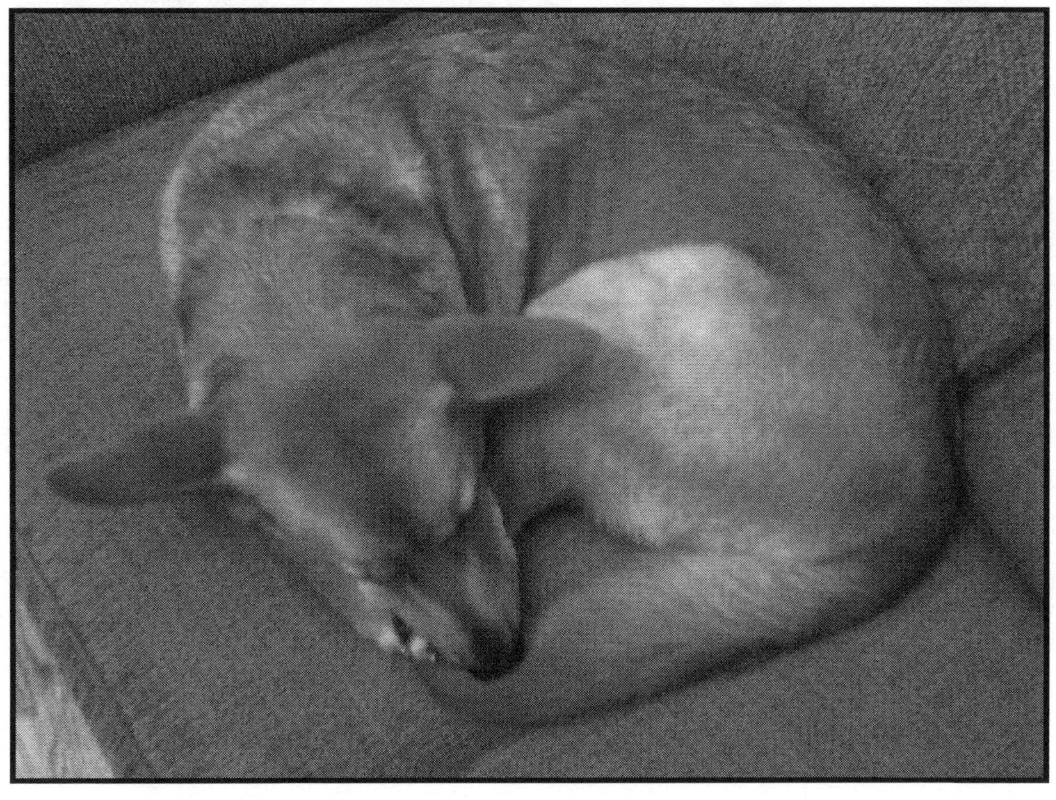

Stella dreaming about destroying things (2007.)

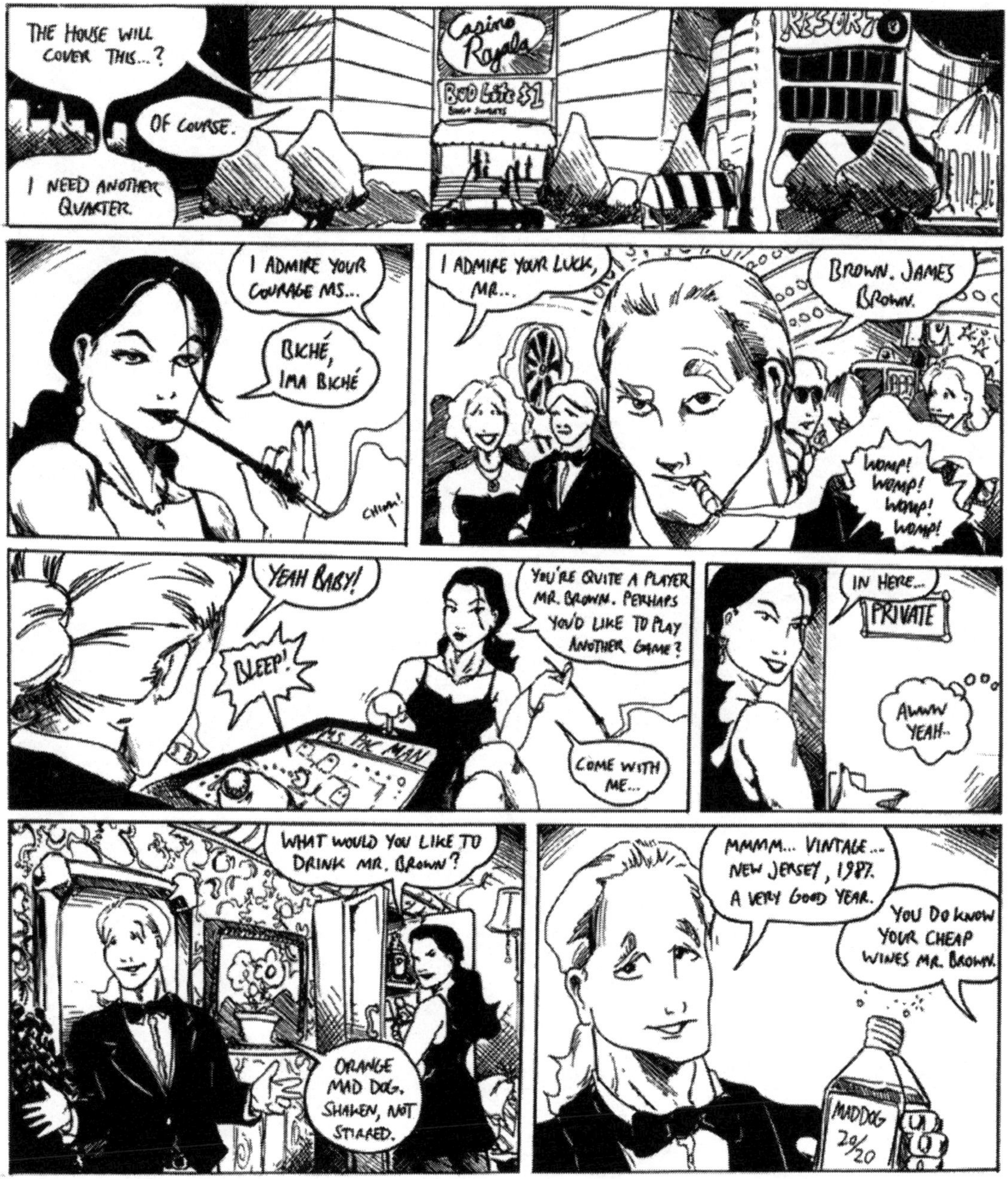

Agent 0040oz (1998)

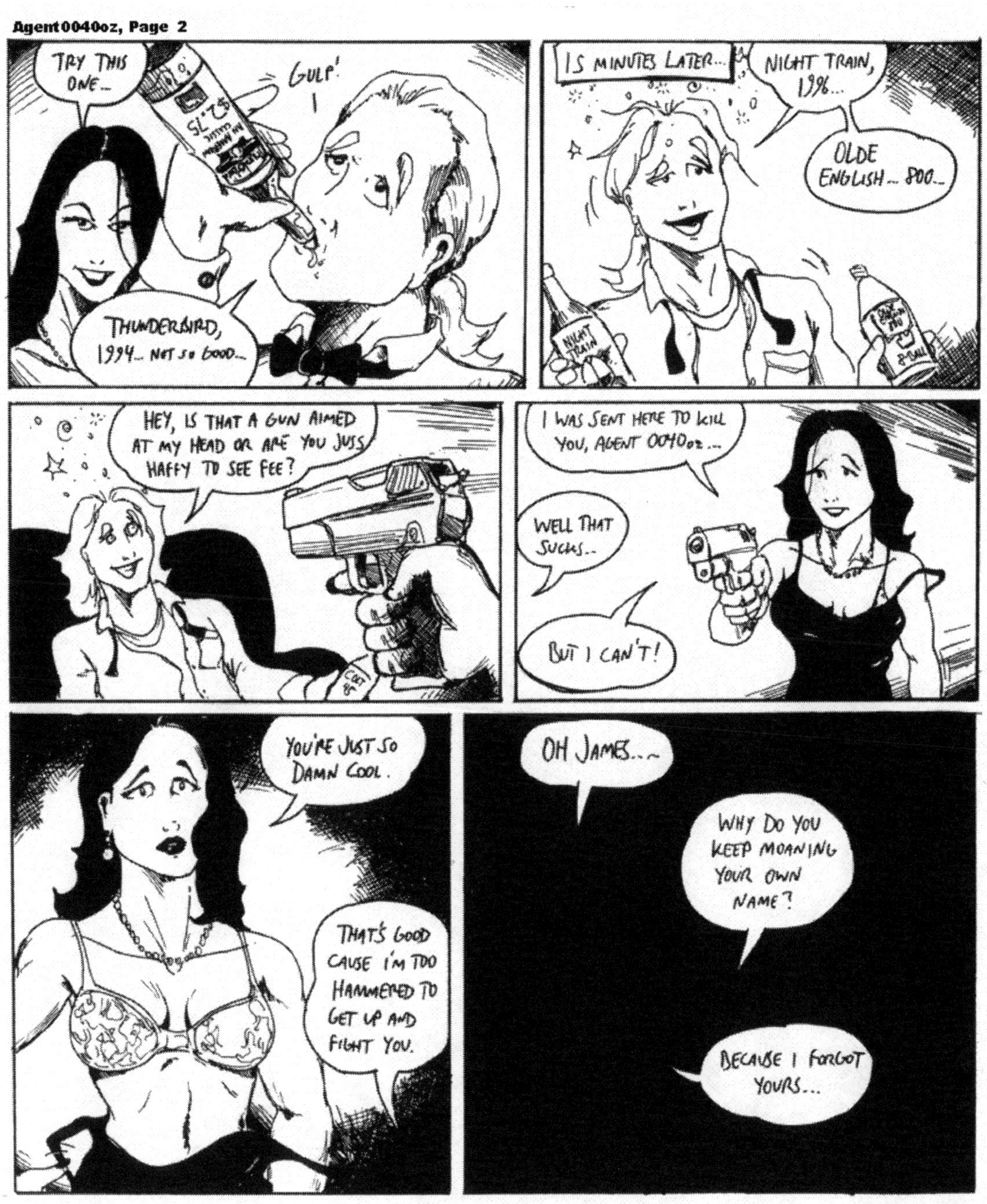

JAMES BROWN MAY RETURN IN...?

Other books from CGR Publishing at CGRpublishing.com

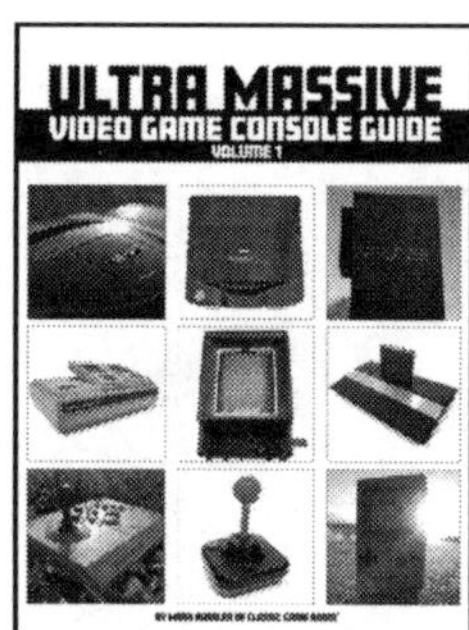

Ultra Massive Video Game Console Guide Volume 1

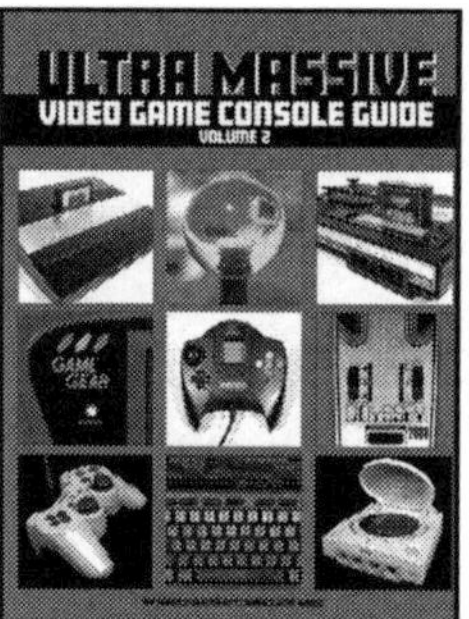

Ultra Massive Video Game Console Guide Volume 2

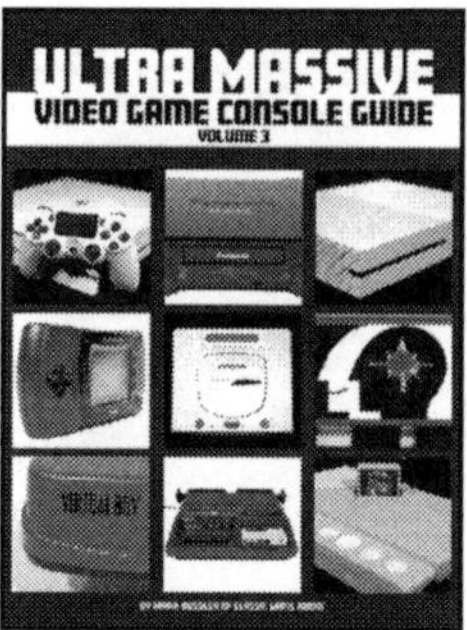

Ultra Massive Video Game Console Guide Volume 3

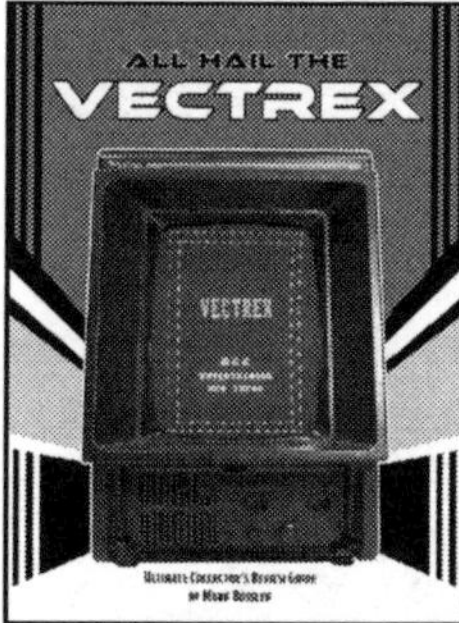

All Hail the Vectrex: Ultimate Collector's Review Guide

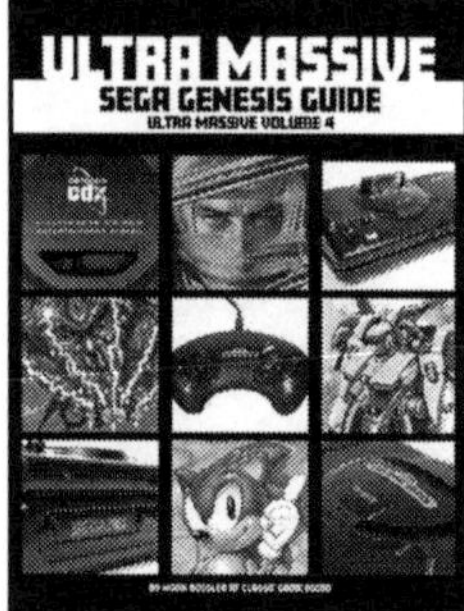

Ultra Massive Sega Genesis Guide: Ultra Massive Volume 4

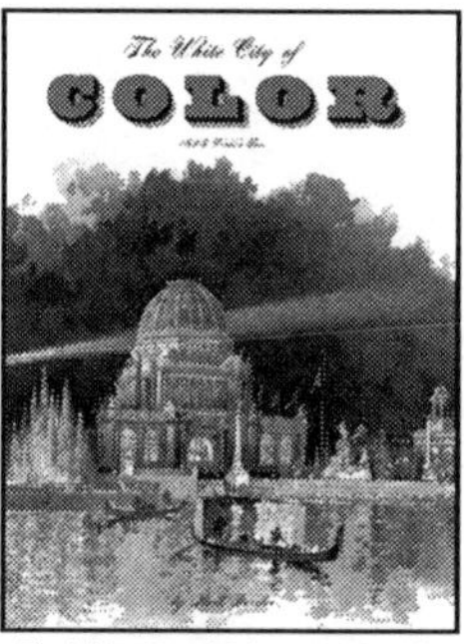

The White City of Color: 1893 World's Fair

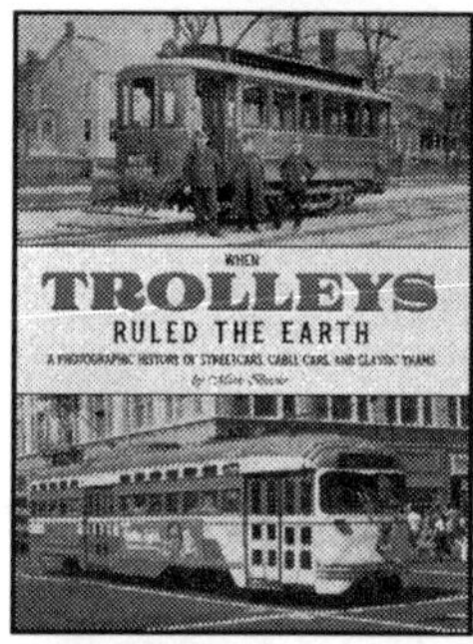

When Trolleys Ruled the Earth: A Photographic History of Streetcars..

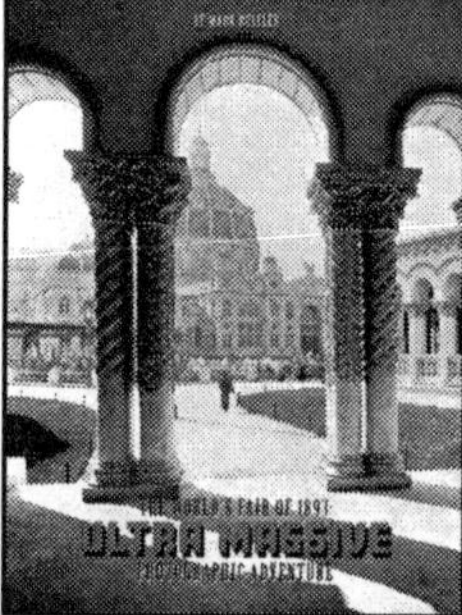

The World's Fair of 1893 Ultra Massive Photographic Adventure Vol. 1

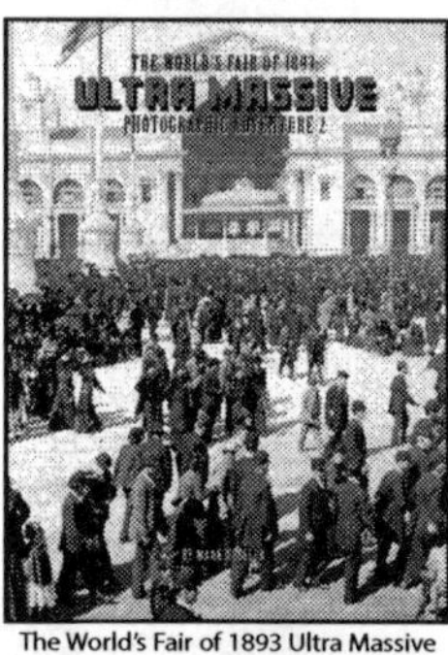

The World's Fair of 1893 Ultra Massive Photographic Adventure Vol. 2

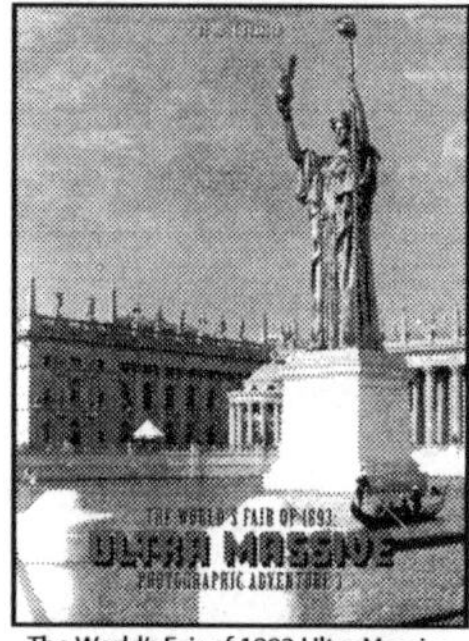

The World's Fair of 1893 Ultra Massive Photographic Adventure Vol. 3

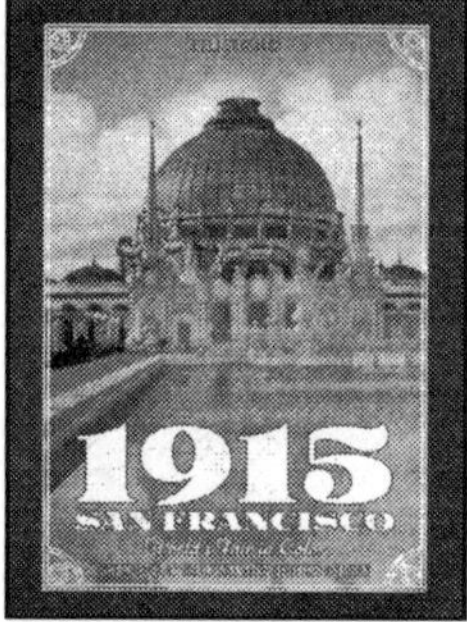

1915 San Francisco World's Fair in Color: Grandeur of the Panama...

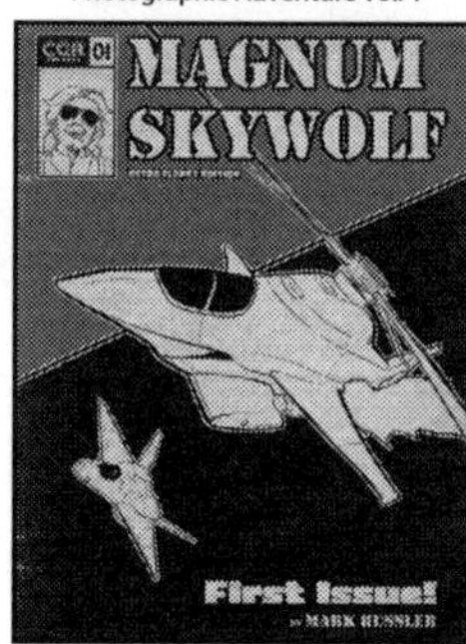

Magnum Skywolf #1

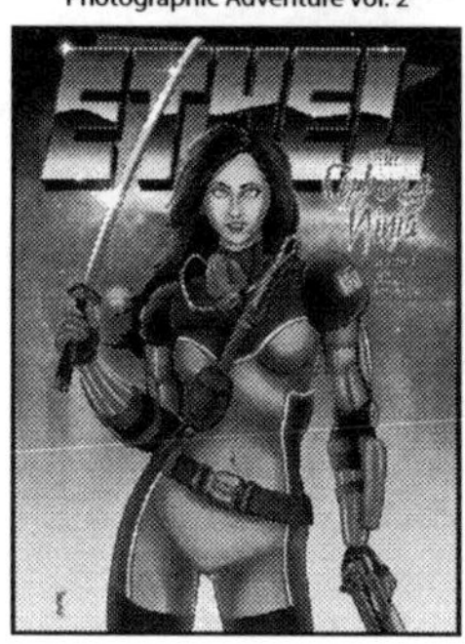
Ethel the Cyborg Ninja Book 1

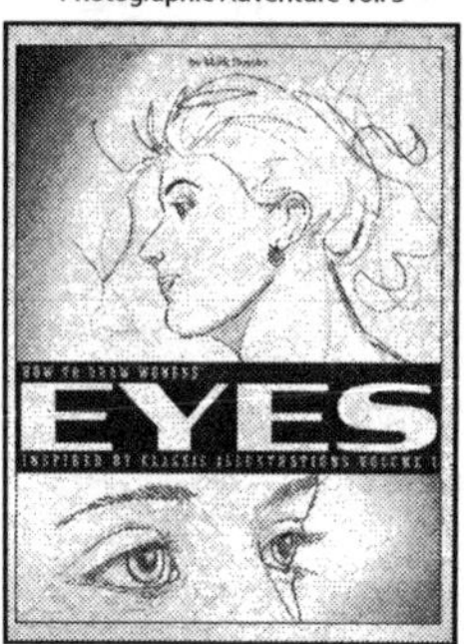

How to Draw Womens' Eyes: Inspired by Classic Illustrations Volume 1

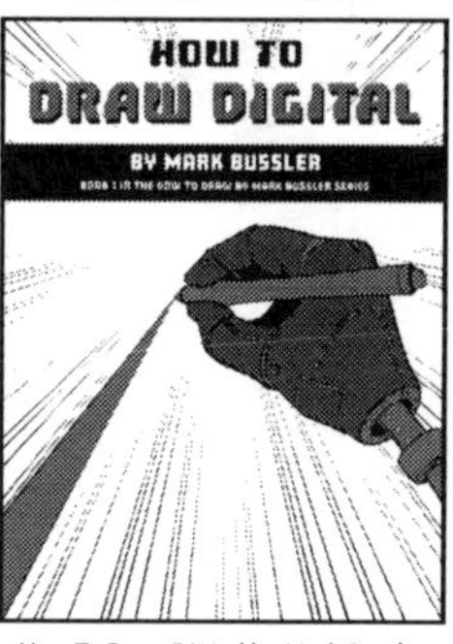

How To Draw Digital by Mark Bussler

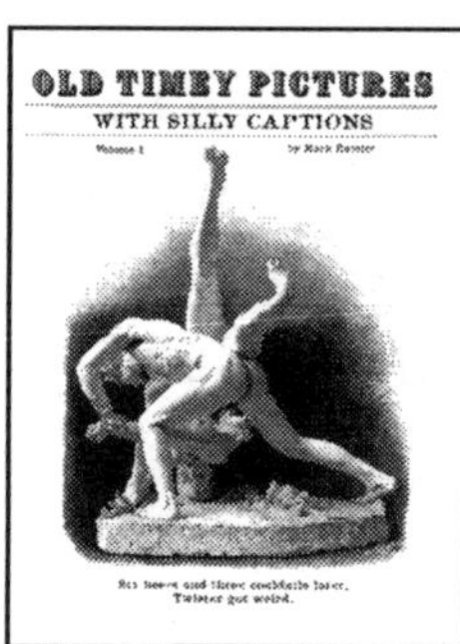

Old Timey Pictures With Silly Captions: Volume 1

Other books from CGR Publishing at CGRpublishing.com

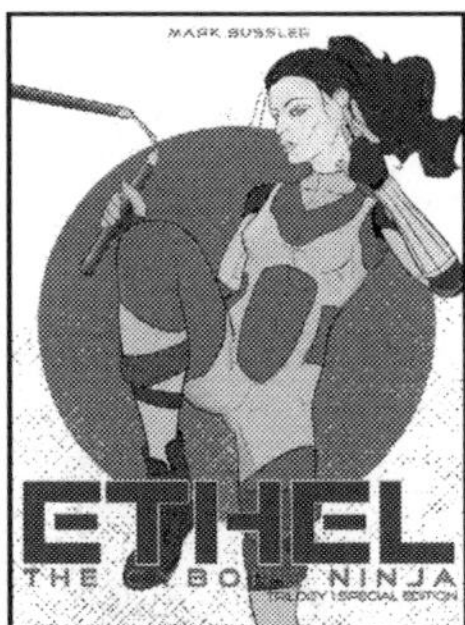

Ethel the Cyborg Ninja: Hardcover Trilogy Edition (Cover A)

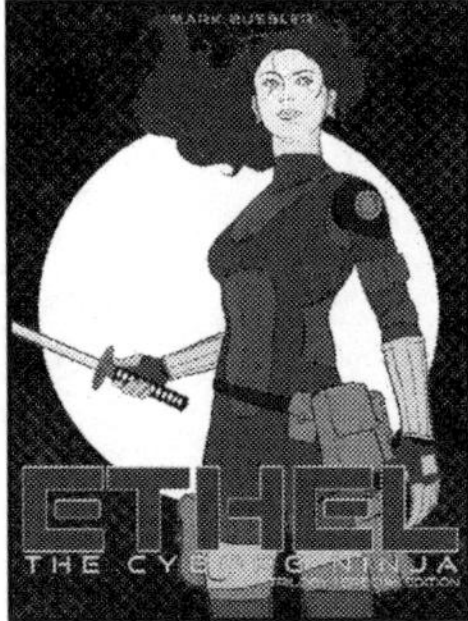

Ethel the Cyborg Ninja: Hardcover Trilogy Edition (Cover B)

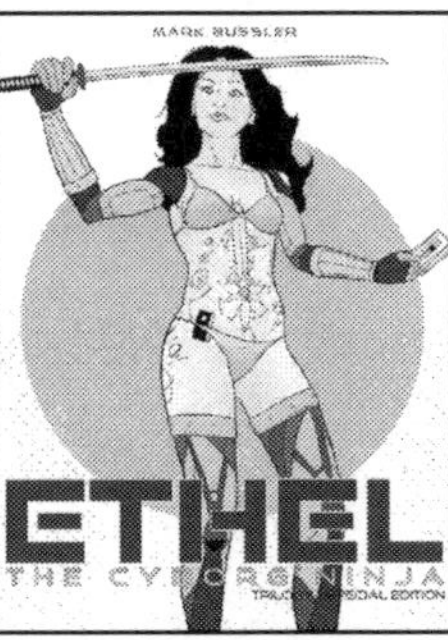

Ethel the Cyborg Ninja: Hardcover Trilogy Edition (Cover C)

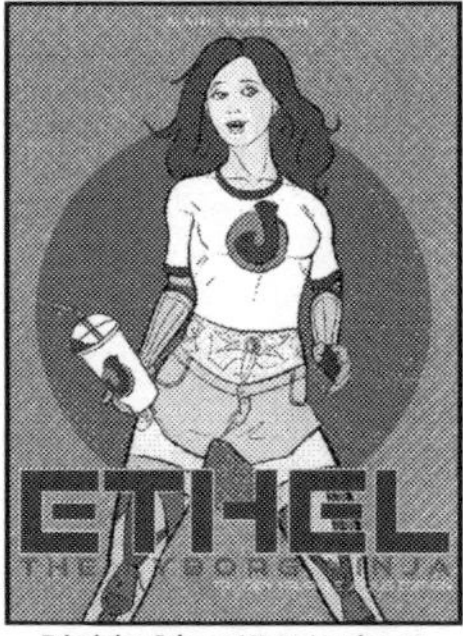

Ethel the Cyborg Ninja: Hardcover Trilogy Purple Julius Edition

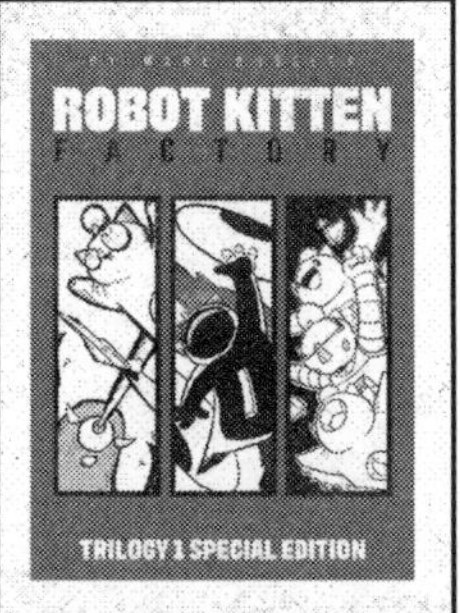

Robot Kitten Factory: Trilogy 1 Special Edition

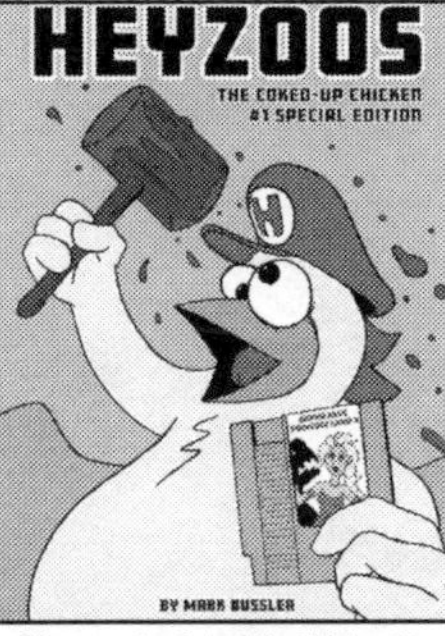

Heyzoos the Coked-Up Chicken #1 Special Edition

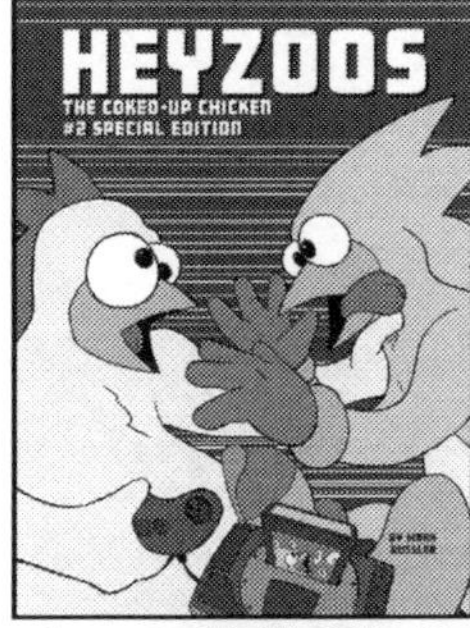

Heyzoos the Coked-Up Chicken #2 Special Edition

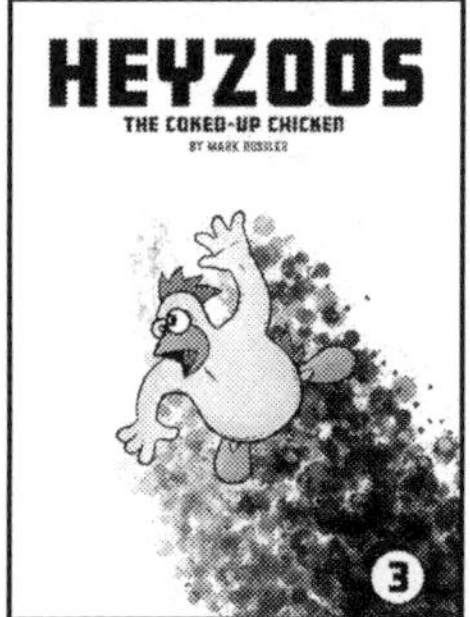

Heyzoos the Coked-Up Chicken #3

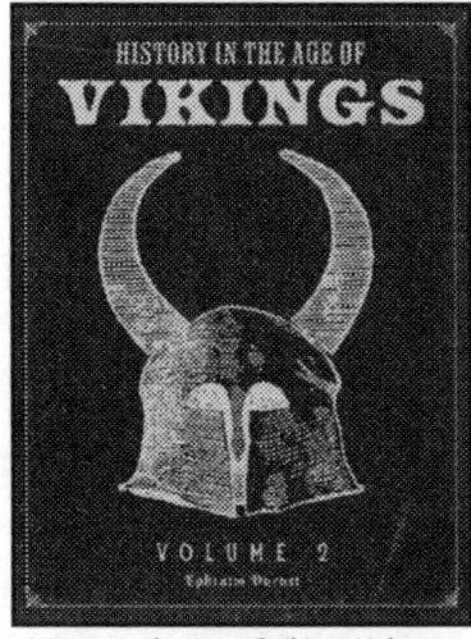

History in the Age of Vikings Volumes 1-3

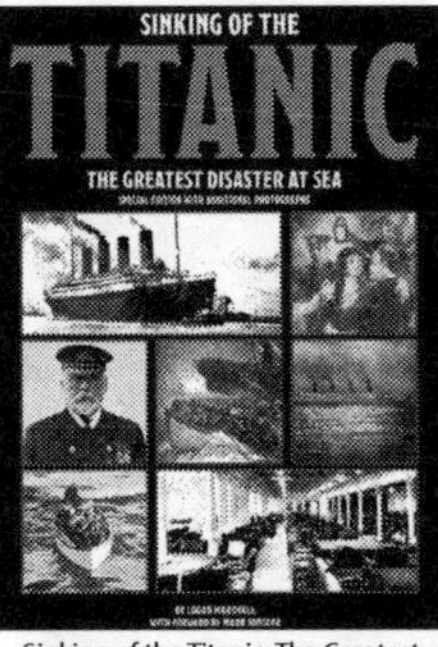

Sinking of the Titanic: The Greatest Disaster at Sea

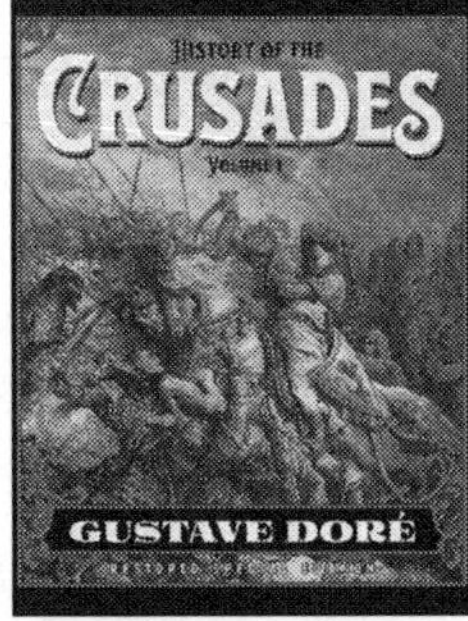

History of the Crusades Volume 1: Gustave Doré Restored Special Edition

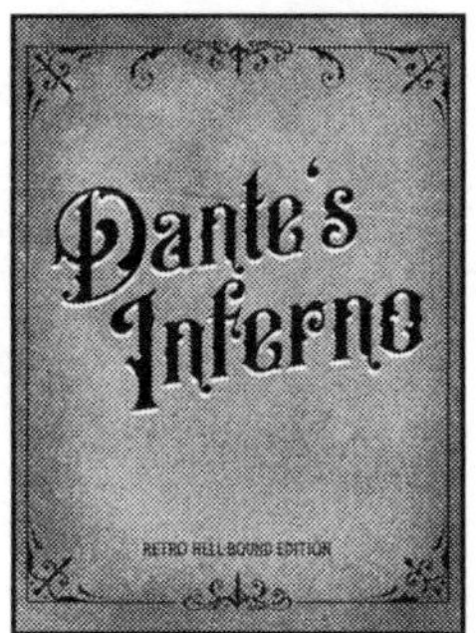

Dante's Inferno: Retro Hell-Bound Edition

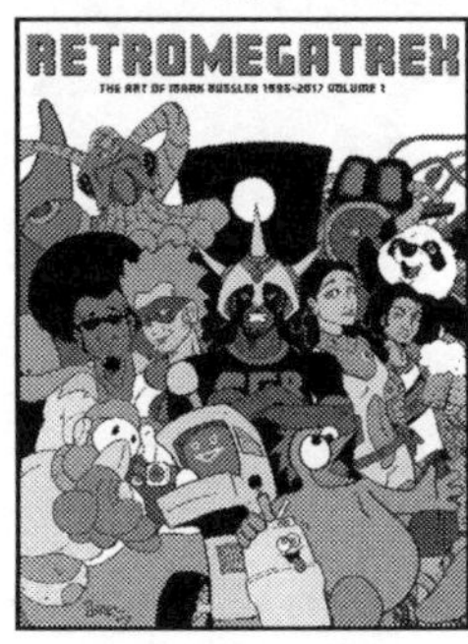

Retromegatrex Volume 1: The Lost Art of Mark Bussler 1995-2017

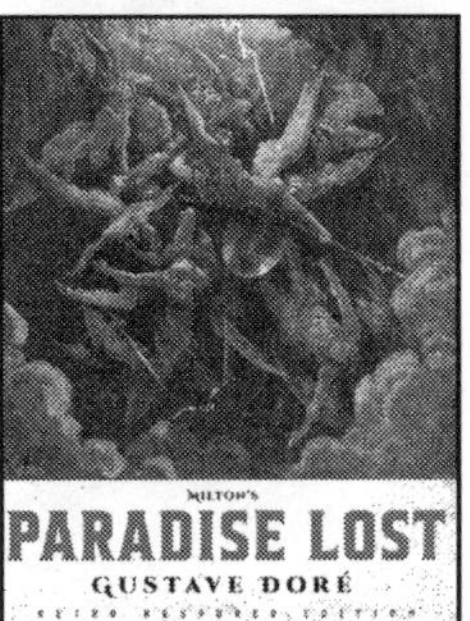

Milton's Paradise Lost: Gustave Doré Retro Restored Edition

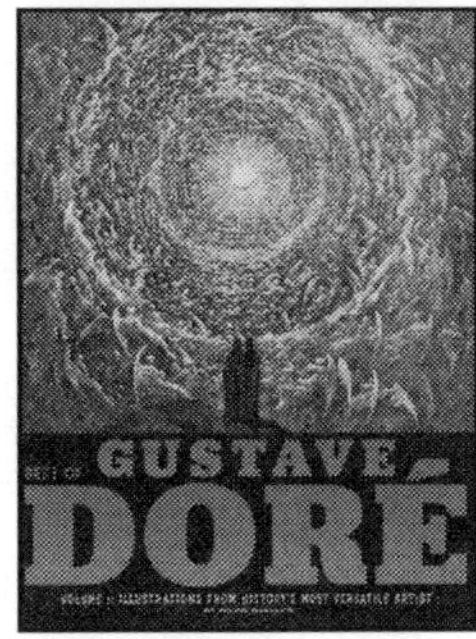

Best of Gustave Doré Volume 1: Illustrations from History's Most Versatile Artist

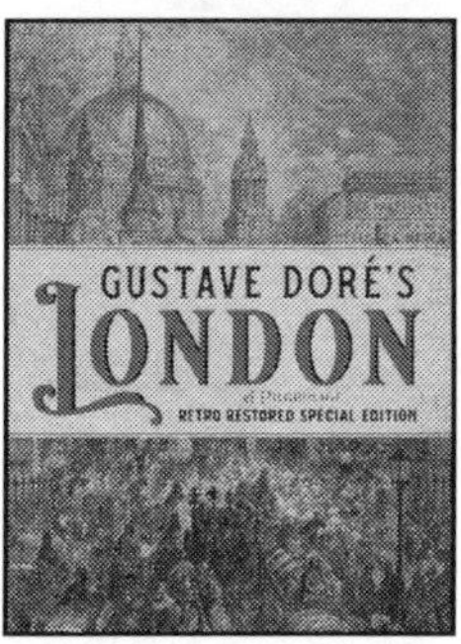

Gustave Doré's London: A Pilgrimage Retro Restored Special Edition

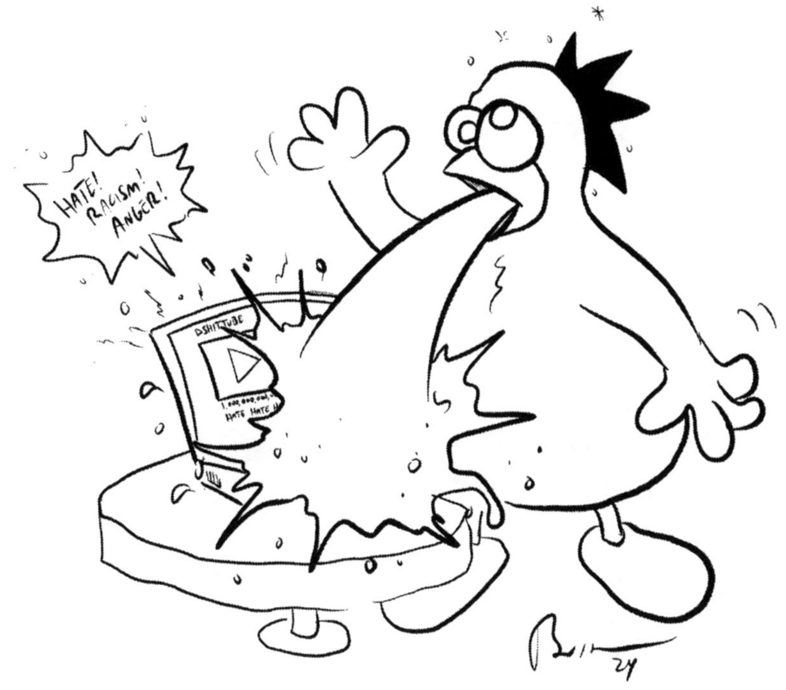
HATE! RACISM! ANGER!
SHITTUBE
HATE HATE

Made in the USA
Monee, IL
05 March 2025

d007fb24-102b-4a4b-b4d1-64326386e693R02